PAT WELSH'S

SOUTHERN CALIFORNIA GARDENING

PAT WELSH'S

SOUTHERN CALIFORNIA GARDENING

A MONTH-BY-MONTH GUIDE

photographs by Steven Gunther

CHRONICLE BOOKS
SAN FRANCISCO

Library of Congress Cataloging-in-Publication Data:

Welsh, Pat.
[Southern California gardening]
Pat Welsh's southern California gardening : a month-by-month guide / by Pat Welsh.
p. cm.
Includes bibliographical references and index.
ISBN 0-8118-2214-1 (pb)
1. Gardening—California, Southern. I. Title. II. Title: Southern California gardening.
SB453.2.C3 W454 1998
635'.09794'9—dc21   99-10043
                          CIP

Printed in the United States

Designed by Patrick David Barber
Typeset in Stempel Garamond, Frutiger, and Interstate

Distributed in Canada by Raincoast Books
9050 Shaughnessy Street
Vancouver, British Columbia V6P 6E5

10 9 8 7 6 5 4 3 2

Chronicle Books LLC
85 Second Street
San Francisco, California 94105

www.chroniclebooks.com

To Louis, in loving memory

ACKNOWLEDGMENTS

This book couldn't have been written without the help and cooperation of many people. I'm deeply grateful to all who so generously gave of their time to help bring it to completion.

First, I remember with gratefulness my dear husband, Louis. He believed this book would go on helping people for many years into the future and cheered me on in all I did for it. I thank my wonderful family—my children, Francesca and Peter Filanc and Wendy and Larry Woolf; my grandchildren, Yvette and Erica Filanc; and Rebecca, David, and Rachel Woolf—for their loving support and enthusiasm. Chief among my helpers has been Lucy Warren, consultant and all-around helper who types a lot better than I do, for whose wisdom, ability, creative ideas, and sense of humor I'm constantly grateful.

It's been great fun working with photographer Steve Gunther. Thank you, Steve, for your glorious photographs, for your cheerfulness and patience with me, and for enduring countless traffic jams and driving hundreds of miles to catch plants or gardens in bloom (some of which turned out not to be when you got there). Most of all I thank you for telling me you'd do "whatever it takes" and for being true to your word.

The following people have generously shared their time and knowledge to help me bring this revised edition up to date with all that is new and important in Southern California horticulture: Vince Lazaneo, Farm Advisor, Home Horticulture, University of California Cooperative Extension, San Diego; Chuck Kline, Horticulturist Emeritus and Landscape Advisor, Sea World; Jerry Stewart of New Leaf Geranium Nursery; Evelyn Weidner, Mary Weidner, and Peggy Bobo of Weidner's Begonia Gardens; Bob Smaus, Garden Editor of the *Los Angeles Times*; Bill Teague, agriculturist and flower grower; Virginia McKenzie, Horticulturist, Hydroscape Products; Phil Lubars, Sales Manager, Drip-In Irrigation; Marnie Mahoney, founder of the Del Mar Garden Club; Becky Dembitsky, member of the Del Mar Garden Club; Linda Chisari, garden designer; Carol Carden, owner of Esmeralda Books; Jack Engberg, Sales Representative, Grow More; Ed Rose, Propagation Manager, Ball Seeds; Sharon Drusch, rosarian, Sharon Splane Drusch Design; Dick Streeper, rosarian and rose columnist of the *San Diego Union Tribune*; Dr. Vic Gibeau, Lawn Scientist, University of California, Riverside; Hugh Wilkerson, ornamental grass gardener; John Greenlee, nurseryman and author of the *Encyclopedia of Ornamental Grasses*; Tim Galardi, owner, Riviera Gardens; Scott Daigre of Hortus Nursery, Pasadena; Janis Blackschleger, Perennial Productions; Tom Carruth of Weeks Roses; David Sakeroff, Hollywood art director; Loretta Foreman, plant lover and observant reader; Libby Doheny, avid gardener; Ruth Boron, avid gardener; Cathy Young, garden designer of "In the Garden," Calabasas, California; Judy M. Horton, garden designer; Katherine Moyers, yoga instructor and expert on the gardens of Silver Lake, Los Angeles; Patrick Anderson, horticulturist and Huntington Gardens volunteer; Shirley Kerrins, garden designer, Huntington

ACKNOWLEDGMENTS

Gardens; Chris Rosmini, garden designer; Agatha Youngblood, gardener extraordinaire with vast knowledge of perennials; and Judy Wiegand, owner of Judy's Perennials in San Marcos, California.

Many people helped me with the first edition and were thanked in detail in that volume. Their contributions remain an integral part of this revised edition; to all these people I say thank you once again for all the time, help, advice, and support you gave me: Evelyn and the late Bob Weidner, Vince Lazaneo, Chuck Kline, Betty Newton, Susan Locke Anderson, Stephanie Bise Shigematsu, Gilbert Voss, Bill Nelson, Tom del Hotal, Victor Voss, Richard Streeper, Tom Cooper, Karen Kees, the late Ernie Chew, Michael MacCaskey, Bob Dale, Bill Teague, Linda Teague, Neil Cassidy, Jim Halda, Craig Miller, Karen O'Toole, Chuck Badger, the late Alice Menard, Dale Kolaczkowski, and Richard A. Haubrich.

Finally I thank my agent, Sandra Dijkstra, whose help and advice I treasure, and all the good people at Chronicle Books, especially my dear friend and editor Leslie Jonath, talented art director Laura Lovett, and Brenda Tucker, public relations.

CONTENTS

PREFACE

to the Revised Edition

Since *Pat Welsh's Southern California Gardening: A Month-by-Month Guide* was first published in 1992, tens of thousands of copies have been sold. Many have become dirt-smudged outdoor references, others dog-eared bedside books. Reader inventiveness and suggestions are heartwarming and utilitarian. The greatest compliment is that many a copy has been worn out and is in need of replacement.

This new edition of *Pat Welsh's Southern California Gardening* retains all that gardeners loved and found helpful in the original edition while reflecting the changes that have taken place during the last ten years. You will find here explanations and recommended controls for new plant diseases and exotic pests, such as the giant whitefly, that few people had ever heard of in 1992. Some other pests, including the ash whitefly, that were frustrating gardeners ten years ago are now almost totally controlled by beneficial insects. Also, since the first edition was written, we've been through yet another periodic drought followed by the usual pattern of heavy rains. Today's gardeners need to know what an El Niño is and how to deal with it; they'll find the answers here.

As with the first edition, I recommend many products by generic and trade names, but some garden products are no longer available and have thus been replaced by others. In other cases, the identical product has a new trade name or is manufactured by a different company than before. Organic gardening has increased in importance, a trend reflected in the equipment and supplies discussed in this book. I've included recommendations of several relatively new products that can help you cope with old problems in innovative, often safer, ways.

Most importantly, I've added a great deal of information on perennials, including when and how to cut them back. You'll find this advice in every chapter, month by month throughout the year under the general heading "Annual and Perennial Flowers." A few plants—gamolepis, for example—are no longer available, but dozens of new plants, especially perennials and flowering subshrubs, have taken their place. And I've added several new "Quick Tips" plus whole sections or boxed features on salvias, botanical geraniums, pelargoniums (those plants known by the common name "geranium"), lilac, clematis, mesclun, ornamental vegetable gardening, and ornamental grasses, with a clear explanation of how and when to cut them back.

Trends in garden design also affect plant choice. New tract houses are often larger, but their garden spaces are smaller. Lawns are often smaller and more drought resistant than they were in the past, but they remain an important part of gardening. I thus include detailed discussions of the new and improved varieties of lawn grasses while not forgetting to address the care of the older types that are still being grown.

Throughout the nineties, cottage gardens and English-style gardens have been the rage. Now our love affair with Provence and Italy has renewed local interest in what is perhaps a more appropriate model, that of the drought-resistant Mediterranean garden harkening back to our

Mission heritage. Bold formal design is also being expressed in new ways. In the twenty-first century I foresee the emergence of an entirely new garden style, a new and innovative formality of design that will provide cheerfulness, excitement, and greater ease of upkeep. All we've learned in the cottage garden can be transferred into a more structured space, combining the greatest formality of design with the greatest informality of planting.

Attention to all these developments has been incorporated into this book. All other material is left intact, though I've streamlined some of the recommendations to balance their current importance. I've also added a few brief plant lists to help with specific needs.

Finally, I've answered the questions most frequently asked when I give talks in Southern California, such as what to do about poor soil (page 22) and how to cope with giant whitefly (page 101), control weeds (page 40), understand and choose fertilizers (page 21), keep wild animals out of the compost pile (page 78), and find manure that's safe to use (pages 27 and 73). Many other current questions—too many to mention here—are handled in detail. An improved and expanded index should make access to the information both quick and easy.

I am grateful to you, the gardeners of Southern California, for taking the first edition of this book into your hearts and making it the local gardeners' bible. I hope you will welcome this newly revised and updated version and find it a helpful guide for many years to come.

Happy gardening!

Pat Welsh
Del Mar, California
April 15, 1999

What This Handbook Includes

For the purposes of this book, Southern California means one large swath of the southernmost third of the state. The map shows that third to be a huge area, most of it sparsely populated. This book addresses the relatively narrow band of heavily populated coastal plains and adjacent inland valleys that begins at the Mexican border, on the south, and extends northward to Gaviota Pass, north of Santa Barbara. Throughout this region, where more than 80 percent of the state's population lives, approximately the same wide array of plants is grown.

North of the Gaviota Pass the climate differs from that in Southern California, and a somewhat different array of plants is grown on a schedule that's not the same as ours. Mexico also has a different climate and differing conditions. Even so, many of the plants discussed in this book can also be grown in the central and northern areas of California and in Baja California. Mountains and desert areas are not themselves the subject here, but they are treated in discussions of plants and methods.

Though this book is written specifically for Southern California, parts of it may be of help to gardeners everywhere who have greenhouses. It can also help those who live in Mediterranean or subtropical climates throughout the world who can use it like an encyclopedia of subtropical gardening. (Gardeners in other parts of the world will need to vary the month-by-month schedule to fit their climates. Temperature requirements will apply anywhere, but some specific recommendations, such as the ingredients of planting mixes and names of products, may be altered to fit what's locally available.) Many of the "Quick Tips" and step-by-step planting and growing directions can be helpful to gardeners anywhere.

Our Unique Schedule for Garden Tasks. Gardening in Southern California offers endless surprises and challenges. It can be a delight, but in order to garden here successfully you have to understand the many problems and solutions that are unique to our region. If you don't have a certain amount of local know-how you won't be able to avoid the pitfalls and reap the rich rewards. Of all the conditions and problems that make gardening in Southern California quite different from anywhere else, there's none more characteristic than our scheduling. Given our climate and our soil, when, what, and how should we plant, propagate, fertilize, and prune?

That's why this book is arranged month by month and why it is meant to be used as a handbook—really to hold your hand as you garden. You'll find step-by-step how-tos and special gardening techniques for the particular plants you grow and, as you apply them, develop the local savvy every Southern California gardener needs.

Special Helps in This Book. While organizing the month-by-month chapters I found that some topics could be covered in only one specific month—pruning roses in January, for example—but other topics could have been discussed in any of several months. For instance, planting and harvesting bananas is discussed in August because it's a hot month, but I could have covered that subject in June or July. So each chapter begins with a brief table of contents and ends with a checklist of what to do in that month, and the page number next to each item tells where that topic is discussed in detail, so you can refer to it easily no matter which month's chapter it's in. Also use these lists to check off jobs after they're completed. Remember as you consult the checklists that no gardener is likely to grow every plant mentioned, and please don't be overwhelmed by the number of jobs they recommend.

For topics of special interest to you, by all means consult other books—guides to native and drought-resistant plants, say, or to pruning. A number that I recommend are listed in the bibliography. This book wasn't designed to aid in plant identification. If you don't know all the plants that are mentioned, the best way to learn them is to search them out at nurseries and botanical gardens or look them up in reference works. Some good aids to plant identification are also included in the bibliography.

You'll also find many "Rules of Thumb" scattered throughout this book. They're designed to help you do things right the first time instead of learning through mistakes. Of course you may think rules are meant for breaking, and there's some sense to that. No rule fits every occasion; an experienced gardener knows when and if a particular rule can safely be broken. But unless you're experienced, rules are helpful guideposts on the road to successful gardening.

Many horticultural terms are defined briefly where first used in the text as well as more fully in the glossary at the back of the book. Because a number of these terms are commonly misunderstood or incompletely understood, just browsing through the glossary may answer many questions. Additionally, for rose growers, there is a chart of the Rose-Pro Method at the end of the monthly chapters. It gives those who choose this highly effective method a quick summation of the tasks throughout the year. There is also a list of seed and plant sources. The index will help you refer to any topic at any time of year.

What You Need To Know First
About Climate, Plant Choice, Soils, Fertilizer, Water, Planting, Pruning, Pests, and Weeds

Gardening is different in Southern California. Anyone who's ever gardened elsewhere will tell you that. It's not like back East, where so many of us came from and I once gardened. It's not like England, where I was born and began gardening at the age of three. It's not even like Florida, that other state that attracts retirees with year-round warm weather. Even people who've never gardened anywhere else soon realize how different Southern California gardening is; all you have to do is flip through any book on basic gardening to realize that much of the advice just doesn't apply here.

The Nature of Our Climate

What It Means to Live in a Mediterranean Climate. Southern California is blessed with a Mediterranean climate, one of the most salubrious growing climates in the world. The main characteristics of a Mediterranean climate are mild winters with enough rain to support plant growth and warm and dry summers with virtually no rain. The factors that create our climate are much like those that create similar climates in other parts of the world: the Mediterranean basin, South Africa, central Chile, and southwestern Australia. Our distance from the equator makes our temperatures subtropical, but our position on the southwest corner of a great land mass—in our case the North American continent—keeps our summers dry.

The Pacific Ocean, with its relatively even temperature, also keeps our climate mild. In general, the closer your garden is to the ocean the cooler it will be in summer and the warmer in winter. The farther inland you live the more extreme the temperatures your garden will undergo.

What's a Climate Zone? Within our overall Mediterranean climate there are many geographical variations. These are called "plant climates," or, more commonly, "climate zones." Each of these is a geographical area in which the yearly temperature range, length of seasons, average precipitation, humidity, amount of sunshine, and other factors combine to make certain plants grow better than others. Climate zones are caused by masses of air moving over our varied topography of coastal plains, hills and valleys, central uplands, high mountains, and deserts.

Much study has been done on plant climates by the University of California Agricultural Extension and others. But because of the technical aspects of agricultural plant climates, many of which overlap, most California home gardeners rely on the zones and maps in the *Sunset Western Garden Book.* When I mention a specific zone in this book by number or name I'm referring to the zones found in this widely respected work. Usually, however, areas are described here in more general terms, such as "coastal" versus "inland" or, in some cases, a little more specifically as "gardens in inland valleys" in contrast to "right along the beach."

How to Recognize Microclimates in Your Garden. In addition to major climate zones there are minizones, called "microclimates." Microclimates are small areas within a climate zone where conditions favor the growth of some plants and not others because of factors of climate particular to that spot. Every neighborhood, every yard has physical characteristics that produce slightly varying climates. Some plants may flourish on the east side of your home but die or do badly on the west. South-facing hillsides collect warmth and are especially good places for growing tropical plants; north-facing hillsides are cooler and thus good for camellias and azaleas.

Gaps on slopes let cold air drain off, while depressions, solid hedges, and walls catch or hold it. Garages, bushes, and walled patios can trap cold air in winter and warm air in summer, creating a more extreme climate than in the rest of the garden. Places that are open to the sky are more likely to be hit by frost than covered areas, because heat absorbed by the earth and by plants during the day radiates up to a clear open sky and is absorbed by the atmosphere.

How Santa Ana Winds Affect Our Weather.
The so-called Santa Ana winds—a climate factor that cuts across several zones in Southern California—temporarily determine the condition of the weather. A Santa Ana is a dry wind, at its worst with gale force, that blows from a vast interior region to the sea and may strike several times a year, most often between October and March. Santa Anas usually last from one to three days. Though Santa Anas disrupt what we think of as "normal" weather patterns, they're as natural to our climate as winter rainstorms. Similar winds are not unknown in other Mediterranean climates.

Santa Ana winds damage plants by their force, drying out their leaves through excessive transpiration and sometimes killing new plantings. When these winds strike, gardeners should make sure plants are well watered. Hanging baskets and delicate container-grown plants should be misted and moved to areas protected from sun and wind.

Plant Choice

The Varied Palette. One of the things that makes gardening in Southern California so much fun—yet also a challenge—is the wide range of plants we can grow. Although we can't grow plants that need a long period of winter chill in order to bloom, such as viburnum and Bing cherries, we are able to grow a great many plants common to cold-winter climates, such as wisteria, lilac, peonies, and privet. Among flowers and vegetables, most annuals and selected perennials flourish here. Native plants and those that hail from Mediterranean climates similar to ours broaden the palette still further. We can also grow many tropicals and subtropicals from all over the world, especially those from higher elevations. This mix of plants from many regions, with strong tropical and subtropical accents, is what gives our gardens their characteristically Southern California look. It's almost impossible to take a photograph of a local scene without a palm tree, an orange tree, a hibiscus, or some other exotic-looking plant in the background.

The Specialty Plants. Among the many species we grow are groups often called "specialty plants" because they require special attention and know-how. These plants and classes of plants include camellias, ferns, fuchsias, begonias, daylilies, hibiscus, pelargoniums (geraniums), irises, roses, orchids, epiphyllums (orchid cacti), cacti and succulents, bromeliads, palms, bonsai, vegetables, herbs, bamboo, rare and tropical fruits, and California native plants.

How to Deal with Bare Bulldozed Ground or Rock-Hard Subsoil

There are two ways to improve bulldozed ground so plants can grow in it. Either will work if done properly.

1. **Add Topsoil.** But when adding topsoil it's important to avoid creating interfaces. Don't just layer it on top; amend the subsoil first. Remove and haul away at least a foot of the existing soil. Create a proper marriage of soils by rototilling the subsurface and mixing into it soil amendments, gypsum if the soil is clayey (as explained on page 19), and some topsoil. Then replace the removed foot of soil with high-quality amended topsoil.

2. **Amend the Soil You've Got.** This method is the less expensive and is used on most commercial and residential sites. First have a soil sample tested (as discussed on page 18). Next, unless you plan to fill depressions or mound the ground, haul away some of the native soil to make space for the amendments. Rototill 8 inches deep, or—better yet—use a backhoe or plow to loosen the ground a foot deep. Add chemicals and fertilizers as indicated by your soil test, plus organic amendments measuring between 25 percent and 50 percent of the volume of soil you're amending. This means working in a 4- to (preferably) 6-inch-deep layer of well-rotted or nitrolized organic amendment, such as wood shavings and manure, into the top 8 to 12 inches of ground. Don't skimp on the organic amendments!

Specialty plants engender such enthusiasm among hobbyists that they have fan clubs—plant societies made up of beginners and old-timers alike—devoted to their culture. One of Southern California's most valuable botanical resources is its incredible number of active chapters of plant societies and the eminent experts who are members. One of the best ways to learn how to grow specialty plants is to join a plant society or simply attend one or two meetings.

Most of us grow specialty plants in our homes and gardens. You'll find advice on their care throughout this book.

Soil Problems and Solutions

How Plants Depend on Soil. Good gardening begins with good soil, the surface layer of earth that supports plant life. Soil is made up of particles of weathered rock, organic matter, air, water, and microorganisms. Plants anchor their roots in it and get most of their nourishment from it; thus the health of your plants is largely dependent on the condition of your soil. *Fertile soils* contain many elements and properties, like minerals, organic matter, and good drainage, that make plants thrive, while *poor soils* are low in them. If you live in Southern California and have poor soil, you're not alone; that's what many of us have to start with.

How to Assess the General Condition of Your Soil. The first task of every gardener is to give plants good ground to grow in. Start out by assessing plant health and the general condition of your soil. If your plants are growing well and looking healthy, if water sinks into the ground readily instead of running off or puddling, and if the soil doesn't dry out too quickly, chances are your soil is in basically good condition. In this case, your concern should be to maintain it. But if your plants are in poor shape, if they look stressed and grow slowly or not at all, and if drainage is either very slow or so rapid that water runs right through, your soil needs improvement.

Improvements Humus Makes in Soil. The best way to improve almost any soil is by working in organic soil amendments. As the organic matter decomposes in the ground it becomes humus, largely decomposed animal and vegetable matter. The decomposition of organic matter, including the chemical properties of humus, improves soil's fertility and structure. Without humus, minerals can be chemically locked up so plant roots can't use them. Humus helps sandy soils hold water, and it helps clay soils to drain.

In the West, where rainfall is sparse, our soils are generally very low in humus, while in the East, where rainfall is greater, most soils contain a high percentage of it. Humus doesn't stay in the ground forever; it gradually breaks down. So nature constantly replenishes her rich organic soils with fallen leaves, rotted twigs, grass, and animal matter. In your Southern California garden, it's up to you to do this job. In small areas you can use a spade to dig the amendments into the ground; in large areas you will need to rent a rototiller to incorporate the amendments into the soil.

When You Begin with Bare Ground. In many cases, owners of new homes start out with nothing but bare bulldozed ground. All topsoil—the uppermost, more fertile layer of soil—has been scraped away. This leaves nothing but bare subsoil, the lower layer that usually has lower fertility and a different texture and color than topsoil. In some cases what's left can hardly be called soil at all. But don't give up in dismay. By working in large amounts of organic soil amendments that will gradually break down in the soil, most subsoils can be eventually turned into topsoil. (See box on page 16 for ways to cope with bulldozed ground.) Additionally, the cycles of wetting and drying of the soil that are a natural part of gardening can actually improve the soil's structure—the arrangement of the variously sized particles in the soil that in turn determines

How to Improve Drainage on a Bulldozed Lot Prior to Planting

Grade the improved soil to a gentle slope; then dig trenches and install drains to carry excess water, by gravity, into the street or a drainage ditch. When properly installed, French and conventional drains can alleviate drainage problems in large areas. Other kinds of drains, such as sleeve drains and chimney drains, are made for individual plants and are discussed on page 34.

French drains allow excess underground water to seep into perforated pipe that's laid in gravel. The perforated side of the pipe is laid face-down (or on the sides, when there are two sets of perforations), so soil particles won't clog the openings, and the gravel is covered with a narrow sheet of plastic. Conventional drains remove excess surface water only. Flexible, unperforated pipe is used for these, and entrance grates are installed in low spots.

how the particles work together. The very process of growing plants with fibrous roots that penetrate the ground can also help to break it apart, and so improve its structure.

Your Soil's pH Value. Another factor that determines how well plants grow in soil is its pH value, its degree of acidity or alkalinity. The pH scale is numbered from 0 to 14; 7.0 is neutral. As values decrease, soil is increasingly acid; as they rise above 7.0, the soil is increasingly alkaline. For most plants a soil pH of 6.0 to 7.0 is ideal, because the elements that are essential for plant growth have their maximum availability in this range. However, a soil pH between 5.0 and 8.0 is usually satisfactory. Certain plants, like azaleas and camellias, are called "acid loving" because they grow best at a soil pH of about 5.0.

In the eastern part of the United States most soils are too acid for cultivated plants, so farmers and gardeners add lime to make them more al-kaline; in other words, they raise the pH level. Many Western soils are too alkaline, so when necessary we make them more acid by adding soil sulfur or such acidifying organic soil amendments as leaf mold, pine needles, peat moss, or wood shavings. To put it another way, we *lower* the pH level.

If you have an established garden and your plants appear to be in good health, it may never be necessary for you to determine the pH value of your soil. However, it's fun, easy, and inform-ative to test pH. You can find an inexpensive kit at almost any nursery or garden supply store. It takes only a few minutes to combine a dry soil sample with the solution provided, wait the re-quired length of time, and check the results on the color chart that comes with the kit.

If you want to test your soil for plant nutri-ents, typically nitrogen, potassium, and phos-phorus, you'll need to purchase a more complicated and expensive kit. Or you can have your soil professionally tested in a laboratory, a service that's available through many nurseries and some offices of the U.S. Department of Agriculture or the U.S. Bureau of Soil Conser-vation. Soil tests don't tell you anything about the structure of your soil or the percentage of humus in it, but they can sometimes pinpoint deficiencies or problems. It's wise to keep in mind, however, that the results of such tests can vary considerably among soil samples from one garden. Don't depend on the results to indicate a simple cure-all, especially not for the whole garden.

Your Soil's Texture. Before beginning any pro-gram of soil improvement, find out what type of soil you're dealing with so you can assess its strengths and weaknesses. Soil is usually classi-fied according to its "texture," which means the size of the particles that are in it. The three basic particle sizes, from largest to smallest, are called "sand," "silt," and "clay." "Loam" is a mixture of all three. All of these basic soil types can be found in Southern California; often more than one occurs in a single garden. Soils with particles larger than sand are often called "gravelly soils." Decomposed granite is a gravelly soil with unique qualities and is found in many parts of Southern California. (Some decomposed granite soils might almost as well be called "sand" or "loam"; what distinguishes the granitic soils is that they contain some particles that are larger than sand.)

The box on page 20 will help you recognize which soil types you have in your garden. Once you know what type of soil you're dealing with, you'll be better able to choose appropriate amendments and techniques to improve its structure and fertility.

Why You Must Never Mix Sand into Clay

Because loam is a mixture of sand, silt, and clay some gardeners think they can lighten clay soil by mixing sand into it. This is a drastic mistake.

It would be necessary to add an enormous volume of sand—well over 50 percent—to clay soil in order to improve it. Smaller quantities of sand would only fill up the spaces between the clay particles and turn good clay soil into some-thing similar to cement. You'd make your soil denser and not improve drainage. The only safe way to improve soil structure is to increase its humus content by adding organic amendments.

When using soil amendments, be aware that organic matter that isn't rotted, nitrolized, or naturally high in nitrogen will rob nitrogen from the soil as it rots, thus killing plants by starvation. (Two rules of thumb for maintaining adequate nitrogen are found on page 25.) Very wet vegetable matter, like melon rind and papaya skins, can be put straight into a 12-inch-deep hole in garden soil. For guidelines, study the list on page 25.

Finding and Solving Difficult Problems and Conditions. Regardless of which type, or types, of soil you have, you may have to overcome several frustrating problems and negative conditions before you can grow a good garden. The problems most often encountered in local gardens are hardpan, rock-filled soil, root-filled soil, and saline soil. Some of these problems may not be obvious at first glance, so it's important to know how to recognize them as well as how to deal with them if they appear.

The box on page 22 can help you recognize which, if any, of these problems you have in your garden and suggest ways to overcome them.

How Gypsum Helps Some Clay Soils Drain Better. Gypsum is a relatively inexpensive soil amendment. Adding it to clay soil often helps and won't hurt.

Sodium pulls clay particles closer together. This makes the soil denser and less easily penetrated by water. In cases where clay particles in the soil have accumulated a high level of exchangeable sodium (alkali), gypsum or calcium sulfate ($CaSO_4$) can loosen the soil and help it drain. Gypsum added to soil releases soluble calcium, which replaces some of the sodium on the clay particles and thereby produces a more open soil structure. Gypsum will not correct poor soil drainage when it is caused by physical conditions, such as fine texture or compaction. Soils that have these problems can be improved by incorporating large quantities of organic matter.

In most cases, apply enough gypsum to

How Often to Add Organic Soil Amendments to Garden Soil

The **Rule of Thumb** is: *Every time you replant an annual bed or vegetable plot, dig in an inch or two (up to 4 inches) of organic soil amendment. Build the humus content of permanent beds and cool-season lawns by topping with organic mulch at least once a year.*

---

make it look as though a light snow has fallen (between 2 and 5 pounds to 100 square feet), and then work it into the ground. As much as 10 pounds per 100 square feet can be used on clay soil prior to seeding or sodding lawns.

How Mulch Helps Soil. Mulch is a layer of organic matter, or such inorganic material as gravel or plastic sheeting, that's applied to the surface of the soil to reduce evaporation and heat or cool the soil. Mulches can also help control weeds, stop the surface of clay soils from cracking, improve water penetration, and increase the soil's biological activity. Organic mulch gradually rots and can then be worked in.

Many organic soil amendments, such as ground bark, wood or bark chips, stable litter, hay, straw, leaf mold, pine needles, dry grass clippings, and compost, can be used as mulch. Lightweight materials like peat moss are less practical since they may blow away. Note that some organic materials that have a low nitrogen content—like hulls, nutshells, and wood or bark chips—are suitable only as mulch and should not be dug into the soil until they are fully decomposed, or they'll rob nitrogen from the soil as they rot (rules of thumb for nitrogen use are included in the box on soil amendments on page 25). Large-textured organic mulches may harbor pests—especially sowbugs, slugs, and snails.

How to Recognize and Deal with Five Basic Soil Types

- **Sandy Soil:** A loose earth mainly composed of tiny particles of rock between 0.05 and 2 millimeters in size. It feels scratchy or gritty to the touch. If you grip a damp handful, it won't hold together. Water and nutrients drain right out before plants can take a gulp. Sandy soils are often called "light" because they're easy to work.
  Virtues: Ease of digging and good drainage.
  Problems: Failure to hold water and nutrients. Apparently "hungry" since it eats up organic materials so rapidly. When completely dry, some sandy soils are difficult to get wet because the individual grains of sand have become coated with organic fats and waxes from decomposing organic matter, such as eucalyptus or acacia litter.
  Solutions: Dig in copious organic amendments. Apply mulch and horse manure that does not contain salt from salt licks. Where necessary, use chemical penetrants (surfactants) to wet dry soils and aid water penetration. Don't let sandy soils dry out completely. Use slow-release chemical fertilizers or organic fertilizers; these won't wash out of the soil as quickly as other types.

- **Silt:** A fine-grained earth mainly composed of particles that are rounder and more weathered than sand particles, and intermediate in size between sand and clay particles. If you rub it between your fingers when moist, it feels smooth, slippery, and soapy but not sticky. Silt holds more water than sand but less than clay. It's often found in river bottoms and on valley floors.
  Virtues: Drains better than clay, yet holds more water than sand. Retains humus and nutrients longer than sand.
  Problems: Compacts when walked on to a much greater degree than sand. When wet it becomes almost like quicksand. Doesn't hold nutrients for long. Cultivating when too wet can make silt dense and restrict the free passage of air and water.
  Solutions: Work in organic amendments at regular intervals. Apply organic mulch. Don't walk on vegetable rows and flowerbeds. Dig and cultivate only when soil is moist and not soggy.

- **Clay:** A firm, fine-grained earth containing a large amount of tiny mineral particles less than 0.002 millimeter in size that have negatively charged surfaces. The electrical charge helps clay retain positively charged minerals, like ammonium, potassium, calcium, and magnesium. Clay feels slippery and sticky when wet. Grip a damp handful and it will hold together in a solid lump. Clay soils bake hard in hot weather and hold moisture when wet. Their color varies from white, gray, and greenish to dark brown (adobe) or red (terra-cotta). Clay soils are often called "heavy" because they're difficult to work.
  Virtues: Mineral richness; water retention during drought.
  Problems: Poor drainage. Hardness in dry weather. Heavy, sticky, and difficult to work when wet. Cultivating clay when wet can worsen drainage.
  Solutions: Work in organic amendments. Apply gypsum. Install drains. Build raised beds.

- **Loam:** A combination of clay, silt, and sand. There are many types of loam, depending upon the percentages of the components. Clay loams (those containing more clay) are heavy soils. Sandy loams are light.
  Virtues: Fertile. Holds water but also drains well.
  Problems: Easily compacted when moist.
  Solutions: Maintain with regular additions of organic soil amendment. Don't walk on moist garden soil.

- **Decomposed Granite:** A grayish or light brown, granular, and sometimes flaky soil mainly composed of variously sized particles of granite rock, some of which are larger in size than grains of sand. It feels loose, gritty, and abrasive to the touch. The unevenly sized particles are easily seen with the naked eye. On bulldozed ground and mesa tops decomposed granite is often packed down hard as rock, but when it's alluvial (deposited by water), in canyons and valleys, it's often loose and friable.

Virtues: Excellent drainage, aeration, and mineral richness. Some alluvial types are easy to work.

Problems: Rocklike hardness when found in subsoils and on mesa tops make the ground difficult to dig. Water and nitrogen leach out quickly.

Solutions: Rototill. Add large quantities of organic matter: nitrolized wood shavings, mushroom compost, green manures, or various animal manures—for example, poultry manure. Where ground is rock hard, plant in raised beds or plow up the surface of hard areas, mix in organic amendments and some topsoil, and then cover with a foot of topsoil.

Black or clear plastic sheeting and some woven plastic fabrics are also used as mulches, but these inorganic mulches warm rather than cool the soil. Clear plastic makes the ground too hot for most crops in Southern California, other than strawberries planted in fall. Black plastic can increase yields of warm-weather crops such as corn and melons. However, unperforated plastic does not allow water penetration and thus requires the use of a drip system beneath it.

Why Plants in Containers Need Special Soil

When planting in containers, always use a bagged commercial soil mix recommended for container-grown plants, or make your own potting mix, though it's easier and often cheaper to purchase a ready-made mix. Growing plants in containers is different from growing plants in the ground. With the possible exception of select decomposed-granite soils (such as occur in the city of Claremont in the San Gabriel Valley), garden soil packs down in containers and doesn't drain, killing plant roots.

Fertilizer Basics

Plants not only need humus; they also need fertilizer. A fertilizer is any material, either organic or inorganic, that supplies elements essential to plants for growth. Our native Southern California soils contain only small quantities of nitrogen, which is probably the most important element plants need. Thus we must add it in some form or our plants will go hungry. (Specific recommendations for feeding particular plants are given throughout the month-by-month chapters.)

The Meaning of the Numbers on a Package of Fertilizer. Every package of fertilizer has a trio of numbers on the label. The first number is the percentage (by weight) of nitrogen in the product; the second is the percentage of phosphorus; the third is the percentage of potassium. These three elements, known simply as N, P, and K, their chemical symbols, are found singly or in combination in many fertilizers. For example, fertilizer labeled 16-8-4 contains 16 percent nitrogen, 8 percent phosphorus, and 4 percent potassium. The remaining 72 percent is made up of other chemicals, such as calcium, sulfur, and oxygen, and some filler, which is added to the product to make it less concentrated and more easily measured and spread.

A high first number (nitrogen) means the product will give plants a lot of top growth, green leaves, and fast growth. Formulas with a high second number or second and third numbers (phosphorus and potassium) give plants the elements essential for flowering and fruiting.

How to Recognize and Solve the Four Most Common Soil Problems

The following soil problems have nothing to do with the fertility or the pH or type of your topsoil. Some are hidden from view and thus often go undetected, but any one of them, if not appropriately solved, could prevent you from growing a healthy garden.

- **Hardpan:** A layer of hard compacted soil of any type cemented together by minerals and almost impenetrable by roots or water. Often buried beneath a layer of good soil; typical of housing developments where a layer of topsoil has been applied over bulldozed subsoil.
  Virtues: None.
  Problems: No drainage. Roots go down, hit bottom, and are stopped cold.
  Solutions: Build French and conventional drains (see page 17). Plant in raised beds. In some localities, you can dig down and break through to a porous layer. When adding a layer of topsoil over hard subsoil, rototill and amend the bottom layer first.

- **Rock-Filled Soil:** Any type of soil that's largely filled with pebbles and rocks or shallowly based on rocky outcroppings.
  Virtues: Rocks may have beauty, practical value, and design potential.
  Problems: Difficult to dig; may have poor drainage; may not contain enough soil to support plant life. Roots of trees may not be able to penetrate the rock substrate.
  Solutions: In some areas, holes suitable for tree planting can be blasted with dynamite. Build raised beds and terraces, and fill them with topsoil or organic materials such as nitrolized wood shavings and mushroom compost. Use hardscape (decks, paths, pergolas, and the like), container plants, and hanging baskets. Grow rock-garden plants and epiphytes. (Epiphytes are plants that grow on other plants but don't sap nourishment from them, as do parasites.)

- **Root-Filled Soil:** Any type of soil made hard, dry, and impenetrable by the roots of such invasive trees as eucalyptus, Monterey cypress

(*Cupressus macrocarpa*), and melaleuca. Often encountered in old gardens.
  Virtues: Shade from the trees is helpful for some plants. Old trees offer charm.
  Problems: Water won't penetrate, the ground can't be dug, the roots invade planters from below, and new plants can't get started.
  Solutions: Plant in raised beds. Cover bare ground with river rock and paving stone. Add hardscape; plant in containers. Also use Biobarrier, a patented fabric containing nodules of slow-release herbicide. Install Biobarrier horizontally under a layer of paving stones beneath raised beds and compost piles or vertically in the ground next to flower and vegetable beds to prevent roots from invading them. (Biobarrier does not harm plants; it only prunes their roots.)

- **Saline Soil:** Soil of any type that contains enough salt to be injurious to plants. A frequent problem in desert areas where salts accumulate in the soil from salty irrigation water, fertilizers, and manures and where rainfall is insufficient to leach salts to lower levels.
  Virtues: None.
  Problems: Salt injures roots and burns foliage; it may kill plants. Limits the types of plants that can be grown to those that are salt resistant. Evaporation can lift salts into the top layers of soil. Capillary action then pulls water to the surface, where it evaporates and deposits a white salt crust.
  Solutions: No matter what type of irrigation is used, apply an adequate volume of water to wash salts out of the top levels of earth down into the ground. Use the furrow system for vegetables, but don't plant in the middle of the top of the mound because salts accumulate there; plant close to the edge of the mound. Construct watering basins for larger plants. Use mulches to reduce evaporation of water from the soil surface. An application of gypsum followed by heavy watering may leach away enough salts to reclaim some sodic (salty) soils.

Both phosphorus and potassium promote overall plant health and stimulate growth of strong healthy roots, though in different ways.

If plants are starved for nitrogen they won't have good health, a satisfactory rate of growth, or enough vigor to produce ample flowers and fruit. On the other hand, too much nitrogen will damage their roots; burn, twist, and deform their leaves; or may even kill the entire plant. Recommendations for fertilizing plants are often given in pounds of "actual nitrogen"—the true amount of nitrogen in a product. For example, a fertilizer labeled 21-0-0 (ammonium sulfate) contains 21 percent nitrogen, so a 10-pound bag of ammonium sulfate contains 2.1 pounds of actual nitrogen. Recommendations given in pounds of actual nitrogen are helpful because one can choose any formula and figure out how much of it to use.

A number of terms are used to describe fertilizers. A "complete fertilizer" (sometimes called a "balanced fertilizer") is one that contains nitrogen, phosphorus, and potassium, though the percentages in different products can vary greatly. An "incomplete fertilizer" contains only one or two of these elements. A product described as "high in growth ingredients" has a high first number and lower second and third numbers, while a "high bloom" formula refers to a product that has high second and third numbers. "Preplant" products have low first numbers and high second and third numbers.

In this book I often use such general terms and give examples of appropriate numerical formulations. This is because products with the formulas I mention are available in Southern California, and it may be helpful to gardeners to know the sort of formula that can fill a given purpose. It doesn't mean you should spend hours looking for a product with those exact numbers. The recommendations are meant only

A Basic Soil-less Potting Mix for Containers

Dozens of potting mixes have been invented by nurserymen, researchers, and gardeners for different purposes. This formula is designed as an all-purpose mix for outdoor container-grown plants. (Some special formulas for specific plants are given in the month-by-month chapters.)

- 1 cubic foot premoistened peat moss (instructions for moistening are given on page 53)
- 1 cubic foot nitrolized ground bark or nitrolized wood shavings
- 1 cubic foot sand or perlite (small lightweight, air-filled granules made from volcanic rock expanded at high temperatures)
- ⅓ cup ground dolomitic limestone or agricultural lime (not quicklime)
- ½ cup 5-10-10 fertilizer containing trace elements

Mix all ingredients thoroughly, and use for immediate needs. If you want to store this mix for a month or two, add a granulated wetting agent according to package directions, and don't premoisten the peat moss.

as basic guidelines and can help you make intelligent substitutions.

Some fertilizers also contain iron and trace minerals, which are necessary for overall plant health and for preventing chlorosis (an iron deficiency that causes yellow leaves and green veins). Whether trace elements are included is usually, but not always, noted on the package. Some fertilizers contain only one or two trace elements, and others contain many. Because fertilizers are made to do different jobs there are great variations in their formulas—the combinations of ingredients and the amounts of each ingredient they contain.

A Gallery of Soil Amendments and How to Use Them

Soil amendments vary in cost and availability, as well as in the characteristics of use cited below. Buy what's carried at a local nursery or, cheaper for you and healthier for the environment, use what's available as discards in your area.

- **Apple and Grape Pomace:** This by-product of wine and cider factories is excellent for working into soil—it's especially good in clay soil—and releases nitrogen slowly.

- **Bean Straw** (a by-product of field-grown California dried lima beans, available from farmers in some areas): Work it directly into soil. Bean straw decomposes rapidly in soil that's damp and is especially good for decomposed granite and clay soils.

- **Chipper Materials** (leftovers from tree trimming): Use as mulch or path cover. They can be added to garden soil when fully decomposed, but watch plants for nitrogen deficiency (telltale signs are yellow leaves, which may drop off, and slow or stunted growth), and add extra nitrogen if necessary. Chipper materials may contain tree seeds. Pull up and destroy unwanted volunteers.

- **Commercial Organic Soil Amendments** (many kinds): Work these into soil or use them as mulch.

- **Compost:** Make it yourself by the slow or fast method. (See page 76.) Work it into garden soil.

- **Grass Clippings:** Work these into soil as "green manure" (see next item) or use them in compost. Either use works best when the clippings are dried first, and they must be allowed to dry first if used as mulch; otherwise the clippings form a smelly, sticky mat. They have a high nitrogen content.

- **Green Manure** (alfalfa, red clover, lupine, crown vetch, and others): Plant the seeds as a cover crop on bare ground in fall; then work the green plants into the ground in spring. They decompose rapidly in warm weather. A **Rule of Thumb** is: *After turning green manure under the ground, wait one to two weeks before planting vegetables or flowers.*

- **Ground Carrot, Apple, and Vegetable Fibers** (from health-food stores or juice factories): Work apple into soil. Add other fibers to compost, or dig them into paths between vegetable rows to build soil and feed earthworms.

- **Kelp and Seaweed:** Hose these off and chop them with a spade before working them into soil or adding them to compost. They decompose rapidly and add trace minerals.

- **Leaf Mold:** Work this into soil or use it as mulch; reserve it for acid-loving plants. Leaf litter under native oaks can contain oak root fungus and shouldn't be used unless it's been sterilized.

- **Leaves, Unrotted:** Add leaves to the compost pile or use them as mulch. All leaves, including eucalyptus and ivy leaves, can be composted, but some take much longer to decompose than others.

- **Manure, Aged:** Work this into the soil, or use it as mulch. It sometimes has high salt content. Don't use it on carrots since it causes splitting. Both aged and raw manures contain nitrogen, phosphorus, and potassium in varying amounts.

- **Manure, Raw and Unaged:** Apply a layer on top of the ground in the furrows between vegetable rows or under trees or berry bushes. Raw manure will burn roots if it's applied too heavily or too soon before planting. Do not use manure chunks that contain salt from salt licks. A **Rule of Thumb** is: *After digging or rototilling raw manure into soil, irrigate thoroughly; wait at least one month before planting.*

To turn raw manure into aged manure, pile it up in a shady place, cover it with plastic (to protect from flies and reduce odors), and leave it to age. The **Rule of Thumb** is: *Age horse manure three months; age cow, chicken, and rabbit manures one year or use them unaged to heat up the compost pile.* (Chicken and rabbit manures are more concentrated and hotter than horse and cow manures and should be used in smaller quantities.)

- **Nitrolized or Composted Wood Shavings:** Work either of these into soil, or use them as mulch.

- **Peat Moss:** Work this into soil. It's highly acid, long lasting, and holds moisture but is difficult to get wet. When using in large quantity, wet it down first. (See how on page 53.)

- **Pine Needles:** Use these as mulch under camellias and azaleas or as path cover in a vegetable garden. Compost formed from needles can be mixed with premoistened peat moss (see page 53) for planting azaleas and camellias.

- **Rotted Hay:** Work it into soil or use it as mulch. (No extra nitrogen is needed if the hay is completely broken down by composting.)

- **Sawdust:** Work it into soil or use as mulch. It does rob nitrogen from the soil as it rots. In order to safely counteract this process, add nitrogen to the sawdust prior to digging it into the ground. One **Rule of Thumb** is: *Add 1 to 1½ pounds actual nitrogen to every 100 pounds of raw shavings.* For a layer of sawdust you've spread 1 inch deep over 100 square feet, the nitrogen required would be that in approximately 1 pound of ammonium sulfate. (The specific recommended ratio by weight is 1.75 parts of nitrogen to 100 parts of unrotted organic matter.)

Besides the nitrogen that you supply when you first apply the sawdust, add nitrogen fertilizer regularly to feed plants. When using raw sawdust as mulch you must compensate by feeding plants more often. The **Rule of Thumb** is: *When using sawdust as mulch, increase the nitrogen fertilizer you would regularly give your plants by one-fourth and feed them at more frequent intervals.*

- **Sludge:** Work it into soil. Though it contains some nitrogen it's not strong enough to burn roots, and it's good for sandy soils. Because it may, in some cases, contain heavy metals, don't add it to vegetable gardens.

- **Vegetable and Fruit Leavings from the Kitchen or Supermarket** (spoiled fruits and vegetables and green outer leaves of vegetables are available through produce managers): Add them to compost or bury them to feed earthworms. Or blend small quantities of fruit and vegetable waste with water in a blender, and pour the resulting liquid directly into garden soil.

- **Wheat and Oat Straw:** Use only as mulch. Don't work these into soil unless they've been composted and are largely decomposed. May contain weed seeds.

- **Wood and Bark Chips** (usually available as bagged commercial products): Use as mulch. They're a useful amendment for heavy soils but dangerous to plants (like sawdust, above, but to a greater degree) unless sufficient nitrogen is frequently added.

Table 1. Conversions: How Much Granulated Fertilizer to Use by Formula

A common recommendation for feeding vegetables is 1 pound of granulated 5-10-10 fertilizer for every 100 square feet of garden soil. Table 1 shows how much granulated fertilizer of other formulas you could substitute, decreasing the amount of fertilizer as the percentage of nitrogen in it increases. The **Rule of Thumb** is: *If you use fertilizer with a different formula, always decrease the poundage as its percentage of nitrogen increases.*

Formula	Lbs. per 100 Square Feet	Oz. per 100 Square Feet
5-10-10	1.00	16
6-18-6	0.80	13
8-12-4	0.57	9
12-6-6	0.40	6½
16-16-16	0.28	4½

Which Formula to Use. When you choose a fertilizer, consider the basic needs of the plant and the way nutrients act in soil. Nitrogen leaches out of soils quickly, but phosphorus and potassium are longer lasting. Thus, when your soil contains adequate levels of phosphorus and potassium, the main requirement of plants is nitrogen. This means that if you mix phosphorus and potassium into the soil prior to planting annual flowers—using a preplant formula high in phosphorus and potassium—there's no need to apply it again that season. Most permanent landscape plants need the addition of phosphorus and potassium only once a year.

Container plants are an exception. They need complete fertilizers at each feeding because most potting soils contain little or no phosphorus and potassium. (Instructions for fertilizing specialty plants—plants that require special treatment, as discussed on page 15—are given in the monthly chapters.)

Many fertilizers are sold under names that specify their intended use, such as "rose food" or "citrus food." There's nothing wrong with using some of these products. High-quality products recommended for acid-loving plants—particularly camellias and azaleas—make it easy to give them the right amount of nutrients in an acid formula that's beneficial for these plants. A good lawn fertilizer also will contain the proper balance of basic elements, including trace elements, for overall lawn health. But it's wise to read and compare labels because a particular fertilizer sometimes can be substituted for another. Often a product with a generic (use unspecified) label is a better buy than one with a specified purpose. You could use 1 pound of 5-10-5, for example, instead of ½ pound of 10-20-10. (Table 1 shows other conversion weights.)

Cheap sources of nitrogen, such as ammonium sulfate, will give you a quick surge of top growth, but they don't feed all parts of the plant, and they aren't long lasting. It's all right to use them for most applications of lawn fertilizer, but for best results be sure to feed your lawn at least once a year with a complete product.

Especially when purchasing lawn fertilizer, read the package to find out what form of nitrogen is contained in it. Nitrogens described by the terms "nitric" and "nitrate" are fast acting.

They'll give you a quick green-up but will soon be gone. "Ammonic" nitrogen is also fast acting, but it's held in the soil until bacteria change it to nitrate and thus lasts about a month during warm weather. Organic sources of nitrogen (discussed below) are slower acting. They stay in the soil longer and are less likely to burn plants. (Many fertilizers contain a combination of types, so you get the benefit of both results.)

Which Forms of Fertilizer to Use. Fertilizers come in many different forms, such as powders to mix in water, powdered or granular solids to add straight to soil, and liquids to dilute with water. There are also slow-release fertilizers, which are plastic coated or otherwise processed so that they release measured small amounts of nutrients over a long period every time the ground is watered. Each form of fertilizer is suited to a particular use or uses.

For home gardeners, the typical powdered or granular fertilizers are the ones you spread on the ground and then water in. You would use them, for example, to toss on ground covers in spring and around citrus and deciduous fruit trees or on the lawn. This is much more effective than spraying on a liquid fertilizer that contains no penetrants. Liquids are useful for feeding seedlings, rooted cuttings, and certain container-grown specialty plants. When adequately diluted, some of them can be sprayed directly on the leaves of plants—this method is called "foliar-feeding." Liquid fertilizers are also useful when added to drip systems to feed all your plants at once.

Slow-release coated pellets are a time-saving way to feed container-grown plants. The steady supply of fertilizer they provide compensates for the lack of nutriments in most potting mixes. Slow-release fertilizers are also available for lawns and general landscape use. They're partic-

ularly worthwhile if your soil is sandy or contains decomposed granite, since nitrogen is quickly leached out of these fast-draining soils. Timed-release pellets, such as Osmocote Tree and Shrub Planting Tablets or Agriform Tablets (the same product sold in larger quantities) or timed-release planting sacks, such as Best-Paks, when used at planting time in the bottom of planting holes, will feed plants for the first year.

What It Means to Be an Organic Gardener. Organic fertilizers are those derived from living organisms, animal or vegetable, such as manure, cottonseed meal, compost, blood meal, hoof and horn meal, bone meal, and wood ash. (Wood ash is often recommended in organic gardening publications as a source of potassium, but the University Extension advises against its use in Southern California because it's too alkaline for most local soils.) Organic gardeners, for either economic or philosophical reasons, feed all their plants with such fertilizers and refrain from using chemical pesticides, other than dormant sprays. Some basic tenets of the organic philosophy are that chemical fertilizers and pesticides harm the soil and environment, kill natural and beneficial organisms, and have a negative impact on the flavor and health-giving properties of food plants, whereas naturally occurring materials have the opposite effects. (Chemical fertilizers and pesticides are "organic" too, in scientific terminology, but the word as it has come to be used in relationship to farming and gardening denotes live rather than synthetic origins.)

Organic fertilizers generally work slower and aren't as concentrated as chemical fertilizers, but knowledgeable gardeners can use them successfully. Some gardeners use the organic method only in the vegetable garden. Vegetables (plus many other garden plants) that grow in full sun can be kept healthy and productive with only the

Table 2. What the Numbers Stand for on a Package of Fertilizer

Main Elements

Chemical	Nitrogen	Phosphorus	Potassium
Symbol	N	P	K
Sample Formula (percentages)	16	8	4
Examples of Chemical Sources	Ammonium sulfate Ammonium nitrate Urea	Single superphosphate	Potassium sulfate
Examples of Organic Sources	Cottonseed meal Blood meal	Bone meal	Greensand Wood ash (too alkaline, saline for local use)
What Each Element Does	Speeds vegetative growth; gives rich green color	Promotes growth of flowers and fruit plus good stems and roots; necessary for photosynthesis; good seed production	Promotes growth of flowers and fruit plus good stems and roots; gives flowers vibrant color; overall plant health
Evidence of Severe Deficiency*	Sickly yellow-green color, stunted growth	Purple or reddish leaf discoloration	Weak stems; browning and yellowing of leaf tips and edges

*Other factors can also cause these symptoms.

standard organic fertilizers—manure, compost, and other organic materials. Unfortunately, manure (particularly bagged cow manure), which is man's most ancient and inexpensive fertilizer, often contains large quantities of salt. Our water and soil are already too salty, and adding too much manure creates a buildup of salts that will retard growth. Chicken and rabbit manures usually, but not always, contain less salt in proportion to the amount of nutrients they supply. (Chicken manure contains more nitrogen and phosphorus than most other manures and can be purchased aged and bagged in many areas of Southern California.) Horse manure that is picked up daily by the horse owner is largely free from salt and safe to use.

Several other organic fertilizers, pelletized and powdered, are available in local nurseries. Always read the labels. (Some sludge products are unsafe for vegetable gardens.)

Irrigation and Water Conservation

Our Dependence on Imported Water. In Southern California rainfall is seasonal and the water we use for irrigation is imported, scarce, and expensive. During the last thirty or forty years our population has exploded while our water supplies have dwindled until the inevitable has at last become a reality: there's not enough water to go around. In good years when rains are adequate—and if we carefully conserve water—we can continue to keep our landscapes properly irrigated. But when there's a severe drought that lasts several years, like the drought of the late eighties and early nineties, water prices escalate, cutbacks are common, and in some areas it's against the law to water for landscaping purposes. These problems are likely to persist unless the state of California changes its priorities. (At the time this book was written agriculture uses almost 80 percent of California's irrigation water; homes and industries use 12 percent; and a relatively small amount—only 4 percent—is used for landscapes.)

But most Southern Californians deeply appreciate the value of plants and gardens and their importance to our quality of life. There's a growing awareness that landscape plants—especially trees—absorb carbon dioxide, give off oxygen, trap dust, muffle sounds, moisten and cool the atmosphere, and save power by reducing temperatures in buildings. Trees, shrubs, and—yes—even lawns make our cities and suburbs pleasant places in which to live instead of cheerless concrete jungles. Under the right conditions there's still a place for a few of the old favorites that need regular watering, including camellias, azaleas, roses, and hibiscus. However, when water supplies are cut back painful choices must sometimes be made between plants worth saving and those that are expendable. In such times use the precious water you have to save the larger plants and let the smaller and younger plants go. Lawns, flower borders, vegetables, ground covers, and young shrubs can be quickly replaced. But mature and graceful trees, shrubs, and vines that add character to the landscape are irreplaceable.

When water supplies are cut back many garden plants, even deep-rooted camellias and roses, can stay alive with much less irrigation than usual. (They'll just pull in their horns, pro-

Keys to Better Fertilizing

Don't feed plants indiscriminately; treat them as individuals. Some plants have low nitrogen requirements and will burn (the leaf tips will shrivel and turn brown) if given too much. Some need extra phosphorus or potassium. Still others require different formulas at various times of year. Container plants need to be fed more frequently than plants growing in the ground, because most potting soil mixes contain little or no nitrogen and only small amounts of other nutrients. Follow specific recommendations found throughout the month-by-month chapters.

Recommendations for fertilizing some specific plants, such as fruit trees, mention only the amount of actual nitrogen needed and give no guidance on additions of phosphorus and potassium. This is because the required amounts of these elements are much more difficult to determine. Various soils contain more or less of them, and they last longer in soils than nitrogen.

After applying fertilizer follow up with water. The **Rule of Thumb** is: *Water pellets and powders into the ground immediately after spreading them, or spread them just before the ground receives an inch of rain.* Dry fertilizer lying on top of the ground releases nitrogen into the air. The longer you leave it the more escapes.

duce no flowers, and stop growing; don't feed them.) But when water supplies are adequate remember that all garden plants need to be watered in order to survive, at least during the summer months. (Some native plants are exceptions.) Most plants need irrigation from time to time during the winter, too, and all plants, even drought-resistant ones, need plenty of water when they're first planted in order to get started.

Right and Wrong Ways to Irrigate. The many methods and the equipment used in irrigation are about as varied as the plants we grow, but—aside from an old-fashioned watering can—they fall into three basic categories. There are conventional underground irrigation systems, drip systems, and plain old garden hoses.

All automatic systems need to be regularly checked for leaks and malfunctioning parts. Also be sure your sprinklers are installed for proper overlap, to keep all the plants evenly watered. A frequent problem with overhead sprinklers is that they can cause water to pour off slopes and dry ground and run into the street. Control clocks that pulse water, applying it in short bursts separated by time intervals, can help prevent this problem by allowing adequate time for the water to sink into parched soil.

Drip, mist, or trickle systems are among the best and newest ways to water plants. Most of these systems feed water at controlled low pressure into an approximately ½-inch-diameter hose, or "header," which in turn feeds smaller spaghetti-sized hoses, or "microtubing," leading to individual plants. At the plants, "emitters" release a measured amount of water to root zones or mist the foliage. Some systems emit water through hoses buried in the ground. These include hoses made from recycled auto tires, which weep water from pores—gardeners call this "leaky-hose"—and perforated plastic drip tubing. Other systems allow you to convert your existing sprinklers to a drip operation. You simply unscrew the sprinkler head from the top of the riser, screw on the new drip attachment, and then connect up microtubes leading to specific plants. It's even possible to convert overhead irrigation of a small existing lawn: you remove strips of grass, install drip hoses a few inches under the soil surface, and replace the sod.

The worst way to water is to stand around, hose in hand, squirting water on bare ground. This only wets the surface, digs up the ground,

Quick Tip

How to Measure Inches of Irrigation Water.
An inch of water from an overhead sprinkler can be measured by setting out empty juice cans here and there, both close to and far away from a sprinkler. Measure the time it takes to fill the can with an inch of water. (This technique can also be used to test a new irrigation system and locate dry spots in your sprinkler pattern.)

and does more harm than good. If you must water with a hose, make watering basins around the root zones of shrubs and young trees, and build dikes of earth or bender board (wooden or plastic lawn edging) around flowerbeds. Lay the hose on the ground inside these areas and flood them.

How Your Soil Type Affects Watering. Some plants with shallow roots, including cool-season lawns, many annual flowers, and vegetables, need approximately an inch of rain weekly for optimum performance. Precise amounts and the intervals between watering can vary according to several factors—for example, when the weather is windy or hot, plants lose moisture from leaves and need more water. On an everyday basis soil type is the most important factor in how much to water.

Once clay soil has gotten thoroughly wet it hangs on to water much longer than sandy soil, which soon dries out. If you have clay soil you should water less frequently but for a longer time than a gardener in the same area but with sandy soil. The percentage of humus in the ground can also affect water penetration and retention. Organic soil amendments help water penetrate clay soils faster and drain more quickly. The amendments do the exact opposite for sandy soil, making water penetrate slightly more slowly and helping soil retain water longer.

In general, water penetrates sandy soil much faster than clay soil, so for sandy soil less is required to reach a given depth. The **Rule of Thumb** is: *One inch of water will penetrate sandy soil about 12 inches, loam about 7 inches, and clay soil only 5 inches, perhaps less.* (Sandy soil that sheds water instead of absorbing it is an exception. See page 20 for an explanation and solutions.)

How to Find Out the Depth of Water Penetration. You can't tell whether plants have enough water by looking at the surface of the ground. Sometimes the ground can look like a swamp on top but be as dry as a desert underneath. At other times the ground may look dusty dry on top but still be soggy wet below. How do you really know whether water reached those roots? The best way is to dig down with a trowel or spade and take a look: if the soil is saturated with water below the roots of plants, there's enough water.

Other ways to test soil moisture are with a soil probe (awl) or with a tensiometer. Though expensive, these instruments are a means to quantify moisture at specific depths of soil. A soil probe is a metal tube with handles on the top and a cut-out section on one side of the lower portion. Wind it manually into the ground a few inches at a time; then pull it up and remove the earth trapped in it. Keep repeating the process until you get a soil sample from the required depth. A tensiometer consists of a dial attached to a long metal probe, usually with handles at right angles so it can be thrust deeply into the ground.

How Shallow Watering Harms Plants. Shallow watering makes roots grow close to the surface; deep watering encourages them to reach far down into the ground. Deep-rooted plants withstand winds and drought much better than shallow-rooted ones.

Always water deeply and infrequently rather than shallowly and often. For trees and shrubs this means watering until moisture reaches 2 to 4 feet into the ground; for vegetables and perennials, 1 to 2 feet; for annuals, 6 to 12 inches; for cool-season lawns, also 6 to 12 inches; and for warm-season lawns, such as Bermuda, perhaps as much as 1 to 2 feet.

Why Overwatering Is as Bad as Underwatering. When plants are underwatered they show such signs of stress as wilting, browning, drying, and dropping of leaves, buds, and flowers—and eventually they die. It's equally as bad to overwater them. Too much water deprives roots of the oxygen they need to function and grow. Overwatering causes root rot and crown rot, which in turn lead to softening, drooping, yellowing, and dropping of leaves. The plants become stunted and weakened, and often they die.

How Frequently Plants Need Irrigation. Most cool-season lawns, vegetables, and annual flowers have shallow roots and need to be watered more frequently than deep-rooted plants—at least once a week in warm weather, more often in hot, dry weather and in sandy soils. Some shade plants, such as container-grown fuchsias and impatiens, may need water every day. Most shrubs are able to go longer between irrigations, perhaps as many as ten or fifteen days. Many mature trees growing in clay soil can go several weeks between irrigations. But when you do water them, water slowly for a long time, so the moisture sinks deeply into the ground. Some established drought-resistant plants may need only one or two irrigations in summer; some native plants must have no irrigation in summer, or they may die from root rot.

How to Conserve Water by Using the Local Evapotranspiration Rate (ET). Gardeners with lawns can conserve water by using an ET chart based on evapotranspiration rate (ET). (The ET rate is a number that stands for the inches of water that evaporate from the soil plus the amount of water that transpires through the blades of grass during a certain period of time.) The philosophy behind ET is that if it's possible to figure out the amount of water that leaves the soil and evaporates from leaves you can then determine how much must be replaced by annual rainfall combined with irrigation. ET rates are calculated by University of California scientists, and they vary by geographical area, from year to year, and even from day to day. Because of the variables involved they aren't perfect, but when used they do help eliminate over- and underwatering. ET rates can't be used in their pure form without doing some fairly complicated mathematics. Fortunately, gardeners can benefit from ET rates without dealing with any of these difficulties. Charts designed for home gardeners are based on ET, but they are easy to understand and don't require you to do any figuring.

To obtain an ET chart, telephone your county's Cooperative Extension office or your local member agency of the Metropolitan Water District and ask for the current ET chart for the area in which you live. These charts tell you when you should water your lawn and for how long according to the time of year. Also check the lawn for signs of dryness. If your lawn goes dry prior to the next suggested watering, you should water cool-season grasses slightly more frequently and warm-season grasses for a slightly longer time at each irrigation. Also, water less when the weather is cool and cloudy and

 Quick Tip

To make artificially softened water safe to use on your houseplants, mix in ½ teaspoon of gypsum per gallon of water. In most cases, this is enough gypsum to replace the calcium that was removed by the softening process.

more when it's hot, dry, and windy. Water much less in winter than summer.

How Planting in Zones Saves Water. Group plants according to their need for water. Grow plants with low, medium, and high water requirements in separate zones. This permits intelligent programming of watering to entire areas. If you mix plants with dramatically different water requirements, either the high water users will die of thirst or the low water users will die from rot.

How Plant Choice Can Save Water. Choose drought-resistant plants for your basic landscape. Place plants that need more water in containers attached to a drip system, or grow them in the ground in small areas close to the house. Use drip systems for irrigating vegetables and annual flowers that need regular water. Grow these plants during years when rains are heavy and water supplies are adequate; cycle them out during drought years. If you need a lawn, plant a drought-resistant grass and keep the lawn area small. Most lawns, other than Bermuda and zoysia, use more water than many shrubs, trees, and flowers, and they're far more labor intensive. When properly designed, small lawns can be just as pleasing as large ones (see the Quick Tip on page 261).

Planting

The act of planting is the most exciting and hopeful moment in gardening, but whether our hopes are realized depends on how well we do the job. Years ago they said a gardener should put a one-dollar plant into a ten-dollar hole. Today we know we should amend and improve all our soil (as described on page 16), not just the planting hole. The aim of proper planting is to encourage roots to get out into the surrounding soil as soon as possible. Except in the case of some specific plants, such as camellias, azaleas, and roses, filling the hole with soil amendments merely creates an underground plant pot; roots tend to stay inside it. In very sandy soil or hard decomposed granite, or when plants have small root systems, it's all right to amend the planting hole, but in general the **Rule of Thumb** is: *When planting trees, large shrubs, and large vines, add no organic soil amendments except as mulch.* Sooner or later those roots are going to have to get out and live in the native soil, and it might as well be sooner. Specific instructions for planting specialty plants are given in the monthly chapters, but here are some basic guidelines:

How to Plant from Nursery Containers. Most of the basic landscape consists of trees, shrubs, vines, and ground covers planted from nursery containers. When planting large areas, first prepare the ground as described on page 17. When planting in unknown conditions, first check the drainage (see the box on page 17). Plant when the soil is moist but not wet. If the soil is dry, water thoroughly; then wait for it to dry out enough so it can be easily worked. (Sandy soils can be worked sooner than clay soils but may be more difficult to moisten, as explained on page 20.) When planting from 5-, 10-, or 15-gallon containers, dig holes approximately twice as wide as the container and 1 or 2 inches shallower than the depth of the root ball. In hard or clay soils roughen the sides of the hole with

your spade, so it isn't like a smooth, hard wall and roots can more easily penetrate the surrounding soil.

Place slow-release fertilizer tablets or sacks recommended for landscape use (Osmocote Tree and Shrub Planting Tablets 20-10-5 or Best-Paks 20-10-5) in the bottom of each hole according to package directions, to feed the plant for the first year and get it off to a good start. In heavy clay soils where drainage is slow, dig several handfuls of gypsum into the bottom of the hole and cover it with a shovelful of earth.

To remove the plant from the container roll it on the ground or strike the sides to loosen them. With a small container, turn it upside down and strike the lip on a hard object, such as the edge of a wheelbarrow. Then slip the plant out—don't pull it out by the crown—and take a look at the roots. If the roots are like a mat on the outside of the root ball, cut the roots apart and loosen them up by slicing through them with a knife in several places across the bottom and on the sides. Next place the plant down into the hole. Check the level to make sure the top of the root ball is 1 to 2 inches higher than the surrounding ground. Backfill with native soil from the hole, unless it approximates pure beach sand. In that case amend the soil from the hole with one-third organic amendment before backfilling. Press the soil down gently but firmly all around the plant with your hands—never with your feet. Make a berm of earth around the hole to act as a watering basin, and cover the surface of the soil with 2 to 4 inches of mulch. Then irrigate thoroughly so that the water reaches the bottom of the planting hole and drains out.

Water frequently for the first week or two to keep the root ball moist until the plant is established. Thereafter manage irrigation according to each plant's individual needs. Just how often and how much you need to water each plant during its early stages depends on your soil and the weather conditions. But more new plants die from underwatering than from overwatering. If the surrounding soil is dry it can act like a wick and pull water out of the root ball, thereby drying it out. Sometimes you can tell for sure that this is happening because a crack will form between the root ball and the surrounding soil.

How to Check Drainage Prior to Planting.
Most plants need good drainage, so after digging a planting hole and prior to planting use this method to check the drainage: First, fill the hole with water and let it drain out. Then fill the hole a second time. Place a yardstick on edge across the hole with its side touching the surface of the water all the way across the hole, and make a note of the time. Return several hours later and use a ruler to measure how far the water level has dropped down below the yardstick. The **Rule of Thumb** is: *If the water level in the planting hole drops one-fourth of an inch or more per hour, drainage is adequate. If the water level drops less than one-tenth of an inch per hour, drainage is too poor for most cultivated plants.* In that case, install a drain, construct a raised bed, or choose another spot.

If the hole doesn't drain well and you're planting on a slope, you can install a sleeve drain (a pipe covered by gravel that drains water from the bottom of a planting hole and releases it farther down on the slope). If hardpan is a problem, try to break through to a level that drains and then install a chimney drain (a narrow hole filled with fir bark or sand that extends below the planting hole into a layer that drains). If you can't penetrate all the way through hardpan, it's better not to dig a hole below the roots as this only creates a basin that will fill with water.

Raised beds need only be 8 or 12 inches high.

🌼 Quick Tip

Help Vegetables Get Off to a Good Start in Heavy Soils. *Instead of covering vegetable seeds with soil, cover them to the recommended depth with packaged soil mix designed for container planting. Rows are then easy to see, the ground doesn't crust, and sprouts break through easily.*

Build the sides of the bed of rock, brick, concrete, or wood; loosen and amend the subsoil under the bed and fill with good amended topsoil. For large trees dig the planting hole down through the raised bed into the lower level. Roots will reach down and out, and your tree will eventually get established in the native soil beneath.

How to Plant Annual Flowers and Vegetables.
When planting transplants of annual flowers and vegetables from color packs, pony packs, and 4-inch containers, prepare the whole bed in advance of planting. Dig deeply—at least a foot deep. Add a layer of organic soil amendment an inch or two thick—up to 4 inches in poor soil—and work it in. Add fertilizer recommended for the flowers or vegetables, according to package directions, and cultivate it into the top 6 inches of earth. Water the ground and let it settle overnight.

Once the soil has been dug up, amended, and cultivated, never step in a flowerbed or vegetable row. Standing on ground compacts it. The **Rule of Thumb** is: *Make flowerbeds no more than 3 feet wide, or 6 feet wide with a path at the back. Make raised beds for vegetables no wider than 5 feet.* That way you can reach to the center. (Wider beds should have a path down the middle so you can work both sides.)

Turn the packs upside down and tap them lightly on a hard object, such as an upside-down flower pot, to loosen the root balls. Don't yank them out by the stem. Some plants, such as marigolds, get very rootbound in containers. Butterfly each of these halfway up from the bottom: stick your thumbs in the bottom of the root ball and tear those tough roots apart. With plants that have tender roots, such as pansies, just fondle the roots a little to loosen them, so they won't get into the ground and sit there thinking they're still in a container.

Make a hole with the trowel and put in the plant; in the case of butterflied roots, spread them over a central mound. Cover the roots with soil up to the original depth of the plant in the container. Press down gently on top of the roots with your palms to give them good contact with the soil. Water deeply after planting. Space the plants according to package directions. (If you're transplanting them to containers, they can be put closer together without ill effects.)

How to Plant Straight in the Ground from Seed. In Southern California many, though not all, annual flowers and vegetables can be planted straight in the garden from seed. Soil must be more thoroughly prepared for seeds than for transplants. Dig deeply, and add enough organic amendment so the top won't bake hard. Then rake and cultivate until the ground has a smooth texture with no lumps.

Sow and cover seeds to the precise level recommended on the package. Some seeds, such as larkspur, impatiens, and stock, need light in order to sprout. Sprinkle these on top of well-prepared ground and press them down gently with the back of the hoe, a flat board, or the palm of your hand so they make contact with soil. (To keep them moist in hot inland areas, cover them with a floating row cover that lets light through, such as Reemay, and remove it as soon as they germinate.) Other seeds, such as

Quick Tip

The "Hat Trick."
When planting transplants on a hot day, avoid letting tender roots get dried out and damaged. After removing one transplant from a pack, lay an old straw hat over the remainder to shade them from the sun.

those for many wildflowers, can be lightly raked into the ground.

Cover seeded areas with netting to protect them from birds; remove the netting when sprouts are 4 inches high. After seeding keep the seedbed damp by sprinkling it once or twice daily—even three or four times in hot interior valleys—until sprouts emerge. Then water it regularly and deeply when rains aren't adequate. Bait against snails and, if cutworms are a problem, sprinkle with Sevin or diazinon granules.

Pruning

No one can prune a plant correctly without knowing how it grows. The best way to learn how plants grow is to refer to a good pruning manual for western plants. Some plants need frequent pruning, others little or none. Some have latent buds lying dormant under the bark, others don't. Some bloom on buds that last from year to year; others bloom on new wood or wood that's hardened for a certain number of seasons. Brief instructions for pruning many of our commonest plants are given in the month-by-month chapters, but here are some general guidelines.

Prune to Stimulate Growth. One of the techniques of pruning is to clip off the growing tips of plants in order to make plants bushier. This is called "pinching" or "pinching back." Fuchsias, azaleas, and some annual and perennial flowers are good examples of plants that benefit from this type of pruning.

Pinch off the tip of a branch and the side shoots will grow longer. Pinch the side shoots but leave the growing tip unpinched and the branch will grow longer. Pinch all but one side tip and the branch will change direction. (This technique can be used to train pine trees into graceful shapes.)

Stimulating growth within a tree, vine, or shrub by cutting back the top or the growing end of a whole branch or branches is called "heading back." The interiors of shrubs, such as hibiscus, can be stimulated to fill out by heading back selected branches (as described on page 100). Some young trees grow stronger when headed back. Bare-root fruit trees (trees sold without earth, when dormant in winter), for example, always need heading back at planting time to make up for the loss of roots and encourage the growth of correctly spaced scaffold branches on a sturdy trunk. Some large shrubs that grow in the shape of a fountain, such as oleander and cotoneaster, benefit from having branches cut down to the ground, to encourage new branches to grow.

Shear Plants to Shape Them. Shearing is similar to pinching, but, instead of removing individual tips one by one, you evenly slice off the entire top or sides of the plant with hedge shears or, in the case of lawns, a lawn mower. One reason for shearing is to keep a small-leafed plant at the same size indefinitely. With some plants this method can be used to remove spent flowers and stimulate growth. It's also used in topiary, the art of training stylized shapes. One of the best uses of shearing is to maintain hedges.

Thin by Cutting Out Branches. Cutting out whole branches or parts of branches at the point where they join another branch or trunk is called "thinning" or "thinning out." Thin with a pruning saw, ratchet pruner, or long-handled lopper. Do this to remove dead or diseased branches, to let light into the interior of plants, and to keep a tree "laced out," so that plants growing underneath will have adequate sunshine.

Brittle shrubs such as acacia should be thinned in fall to prevent top-heaviness and consequent storm damage. Dense trees sometimes need thinning in order to let light in and permit wind to pass through. Plants can be made into special shapes, such as trained two-dimensional espaliers, by controlled thinning and training.

Finished cuts should be made flush with the outside of the branch collar, the swollen area surrounding the branch where it meets the trunk or larger branch. (If you cut off the branch collar the wound won't heal properly.) In order not to tear the bark start the cut from below. Then finish with a second cut from above. With very heavy limbs make cuts at three places. Make the first cut on the bottom side about 1 foot out from the trunk. Cut halfway through the branch (this is the cut that keeps the bark from tearing). Make the second cut on top of the branch 6 inches out from the first cut, to remove the end of the branch. Then cut off the remaining stub at the branch collar, starting from below and finishing from above.

Prune to Encourage Flowers and Fruit. Almost all fruiting vines and fruit trees, especially deciduous fruit trees, require special pruning in order to encourage proper growth, fruiting, and flowering (as discussed on page 43). Many annual and perennial flowers will stop blooming unless they're deadheaded. ("Deadheading" means clipping off faded flowers before they can set seed.) Pruning hard after the bloom or removing seed capsules can encourage many flowering vines, shrubs, and, in some cases, trees to bloom better the following season, or even repeat bloom in the same year.

Prune to Control Size. Many gardeners do a great deal of pruning to keep plants down to desired size. This is probably the worst reason for pruning and produces the ugliest results. We all do it, however, because we choose plants that are too big for the spaces we put them in; then we have to chop at them continually to keep them in bounds. Most hedges, of course, need frequent pruning or they'll grow too tall and wide, but shrubs should be chosen so that, at full size, they will fit the spaces allotted to them.

Controlling Pests and Diseases

In Southern California we work in our gardens year-round, but so do the bugs. Pests such as caterpillars, mites, whiteflies, snails, and slugs are part of the environment we regularly deal with. Animal pests may be a challenge. Plant and soil diseases, too, sometimes present problems, especially with specific types of plants. Successful gardeners outwit animal pests and minimize diseases through good cultural practices. They balance the environment in order to live in harmony with a few pests without having a garden that looks like a chewed-up disaster. This book isn't a handbook on pests and diseases, though tips for controlling many problems are included in the month-by-month chapters. But here are a few basic principles and rules that will help you deal wisely with this aspect of gardening:

Control Pests Through Integrated Pest Management. Prior to the 1960s many Southern California home gardeners thought that regular spraying with pesticides was the right way to control pests. That was before Rachel Carson's book *Silent Spring* alerted our society to the dangers inherent in the irresponsible use of insecticides, especially DDT. Formerly gardeners often sprayed with DDT to control caterpillars and ants, totally unaware of the hazard it posed to birds and other wildlife, not to mention humans. Today the approach has completely changed. Wise gardeners now know that use of toxic pesticides should be kept to an absolute minimum. Chemical sprays are possible health hazards, and their frequent use can upset the balance of nature, killing beneficial insects and creating new strains of pests that are resistant to pesticides. The alternative is integrated pest management (IPM), a multipoint strategy. It involves spraying only when absolutely necessary and using specific sprays against specific pests instead of broad-spectrum sprays that kill the good guys along with the bad. IPM also involves working with nature and trying not to upset its balance—by using, for example, environmentally safe pest controls like mechanical traps, Safer soap, and BT (*Bacillus thuringiensis*, a bacterium that kills certain leaf-eating caterpillars and nothing else).

Release Beneficials and Help Them Fight Pests. Our environment has not only a resident population of pests but also armies of beneficial organisms that are constantly on the hunt for caterpillars, beetles, and bugs. These creatures—often lumped together under the catchall term "beneficials"—include spiders, ladybugs, praying mantises, several nematodes, various types of predatory mites, green lacewings, syrphid flies, various whitefly parasites, and many types of wasps, including trichogramma wasps. Gardeners who practice IPM help nature along by releasing additional populations of beneficials; they also take care not to kill such conspicuous helpmates as birds, frogs, lizards, and toads, as well as the nearly invisible larval forms of beneficial insects and arachnids that may occur in their gardens.

In my garden I've found that releasing ladybugs, trichogramma wasps, and lacewings several times beginning in early spring reduces pest problems to such an extent that spraying is unnecessary. It's not the adult ladybug or lacewing that kills the pests but the immature, larval stage of the insect. Although ladybugs are sold mainly as a control for aphids it's been my experience that they may also control immature stages of whiteflies and mites, including fuchsia gall mites. Prior to releasing ladybugs, I always chill them in the refrigerator (see the Quick Tip on page 128). Every year millions of other types of beneficials are released by botanical gardens, zoos, and governmental and agricultural agencies. Because all beneficials travel from place to place, we can cooperate with nature by not killing those that settle in our gardens.

To work with nature in this way, one needs to understand that some pests must be allowed to coexist along with the beneficials; otherwise, the beneficials would have nothing to eat! The goal is to work toward a natural balance between pests and predators. Gardeners who release several types of beneficials and talk their neighbors into adopting IPM as well may see dramatic results.

Ladybugs, green-lacewing eggs, and the egg cases of praying mantises can be purchased at many local nurseries in spring. Many other types of beneficial insects, arachnids, and nematodes can be purchased by mail. Because birds, too, can be a help in controlling caterpillars and other pests, encourage them to set up housekeeping. Provide shrubs for nesting, birdhouses of correct design and placement, and a safe source of water for them to drink. Water in motion—a fountain or a birdbath with a dripper, for example—is more attractive to birds than still water in a birdbath.

Control Disease Through Good Cultural Practices. Plant diseases are caused by microscopic organisms in the air and the soil that attack plant tissues. There are many different kinds of diseases. Fungal diseases, such as rust, mildew, and botrytis, are usually the most readily observed and easily diagnosed by gardeners because they disfigure leaves, stems, or flowers. These diseases tend to occur at particular times of year, during certain kinds of weather, and on some host plants more than others. They can be controlled through spraying or by such good cultural practices as growing resistant plants, watering early in the day, not planting sun-loving plants in shade, and keeping a clean garden.

Viral diseases are sometimes caused by pests that carry the disease from plant to plant. Leafhoppers, for example, can carry viral diseases that infect tomatoes and other plants. Bacterial diseases are caused by single-celled organisms that prey on larger plants. Fireblight, a bacterial disease that causes blackening and dieback of members of the rose family, can be controlled by cutting off diseased portions 12 inches beyond the damage and spraying.

Soil diseases, such as various root rots and crown rots, can be caused by overwatering and by growing plants in insufficient drainage. Therefore, when you adjust lengths of watering times, take into consideration the time of year and also the weather. Good cultural practices that will help cut down on root rots include improving soil, providing good drainage, and growing resistant plants. Wilt diseases, such as verticillium wilt and fusarium wilt, can affect entire plants (such as tomatoes), gradually causing death. The best solutions are crop rotation and growing resistant varieties.

Learn to Diagnose Plant Problems. The first step in proper pest and disease control is always to inspect the ailing plant carefully and make an intelligent diagnosis of the cause. Once you've found out what's wrong with the plant, you can then choose an appropriate solution, whether chemical or organic.

For example, if leaves are chewed, leaving large holes, go out at night with a flashlight and find out what's doing the damage. Nine times out of ten the problem will be slugs, snails, or caterpillars. Control slugs and snails with bait or organic controls (as described on page 91); spray caterpillars with BT or introduce beneficials such as trichogramma wasps. If plants show telltale signs of sickness, such as mottled or browning leaves, wilting branches, or lesions oozing sap, the source of the problem might be either pests or disease, or even animal damage, depending on the specific plant, the time of year, the place where the plant is growing, and the precise appearance of the damage.

One good way to diagnose a problem is to list the signs of damage, wrap a sample leaf in plastic, and compare these with the text and pictures in the *Ortho Problem Solver* (edited by Michael D. Smith). This thick volume can be used for reference free of charge in most nurseries, discount stores, and garden supply centers. It contains hundreds of colored photographs showing pest and disease problems on specific plants. It also suggests controls, including proper cultural practices and chemical sprays. Once you've diagnosed the problem, you may want to compare the accompanying solutions with those in other sources—for example, an organic guide. You might also consult with a local Cooperative Extension Office regarding the

How to Clean Up a Vegetable Garden or Flowerbed That's Entirely Overrun with Devilgrass

When an entire vegetable garden or annual flowerbed has been taken over by devilgrass (common Bermuda grass), sacrifice the area in late August. Pull up all the flowers or vegetables. Water the devilgrass so it's growing energetically; then spray with glyphosate (Kleenup or Roundup) to kill it. (It may be necessary to spray more than once.) Wait one or two weeks; then pull up the devilgrass, roots and all, bag it, and send it to the dump. Follow up with preemergent herbicide to kill any remaining seeds. Install edging to prevent a reinvasion of devilgrass from lawn or paths or install Biobarrier, buried vertically in the ground to prevent invasive roots from reentering the bed. Replant with flowers or vegetables in October. (When using glyphosate, take care that spray doesn't blow into other areas. It will kill any plant it touches.)

wisest course of action. You could also ask advice from a knowledgeable nursery person, but don't take every nursery person's advice as gospel truth. Some are fonts of wisdom, but much wrong advice is handed out by nursery employees who, though they may love plants, may know nothing whatsoever about growing them.

If You Must Spray, Practice All Precautions. If all else fails and a specific plant or plants need occasional or onetime spot spraying with a chemical control, follow the directions on the package precisely. Never use more of the product than the label recommends. Use it only for the specific problems listed and only on the plants that are suggested for treatment. Wear protective clothing, such as mask, rubber gloves, long-sleeved shirt, trousers, and boots. Do the job in the early morning or evening when there's little or no wind. Use an appropriately sized sprayer, and make up only a quantity of spray sufficient for the job.

After spraying, thoroughly wash the sprayer, and lubricate the metal parts with an all-purpose oil. Wash your protective clothing and your hands and body.

Controlling Weeds

The best and safest way to get rid of weeds is by pulling, hoeing, or digging them up before they make seeds. Black plastic mulch can also be used, especially in the vegetable garden and under paths, to shade out many weeds. (This is one way to get rid of Bermuda grass.) Landscape fabrics, including Biobarrier, which is impregnated with herbicide, can be installed under mulch and pathways to control weeds. However, when planting seeds, sod, or a whole garden in an area known to be full of weed seeds it's possible to get rid of the problem before you plant. One way is to water the ground first to germinate the seeds, wait until the plants grow,

and then kill them by tilling them under or applying glyphosate (Kleenup or Roundup). (For extreme cases, see the accompanying box.) Or you may opt to use a preplant or preemergent herbicide that's recommended for use prior to planting vegetables or flowers.

Many weed killers are designed for specific purposes. Several of these are discussed in detail in the month-by-month chapters. Some kill weeds in lawns; others kill weeds in ground cover or among woody plants. Always follow the label instructions exactly and use only as directed. Most of these products are dangerous to people and animals. Protect children, pets, wildlife, and your own health.

No pastime provides better exercise or is more rewarding than gardening, especially in Southern California—if you know what to do and when to do it. After a year or two of combining the information in the month-by-month chapters of this book with practical application in your own home garden, you'll be a seasoned, experienced, and knowledgeable gardener. What's more, you'll be getting results and having fun. And isn't that what it's all about?

JANUARY

The Bare-Root Month

n cold-winter climates gardeners rest from their labors in winter, but in Southern California we garden year-round. Our gardening year starts in January, and it begins with a flurry of activity. Many tasks throughout the year are seasonal, so if you don't get to them one month you can do them the next. But January's jobs can't be put off. The main tasks—pruning deciduous fruit trees if you haven't already done so, pruning roses, dormant spraying, and bare-root planting—must be done now. February will be too late. Coastal gardeners can start this month to feed their citrus trees. (If you live in an inland valley wait until March.) There are also many flowering plants to care for and, as in every month, chores for keeping up lawns and vegetable gardens.

Even though January is our coldest and sometimes wettest month, it's often one of the nicest times to work outdoors. Good days are crisp and clear, perfect for gardening and for making the gardener feel even more optimistic than usual. So rejoice that the holidays are over, dig in, and enjoy the promise of a New Year, which to the true gardener is always the same: this year the garden will be better than ever before.

Bare-Root Planting

January is often called "the bare-root month" because a great many plants are available at local nurseries during January in bare-root form. "Bare-root" describes a plant that has had all the soil taken off its roots before shipping. Only plants that go dormant in winter can be sold in bare-root form. In our region the major items sold this way are roses (discussed in a separate section, below); cane berry bushes; deciduous fruit trees; ornamental deciduous trees and vines, including wisteria; strawberries; and a few vegetables, including artichokes, asparagus, horseradish, rhubarb, and short-day onions.

There are definite advantages to buying bare-root plants. Not only are they usually cheaper than plants in containers, but the selection of plant material, especially of roses and fruit trees, is also far greater. (See the accompanying boxes for how to plant bare-root trees and roses.) But before you dash out and start recklessly filling your car with bargains, a word of caution: more mistakes are made in plant choice now than at any other time of year. Unfortunately, some local nurseries, discount houses, and do-it-yourself centers still carry bare-root varieties that are poor choices for our climate. Asking for help may do no good, because the salesperson may know less than you do about gardening and may never have heard of a chilling requirement.

Choose Low-Chill Varieties. A "chilling requirement" is the number of hours between 45°F and 32°F that a deciduous plant needs in order to grow, flower, and fruit. It applies particularly to deciduous fruit, nut, and ornamental flowering trees and to berries. It's not the depth of cold that does the job but the length of time in hours that the plant undergoes the cold temperatures. Lengths of time necessary for proper performance may vary, according to variety, from hundreds to even thousands of hours.

If a plant suffers lack of its required winter chill, buds won't open properly or will open unevenly. Leaf buds need even more winter chill to break their dormancy than flower buds. If a tree doesn't have enough leaves it won't grow well,

and its fruit will sunburn. Fortunately there are many fine varieties of deciduous plants with low chilling requirements, those that need few, if any, hours of cold in order to bloom and bear. Refer to the lists in the encyclopedia section of the *Sunset Western Garden Book.*

Choose Cane Berry and Blueberry Bushes Adapted to Our Climate. Bare-root cane berries, grapevines, and blueberries are available at many nurseries now, but again, some nurseries still sell varieties that won't bear fruit in Southern California. Look especially for Rabbiteye or Southern High Bush blueberries. These were developed in Florida and Georgia and bear delicious berries here. You'll need at least two bushes, for cross-pollination. Plant them so the root ball is slightly high. They need acid soil mix, acid fertilizer, good drainage, and ample moisture—in short, care and planting much like that for azaleas, except with full sun.

Check Whether You Need a Pollinator. Pollination is the transfer of pollen from the anthers (the male part of flowers) to the stigma (female part). Some fruit plants are self-pollinating; bees and other insects carry the pollen from flower to flower on the same plant. Others are cross-pollinating; they need another plant, called a "pollinator," in order to bear fruit. The lists in the *Sunset Western Garden Book* will tell you which these are.

Don't Let Bare-Root Plants Dry Out. Purchase bare-root plants early in the month. The early shopper gets the best plants. If you buy them with roots wrapped by the shipper leave them in their containers, and keep them in a shady place until you're ready to plant. The packages usually contain enough moisture to keep the roots in good condition until the end of the month, but the sooner you plant, the better. (Beware of packaged plants on display in full sun, since the roots may be dried out or damaged by heat.)

If you purchase your bare-root plants at a nursery that sells them loose in a bin of shavings, you have the benefit of choosing specimens with good, strong root systems but also the responsibility to keep them moist. Once you get the plants home, soak the roots in a pail of water for an hour or two and then plant right away. If that's impossible, heel the plants in. To "heel in" means to dig a shallow trench in a shady spot, lay plants on their sides with their roots in the trench, cover the roots thoroughly with soil up to the soil line, and water well. Heeled-in plants can survive at least six weeks, though it's best not to leave them that long because by then they'll have started to grow.

Deciduous Fruit Trees

All deciduous fruit trees need to be pruned for good shape from "childhood" up, and to bear well they need to be pruned at least once a year. The time to do the major pruning is January (unless you already did the job in December). The **Rule of Thumb** is: *Deciduous fruit trees should be pruned during winter while the trees are dormant and after the leaves have fallen to the ground but before new buds have swelled.*

Each type of fruit tree needs to be pruned differently, so it's important to know which kind of tree you're pruning and how to prune it properly. For example, apples bear their fruit on spurs that bear again and again, sometimes for as long as twenty years. If you whack off all the spurs you'll have no fruit. In general apple trees need very little pruning once a main framework of branches has been established. It's important, however, to cut off all the leaves even from low-

chill varieties, such as 'Anna', that may not lose all their foliage in winter. Leaving old leaves hanging on while new ones form can lead to apple scab, a fungal disease that causes black blotches on leaves and then, subsequently, causes the fruit to rot. Apple scab is at its worst during rainy years. Dormant spray also helps prevent apple scab.

Plums also bear on spurs. The pruning of mature European plums is minimal, as for apples, but Japanese plums grow so vigorously that they need heavy pruning of new growth. Apricots bear partly on one-year-old wood and partly on spurs that continue to bear well for four or five years. The older branches must be headed back so that one-fifth of the bearing wood will be replaced. Peaches and nectarines need the heaviest pruning of all: their fruit is borne on one-year-old wood. By pruning them hard, you encourage new growth to replenish fruiting wood. Figs need very little pruning at all except to control tree size and the density of foliage.

Not only different varieties but also individual trees vary in the pruning they need. And no two trees can be pruned exactly alike; basic guidelines will apply differently according to the placement of their branches, their age, and their overall vigor.

Only an expert can keep all the complications of pruning clearly in mind. If you're not an expert, follow a pruning manual that applies to mild climates and contains charts. (Martin's *How to Prune Fruit Trees* is one; I often consult more than one book, because each one says things differently.)

After pruning deciduous fruit trees, clean up the ground under the tree and follow up with dormant spray, as explained on page 47.

How to Plant a Bare-Root Deciduous Fruit Tree

- Choose a spot in full sun with good drainage and adequate space for the tree to grow. (If space is limited, choose a dwarf tree or plant so you can espalier, training it on wires, on an arbor, or against a wall.)

- Prune off any damaged or broken roots, and plunge the remaining roots into a bucket of water to soak while you dig a hole.

- Dig a planting hole and check the drainage (as described on page 33).

- If you are planting in heavy clay, work at least 2 pints of gypsum into the soil in the bottom of the hole. It will do no harm, and it may improve drainage (see page 19 for explanation).

- If gophers are a problem, line the hole with a basket made of chicken wire (sometimes sold as "poultry wire") to protect the roots while the tree is young.

- Hold the tree in the hole so that the bump on the bud union faces north, to shade it from the sun, and the original soil line (look for it below the bud union) is 2 inches higher than the surrounding ground. (The bud union is the location where the variety was grafted onto the rootstock; on trees it usually appears as a slight bend in the trunk or a change in its width.)

- Backfill the hole by sifting the native soil you took from it back into the hole around, through, and over the roots. (Don't add soil amendment unless you're planting in pure sand.) Plant high, so that as the tree grows the area where the trunk meets the ground is high and dry.

- Press down with your hands to compact soil around and over the roots.

- Make a watering basin. Mulch the ground around the plant and in the basin.

- If the tree does not already have a good branching habit, prune it immediately after planting: cut the tree to a height of 30 to 36 inches above ground. Remove most of the side branches (if present) except those needed for main-scaffold limbs. You can produce a low-branching tree by choosing to keep three low branches that are not exactly opposite each other.

- Water deeply by allowing the hose to lie on the ground and trickle into the hole until it penetrates around the roots. In fast-draining sandy or decomposed granite soil, water often until the tree is established. If drainage is poor or if the soil is heavy clay, check once a week and water when the soil begins to dry out. Gradually lengthen the intervals between waterings.

Roses

January is an important month for rose care because this is the time to choose and plant bare-root roses, prune the ones you already have, and spray with dormant oil. It's also the time to choose a method of fertilizing your plants, though not to feed with nitrogen.

Choose a Method of Fertilizing. Most gardeners don't fertilize roses this month, because the **Rule of Thumb** for beginning to fertilize roses is: *Wait until the leaves unfurl and change from red to green before feeding roses with nitrogen.*

(All commercial fertilizers for roses contain nitrogen.) Throughout the monthly chapters you'll find a choice of two fertilizing systems for roses. One is to purchase a commercial rose food and use it according to package directions. This is the easier method and requires no thinking other than remembering to feed your roses monthly throughout the growing season. If you use commercial rose food, you will not fertilize your plants this month. Your other choice is to feed your roses with generic fertilizers according to a system I call the Rose-Pro Method (based largely on the work of San Diego rosar-

The Basic Categories of Roses

Hybrid teas are the most popular garden roses. They usually produce one flower per stem, on plants from 2 to 6 feet high. Grandifloras are bigger and taller, sometimes 8 to 10 feet high. Floribundas produce quantities of flowers in clusters on bushy plants that are usually shorter than hybrid teas. Polyanthas have smaller flowers than floribundas and are carried in larger bunches on many canes.

Climbing roses come in several types. Some, such as climbing "sports" (mutations exactly like the parent except for growth habit) of hybrid teas, are everblooming. Many old-fashioned climbing types bloom mainly in spring. Climbing roses send up long, bendy canes that usually don't end with a flower bud like standard roses; most of the flowers occur on side shoots that spring from the canes. Some types of climbers can be used as ground covers, and some can be grown as large freestanding shrubs, but most need support, such as a large tree, a fence, or an arbor. Pillar roses are similar to climbing roses. They have tall canes that are less bendy than those of climbing roses. They can be trained straight up a post or pillar or the corner of your house and will bloom all the way from the ground to the tops of their canes.

Miniature roses are natural dwarf versions of all the above types of roses. The only difference is that their canes, stems, flowers, and leaves are scaled down in size.

Heirloom old roses are favorites of the nineteenth and twentieth centuries prized for their hardiness, fragrance, romantic flower form, disease resistance, and rugged constitutions. Some old roses bloom only once a year; others repeat bloom. Species roses are those that were originally discovered in the same or similar form in the wild.

David Austin's English roses are an entirely new class of roses that combine the romantic flower form, fragrance, and other good qualities of old shrub roses with the bright colors and everblooming flowers of modern hybrids. Modern landscape roses, another somewhat vague category, include shrub roses, ground cover roses, and Romantica roses. Romanticas, developed in the south of France by the House of Meilland (introduced here by Conard-Pyle Co.), blend the best qualities of old roses with modern ones. Romanticas have disease resistance and bright or unusual colors; several have compact growth habits that fit into small gardens.

---

ian Richard Streeper and summarized for the whole year in the Rose-Pro table on page 308). You'll find this system slightly more complicated and time consuming than using rose food, but it's very effective and much less expensive, which can be a help if you grow many roses.

If you opt to follow the Rose-Pro Method, feed your roses now as follows: Give all the plants 2 tablespoonfuls of Epsom salts (magnesium sulfate) to provide magnesium. Also give all newly planted roses 1 cup of superphosphate and all established plants ¼ cup of superphosphate. (Phosphorus is longer lasting in soil than nitrogen; this is the only time during the year when you'll need to give your plants this nutri-

ent.) Sprinkle the Epsom salts and superphosphate on the ground over the roots and water them into the soil. (When planting bare-root, work the superphosphate into the soil under the roots at planting time.) Don't use more than the recommended quantities of Epsom salts: too much can cause soil compaction and tie up nutrients.

Select Bare-Root Roses. To get the best choice of rose varieties and plants, go to the nursery as soon as possible this month, but study a good handbook first. (Also see the lists on page 72.) Choose not only for color and fragrance but for basic categories of growth habit

How to Plant a Bare-Root Rose

- Examine the roots. Prune off any broken or damaged portions. Then place them in a bucket of water to soak while you dig a hole.

- Choose a spot in full sun, and dig a hole approximately 1½ feet deep and 2 feet wide.

- Be sure to check the drainage (as described on page 34) and make sure it's adequate. It's possible to grow roses in red clay or adobe—they thrive in heavy soil—but they won't grow in a swamp.

- Unlike with trees, you need to amend the soil before planting roses because the root system is smaller. So unless your soil is superior loam, you'll need some good organic soil amendment, either a bagged commercial type or homemade compost, to mix with the earth you take from the planting hole. (Manure can be used as mulch but not in the hole.)

- Build a cone of mixed soil on the bottom of the hole, firming it with your hands. Set the plant on top, and spread the roots out over the cone. They shouldn't bend on the bottom of the hole. If they do, start over and dig deeper.

- Check your soil level with a stick. The bud union should end up 2 to 3 inches *above* ground level. Most roses do better with the bud union (that knob at the base of the plant) aboveground, so don't bury it, as they do in the East or Midwest. Plant high, because if you add mulch yearly, as you should, the bud union can get buried.

- Backfill the hole to the correct planting depth, firm the ground around the roots with your gloved hands, mulch the ground over the roots, and build a watering basin.

- Place the hose into the watering basin and let the water trickle in slowly, to water the roots thoroughly. In fast-draining soil, water daily for the first three days and twice a week for the next three weeks. In moist, heavy soils, check the soil twice a week and water when needed. Thereafter apply adequate water—preferably by means of a drip system—to saturate the root zone once or twice a week, depending on the weather, your climate zone, and your soil.

(see accompanying box), disease resistance, vigor, and your climate zone. Some roses are more heat resistant than others. Roses with fewer petals generally do better along the coast than those with many, because there isn't enough heat for many-petaled roses to open completely. It's possible to save money by purchasing old varieties that are no longer patented, but it's not wise to skimp on grade, which is determined by law and labeled on each plant. Always buy No. 1 grade plants. They have more roots, bigger canes, and a better shape, so you end up with healthier and more vigorous plants.

Also consider water conservation. Limit the number of roses you plant by the amount of irrigation you'll be able to give them. Grow roses in a zone devoted to plants that have similar high requirements for water; don't put them close to drought-resistant plants. One way to irrigate roses is to provide a watering basin for each rose plant and flood these by means of bubblers (rather than sprayers) connected to a conventional irrigation system. Another way is to install a drip-irrigation system with a header (main line) leading to each rose. Surround each plant with a circle 1 or 2 feet in diameter, depending on the size of the plant, of water-emitting hose, such as Drip-In, a ¼-inch soaker line. Place Drip-In on top of the ground but under the mulch. Drip-In won't clog when covered with mulch, but roots might invade it if you bury it in the ground. There is also a ½-inch

Drip-In Dripline that will deliver a larger volume of water in less time, but you may need to order it. For a hedge of roses, use one Drip-In line on each side of the hedge.

Prune the Roses You Already Have. Prune your rosebushes in January before new growth starts. (See the large box for directions.) Assemble your tools. You'll need pruning shears (the blade type that slices like scissors, not the snap-cut type that can squash the bark), long-handled shears, a keyhole saw, pruning compound or a white latex glue, a pair of leather gloves, and some knee pads. You'll also need to know what kind of roses you've got.

Dormant Spray

Dormant spray is any insect or disease-control spray—such as horticultural oil (Volck Oil), lime sulfur, or fixed copper—that's applied after a deciduous plant has gone dormant and dropped its leaves. (Deciduous plants are those that drop their leaves during dormancy. Many other plants are said to be dormant in winter even though they may not be deciduous. Don't spray these, because strong concentrations of oil sprays are damaging to leaves and can burn them.)

If you grow roses or deciduous fruit or ornamental trees you should apply dormant spray to these plants every winter after their leaves have dropped to prevent a buildup of disease. If any leaves are still clinging to the plant in January, they should be clipped off prior to spraying.

Even organic gardeners who eschew chemical sprays should use dormant sprays. Because they're applied in winter they don't harm beneficials and can't contaminate fruits; and it's virtually impossible to grow certain plants, particularly peach trees, without using them. Of

🐾 Quick Tip

How to Keep Skunks Out of Flowerbeds.
Protect your spring bulbs and annual flowers from being crushed by skunks. Don't throw away the thorny canes you prune off climbing roses; bend them around the borders of your flowerbeds to make a low fence. Peg them in place with bent sections cut from coat hangers. The canes will soon be hidden by foliage and flowers, but skunks won't cross the thorny barrier.

course you should always follow label directions and use safety measures when handling chemical sprays. Wear protective clothes, boots, rubber gloves, goggles, and mask.

What Dormant Sprays Do and How They Work. Dormant oil sprays are used to control overwintering mites and insects, such as scale and certain caterpillars, by coating their bodies and suffocating them. Various types are available, so choose one that's recommended for the specific plant or plants you want to treat. In the case of peach trees and nectarines it's important to use lime sulfur, to prevent peach leaf curl. This is a fungal disease that causes the leaves of peaches and nectarines to become curled and misshapen and then drop off the tree. The fruits may have warty areas on them. Severely infected trees that aren't treated for several years will decline and may die. Lime sulfur also controls certain mites and overwintering spores of other fungal diseases. You can mix lime sulfur spray with Volck Oil and smother overwintering plants at the same time.

Timing of Spray for Peach and Nectarine Trees. Peach trees and nectarine trees should be sprayed with dormant oil twice: once after the leaves fall in November or December and again in January before the buds begin to swell. If you

How to Prune a Rose

The Basic Principles

If you moved to Southern California from a cold-winter climate, forget what you may have learned there about rose pruning. In the East and Midwest roses are pruned hard in fall—down to 12- or 18-inch stubs—so they'll survive the winter. Here we should never shorten a healthy, productive cane. The more good wood left on the plant, the earlier it flowers and the longer it lives—so don't cut your plants way down. Try never to cut lower than your knee. Many of our roses can be left 4 feet tall after pruning, but the canes that remain should be thick and healthy ones. When making all cuts, in order to slice cleanly, put the blade of the pruner, rather than the anvil, next to the part of the plant that's going to remain. Cut closely above a promising outside bud, so new growth will point outward. Cut ¼ inch above the bud, even closer if you can do so safely. Make your cut straight, not slanted. A sharp angle can dry out wood and kill the bud.

Bush Roses

- Start by removing all wood that is dead, damaged, or diseased.

- Remove all twiggy growth (smaller than the thickness of a pencil). It simply won't produce.

- Remove all old, spent canes. These are the ones that look tired and woody and produced nothing but spindly wood and inferior flowers last year. Get down on your knees and saw off the old canes right at the bud union—here's where your keyhole saw and knee pads come in handy. Saw off any old stubs, too. Sawing is not only easier than cutting, but it also stimulates production of new canes. However, if you have a great many roses and not much strength, it's better to use a ratchet-type pruner than not to take off old stubs and canes. (Ratchet-type pruners are long-handled blade-cut pruners with a built-in ratchet device that makes it easy to cut through thick, hardwood branches.)

- Leave all the good strong canes in place, at least four or five per plant (five to seven for plants over five years old; more for some floribundas).

- For all bush roses remove all branches that cross. Try to open up the centers so each plant takes the shape of a vase. In interior valleys it's a good idea to leave a few branches that cross the center in order to provide shade, but gardeners elsewhere should cut off all branches that cross the center.

- For floribundas cut out the center branch from each cluster of branches, and cut the other ones back to three or four eyes (undeveloped buds). On floribundas leave more twiggy growth—you can even use hedge shears on them to get the right shape.

- For tree roses cut back the branches so they are between 1 foot and 18 inches in length, depending on the age of the rose. (As tree roses age, leave their branches longer.) Remove all sprouts arising from the roots or trunk. Aim for symmetry: a rounded bush on top of the upright trunk.

- Miniature roses resemble large roses in every way except size, so for these follow the instructions for full-sized roses but scaled down proportionally. Shape ground-cover types with hedge shears.

- For full-size roses remove about one-third of all growth that was new last year, but don't cut into any new growth that's thicker than your thumb.

- For English roses and old roses, during the first two years after planting, remove dead wood and leaves only. Allow the shrub to build its size and strength with no pruning until it is three years old. As the rose matures, remove enough old growth to keep the plant producing on young and vigorous growth. Prune Romanticas like floribundas or hybrid teas, according to the growth habit of each rose.

Remove the Suckers. Suckers on roses are canes

that spring from below the bud union. Instead of growing from the bud union like the canes of the variety you want, they grow from the rootstock. Suckers are usually easy to recognize because they're thinner and more prickly than the canes that arise from the bud union, and their leaves are usually smaller and shaped differently from the other leaves on the plant. If allowed to persist they'll sap strength from your varietal rose.

Suckers are easiest to reach after the major pruning is complete. The best way to get rid of one is to grasp it firmly with a gloved hand, work it back and forth and around and around to loosen it, then pull it off with a mighty yank. If you can manage this you'll get the bud cells along with the stalk, but if instead you cut it off two or three more suckers are likely to spring from the same spot.

Let Them Stand Tall. Finish the major pruning by cutting the tops of the canes so they're roughly equal in height. If any leaves remain on your plants when you are through pruning, clip—don't pull— them off. Removing the leaves prevents the buildup of disease.

After pruning:

- Your hybrid teas should stand 2 to 3 feet tall.

- Grandifloras should be 4 to 5 feet tall.

- Floribundas and polyanthas should end up about knee high with a round, bushy shape.

- Miniature roses should be between 6 inches and 3 feet tall, depending on their age and variety.

- Old roses, English roses, and shrub roses vary greatly in height and size. Never cut old roses and English roses short; they may never recover.

Finish Up. Paint all cuts on the bud union with pruning compound or white glue to protect them from rot. (This treatment is unnecessary for cuts higher on the plant.)

Clean up the ground under and around the plants. Destroy all leaves and debris. Then mulch under your plants with steer manure or—better yet—with compost. Follow up with a dormant spray (as discussed on page 47), such as Ortho Dormant Disease Control Lime-Sulfur Spray. Wait until new growth unfurls and turns from red to green before feeding with a fertilizer containing nitrogen.

Climbing and Pillar Roses

Young climbing roses (particularly those less than two years old) should be pruned little or not at all. Do prune all everblooming climbing roses that are more than three years old now.

Climbers that bloom only once a year should be pruned when they finish blooming, but if this task was neglected old spent canes and all sucker growth should be removed now. Clean up and apply dormant spray to those that drop their leaves in winter. (Before spraying, clip off any leaves that remain except from species roses that are evergreen in mild climates, like *Rosa banksiae*, Lady Banks' rose. Do not prune these now; see page 151.)

Climbers that are arranged sideways on arbors and fences and espaliered on walls can bloom for many years on the same old canes. If this is the method you choose then be sure to remove unwanted canes as they arise throughout the year. Eventually, if the roses decline in vigor, allow new canes to grow and replace the old ones. With pillar roses it's better to cut out one or two old woody canes yearly and allow new, vigorous canes to replace them.

Here's the procedure.

- Remove all dead or twiggy growth extending from the bud union.

- Leave all good, well-placed canes on the plant.

- Remove any suckers that arise from below the bud union.

- Cut back all laterals (side branches) to two or three buds each.

- Clip off all remaining leaves. (In cold climates rose leaves fall in winter. Here we often have to defoliate most or all by hand.)

- Untie the rose and reposition it on its support. Climbing roses bloom mainly on laterals that spring from the canes. In order to encourage them to put out more laterals and thus to bloom more, train the canes as horizontally as possible, either onto a fence, into an existing tree, over an arbor, espaliered on a wall, or with the tips of the canes pegged to the ground, giving the plant the shape of a fountain. Pillar roses are an exception. You can tie all the canes of a good pillar rose in a vertical position, onto a post, say, or the corner of your house, and it will bloom massively all the way from the ground to the top of its canes.

- Clean up and mulch the ground, and follow up with a dormant spray, such as Ortho Dormant Disease Control Lime-Sulfur Spray mixed with Volck Oil.

didn't spray in November or December, spray twice in January, once early in the month and again two weeks later. If you use lime sulfur and rain occurs within forty-eight hours, treat again. It's best not to spray if a heat wave is expected, because if temperatures rise above 90°F soon after treatment lime sulfur may injure buds. Use a proper sprayer—one that allows you to aim the spray onto the tree rather than broadcasting it into the air—and go over the tree carefully, reaching all parts (see page 281).

Dormant Spray for Sycamore Trees. Sycamore trees (*Platanus* species) are hosts to a flock of pests and diseases, among which sycamore scale (*Stomacoccus platani*) is one of the worst. Sycamore scales overwinter on bark as eggs, then in spring attach themselves to the undersides of leaves and suck out plant juices. This creates yellow spots that eventually turn brown and cause leaves to drop prematurely. The scales also feed on young twigs and limbs, causing dieback and weakening the tree.

To find out whether your tree suffers from scale, look for cottony white masses of material bulging from cracks and crevices in the bark. This cottony substance protects overwintering eggs. Affected trees must be thoroughly sprayed now with a high-volume, high-pressure spray in order to get rid of the eggs. It's best to hire a reputable company with professional equipment to do this job. The procedure is to use dormant oil at the rate of 2 gallons of oil to 98 gallons of water, with a wetting agent (surfactant) also mixed into the spray. Make sure all precautions are followed during the spraying, and finish by cleaning up fallen leaves, twigs, and debris. (See page 69 for more about sycamores.)

Citrus Trees

Start Fertilizing Citrus in Coastal Zones. If you live in a coastal zone, January is the time to start feeding your citrus trees. (See the accompanying box for directions.) By fertilizing your trees now you'll promote more blossoms in February and thus a more abundant crop. If you live in an interior zone where frosts continue through February and sometimes into March, don't start feeding your citrus trees until March. Feeding too early might encourage a flush of growth that could be damaged by frost.

Citrus trees are heavy feeders. A mature tree growing in clay soil needs 1 pound of actual nitrogen per year, but that's not the same as a pound of dry fertilizer. Let's say you choose a balanced granulated fertilizer such as 16-8-4 or a slow-release fertilizer such as 17-6-10. Since the first number stands for the percentage of nitrogen in the mix, you'll need to feed about 6 pounds of either of these products to each full-grown tree. Feed young trees proportionately less. For example, a one-year-old tree could be fed ¼ pound of actual nitrogen per year. A three- or four-year-old tree can use ½ pound of actual nitrogen per year. When a tree is six or eight years old it can usually be given the full amount. In fast-draining soils, such as sand or loose decomposed granite, use more fertilizer—up to 1½ pounds of actual nitrogen per year.

If you live in a coastal zone, divide the total amount of granulated fertilizer needed for each tree into six equal portions. Give one feeding per month from January through June. If you live in an interior climate zone, divide the total amount of granulated fertilizer needed into four equal portions. Apply the first dose in March and the remainder at monthly intervals through June. Slow-release fertilizers are more expensive but more convenient because they require less-frequent application. Divide slow-release fertilizer into two equal applications. Apply the first in January if you live in a coastal zone, late February inland, and the second in June if you live on the coast, July in the interior.

🐾 Quick Tip

How to Keep Mulch and Water Away from the Trunk of a Citrus Tree. *Cut the bottom out of a 5-gallon plastic plant container. Use a can cutter to make a slit up the side. Slip the container upside down around the trunk, with the slit side facing away from the water source. The container can keep the trunk high and dry.*

Correct Chlorosis. Give iron and zinc to citrus trees now if they show signs of chlorosis (iron deficiency). Plants suffering from chlorosis have light green leaves with dark green veins. Don't use iron sulfate. It can't be absorbed by the tree because it combines with minerals in the soil and becomes insoluble. Get the chelated kind

How to Fertilize Citrus Trees

- Determine how much fertilizer a tree will need during the year and divide this quantity by the number of applications you want to make during the year.

- Use a coffee can and a bathroom scale to weigh the amount needed for each application. (Mark the level and poundage on the can and keep it for reuse. That way you won't need to weigh the fertilizer each month.)

- Scatter the contents of the can evenly on the ground in a 3-to-4-foot-wide, doughnut-shaped band centered under the drip line (an imaginary line directly under the branch tips). The main feeder roots of a mature citrus are in the top 2 feet of soil beginning 2 or 3 feet from the trunk and extending out twice as far as the drip line. You can, if you wish, distribute the fertilizer over this entire area.

- Water the fertilizer deeply into the ground, right away. (Don't work it into the soil.)

that's combined with zinc. Apply it, according to package directions, evenly to the ground around the tree, along with the fertilizer when you apply it. For faster results purchase a product for foliar application and spray it onto your tree. Overwatering can cause chlorosis, so proper irrigation is often the best treatment.

Irrigate Citrus. Water mature citrus deeply and infrequently—perhaps once every two or three weeks depending on the weather and your soil type and drainage—rather than shallowly and often. Frequent shallow watering can harm citrus; it encourages shallow rooting and causes root and trunk rot.

Make sure sprinklers don't hit the trunk of any citrus tree. A wet trunk can lead to gummosis (oozing sap and sunken lesions on the trunk,

---

How to Plant Camellias and Azaleas

- Choose an area in semishade. Most camellias and azaleas need some sun in order to bloom. Morning or evening sun is best—not midday. Good spots are in dappled light under lath, shade cloth, or an open tree, or to the north of a house, hedge, or wall.

- Choose an area with good drainage, especially for azaleas. If you don't have such an area, use raised beds or tubs filled with an acid-type potting mix.

- Dig a planting hole 1½ times as deep as the root ball and twice as wide.

- Amend the soil removed from the hole by mixing it with one-half acid-type soil amendment, such as commercial camellia-azalea mix, leaf mold, or premoistened peat moss. (Be sure to moisten peat—see the Quick Tip on page 53—because dry moss sheds water. If you plant with dry moss, it will stay dry and kill your plants.)

- Slide the shrub out of the container and plant it high. Camellias and azaleas can't stand to have soil collecting around their trunks. Measure the height of the root ball and the depth of the hole. Add as much amended soil as needed to bring the top of the original root ball 2 or 3 inches higher than the surrounding soil.

- Gently lift the plant into the hole, position it with the best side to the front, and backfill the hole with amended topsoil.

- Use your hands to press the soil mix firmly around and over the roots.

- Form a watering basin, and cover the entire bed with an acid mulch, such as 2 or 3 inches of pine needles.

- Place the hose, running gently, into the watering basin and allow the water to thoroughly penetrate the root ball and the surrounding ground while you go on to the next plant.

- Water daily for the first three days and frequently thereafter until the plants are established. Then lengthen the periods between irrigations.

---

caused by fungal disease). (See the Quick Tip on page 51.) The **Rule of Thumb** for watering citrus is: *Apply water so it sinks into the ground around the tree in a broad doughnut-shaped band beginning one-third of the distance from the trunk to the drip line and extending an equal distance beyond the drip line.* The area of ground next to the trunk of the tree should be kept high and dry, with no soil pushed up against the trunk. If water is collecting in the wrong places, build a wide double-walled watering basin around the tree at the drip line to keep the irrigation water there and away from the trunk.

Control Citrus Pests. Check trees for insect and disease damage (as described on page 67). Be on the lookout for snails. In inland valleys snails often spend the winter snuggled together in the crotches of orange trees. You can clean your entire tree of snails now by picking them off, tying them into a plastic bag, and tossing them into the trash. Once snails have been removed, clip off bottom leaves that brush the ground. Some gardeners find that surrounding the trunk of each tree with a copper band prevents snails from crawling back up it. (These and other snail and slug controls are discussed on page 91.)

Camellias and Azaleas

Select and Plant Good Varieties. Camellias and azaleas are two of our most prized plants for permanent winter color in semishade. Both camellias and azaleas have a long bloom cycle that starts in fall and lasts through spring, but not all varieties flower at the same time. Some varieties may open as early as October; others don't flower until April or May.

As a general rule you can safely plant any camellia or azalea during a cool winter month, including this one (see the accompanying box for directions). But the best time to plant them is while they're actually bearing flowers. This is because the roots and branches of camellias and azaleas rest rather than grow during their bloom cycle, and the minute they finish blooming they start a spurt of growth. If you plant them while they're in bloom they get off to a good start; planting later disturbs roots and interferes with normal development.

When you shop for azaleas, don't just fall for a pretty face; select good varieties. To find them, refer to lists in the *Sunset Western Garden Book* and ask experts for recommendations. Belgian Indicas, developed for florists, are often difficult to grow. 'Alaska', 'Phoenicia', and 'Formosa' are easy for beginners. (The last two, sometimes taken to be identical, are not the same. 'Formosa' has larger leaves and is often used as understock.) Don't be misled by the term "sun azalea." These varieties can take more sun and interior heat than most azaleas, but they will die if you put them in full sun. The exception is in the fog belt along the coast. Some camellia and azalea varieties can stand full sun along the coast if grown in the ground, not in pots.

Protect Camellias from Petal Blight. Pick up dead and fallen petals and flowers from camellias, daily if possible, in order to prevent petal blight. Petal blight is a fungal disease that causes brown, discolored, rotting blooms—not just at the petal tips, as can be caused by wind or rain, but brown to the center. Blighted blossoms that fall to the ground permit the fungus to live and

Quick Tip

How to Get Peat Moss Wet. *Pour a soup pot full of boiling water on a wheelbarrow full of peat moss, add water from a hose, and mix with a shovel. Let this sit several hours to cool. When using a lot of peat moss wet it in batches, and cool the batches by spreading them on a paved area such as the patio or driveway.*

reproduce in the soil for years. Spores can be carried by the wind from nearby gardens.

Cleanliness is the best way to avoid petal blight, but if you're troubled with a serious outbreak spray with Ortho Multi-Purpose Fungicide (Daconil 2787) or Ortho Funginex Rose Disease Control. Add a spreader-sticker such as Spraymate, according to package directions, when you mix the spray. (A spreader-sticker is an additive that decreases surface tension of water, making sprays cover plant surfaces more evenly and effectively.)

Quick Tip

A Time-Saving Way to Foil Petal Blight. *Cut shade cloth in circles, with a hole in the center and a slit from the outside of the circle to the center hole. Place under potted or ground-grown camellias during the flowering season. When blossoms fall pull out the fabric, shake it into a waiting trash can, and replace it under the bush.*

Protect Azaleas from Petal Blight. Petal blight also attacks azaleas. To control it remove dead and brown blossoms—and while you're about it, snap off the little seed capsule inside each flower with your thumbnail rather than leaving it on the plant. Long-blooming varieties, such as 'Alaska', 'California Sunset', and 'Nuccio's Happy Days', will be stimulated to produce even more flowers.

🐚 Quick Tip

Prune Camellias as You Pick Them. *Whenever you leave the house break off a few blossoms, each with a short piece of stem and a few leaves. Give them to whomever you meet at work, the bank, the store—you name it. It's all the pruning most camellias need.*

Watering

It's tempting to neglect watering chores when the weather's cool and plants aren't growing, but properly irrigated plants stand up better to frost than plants with dry roots. Even when it rains don't forget those specimens under the eaves that aren't getting a drop. Many a poor camellia or tree fern has died an untimely death just because the gardener forgot that no winter rains could reach them.

Coping with Frost

Move Container Plants to Safety. Many a balmy December is followed by a sudden cold snap in January. Protect tender container-grown plants such as impatiens, fuchsias, and cymbidiums from frost by moving them under the eaves of your house or beneath a sheltering tree. Injury is more likely for plants exposed to open sky. Cold air can often be trapped in an atrium or a courtyard surrounded by walls, or even hedges, and can build up like water in a swimming pool. So don't choose these spots for sheltering treasured tropicals. Move them to places from which cold air can escape.

Cover Plants in the Ground. Protect tender plants growing in the ground, such as agaves, aloes, Natal plum, bougainvillea, and cineraria, by throwing old sheets, towels, canvas drop-cloths, car covers, or cardboard boxes over the plants. In interior zones use tall pea stakes (as described on page 259) or hoops of heavy-gauge wire to support cloth above the plants, since the fabric may sometimes become cold enough to damage the foliage it touches. Dash out first thing in the morning and uncover the plants before sun strikes. Heat builds up quickly under covers and can burn foliage as badly as frost.

Don't Prune Off Frost Damage. If, despite all your care, some tropicals are damaged by cold, resist the urge to prune off the unsightly dead parts. The frost-burned portions will protect the rest of the plant. Removing frost-burned leaves and twigs now can be disastrous, causing the plant to grow and then be hit again, worse than ever, if more cold follows. So hold off until the weather warms up and all danger of frost has passed. (Then, you may find plants not as badly damaged as you think.) The **Rule of Thumb** is: *Wait until you see signs of regrowth before cutting off frost-damaged growth.* Large branches may not recover until summer.

Epiphyllums

Start feeding epiphyllums (orchid cacti) with 0-10-10 or 2-10-10 liquid fertilizer every two weeks to encourage spring and early summer bloom. Even if you've neglected them and they look scruffy, don't feed with higher than 2 percent nitrogen now or you'll trigger growth instead of flowers.

Don't prune epiphyllums until after the bloom cycle. It's all right to cut off badly diseased or rotted branches, but like excess nitrogen, extensive pruning will make your plants grow rather than bloom. Plants should have some sun now, not solid shade.

Cymbidiums

Purchase cymbidium orchids now, while they're in bloom. Continue to feed those that haven't yet bloomed with a high-bloom formula (as described on page 23). Stake bloom spikes, and protect the plants from snails and slugs. Once blooms open, stop feeding the plants but keep them well watered. Put plants that are blooming in a cool, shady spot to lengthen flower life.

Enjoy some cymbidiums in the house, too, but don't let them sit in puddles. Put gravel in plant saucers and cachepots to hold roots safely above water that drains out the bottoms of the pots.

Color from Permanent Plants

A well-planted garden in our area can have perennial color year-round. If your garden needs some pepping up, consider adding one or more of the following January-blooming plants. Among drought-tolerant plants that give color now are many named varieties of New Zealand tea tree *(Leptospermum scoparium)*, Bailey acacia *(Acacia baileyana)*, Kaffirboom coral tree *(Erythrina caffra)*, and many species of aloe. By choosing aloes with care you can have varieties in bloom any month of the year, but most of the aloes we grow here are from South Africa so they flower in winter, a time when the insects that pollinate them are most active.

Less drought resistant but still beautiful are deciduous magnolias, such as saucer magnolia *(Magnolia soulangiana)* or star magnolia *(M. stellata)*. These trees stay small for a long time and are good in flower and bulb beds, entryways, and small-space gardens; against a dark wall; or in Oriental gardens. A striking shrub for winter bloom is the pink powder puff *(Calliandra haematocephala)*, at its best espaliered on a sunny wall. Marmalade bush *(Streptosolen jamesonii)* needs plenty of water but gives bright orange bloom at this time of year in frost-free zones. (It's lovely when planted above a retaining wall and allowed to cascade down it.) Outstanding choices for purple bloom are the vine *Hardenbergia violacea* 'Happy Wanderer' and the Brazilian shrub called princess flower *(Tibouchina urvilleana)*.

Annual and Perennial Flowers

Mulch, Cut Back—Perhaps Even Plant—Perennials. Perennials are working on their roots in winter; those you planted in fall are getting established now. Fix up the soil by adding a mulch before the tops get growing and spread out to cover the ground. Continue to deadhead plants like pentas that may bloom year-round. Cut back to the ground, or almost to the ground, plants that bloomed in fall and winter, such as Japanese anemones, perennial marigold *(Tagetes lemmonii)*, perennial asters, and Russian sage *(Perovskia* 'Blue Spire'). Trim back the woody branches of yellow flax *(Reinwardtia indica)* that have bloomed; it will keep on putting out its golden, trumpet-shaped flowers into March. If you haven't cut back *Hypoestes aristata* 'Lavender Cloud', do it now; cut stems that have bloomed to 16 inches. Young buddleias can be cut almost to the ground, but old woody ones will probably die if you cut them too short. Wait until they show growth and then cut to that. "Cut to basal foliage" (the foliage at the plant's base) is always a safe rule to follow. When you see plenty of basal growth on *Verbena bonariensis*, cut down to it. Common sneezeweed *(Helenium autumnale)*, false dragonhead *(Physostegia virginiana)*, veronica, gayfeather *(Liatris)*, balloon flower *(Platycodon* *grandiflorus),* and California fuchsias *(Zauschneria)* are among other perennials and subshrubs that can be cut back to the ground or nearly to the ground now. The easiest way to attack mounds of Santa Barbara daisy *(Erigeron karvinskianus),* Mexican evening primrose *(Oenothera berlandieri),* and botanical geraniums, including *G. sanguineum,* is with hedge shears. Shear lavender into nice rounded forms now in January, and you won't interfere with its spring bloom.

All this cutting will leave plenty of bare spaces to mulch. Maybe you can even add a few new varieties. So if you're just dying to visit nurseries to see what they've got, there's no need to resist. But what perennials to plant now? The answer is simple: whatever you find.

Plant Cool-Season Annual Flowers. If you planted winter and spring bedding flowers in September and October, you can congratulate yourself now because many should be flowering, especially in coastal zones. But in January nurseries are brimming with cool-season flowers (annual and perennial bedding plants that bloom in winter) already in bloom. These include foxgloves, cyclamen, English primroses, malacoides or fairy primroses, obconica primroses, calendulas, pansies, johnny-jump-ups and other violas, stock, and snapdragons. So if you didn't plant before and your flowerbeds and pots need sprucing up, or if you have bare patches in your beds, use nursery transplants to fill them with instant color.

Fertilize Cool-Season Flowers. The trick with cool-season flowers, other than wildflowers, is to give them plenty of nitrogen for strong growth, as well as high phosphorus for bloom and some potassium for general plant health. The reason for the extra nitrogen is that it tends

to leach from the soil during the rainy season. Also, fungi and bacteria in the soil are less active in cooler weather, so nutrients are not released as quickly from organic matter. This is especially true of plants growing in containers. (In general, use liquid or slow-release fertilizers for winter flowers in containers, pellet or liquid fertilizers for plants in the ground. See page 27.)

Feed Cineraria. Feed cineraria *(Senecio hybridus)* once every two weeks for growth, with a liquid fertilizer high in nitrogen. Once buds show, switch to a high-bloom liquid fertilizer, such as 2-10-10, to stimulate production of large flowers. Watch for leaf miners; if necessary, spray with a systemic such as Orthene to control them. (Mix it with a spreader-sticker such as Spraymate in order to increase effectiveness. Also check that your bottle isn't outdated.)

Should You Plant Seeds? January isn't one of the best times for planting seeds, but that doesn't mean it's impossible to plant. Seeds of California poppies, lupines, and other wildflowers, gaillardia, clarkia, godetia, and sweet alyssum *(Lobularia maritima)* will sprout and grow if sprinkled onto well-prepared ground and raked in prior to rain. It's better, however, to plant wildflowers in fall (as described on pages 259 and 278). (When rains aren't adequate, water seeded areas daily to keep them damp.)

Coral Trees

Prune Naked Coral Trees. The naked coral tree *(Erythrina coralloides)* is one of the best coral trees for local gardens in Zones 21 to 24. Though slower to start, it's a much better choice for home gardens than Kaffirboom coral tree *(Erythrina caffra).* It blooms spectacularly in spring on tip growth. Once a tree has become established, prune it judiciously in January (heavily, when specimens get out of hand), during its brief dormancy, in order to bring out its artistically bizarre shape and stop it from becoming a tangled mess. Cut out branches that cross. Control size by cutting out unwanted branches. A word of caution: Don't whack off all the tip growth or you'll lose all the flowers.

Don't Prune Kaffirboom Coral Trees Now.

Many Kaffirboom coral trees (*Erythrina caffra*) are pollarded in winter—all branches are cut back so hard that only stubs are left at the top of a bare trunk. Pollarding coral trees permanently ruins their shape, makes them subject to rot, and prevents them from ever blooming. Prune Kaffirboom coral trees, if necessary, by thinning out a few unwanted branches back to a main scaffold branch or trunk while leaving all desired growth in place, and do the job after rather than before bloom.

Kaffirboom coral trees eventually become giants, 30 feet high and 40 feet wide. Plant them in places where they'll have room to grow to full size, and don't plant them on lawns. The frequent watering lawns need is bad for Kaffirboom coral trees; it causes overly rapid growth with dangerously brittle, top-heavy branches. Most coral trees do better and bloom more beautifully when subjected to benign neglect once they are established. When winter rains are adequate, and depending on the soil, mature trees in coastal zones can often go without irrigation until late summer before showing stress and needing a deep application of water.

Jobs for a Cold or Rainy Day

Start a Garden Notebook. If you don't know much about gardening, keep a notebook to help yourself learn. If you're a seasoned gardener, keeping notes can help you remember things you'd otherwise forget. There are several printed diaries on the market, but any notebook or calendar will do as long as there's plenty of room to write.

Clean Out the Potting Shed. Another good task for a rainy day is to clean out the potting shed or tool shed if you have one. If you don't, this is a good time to consider building one and getting the messy accumulation of garden supplies and equipment out of the garage. A serviceable shed for supplies and tools can often do more to promote domestic harmony than flocks of psychiatrists.

Order Seeds from Catalogs. Most seed catalogs arrive in January. (See the list of seed and plant sources on page 307.) Order now so you'll have the seeds in time for spring planting. If you've ever gardened in a cold-winter climate, you probably remember the joy and temptations of poring over a seed catalog on a snowy day.

The danger of ordering from catalogs when you live in Southern California is ordering not only too much but also the wrong items for our climate zones. Check all new-to-you ornamentals by looking them up in the encyclopedia section of the *Sunset Western Garden Book*, so you won't be disappointed by trying to grow something that isn't suited to your climate zone or that needs to go through a freezing winter in order to perform.

The plus side of catalog buying is that you can sometimes find rare items that aren't locally available. If you care about color schemes and don't always want a mixed packet, you can get flowers in specific colors. Many gardeners order vegetable seeds because they enjoy growing gourmet varieties that they can't buy in the grocery store. Don't forget to add a package of nitrogen-fixing bacteria, such as Legume-Aid, to your order. If you plan to plant beans in March you'll need this product, which usually isn't available in local nurseries (see page 109).

Studying seed catalogs can help beginners learn about annuals and vegetables, but be fore-warned: many cool-season plants and flowers that are planted in early spring in the East are planted in fall here. When you live in Southern California you should think ahead and order seed for fall planting now along with the seed for spring. (Keep the seed cool and dry during the summer.) Or, if you prefer, order from cata-logs again in summer for fall planting, though by then some items may be sold out.

Lawn Care

Cool-Season Lawns. Cool-season lawns, such as bluegrass, tall fescue, and ryegrass, are at their best now, so keep mowing them regularly and feeding them, at intervals of one month to six weeks, with a soluble lawn fertilizer or with other products as directed. (Bluegrass unmixed with other grasses is a poor choice for Southern California, but some lawns survive from an ear-lier era.) Water all cool-season lawns when rains aren't adequate.

A healthy, well-fed lawn is more resistant to disease. If you notice unsightly red-brown pig-ment on grass leaves plus red dust on your feet after walking across your lawn, it's suffering from rust. This is a sign it needs feeding. You don't need to spray—just fertilize with nitrogen and mow regularly to remove the older, infected portion of the grass blades. The rust will disap-pear and the lawn will green up like magic.

Choose a Good-Quality Fertilizer. Low-cost soluble fertilizers containing nitrogen alone or in combination with other nutrients will give your cool-season lawn a quick green-up. Slow-release fertilizers and organic fertilizers are more expensive, but they last longer and are less likely to burn the grass. Heavy rains won't wash them out of the soil. When using chemical fertilizers, spread them carefully, according to directions, and beware of dumping when going around cor-ners with a push-type feeder. Burn patterns re-sulting from excess fertilizer are ugly and difficult to eradicate.

Warm-Season Lawns. Warm-season grasses, such as Bermuda, St. Augustine, 'Adalayd' (seashore paspalum), and zoysia, are dormant now. They need no feeding or mowing. ('Adalayd' may continue to grow along the coast; if so, mow it.)

Control Crabgrass with a Preemergent Herbi-cide. If annual weeds such as crabgrass were a problem last year, use a preemergent herbicide now or in early February to stop seeds in their tracks. Generally you'll be safe if you treat dur-ing the last half of January in coastal zones and in early February inland. Treat twice, with the second treatment two weeks after the first. You can, if you wish, be highly scientific about this task and use a soil thermometer. When the soil temperature reaches 63° to 65°F, that's the time to treat the lawn with a preemergent herbicide. If in the past you've had a terrible crabgrass problem, treat a third time in late March along the coast and in early April inland to catch the plants that come up later. Not all the seeds ger-minate at the same time, and even long-lasting products can wash out of the soil.

Some products have to be sprayed on. Others come in dry form. Always read the label care-fully and follow directions exactly. Rate and time of application and safety precautions (such as keeping children and dogs off treated areas) differ from product to product. But be aware that most of the timing directions are aimed at gardeners in cold-winter climates. Thus, many Southern California gardeners make the mistake of treating too late for local conditions.

Check the Lawn Mower. January is also a good time to check over the lawn mower and make sure the blades are sharp. If necessary, have them sharpened.

Vegetable Gardening

Fill in with Transplants or Seeds. As you harvest rows in your vegetable garden refill them with winter vegetables; use either transplants of broccoli, Brussels sprouts, cabbage, cauliflower, celery, lettuce, parsley, peas, and Swiss chard or seeds of beets, carrots, lettuce, mesclun, peas, radishes, and turnips. Short-day onions, artichokes, asparagus, strawberries, rhubarb, and horseradish can be bought bare-root. I list the last three with reservations. November's a better time to plant strawberries (page 285), and rhubarb is difficult in Southern California. I don't recommend growing it, because along the coast it doesn't get the frost it needs to develop good flavor, and inland it usually succumbs to root rot during the summer. (See pages 112 and 84 for artichoke and asparagus planting directions.) Horseradish grows like a weed here. It's well worth growing but needs ample water plus room to grow. Confine it in a special place, such as a raised bed, or it can become a noxious and invasive pest.

Side-Dress Vegetable Rows with Fertilizer. Nitrogen is less active in winter. Rains also wash soluble nutrients down to deeper levels where plant roots can't reach them. This makes it doubly important to remember to side-dress your vegetable rows with more fertilizer if you didn't do so in December. "Side-dressing" simply means to sprinkle fertilizer on top of the ground around individual plants or down the sides of rows. Spread the fertilizer just before a rain or water it into the ground. Harvesting is also a cue to fertilize. For example, after cutting the central head from broccoli, feed the plant so it can produce good side sprouts. After cutting all the outside leaves from a row of lettuce, side-dress the row so the plants can keep producing. Onions also need regular fertilizer now to make them produce plenty of green growth. With onions, the trick is to feed them early in the season so they'll have lots of sturdy green leaves, and then to stop fertilizing them a month or two before they're ready to make a bulb; otherwise, their skins will split open and they may rot instead of keeping well after harvest. Liquid fertilizers, like fish emulsion, are the safest way to feed onions now because liquids don't hang around in the soil.

Plant Lettuce. This is the best time for lettuce. It's easy to grow and a money saver. Plant either from transplants, which will give you a faster harvest, or from seeds (see box), which will give you more lettuce over a longer period of time. Lettuce seeds germinate within a wide range of soil temperatures (from 35° to 80°F) but sprout quicker at cooler temperatures than warm ones, so this is a good time to plant them. Growing from seeds also gives you more interesting varieties to choose from, such as 'Rouge d'Hiver', a red romaine, or mesclun, a mixture of various lettuces, salad greens, and herbs that's expensive to buy in the grocery store but easy to grow in your garden. (For instructions, see page 85.)

Force Fava Beans to Bear a Crop. If you planted fava beans last October, by now they

How to Plant, Grow, and Harvest Lettuce from Seeds

- Plant in full sun. (Lettuce can take some shade in summer but not in winter.) Don't plant it in the same spot twice, or it may succumb to wilt.

- Dig deeply prior to planting. Mix in organic soil amendment and add fertilizer that's recommended for vegetables to the top 6 inches of soil, according to package directions.

- Distribute the seed down a wide row, or broadcast it on a raised bed at the approximate rate of 3 seeds to every 2 square inches of soil surface.

- Cover the seed very lightly with potting soil (about ¼ inch), and water by sprinkling lightly. Use a misting valve. Continue to keep the seedbed damp by sprinkling daily until the seeds sprout—three to seven days. Then lengthen the watering times and water more deeply. (If your lettuce seeds don't germinate, your soil may be too salty. Give the soil a long deep soaking to leach out salts. Plant again with fresh seed.)

- Stimulate fast growth with plenty of water and fertilizer. (Fast growth means sweet, crunchy lettuce, while slow growth makes it tough and bitter.)

- Protect the plants from slugs (page 91).

- Thin seedlings according to package directions. Either eat the little thinnings or transplant them to an adjacent row.

- If you'd like to grow lettuce but don't have space, plant it in pots and half barrels filled with potting soil. Feed every two weeks with liquid fertilizer recommended for vegetables.

- Harvest whole heads of lettuce, leave the roots in the ground, and feed and water them; they will grow new heads. Or lengthen your harvest by taking off only the outside leaves as needed.

should be waist height. Protect them from being pushed over by rain or wind by adding a few bamboo stakes and connecting them with twine.

In some climate zones fava beans will bear crops without the aid of the gardener, but for a variety of reasons (including too much shade, water, or fertilizer) they may bear flowers but no beans. If that happens, pinch off the growing tips of the stems. It's all right then to side-dress the rows with vegetable fertilizer according to package directions; gently cultivate it into the ground and water deeply. Within a week of pinching, the favas will start to bear beans. Wait until the pods are between 5 and 8 inches long and filled with beans before you begin to harvest. (The tips of the stems you pinched off are very good to eat; steam or stir-fry them.)

Harvest Cole Crops. Here's how to harvest cauliflower, cabbage, and Brussels sprouts. When it's done correctly all but cauliflower will continue to produce.

As soon as you see the white curd (head) beginning to form on cauliflower, tie the leaves together over the top to protect it from sunshine. Sun turns cauliflowers green. (Even "self-blanching" types are best treated this way in our strong sun.) Untie and check them every few days. Suddenly a head will start to fill out. Then check that one daily for readiness.

A head of cauliflower is a flower in the bud stage. Harvest it just when the snowy white buds are all filled out but before they open. When you see the sections just beginning to loosen up and separate around the outside, cut the head with a knife below the curd. If you wait too long, it will be overdone and ricey.

Homegrown cauliflower cooks more quickly than bought. Steam the whole head for three to five minutes; then test with a fork. No need for sauces; straight from the garden it's a tasty treat, one of the best vegetables.

After harvesting pull out and compost the plant. Replace it with something else, such as bare-root short-day onions, carrots, or lettuce, not another cole crop (member of the cabbage family)—they all share the same diseases, so you shouldn't plant them in the same spot for two or three years.

Broccoli is another edible flower bud that needs checking daily. Harvest by cutting stalks with a knife when the buds are filled out but still tight. Don't pull up the plants when you harvest; leave them in the ground and side-dress the row with fertilizer. Unlike cauliflower, broccoli will branch and give you more crops. The farther down on the stalk you cut, the fewer but the fatter will be the side branches you get. Many home garden varieties—'Bonanza' is one—are known for their ample manufacture of such second, third, and fourth crops.

Harvest cabbage as soon as the heads fill out and feel firm to the touch. If they give when you squeeze them they're not quite ready. As soon as they feel hard as a bowling ball, pick them by cutting just below the head. If you wait too long they'll split.

To keep the plants going, cut off the outer leaves but let the roots remain in the ground. Fertilize and water them and they'll form three or four baby heads. Though these have a stronger flavor than the first harvest, they're good for soup.

There's a trick to harvesting Brussels sprouts, and unless you practice it you may not even get a crop. As soon as the plant begins to manufacture sprouts, pull off its lower leaves with a downward twisting motion, and take off a few of the tiny sprouts at the bottom of the stalk. This stimulates sprouts farther up on the stalk to grow faster. As the sprouts grow, pull off all the remaining lower leaves that have sprouts above them, leaving a topknot of leaves at the peak of the stalk rather like a mini palm tree. This provides more room for sprouts and forces the energy of the plant into sprout production.

Harvest Brussels sprouts as soon as they're big enough to eat. Always take them from the bottom to the top. Side-dress the row with fertilizer and continue to water the plants when rains aren't adequate. They'll grow and continue to produce sprouts throughout cold weather.

Purchase/Plant

❑ Purchase and plant bare-root roses, trees, vines (including wisteria), berries, and vegetables, 41

❑ Choose and plant camellias and azaleas, 52

❑ Purchase cymbidiums, 55

❑ Purchase and plant cool-season flowers to fill in bare spots, 56

❑ Plant seeds of warm-season flowers for transplants to put out in spring, 56

❑ Continue to plant winter vegetables from transplants and seeds, 59

❑ Many succulents, including cacti, bloom in winter and spring; purchase new types now, 194

Trim, Prune, Mow, Divide

❑ Prune deciduous fruit trees, 43

❑ Prune roses, 47

❑ Pick camellias, 53

❑ Deadhead azaleas, 53

❑ Don't prune off frost damage, 54

❑ Prune naked coral trees, 56

❑ Mow cool-season lawns. Most warm-season lawns are dormant now and don't need mowing, 58

❑ Cut back Japanese blood grass, 240

❑ Prune conifers, 191

Fertilize

❑ Choose a system for fertilizing roses (Rose-Pro gardeners feed with Epsom salts and superphosphate), 44

❑ Begin to feed citrus trees in coastal zones only, 50

❑ Treat citrus trees to correct chlorosis, 51

❑ Start feeding epiphyllums for bloom with 0-10-10 or 2-10-10, 54

❑ Continue to fertilize cymbidiums that have not yet bloomed with a high-bloom formula, 55

❑ Feed cool-season flowers (other than wildflowers), 56

❑ Feed cineraria, 56

❑ Fertilize cool-season lawns, 58

❑ Side-dress vegetable rows with fertilizer, 59

❑ Treat the ground under royal purple brunfelsia with nitrogen fertilizer mixed double-strength, 296

Water

❑ When rains aren't adequate water all garden plants according to their individual needs. (Succulents don't need water now, but native plants will perform better if given water in dry weather during their growing season.) 54

❑ Irrigate citrus trees, if rains aren't adequate, 51

❑ Remember to water plants under eaves where rains can't reach them, 54

❑ Water cool-season lawns when rains aren't adequate, 58

Control Pests, Diseases, and Weeds

❑ Apply dormant spray to roses and deciduous fruit trees, 47

❑ Apply dormant spray to sycamore trees, 50

❑ Check citrus trees for pests, 52

❑ Pick up dead camellia blossoms to prevent petal blight, 53

❑ Protect cymbidiums from slugs and snails, 55

❑ Control rust on cool-season lawns, 58

❑ Control crabgrass with preemergent herbicide, 58

❑ Check trees, shrubs, and ice plant in coastal zones for overwintering whiteflies. Control by spraying, 47

❑ Pull weeds, 40

❑ Spray peach and apricot trees for peach leaf curl, 47

❑ Control ants, 68

Also This Month

❑ Protect tender plants from frost, 54

❑ Stake cymbidium bloom spikes, 55

❑ Start a garden notebook, 57

❑ Clean out the potting shed, 57

❑ Order seeds and supplies from seed catalogs, 57

❑ Check the lawn mower; have the blades sharpened if necessary, 59

❑ Pinch tips of fava beans if they fail to bear crops, 59

❑ Harvest cool-season vegetables as they mature. Harvest cole crops by individual methods, 60

❑ At month's end begin to check bamboo in coastal zones to see if it's time to propagate, 103

FEBRUARY

A Month for Waiting

In Southern California February feels like spring. Acacias decorate the roadsides, orange blossoms scent the air, the first bulbs come into bloom, and gardens smell inviting after rain, which may be frequent this month. Native plants are in a season of growth, and cool-season garden flowers such as primroses, cyclamen, linaria, annual African daisies, pansies, and cineraria are at the height of their beauty. But despite appearances it's still winter. Most plants are growing slowly now, and the wise gardener knows never to rush the seasons. February is not a major planting month. If spring is in your blood, concentrate on putting in those few items that can be planted now.

Though there are many interesting jobs to be done in February, it's also a time for waiting. Certain plants can be pruned now, but wait until

How to Feed an Avocado Tree

- Weigh the total poundage of fertilizer you need for each monthly feeding on your bathroom scale and divide it equally into four coffee cans.

- Using gypsum as a marker, divide the ground under the tree into four equal pie-shaped areas. Place one coffee can in each pie-shaped section.

- Sprinkle the contents of each can evenly over the ground under the tree from about 1 to 2 feet away from the trunk to the branch tips, or drip line. (Avocados have feeder roots just under the soil surface beneath their entire leaf canopy.)

- Water deeply immediately after fertilizing.

the weather warms up before cutting off frost-bitten branches. In cold low-lying gardens and interior valleys, wait until all danger of frost has passed before you move those tender plants safely sheltered under eaves. Fertilize deciduous fruit trees—and avocados too, in coastal zones—but wait until next month to feed most of the landscape. Throw off your coat, dig in the garden, prepare the soil, spread manure, start a compost heap, but wait until March to put in summer vegetables and flowers.

Avocado Trees

If You Use Commercial Fertilizer. A mature avocado tree needs at least 2 pounds of actual nitrogen per year and varying amounts of other nutrients, like phosphorus and zinc, periodically. For the home grower the easiest way to go is to use a commercial fertilizer specifically recommended for citrus and avocados that contains nitrogen, phosphorus, potassium, and zinc. If you do opt for bagged "citrus and avocado food" follow the package directions, which usu-

ally tell you to measure the girth of the tree 24 inches up from the ground and feed ½ to 1 pound per inch of girth. But if you have several trees it may be less expensive to purchase a large bag of generic fertilizer, with a formula such as 25-18-10 or 16-8-4 or slow-release 17-6-10—good formulas for avocados but not magic numbers you absolutely must find. Feed young nonbearing trees lightly. They require much less nitrogen and can be damaged by too much fertilizer.

When you use a product with 25 percent nitrogen, you need to give 8 pounds of it to each mature tree (eight or ten years of age) per year. Give 12 pounds if you have selected a product with 16 or 17 percent nitrogen. Give young trees proportionately less. (For example, you could give a three-year-old tree one-quarter of the total amount, a five-year-old tree half the total amount, and a large tree over fifteen years old—especially if it is growing in fast-draining soil—as much as 3 pounds actual nitrogen per year.)

Gardeners in coastal zones should divide the total amount of fertilizer for the year into five equal applications and give one feeding each month from February through June. Interior gardeners should divide the total amount into four monthly applications and give one feeding per month from March through June. With slow-release fertilizers you can divide the fertilizer into two equal doses. Give the first dose early this month if you live along the coast, late this month if you live inland, and give the second dose in June.

If You Use Organic Fertilizer. Organic gardeners can feed avocados by spreading 25 pounds of aged chicken manure (available bagged in some Southern California nurseries) under each mature tree in February. Beginning in March, give each mature tree one trowelful of blood meal and one of bone meal every six weeks, through August. If mulch is thick, sprinkle fertilizers underneath and then replace the mulch on top.

Other Basic Requirements of Avocados. The main requirements of avocados are rich soil, excellent drainage, and a thick layer of mulch over the roots. Allow the leaves that fall to remain under the tree; don't rake them up. (Avocados are best planted at the back of the garden, where their large leaves won't look untidy.) Add additional mulch to young trees.

Never cultivate or dig under avocado trees, because that would damage the roots and all your fruit might fall off. It's best not to grow anything under an avocado tree, especially if it needs frequent irrigation. Wet soil promotes root rot of avocados.

Citrus Trees

Feed Citrus in Coastal Zones. If you live in a coastal zone, fertilize citrus trees again this month (and every month through June, as described on page 50). If you live in an interior zone, hold off fertilizing until March.

Control Citrus Pests. Citrus pests often step up their activity now. Books such as the *Ortho Problem Solver* contain colored photographs to help you recognize specific pests and diseases. Use a magnifying glass to identify such pests as aphids, which cause curly leaves and sooty mold; mealybugs, which also cause sooty mold; and woolly whitefly, which can be recognized by fuzzy white residue under leaves. Rust mites (the same pest as silver mite on lemons) cause reddish brown fruit that spoils easily. Various scales attach themselves to trunks, twigs, and fruit.

 Quick Tip

Control Ants with Homemade Bait Stations.
For each station you will need a small bottle or jar, such as a jam jar. Use a roofing nail to drive a hole in the top that ants can enter. Make the following solution: ½ teaspoon boric acid, 3 tablespoons sugar, 1 cup water. Stir until all crystals are dissolved. Fill the jar half full with the mixture. Screw top on tightly. Place the bait station on its side, nestled halfway into the ground for stability. Renew weekly. (Note: Boric acid is a dangerous poison. Ingestion could be fatal. Do not use where young children play. For a slower-acting but effective long-term control, use half the amount of boric acid in the formula above.)

Wash Citrus Trees. Of course you could have your trees professionally sprayed with chemicals specific to whatever pests you find. But one of the pleasures of growing your own fruit is knowing it hasn't been sprayed. Fortunately many calamities can be avoided by keeping trees clean. It's been proved that beneficial insects can't reach the harmful ones if the latter are hidden beneath a layer of dust. If the trees are dusty even after rain, spray them with soapy water made with an insecticidal soap, such as Safer soap, or a solution of 1 to 2 tablespoons of dishwashing liquid—the kind you use in the sink, not in a machine—per gallon of water. (Before spraying, cut off the tips of branches that brush the ground, as described below, because they're a ready highway for ants.)

Washing trees can also help rid them of certain pests directly. Aphids, woolly whiteflies, and mealybugs can be washed to the ground with a soapy spray. An even better job can be done if you're willing to get right under the leaves and manually scrub off aphids and other pests with a sponge or paintbrush. I've done this myself, and it doesn't rank high on my list of favorite jobs, but rubber gloves, a rain suit, and boots can make it bearable.

Cut Ants Off at the Pass. Although washing and sponging under the leaves can get rid of most pest problems on citrus, the problems will come back if you don't get rid of ants. Ants are determined little dairy farmers who manage immense herds of sucking insect "cows," such as aphids, mealybugs, woolly whiteflies, and scale. Ants protect pests from predators, carry them from plant to plant, and milk them for the honeydew they produce. If you can get rid of ants, your pest problems will be almost completely gone. This requires a special strategy.

Before washing the trees, carefully cut away any branches that are lying on the ground. (Don't cut up too high. It's good for a citrus tree's branches to hang low, not only because of all the extra fruit they bear, but also because this "skirt" of low branches protects the trunk from sunburn.) Now the only avenue left for ants will be up the trunk. You can cut off that route by applying a sticky product such as Tree Tanglefoot Pest Barrier.

Don't put these products directly onto bark. Wrap quilt batting (available at fabric stores) around the trunk so that ants can't climb under it, cover it with a strip of plastic, and apply the substance to that. Wear an old pair of rubber gloves to keep the product off your skin—it's quite hard to get it off! Renew the coating frequently to keep it sticky.

You can also spray the ground with diazinon to control ants. (Regular professional spraying is best.) But you can control ants and avoid releasing diazinon into the environment by using baits. An especially strong type is called MAXFORCE, available as granules or in bait stations. (If you're worried that your dog might chew on these, place them inside tin cans, bent partially closed. Or put the granules inside glass jars with holes punched in the tops. Place jars on their sides so rain won't enter.) COMBAT is another brand of bait station, with a choice of indoor or outdoor containers. Ants can also be controlled by distributing homemade bait stations (see the Quick Tip on page 67). Ants are more likely to use baits when placed directly on their trails and when avenues up trees are cut off with a Tanglefoot product. Once you're rid of ants, the beneficials can go to work to clean up your grove.

Protect Honeybees. When gardeners tell me their citrus trees were loaded with flowers but they got no fruit, I always ask, "Did you spray with malathion?" Invariably the answer is "Yes, I was told it would get rid of the aphids." Malathion will indeed kill aphids. It will also kill honeybees, and if you don't have any bees you won't get any fruit. A good **Rule of Thumb** is: *Don't spray citrus with pesticides like malathion when the trees are in bloom.* (An environmentally friendly way to rid your trees of aphids is to distribute ladybugs on them; see page 38. For more on bees, see pages 199–203.)

Cooperate with Beneficials. It's remarkable that even difficult pests such as scale insects and rust mites will be killed by beneficial insects on a clean, well-kept tree. However, if your trees are in such bad shape that you feel you must spray against rust mites, then spray twice a year—spring and fall—with a miticide. Be sure to choose one recommended for citrus. If scale is also a problem, mix the miticide with oil so your spray will control scale at the same time. Try using SunSpray Ultra-Fine Spray Oil, which does not burn when used as directed and smothers pests without poison.

Deciduous Fruit Trees

Feed deciduous fruit trees when the weather warms up in February and the flower buds swell just prior to bloom. The reason for fertilizing now rather than throughout the spring and summer months, as is done in cold-winter climates, is that fertilizing in summer could produce unseasonal flowering, irregular fruiting, or a spurt of growth that could shorten or prevent winter dormancy.

Feed no more than 1 pound of actual nitrogen per year to each mature deciduous fruit tree growing in fast-draining soil. Feed less to trees in clay soil, and feed young trees very lightly. Too much nitrogen can overstimulate growth. Most experts say deciduous fruit trees need only nitrogen, not phosphorus or potassium, when grown in deep fertile soils, but my own experience indicates that they respond well to a complete formula like 16-8-4, or whatever the gardener may have used to feed citrus and avocados. Vary the amount and formulas depending on local conditions, the fertility of your soil, the size of your tree, and the results you get after the first yearly feeding.

Water deeply and well after fertilizing. If you are an organic gardener, spread a deep layer of aged horse manure over the tree roots at this time. If rains are inadequate, watch the leaves for brown edges, indicating possible salt burn. Water to flush salts to deeper levels. (The safest, least-salty manure is that which is picked up daily by a conscientious horse owner.)

Sycamore, Ash, and Alder Trees

Continue control of pest and disease problems on sycamore *(Platanus)* trees, and now include ash *(Fraxinus)* and alder *(Alnus)*. Refer to the *Ortho Problem Solver* and ask your Cooperative Extension for advice on applicable fungicides and pesticides in your area. The best solution is to clean the ground, prune out dead and diseased wood, and have your trees professionally sprayed. Problems are worse in some areas than others. Don't plant without prior investigation.

Spray Sycamores. Sycamore anthracnose *(Gnomonia platanus)*, a fungal disease often called sycamore blight, can completely ruin the appearance of sycamores unless controlled now. If you wait for damage to occur, there's no solution. Anthracnose causes dieback of young shoots and leaves; brown, scorched-looking mature leaves; and cankers on stems and branches that can girdle and kill them. Spray with a fungicide containing chlorothalonil (Ortho Multi-Purpose Fungicide [Daconil 2787]) three times: once when buds begin to swell, again when leaves reach full size, and finally two weeks later.

Use oil sprays when trees are dormant to control scale and sycamore lacebug *(Coythucha)*, which overwinters in bark and branch crotches and later causes whitening and dropping of leaves. (Spray later with a systemic at the first signs of any damage.)

Spray Ash Trees. Ash anthracnose *(Gloeosporium aridum)* can infect some ash trees, such as Modesto ash *(Fraxinus velutina* 'Modesto'), so severely that all the leaves sometimes go brown and drop off after the tree leafs out in spring. Usually new leaves grow in summer, but if the disease isn't checked large portions of the tree can die. Clean up all debris under the tree. Cut out dead branches. Spray three times with a product containing chlorothalonil (Daconil 2787): spray once when leaves unfurl, again two weeks later, and once more two weeks thereafter. Fertilize just prior to leaf emergence to promote vigorous growth.

Spray Alders. The main pests are aphids and alder flea beetles *(Altica ambiens),* which overwinter in debris. Clean up the ground. Follow up by spraying with a product such as Sevin (carbaryl).

Kiwi Vines

Prune kiwi vines in February, during dormancy. Kiwis bear mostly on new canes arising as laterals from fat buds on canes that grew last year. Prune young kiwis lightly, to develop a primary trunk and to create a structure on a pergola, overhead wires, or espalier. Head back canes to create fruiting wood. Prune mature kiwis hard, to remove old wood and produce fresh fruiting growth. Here are the basic steps for mature plants:

- Remove all twiggy, dead, diseased, and tangled growth.
- Remove a few two- or three-year-old branches each year, to reduce crowding and encourage growth of new branches for the future. (These cuts won't produce much fruit this year but are necessary for renewal.)
- Cut off all but twenty-eight or thirty canes with smooth wood (those that grew last year). Shorten the remaining canes to four or five buds.
- Shorten fruiting spurs (short side branches) to two buds each.

Camellias

Continue to buy, plant, and transplant camellias now, while they're still in bloom and before they start to grow. (See the box on camellias on page 52 for how to plant.) Most people choose camellias simply by picking out something that looks pretty. It's better to select them for your climate zone and ease of growing. Some are slow growers, others vigorous. Some are good along the coast, others better inland. Many varieties need extremes of temperature in order to open their blooms and thus do better in inland valleys than they do along the coast.

Among varieties that do well inland but have difficulty opening in coastal gardens are 'Mathotiana', 'Ballet Dancer', 'Mrs. Charles Cobb', 'Chandler Elegans', 'C. M. Wilson', and 'Shiro-Chan'. Easy to grow either on the coast or inland are 'Debutante', 'Pink Perfection', 'Herme' ('Jordan's Pride'), 'Professor Sargeant', 'Lady Claire', and 'Ace of Hearts'. The last can take full sun when grown close to the coast.

As a general rule, singles and semidoubles do best in milder areas, though many formal doubles will open. Anemone-form and peony-form camellias usually won't open in coastal gardens, because the winters are too warm. Get more information from knowledgeable gardeners, nurseries that specialize in camellias, and your local camellia society.

Deciduous Magnolias

Purchase deciduous magnolias now, while they're in bloom (before leaf-out). Saucer magnolia *(Magnolia soulangiana)* and star magnolia *(M. stellata)* eventually become large, but they grow so slowly they're good choices for small gardens. Use them as focal points in corner beds. They're best against a dark background. They grow best in interior valleys or the Los Angeles basin, where they get some winter chill. A pink saucer magnolia underplanted with spring-flowering bulbs can be breathtaking.

Clivia

Purchase clivia now while they're in bloom to get the shade of orange and the size of flowers you want. Belgium hybrids are more handsome than chance seedlings, and there are several exciting new varieties and colors, including white and yellow. 'Flame', developed by a local nurseryman, has unusually wide, shiny foliage and brilliant, flaming orange blooms, with twenty-four individual flowers in each cluster compared to the usual fourteen. (Your local nursery can order it from Monrovia Nursery.)

Clivia are easy to grow in pots or the ground and are good multipliers. They flower most when crowded, and they'll bloom in northern exposures under overhangs with too much shade for almost all other winter flowers. If you grow enough of them they make dramatic, long-lasting cut flowers.

Bait now for slugs and snails. They don't often damage the leaves but do like to hide in them and sneak out at night to eat the flowers. A time-honored **Rule of Thumb** is: *Don't plant clivia next to red or pink tones of azalea. They clash.* (White azaleas are beautiful near clivia.)

Gerberas

Plant Transvaal daisies *(Gerbera jamesonii)* now through April. New varieties are freer blooming and have a wider range of colors than older types.

Gerberas are easy to grow in pots or the ground but need good drainage, sun along the coast, and part shade inland. When planting take care to bury all the roots but not the crown (the place where the roots join the leaves). They rot if planted too deeply. Allow gerberas to dry out slightly between waterings. Protect them from snails and feed often with a complete fertilizer.

Gladioli

Start planting gladioli early this month. By continuing to plant a few more every week between now and the end of March you can have a continual display lasting from early June through summer. The ones that go in now will be less subject to thrips, and you may not need to spray them. This rasping insect that disfigures leaves and flowers particularly favors gladioli, but it's most active in hot weather.

Gladioli are easy to grow if you give them what they need: full sun; light, sandy loam; bone meal worked in under the corms and covered with a handful of earth; plenty of water; and good drainage. Buy the best corms and plant them in drifts at the backs of beds—they look gawky in rows. Or use dwarf types up front. Plant small corms 3 to 4 inches deep, larger corms 4 to 6 inches deep. (Mark the spots so you won't plant something else on top.) They do well in pots if you shade the containers from burning sun. A few giant red ones can spark up a patio.

Roses

Water and Fertilize Roses. Keep roses irrigated with 1 inch of water per week beginning at mid-month when rains aren't adequate.

If you've chosen to fertilize your roses with a commercial rose food, wait for the leaves to unfold before feeding them. As soon as the leaves lose their reddish hue, fertilize your roses with a complete fertilizer recommended for them, and mark the date on your calendar so you can feed them again on approximately the same date next month. Do this fertilizing just prior to a regular irrigation or heavy rainfall. You can, if you wish, choose a fertilizer that contains a systemic pesticide as discussed below under pest control.

Throughout this book I also recommend an alternative method for fertilizing roses, the Rose-Pro Method (as summarized on page 308). If you've chosen to feed your roses according to

Easy, Disease-Resistant Roses

Hybrid Tea Roses
'St. Patrick'—light yellow
'Color Magic'—pink to red
'First Prize'—pink
'Brandy'—apricot
'Olympiad'—red

Floribundas
'Iceberg'—white
'Carefree Wonder'—pink
'French Lace'—white
'Flutterby'—yellow, tangerine, pink
'Angel Face'—fragrant lavender
'Bonica'—pink

Climbers
'Lady Banks'—yellow or white
'Eden'—pink
'Sombreuil'—white
'Sally Holmes'—white single, pink tinges
'Altissimo'—red single
'Handel'—pink blend

English Roses
'Belle Story'—apricot blend

Hybrid Musks
'Cornelia'—coral pink
'Penelope'—light shell pink

Grandiflora
'Gold Medal'—yellow, with pink touches

the Rose-Pro Method, apply 1 cup of gypsum to the ground over the roots of each rose in early February. Follow up with deep watering to leach accumulated salts down into the ground. Later, in mid-February, give each of your rose-bushes and young climbing roses 1 cup of Milorganite (6-2-0), an organic fertilizer, to contribute to a good organic soil. Give established climbers (over three years old) 2 cups of Milor-

ganite. Sprinkle this over the root zone and follow up with irrigation. (If you didn't start your Rose-Pro regime last month it's not too late to begin; early this month, feed Epsom salts and phosphorus fertilizer to your roses as recommended last month. Follow the directions on page 45.)

Protect Roses from Pests and Diseases. It's an unfortunate fact that roses, one of our most loved garden plants and the national flower of the United States, are also host to a flock of pests and diseases. It's almost impossible to grow healthy roses without spraying them with chemicals. It can be done—I've done it myself for years—but to do so you have to grow only the most disease-resistant roses and be content with somewhat ratty-looking plants for the second half of the year.

If you're not satisfied by anything less than pristine rose plants unblemished by pests or diseases, you simply have to use chemical sprays. In that case, start spraying this month against fungal diseases with RosePride Funginex Rose & Shrub Disease Control. It will control mildew and rust, but because it controls rust only as a preventative you must start spraying before the onset of the problem. The best times to spray are either in the early morning or late in the evening when the wind's died down. Whenever you spray with chemicals, be sure to wear protective clothing, including a shower cap, boots, face mask, and waterproof gloves. After spraying put your clothes into the wash and immediately take a shower, washing not only your body but also your hair; even perfect roses aren't worth risking your health. Most rose pests aren't active yet, so it's not necessary to start pesticides until next month. (If aphids are a problem, wash them off with a squirt of the hose.)

If you too prefer not to spray roses with toxic

chemicals, plant disease-resistant varieties. Once established, Lady Banks' rose is completely resistant to diseases and to pests, including aphids. (For other suggestions, refer to the list on page 72.) Environmentally friendly pest and disease controls you might want to try include Sun-Spray Ultra-Fine Spray Oil, the Cornell Fungicide Formula (see the accompanying box), and products, such as Green Light Rose Defense, containing neem oil (which is derived from the neem tree).

You can, if you wish, control sucking pests (those, like aphids or scale, that attach themselves to plants and suck out their juices) by using a systemic pesticide in the soil (but this practice kills earthworms). Some commercial rose fertilizers, such as Green Light Rose and Flower Food, contain systemic pesticides along with the fertilizer. In general, systemics are safer than sprays but their use nonetheless requires certain precautions. Never use systemics close to food plants, such as herbs, fruit trees, or vegetables, because the poisons can be picked up by their roots; don't breathe in the dust, and wear rubber gloves while measuring them. Because of these dangers I no longer use systemics, and I have found that ladybugs do a good job on aphids.

Bulbs

When rains aren't adequate keep spring bulbs well watered. Dryness can damage flowers. After ranunculi are 3 or 4 inches high, remove the netting (see page 278) that's covering them. Birds love the sprouts when they're young and tender but turn up their beaks at them later.

Try growing lilies-of-the-valley (*Convallaria majalis*). You can buy prechilled roots, called "pips," at nurseries now. Plant the pips in pots of high-quality potting mix, water them, and

🐾 Quick Tip

Control Rose Diseases with the Cornell Fungicide Formula. *For control of blackspot, mildew, and several pests on roses and for control of early blight on tomatoes: Mix together 1 tablespoon baking soda, 1 tablespoon light summer oil (SunSpray Ultra-Fine Spray Oil) and 1 gallon of water. Spray once every four or five days, shaking spray frequently.*

keep them in a warm eastern window. Give the pots a quarter turn daily. They'll bloom fragrantly in three weeks. (Once in bloom, keep them in bright light with no sun, and give them cool nights.)

Fuchsias

Fuchsias bloom only on new wood. They need to be cut back annually to stimulate growth (see directions in boxes). In mild, frost-free coastal zones you can cut them back in November and allow regrowth during the winter, but for most other Southland gardeners February's the time to cut them back. Wait until you see some green growth begin and then prune and begin fertilizing.

The Use of Manure as Mulch

Manure has been much criticized for its high salt content. If you've ever had a problem with salt damage on plants or had a soil test showing a high salt content in your soil, don't use it. But bagged steer manure is an inexpensive and readily available soil amendment that has some good applications when used wisely. On certain plants it can be beneficial, especially when they're growing in fast-draining soil and when the application of manure is likely to be followed by

How to Cut Back Standard and Shrub Fuchsias

- Cut back standard and shrub fuchsias into old wood now. Look at the bark. The twiggy growth with smooth bark is what grew last year. The bark with darker color and rougher texture is the old wood. Cut off the twigs along with an inch or two of the older wood.

- Go easy on very old specimens that haven't been pruned in years. Cut back these one-third now. Then wait a month to six weeks for the plants to regrow. When they're leafed out, cut back a third more, and wait for that to regrow before finishing the job. (If you cut back a venerable old fuchsia all at once, you might kill it.)

- Clean up the ground beneath the plant. Water, fertilize, and pinch back as described in the box on hanging-basket fuchsias. If you use slow-release fertilizer, increase the amounts in proportion to the size of the plant. For instance, sprinkle ¼ cup of the slow-release type all over the soil under the plant where irrigation water will hit it, or soak the roots with 2 gallons of liquid fertilizer.

- As plants regrow pinch to make them bushy, as described last in the box on hanging fuchsias.

How to Cut Back Hanging-Basket Fuchsias

- Cut fuchsias growing in hanging baskets back to pot level or 4 inches above the soil. If the plant is young and vigorous, take off all green growth.

- Turn the basket on its side and, with your gloved hand, clean off the surface of the soil. Remove all old leaves and debris, including dead bodies of slow-release fertilizer.

- Dig out and remove about one-quarter of the old potting mix, roots and all. Replace it with fresh fast-draining acid soil mix. Press it down firmly. Rehang the plant in semishade.

- Water well after pruning. Don't let the roots dry out.

- Start to fertilize immediately, and fertilize regularly thereafter, with a balanced fertilizer high in growth ingredients. For example, use 1 tablespoon slow-release 14-14-14 or 18-18-6 on the top of the soil once per month or use 20-20-20, 18-24-16, or 30-10-10 liquid every two weeks.

- As plants regrow, pinch them to make them bushy; when a sprout has made three pairs of leaves, clip off the top pair. This makes the plant branch. When it's really full, stop pinching and let it bloom.

rains. (Some plants, such as asparagus, are more resistant to salt than others.)

Horse or cow manure adds low-level nitrogen and life-giving humus to soils. Horse manure picked up daily by a conscientious owner is free from the chunks of salt from broken salt licks that cow manure often contains. Also, cattle feed is heavily salted, unlike the alfalfa hay commonly fed to horses. On sandy ground I often lay horse manure straight on top of the ground over the roots of plants as mulch and let it age right there while winter rains wash the nutrients into the ground. In a month or two I cultivate it into the ground prior to planting flowers or vegetables. Manure is especially good for fast-draining soils, but it will improve clay soils too if water from rain or irrigation is adequate and the manure isn't salty. Rabbit manure is not salty and doesn't burn.

A few cautions: Every gardener should have an up-to-date tetanus shot, but particularly those using manure. Always wash vegetables carefully prior to eating them. Hog manure is unsafe for vegetable gardens; dog and cat manure contains dangerous pathogens; hot-composted manures, including bagged cow manure, contain fewer pathogens than fresh manure. Some experts say that pregnant women and people with low immune systems shouldn't eat raw vegetables grown in manured soils, but also that cooked vegetables are fine.

Observing these precautions, spread manure over the roots of the following: bananas, ginger, cannas, asparagus, perennials, and old clumps of geraniums. Also spread it under bushes, trees, and ground covers, especially gazanias, ivy geraniums, and small-leafed ivy. (Don't use manure on camellias, azaleas, ferns, succulents, or specialty plants other than those listed.) Water thoroughly after spreading.

Pruning Chores for Washington's Birthday

Washington's birthday is the time-honored day for cutting back certain tropical and subtropical plants, including begonias, ginger, and cannas. Gardeners in mild areas, such as Rincon, Malibu, Long Beach, Laguna, and coastal San Diego County, can do these jobs a week earlier, on Lincoln's birthday. But if you live in a low-lying interior valley where you may still get a late frost, it's safer to wait until early March.

Prune Begonias. Cut back *Begonia* 'Richmondensis' to pot level or 4 inches above the ground to keep the plants from getting leggy in summer. Or you may opt to use "progressive pruning." This means cutting back a few of the longest branches every month throughout the growing season. Feed lightly with a balanced fertilizer mixed half-strength. They'll soon regrow. Richmondensis begonias grow best in the ground or in large containers—they dry out too soon in small ones. When ground grown they can be used as a tall ground cover and can go two or three years before being cut back, if desired. Cut

Quick Tip

How to Make a Green Shrub or Tree Bloom with Pink or Red Flowers. *Conceal large tubs of cane begonias under tall informal shrubs, such as Victorian box* (Pittosporum undulatum). *Train the begonias into the shrubbery so flowers cascade among the branches in a natural way. The shrub will appear to be blooming with pink or red blossoms for most of the year.*

back container-grown angel-wing and other cane begonias to pot level now, for a bigger flower display in summer. Spectacular varieties such as 'Irene Nuss', which bears the largest bunches of flowers of any cane begonia, especially benefit from this treatment. Flowers will be larger and plant size more controlled.

Clean up old-fashioned, tall-growing cane begonias and cut out one or two old canes to encourage new canes to arise. Cane begonias can be grown in moist acid ground away from invasive tree roots or, if trees are a problem, in large tubs.

Prune Ginger, Cannas, Asparagus Fern, Ivy, and Pyracantha. If you live in an interior valley, remember to hold off pruning these plants until the weather has warmed up for good and there's no more chance of a late frost.

Ginger is "monocarpic," which means it blooms just once on a stalk and then dies. If you don't cut back stalks that have bloomed the clump will tend to stop sending up new growth. You won't get much, if any, bloom.

- **Algerian Ivy** (*Hedera canariensis*). Renew thick, woody stands by cutting them to the ground by hand or rented machine. Follow up with fertilizer.

- **Cannas.** Cut all stalks that have bloomed down to the ground now, to encourage new stalks to grow and make plants look as good as new. Deadhead them throughout the year (remove individual dead blossoms after bloom).

- **Kahili Ginger** (*Hedychium gardneranum*). Cut back to ground level now all stalks that have bloomed, to encourage growth of new stalks that will bloom this year. Leave stalks that have not yet bloomed.

- **Pyracantha.** Cut off branches that have borne fruit this year to the base of the plant or to strong side branches. Pyracantha only bears on one-year-old wood, so don't cut off last year's wood that will flower this spring and bear fruit next winter.

- **Shell Ginger** (*Alpinia zerumbet*). Beginning now, cut down to the ground all stalks that have bloomed when the blooms have finished. Continue this throughout the year. After blooms fade, some varieties make little plantlets that you can use to propagate more plants.

- **Sprenger Asparagus Fern** (*Asparagus densiflorus* 'Sprengeri'). Renew ratty-looking clumps by cutting them to the ground now. Fertilize for quick bounce-back.

Compost

A compost pile can be a great way to use up vegetable wastes from garden and kitchen and return them to the soil. In general there are two ways to go: slow (cold) composting and rapid (hot) composting. Slow composting involves much more time and more space but less effort, and it works eventually even if you don't have the perfect combination of ingredients. (Serious composters should consider purchasing a garden chipping machine, since small particles decompose much faster than large ones.) Rapid composting is indeed fast but takes considerable work; it kills most disease and pest organisms, but you need scientific know-how and a ready supply of the necessary ingredients.

Slow Compost. Choose a hidden area at least 10 feet square. Dig within it a hole 1 or 2 feet deep and 3 or 4 feet square, and pile in such garden refuse as leaves, vegetable peelings, lawn clippings, and chopped remnants of garden plants. If you find you have too many dry materials and not enough wet ones while you are making a pile, sprinkle on some sulfate of ammonia to provide extra nitrogen and speed up decomposition. Wet the pile often to keep it damp.

When adding such wet materials from the kitchen as fruit and vegetable peelings, first dig a deep hole in the pile and pour them into it; chop them up a bit with a spade and then completely cover them over with other materials to prevent odors. Topping a cool compost pile with a thin layer of moist earth can also destroy odors and additionally prevent flies from laying their eggs. Technically, the best compost is made without the addition of earth, but if an occasional topping of it saves you from the horror of finding maggots in your compost pile, changing the rule in this case is worthwhile.

Keep adding to the pile until it is about 3 feet high and 3 feet wide; then start another. Leave the first for another six months or a year to rot. Slow composting is hit or miss. Some slow compost piles heat up part of the time depending on the ingredients that have gone into them, and they decompose faster than others. Others never go through a hot stage. Many cold compost piles become earthworm factories; the worms slowly devour all the organic materials and eventually turn them into rich soil. Sooner or later you'll end up with a heap of finished compost, and it will be about half the size of the pile you started with. When your compost has become even-textured, soft, crumbly, dark brown, and sweet smelling, and you can no longer discern what went into it, then it's sufficiently decomposed to safely add to garden soil. Use homemade compost like any other soil amendment—it's better than most you can buy. (This pit system of making compost is unconventional, but it's an excellent way to make a low-profile compost pile and keep it damp in our dry climate.)

Rapid Compost. Choose an area for composting or build a system of three wooden bins. A plan for bins is included in Sinnes' *All About Fertilizers, Soils and Water.* University of California Leaflet #21251, *The Rapid Composting Method,* tells you how to make compost in one to two weeks.

Basically, to make a good, active pile it's necessary to mix equal amounts of carbonaceous wastes with nitrogenous wastes until you have a pile approximately 3 feet square. Carbonaceous wastes are woody materials, such as dry leaves, cornstalks, hay, and wood shavings. Nitrogenous wastes are fresh manure and damp green or wet plant materials, such as grass clippings, green leaves, and kitchen peelings. (Grass clippings do an excellent job of heating up compost, but don't layer them like other materials or they'll stick together in a leathery wet mat that won't properly decompose. Instead, separate them with dry materials; thoroughly mix grass clippings with an equal volume of hay or dry leaves.) Don't add earth to hot compost piles; earth only slows down the composting process and makes the final product too heavy.

Suburban and Small-Space "Composting"

Even without room for a compost pile you can have some of compost's benefits. Mix vegetable wastes from the kitchen with unsoftened water, and purée them in a blender. Dig a hole with a trowel, and pour the contents of the blender straight into the garden soil. Cover it with earth to discourage flies. (This is a good way to feed earthworms and increase their numbers.)

You can also chop up vegetable and fruit wastes from the kitchen and bury them in flowerbeds and under the paths in your vegetable garden. They will slowly decompose, adding soluble nitrogen straight into garden soil.

Keep the pile damp. Covering the pile loosely with a sheet of black plastic can help hold in moisture and discourage flies from being attracted by odors. (With hot composting flies are usually not a problem; all their eggs are killed by heat.) As soon as the pile heats up to approximately 160°F, begin to toss and turn it with a garden fork every day or two to keep it from getting too hot. (If the compost heats to over 160°F, the microorganisms that break down the organic materials will be killed and the process will have to start over.) As you work, try to get the inside portions onto the outside and the outside portions into the middle. Tossing also aerates the pile, which keeps the decomposition process functioning. In two to three weeks, when your compost has thoroughly cooled down and is fine-textured, dark, and sweet smelling, stop tossing it and use it in the garden as a soil amendment.

Warning: The following items should *never* be added to compost: dog or cat manure, meat, bones, fat.

How to Keep Wild Animals and Tree Roots Out of Compost Bins

Once wild animals, such as raccoons, opossums, mice, and roof rats have discovered an open compost pile or wooden compost bin they may use it as a convenient larder, visiting nightly to devour worms and freshly added kitchen peelings. To foil them, cover the floors inside your compost bins with concrete pavers. To prevent tree roots from invading from below, bury a sheet of heavy-gauge plastic or Biobarrier, a patented fabric impregnated with root-stopping herbicide, beneath the pavers. (Place the cloth with the rounded bumps facing up and the flat side facing down.) Cover the sides of the compost bins with ½-inch hardware cloth. Complete the project by building a hinged frame for the top of each bin. Cover these also with ½-inch hardware cloth. In rainy weather or to provide shade, throw a tarp over the top.

Annual and Perennial Flowers

Deadhead and Feed Cool-Season Flowers. If you planted cool-season flowers in October, they should have started to bloom before Christmas and be in full bloom this month. If you got them in late, they'll start to bloom this month.

Continue to feed with a balanced fertilizer and deadhead the plants or pick the flowers to promote bloom. Nitrogen is less active in cold soil, so choose a fertilizer with a high first number as well as bloom ingredients. Most of the new pansy varieties with smaller flowers don't need deadheading, but larger-flowered varieties look better if seedpods are removed. Older varieties need this care to keep them blooming. Among winter flowers that need to be deadheaded or picked to promote continuous flowering are calendulas, tall varieties of cineraria, foxgloves, Iceland poppies, linaria, snapdragons, and stock.

Plant More Flowers if Necessary. Fill bare patches and containers with transplants of such cool-season flowers as calendulas, evergreen candytuft (a perennial), foxgloves, primroses, pansies, and violas. If you planted these and other cool-season flowers at the right time (September through November) you won't need to plant many flowers now, because all available space will be taken. People who fill whole beds this late don't get their money's worth, because flowers won't bloom as long. But there are some exceptions. Evergreen candytuft (*Iberis sempervirens*) is an admirable plant for edging a bed and is often available only in spring when in bloom. New varieties of viola and pansy are both heat and cold resistant. They go through winter better and last longer in hot weather.

It's too early to plant most warm-season flowers, such as lobelia, marigolds, or salvia. They won't get off to a good start. One exception is petunias. They won't bloom in February but will make strong roots for better bloom later. So if you still have a whole flowerbed or tub to fill in a hot spot in full sun, choose petunias. Protect them from frost and snails. Feed for growth.

If you've been feeding cinerarias with nitrogen all winter, they should be large and healthy. Watch them now for the first flower buds, and the moment you see them, switch fertilizers to liquid 2-10-10 or 0-10-10 and feed every two weeks until flowers open. This will give you a huge display. Then stop fertilizing but continue normal watering. Bait for slugs and snails; control leaf miner, if necessary, with Orthene. Control aphids with insecticidal soap.

Cut Back Woody and Overgrown Perennials.
By midmonth you can cut back perennials that
are woody and overgrown to basal growth
(fresh new growth springing up close to the
roots). Mexican bush sage *(Salvia leucantha)*, for
example, may die if you cut it back in fall when
the basal growth is only an inch or two high, but
by February basal growth should be 6 to 8
inches long and actively growing. Now you can
safely cut all the woody parts off, leaving the
new growth. Follow up with a little balanced
fertilizer, add a layer of fresh mulch over the
roots, and you'll soon have a fresh new plant on
the old roots.

Any plant that has a similar show of fresh
basal growth can be cut back safely now.
Artemisia 'Powis Castle', for example, grows
huge, flops open in the middle, and looks ugly.
Cut it back now if you see new growth springing from the middle. You can keep artemisia
from flopping open by cutting the bottom
branches off from below in spring and fall (as
described on page 190), but once it's happened
you have to attack it from the top. Also cut back
to basal growth plants that bloomed late last
summer and fall, including penstemon and *Verbena bonariensis.* It's too late to cut back plants
that bloom mainly in spring, including lavender.
With lavender, just pinch back its rangy tips to
keep it compact and bushy, but wait until after it
blooms to shear the whole plant. Achillea (also
called yarrow) and New Zealand brass buttons
(Cotula squalida) will bloom soon, but you can
cut back outer portions of these and other
creeping plants that are overwhelming their
neighbors; transplant some if desired. Clean up
coreopsis, cutting to the ground those short
stalks that stick up above the rest of the leaves
and have plantlets on top, sometimes with roots
that you can stick into the ground.

Plant Perennials and Biennials. Many fine
perennials and biennials reach nurseries this
month, and some are in bloom. The following
selections, all available now, will give you an almost instantly colorful perennial border in hues
of pink, yellow, blue, lavender, gray, and white:
Gaura lindheimeri 'Siskiyou Pink', yarrow
(*Achillea filipendulina* 'Gold Plate'), blue marguerite *(Felicia amelloides)*, *Salvia* 'Indigo
Spires', Santa Barbara daisy *(Erigeron karvinskianus)*, French lavender *(Lavandula
dentata)*—one of the easiest lavenders to grow
here—and wallflower *(Erysimum* 'Bowles
Mauve'). The last, a fine filler, makes a mound of
gray-green foliage 2 or 3 feet tall and often 6 feet
wide with nonstop mauve flowers arranged at
equidistant intervals all over the top. In three
years it wears itself out from flowering and suddenly dies, but by then you'll be bored with it.

If you didn't plant California poppies last fall,
don't despair; you'll find them in nurseries by
month's end. (Though usually treated as annuals, they're actually perennials.) Orange California poppies won't mix well with the colors of
the border suggested above, but you could create a stunning arrangement in another spot with
three 5-gallon Spanish lavenders (*Lavendula
stoechas* 'Otto Quast') planted in a triangle and a
drift of seven 1-gallon California poppies in
front. Deadhead both these plants to keep them
blooming.

Delphiniums are perennials that are usually
treated as annuals here. When planting delphiniums, prepare a rich planting hole; put plenty of
compost with some fertilizer mixed into it under
their roots. Either use a tablespoon of slow-
release triple-14 or a sprinkling of organic fertilizers of your choice, such as bone meal for
phosphorus, greensand for potassium, and
blood meal or cottonseed meal to provide nitrogen. (See below for more about fertilizing

perennials.) After delphiniums have bloomed, cut them back; they may bloom again in summer. Foxglove is another biennial to plant now, though they may bloom later than if you'd put them in last fall.

Divide Plants That Die Down in Winter. In late February, divide plants, such as saponaria (soapwort; *Saponaria ocymoides*), that act like true perennials and die down to their roots in winter. Saponaria is a low mounding plant for the front of the border and interior zones with bunches of pink, phlox-shaped flowers over a long season through summer and fall. It's a real "workhorse," blooming long with little care. Other plants that can be divided now include Japanese anemones *(Anemone hybrida),* true, or botanical, geraniums and Stokes aster *(Stokesia laevis),* which thrives in interior gardens given adequate irrigation, good drainage, and full sun. Wait to divide until you see little plants coming to life and sprouting up; you may have plenty to share with friends. If rudbeckias live from year to year in your garden—they don't for everyone—divide these now or as soon as you see growth begin again. Do the same with clumps of echinacea and gaillardia. *Gaillardia* 'Yellow Queen', which is yellow throughout and great for bouquets, may still be in bloom now. Nevertheless, if the clump is too large, this is the time to divide and replant it. 'Yellow Queen' reestablishes quickly and keeps right on blooming. There's a **Rule of Thumb** that applies to all these plants, and perhaps some others I haven't thought of: *When perennials begin to grow again and show some life, it's safe to divide them.*

Fertilize Perennials. In good years winter rains will have washed nutrients to lower levels, so fertilize all perennials now in preparation for spring flowers. Alstroemeria, daylilies, pelargonium, and penstemon are among the plants that will reward you with much finer displays. One of the best things to use is cottonseed meal. Buy a sack and sprinkle it around. (It's difficult to prescribe exact amounts when discussing organic fertilizers, but because they're milder they're also less likely to burn.) Organic gardeners eschew strong nitrogen fertilizers because they kill earthworms and swear that organically nourished plants suffer less from pests and disease. If you decide to go this route, build up the humus content of your soil with homemade compost and other organic amendments. For nitrogen, rely on manure, cottonseed meal, and alfalfa meal. When a liquid fertilizer is called for, use fish emulsion. Sandy soils may be deficient in phosphorus and potassium. Bone meal and greensand, respectively, can correct these deficiencies and should be added early in the growing season. Provide trace minerals by spraying with seaweed emulsion and spread chelated iron. (For all these products, follow package directions regarding amounts.)

Also feed Madeira geranium *(Geranium maderense)* to keep it growing strongly now in readiness for flowering in late March or early April. Give it organic fertilizer for bloom and growth or sprinkle a handful of slow-release triple-14, such as Apex Blue or Apex Red. Apex Blue is formulated for coastal gardens, Apex Red for interior gardens. (For more about Madeira geranium, see page 132.)

Seeds for Flower and Vegetable Transplants

Although February is too soon for planting warm-season annuals and vegetables in the ground, it's not too early for seeds. Ambitious gardeners with lots of space to fill can grow their own transplants in flats or peat pots filled

✿ Quick Tip

How to Test the Thickness of Thatch. *With a sharp knife cut a small triangle into the soil and pull out the resulting plug of turf. A layer of thatch between ¼ and ½ inch deep is normal. Thatch thicker than ½ inch will harm the lawn.*

with sterilized potting soil. Use bottom heat (70°F) from a heat cable to germinate seed. (Alternatively, a 15- or 20-watt bulb in a "trouble light," protected from moisture by several layers of plastic, can be used under flats raised on bricks or flowerpots.) Bright light for healthy transplants can be provided by a fluorescent shop light hung 7 to 10 inches above your flats. Leave it burning from fourteen to sixteen hours per day.

Give plants a gentle transition into the garden—first a week in the shade, then one in full sun, during daytime only. The third week leave them out at night, too, to harden them off. Grow varieties, colors, and sizes not found in the nursery.

Lawn Care

Check Warm-Season Lawns for Thatch. Thatch is a layer of partially decomposed leaf sheaths, stems, and roots that forms between the earth below and the grass blades above. It's not made up of grass clippings. Certain subtropical grasses that spread by runners, like Bermuda, make lots of thatch. Bluegrass is intermediate in thatch production, while tall fescue and perennial ryegrass make little, if any. If thatch is more than ½ inch thick, it harms the lawn by preventing water and fertilizer from passing through (see the Quick Tip). Roots may even "move upstairs" and live in it. Thatch dries out fast, causing dead patches of lawn in summer. A thick layer gives a

How to Reduce Lawn Thatch and Landfill Waste

- Follow the **Rule of Thumb** for mowing, which is: *Never mow off more than one-third to one-half of the leaf length of grass at any one time.*

- Instead of using a grass catcher, allow your lawn clippings to fall where they are mown.

- The lawn clippings will fall through the grass and decompose quickly.

- This continual mulching will actually help nourish your lawn with an organic source of nitrogen, reducing its need for fertilizer by almost a third, and slowing the growth of thatch.

- By not tossing out your grass clippings you will be doing your part in alleviating the serious problem of urban waste.

lawn a springy texture and makes mowers bounce, causing scalp marks.

Dethatch warm-season lawns such as Bermuda (see directions in the box on page 82) every two or three years, when they wake up and start growing again in late winter or early spring. If you dethatch your lawn just after it greens up, it will bounce back quickly. (Dethatch cool-season lawns in early fall, as described on page 263.)

Controlling Nutsedge in Lawns and Flowerbeds

Nutsedge is a troublesome weed in lawns and flowerbeds that thrives in waterlogged soils; once established, it can survive drought. Though often called nutgrass, nutsedge is a true sedge. (Sedge stems are solid and triangular; their leaves are thicker and stiffer than most grasses and are in sets of three at the base. Grasses have round hollow stems, and grass leaves are in

How to Dethatch Warm-Season Lawns

- Wait until the weather in your area has warmed up for sure and your lawn has greened up and begun to grow. This is mid- to late February in coastal areas and early March in inland valleys.

- Rent a professional renovator or dethatching machine, called a "vertical mower," which will cut down into the thatch. (It may be necessary to reserve one in advance.)

- Mow the lawn short at least twice, first back and forth in one direction and then across it from side to side. Adjust the blades lower each time.

- Drive the vertical mower over the area. Go in both directions and then diagonally. Start on the highest setting; then lower the level of the blades. (If the thatch is very deep, don't try to do the job all at once. Renovate the lawn by degrees over one or two years; with each treatment remove ½ inch of thatch.)

- Rake up the thatch, bag it, and send it to the dump. Don't compost it—it would take a blowtorch to kill the stolons.

- Follow up by leveling, if necessary. (See directions in the accompanying box.)

- Evenly sprinkle on fast-acting fertilizer at the rate of 6 pounds of sulfate of ammonia for each 1,000 square feet of lawn. Use a spreader if you have one. (There's no need to use an expensive fertilizer at this time.)

- Follow up by watering thoroughly. Keep the lawn well watered until it's completely regrown.

opposite sets of two.) Two types of nutsedge grow here: yellow nutsedge, which has light brown flowers, and purple nutsedge, which has reddish flowers and black or dark brown seeds. Both produce tubers on rhizomes that can be 8 to 14 inches underground. Because buds on the tubers sprout into new plants, patches grow to 10 feet or more in diameter. Nutsedge may arrive in your garden with a load of topsoil, unless you specified weed-free soil, or in potted plants. Hoeing or digging can get rid of the tops but spread tubers farther. Hand-pulling takes off the tops, but the tubers stay in the ground to sprout again, though repeated pulling can weaken the tubers. Roundup doesn't kill nutsedge.

To get rid of nutsedge in your lawn, apply Manage Turf Herbicide (halosulfuron), a product specifically designed to control nutsedge in established lawns. Don't apply Manage to freshly planted lawns. Also, do not use Manage on food crops, flowers, shrubs, or trees. Spraying the lawn won't harm nearby plants, however. Follow package directions carefully and apply it at the right time of year. When nutsedge has between three and eight leaves, that's the time to treat it with Manage herbicide.

Manage comes in a water-soluble packet containing a premeasured quantity that will treat 1,000 square feet of lawn. Just drop the sealed, self-dissolving packet into a handheld or backpack-type sprayer containing a gallon of water. Add 2 teaspoons of non-ionic surfactant, such as Monterey's Herbicide Helper or No Foam, at the recommended rate to increase the spray's effectiveness. Then shake the spray and apply. If the infestation is dense, you may have to treat again in six to ten weeks. Also watch for a second—perhaps even a third—growth of new nutgrass plants sprouting from previously dormant tubers.

Get rid of nutsedge in flowerbeds by continual weeding until the tubers are weakened, by shading the ground with a layer of mulch, and by maintaining an abundant growth of plants.

How to Level Your Lawn

When you mow your Bermuda lawn in summer, do you end up with brown, scalped areas? These mower marks may result from the machine bouncing on a thick layer of thatch, but many times they result from dips and bumps in the grade. One method for keeping golf courses smooth and their hills so gently rolling is to top them with sand at least once a year and let the grass grow up through it. You can correct bumpy lawns in the same way, and you won't need to do it as often. Do this job just after the grass begins to grow; your lawn should bounce back fast and won't have scalp marks after mowing. Here's how.

- Measure the lawn and order sand and soil amendment. For each 200 square feet of lawn you'll need at least 1 cubic foot of good washed plaster sand and 1 cubic foot of dark-colored, fine-textured soil amendment, such as ground nitrolized wood shavings or ground bark. (The dark color attracts heat and speeds growth.)

- Totally scalp and, if necessary, dethatch the lawn (as also described in this section).

- Mix the sand equally with soil amendment by putting a shovel of one, then a shovel of the other, into a wheelbarrow and mixing the contents.

- Arrange the sand mixture in piles all over the lawn. (This will look like the attack of a giant gopher.)

- Attach a 4-foot piece of 1-by-4 lumber to a garden rake (not a grass rake) to construct a leveling device. (Drive half a dozen nails into the lumber and bend them over the teeth of the garden rake.) Push and pull your leveler evenly over the lawn, filling in the depressions.

- Sprinkle a fast-acting fertilizer over the top. Use a spreader if you have one. Apply 6 pounds of sulfate of ammonia for each 1,000 square feet of lawn. (There's no need to use an expensive fertilizer at this time.)

- Water thoroughly and continue to keep the lawn well watered, if rains aren't adequate, until the grass comes through.

Another method is to weed out the tops and then use a geotextile, weed-block fabric, such as Biobarrier, to cover the ground between plants. (Nutsedge can pierce some nontreated fabrics; inquire when purchasing.) Place Biobarrier flat on the ground around ornamental plants, with the bumps facing up and the flat side down. Or cover bare ground prior to planting with Biobarrier, fix it to the ground with stakes provided for the purpose, cut X-shaped holes in it, and plant through them. Finish by hiding the fabric under a thick layer of organic mulch.

Mow, Feed, Aerate, and Spread Mulch on Cool-Season Lawns. Cool-season lawns are still growing fast this month. Water them regularly when rains aren't adequate, to keep them grow-ing. Mow them frequently with the mower blades set short, to 1½ or 1¾ inches. Fertilize every six weeks or, with a slow-release formula, less frequently. To increase the humus content of the soil, top cool-season lawns with a fine-textured organic soil amendment.

Grass that's mulched now will withstand hot weather better in summer. You'll need about 1 cubic foot of mulch for each 100 square feet of lawn. In fast-draining soils where salt damage has not been a problem it's probably all right to use steer manure, despite its possible high salt content. If you have clay soil, it's wiser to use fine-textured nitrolized wood shavings or nitrolized ground bark. If soil compaction has been a problem, rent an aerator prior to mulching and run it over the lawn to remove

How to Plant Bare-Root Asparagus

- Choose a good variety that will produce reliable crops in our mild climate. (Most asparagus varieties need freezing winters, which we don't have.) 'UC 157', 'UC 157 F1', and 'UC 157 F2' were especially developed for conditions in California and are available bare-root in February. These varieties are mostly male and will thus produce all, or almost all, fat, tender spears and lots of them. (Female spears make the berries and are more stringy.) 'California 500' is another fine variety but only for coastal gardens. It produces good crops in frost-free zones, but it cannot abide summer heat.

- Put the plants in a bucket of water to soak while you prepare trenches in well-drained soil 1 foot deep, 1 foot wide, and 3 feet apart. (Amend the soil with organic amendment if necessary.)

- Put 4 inches of well-aged manure mixed with

- one handful of bone meal per linear foot in the bottom of each trench, or mix in 15 to 20 pounds of 5-10-10 or 5-10-5 fertilizer per 100 feet.

- Cover the bone meal with 2 inches of soil, and form mounds 4 inches high and 18 inches apart in the trench.

- Place the plants on the mounds with their roots arranged out over the sides. Cover them with soil so that each crown is an inch below the soil surface.

- Water the plants well when rains aren't adequate. As they grow, add more soil to cover them until the trench is filled.

- Mulch with manure in February. Wait two years before starting to harvest.

---

plugs of earth and sod. Rake up the plugs; then spread the soil amendment and rake it into the holes. (For a long-term solution, use Profile Professional Soil Conditioner, discussed on page 210.) After aerating, mulch with nitrolized ground bark or nitrolized wood shavings, not manure. Water thoroughly after spreading it.

Continue to Control Crabgrass. In inland areas control crabgrass by treating your lawn with a preemergent herbicide in early February and once again two weeks later (as described on page 58). If you live in a coastal zone and you failed to use a preemergent in late January, it may be too late now for preemergent control. Remember to start earlier next year.

If plants are already up and growing, control crabgrass instead with a postemergent herbicide such as methanearsonate. Use it before seed sets. Follow package directions to the letter, and be especially careful to follow the safety precautions. Keep children and dogs off the area for the recommended period of time. Gardeners who prefer not to use selective postemergent herbicides because of the dangers involved can still win the war against crabgrass. By pulling up the plants in fall (as described on page 221), using preemergent herbicide earlier next year, and applying it again in April, you will eventually be able to get rid of the problem.

Vegetable Gardening

February offers the last chance for planting winter crops. Whether to plant more at this time depends on how much ground you have, how close to the ocean you are, and how much your family likes winter vegetables. If you're crowded for space, it's much easier this month to continue to pick and eat the winter vegetables

How to Plant, Grow, and Harvest Mesclun

"Mesclun" (pronounced mess-cloon) is the colloquial term for "mixture" in Provence and refers to mixtures of young lettuces and salad greens. Traditional Provençal mescluns contain chervil, arugula, lettuce, and endive in precise proportions. American mescluns and those from northern France include a wide selection of exotic greens and even edible flowers.

• Purchase ready-made mesclun mixes or individual packages of salad greens for making your own mix. Choices include lettuces, arugula, endives, mustards, purslane, chicory, cresses, parsleys, fennel, escarole, mache (lamb's lettuce), miner's lettuce *(Claytonia perfoliata, Montia perfoliata),* and others. (Shepherd's Garden Seeds and The Cook's Garden carry seeds. Addresses are listed on page 307.)

• Prepare a wide row in full sun. Or plant in a raised bed, half barrel with holes drilled in the bottom, or pots. Dig wide rows or raised beds deeply, mix in a 4-inch-thick layer of well-aged compost or nitrolized soil amendment. Apply organic fertilizer recommended for vegetables according to package directions, work this into the top 6 inches of ground, and rake smooth. For barrels, cover each drainage hole with a piece of broken crockery and fill with potting soil appropriate for vegetables. Mix in 1 gallon of commercial bagged chicken manure and an organic vegetable fertilizer according to package directions. Fill other containers with the same mix. Water seedbeds and containers deeply and let the ground settle overnight.

• Divide the seeds into two or three batches so that you can plant successive crops. (Store remaining seeds in a cool, dry place.) Thinly broadcast the first planting of seeds in a block and rake gently into the ground, or cover seeds lightly by sprinkling the ground with fine compost or potting soil. Pat down.

• Some greens, including mustards, kale, chicories, and certain lettuces, grow larger and more vigorously than others. Plant these separately so you can harvest some when they are young to add to mesclun and let others grow larger for use in salads and other dishes.

• Sprinkle the bed and bare areas surrounding the bed with a bait labeled for the control of slugs, snails, and cutworms in the vegetable garden. Or use organic controls (as described on page 91).

• Optional step: Cover the seeded area with floating row cover, such as Reemay, available by sheet or roll at garden centers or through mail-order catalogs. Peg down the edges to protect from wind and birds, or build a lightweight, reusable wooden frame the size of the seeded area. (Use a staple gun to attach the floating row cover to this frame.) Remove row cover when plants are 1 or 2 inches high.

• Sprinkle daily or twice daily to keep seed moist. Water regularly by drip system, overhead watering, or hand-watering. Continue to control slugs and snails.

• Begin harvesting by thinning to package directions (pulling up whole plants) when they are 2 to 3 inches tall. When the plants are up 5 or 6 inches, begin regular harvesting by shearing the greens 1 inch above the roots; the plants will regrow and you can continue harvesting for several weeks. Or, for slightly larger plants, 5 to 6 inches tall, harvest by picking individual leaves from the outside edges of plants.

• Feed the bed once a week with a balanced liquid fertilizer diluted according to package directions. Or, alternatively, apply dry organic fertilizers onto the ground around the plants after harvesting and before rain. When rains aren't adequate, wash the fertilizer into the ground by watering overhead.

• Plant another patch for future harvests. Meanwhile, your first seeding of mesclun will provide salads for several weeks.

you have and hold off major planting until March. That way most of the garden can be dug up, the soil prepared, and the first planting of summer vegetables put in all at one time. But if your family adores a specific winter vegetable, such as peas, a last crop could be put in now, especially if you live near the coast. Hot temperatures will ruin peas, but cool coastal conditions will permit much later harvesting. (When planting peas this late, be sure to choose a disease-resistant variety. Mildew problems increase as the weather gets warmer.)

Other vegetables that can be planted now are lettuce, mesclun (see box), beets, broccoli, cabbage, carrots, cauliflower, celery, kale, kohlrabi, potatoes, radishes, spinach, Swiss chard, and turnips. Asparagus, artichokes, horseradish, and rhubarb can be put in bare-root. With asparagus, equally good and sometimes better results can

be had from planting in March from seeds. To do so, dig and prepare the trench as described in the box on page 84 for bare-root planting, plant the seeds in the bottom of the trench according to package directions, and fill in with soil as the plants grow. The difference is you'll have to wait three years instead of two before starting to harvest.

Harvest your winter vegetables regularly. Continue side-dressing the rows with fertilizer to keep them growing (as described on page 59). Water when rains aren't adequate, and vigilantly protect your crops from slugs and snails. Blanch your celery now (as described on page 302), and don't let slugs climb inside the stems or they'll ruin your crop. Lettuce also needs special protection from those slithery marauders (see page 91 for ways to control them).

Purchase/Plant

❏ Continue to purchase and plant camellias and azaleas, 70, 52

❏ Choose and plant deciduous magnolias, 70

❏ Purchase clivia, 70

❏ Plant gerberas, 71

❏ Begin to plant gladioli, 71

❏ Plant lilies-of-the-valley, 73

❏ Fill in beds and pots with cool-season bedding plants, if necessary, 78

❏ Start seeds for flower and vegetable transplants, 80

❏ Plant more winter vegetables, including mesclun, if desired, 84

❏ Plant bare-root asparagus (but wait until March to plant seeds), 84, 86

❏ Many succulents, including cacti, bloom in winter and spring; continue to purchase colorful types, 194

❏ Purchase and plant perennials in coastal zones, 79

❏ Plant mesclun, 85

Trim, Prune, Mow, Divide

❏ Prune kiwi vines, 70

❏ Cut back fuchsias after they begin to grow, 73

❏ In coastal zones prune begonias, cannas, ginger, ivy, pyracantha, and Sprenger asparagus, 79

❏ Deadhead cool-season flowers to keep them blooming, 78

❏ Mow cool-season lawns, 83

❏ Check warm-season lawns for thatch. Dethatch if necessary but wait until the lawn begins to grow, 81

❏ Level Bermuda lawns that need it, to prevent scalp marks from mowing, 83

❏ Propagate running (usually hardy) bamboos in coastal zones, 103

❏ Cut back Mexican bush sage, 79

❏ Cut back woody and overgrown perennials, 79

❏ Mow to reduce thatch and cut down on landfill waste, 81

❏ Finish pruning conifers, 191

Fertilize

❏ Continue to feed citrus trees in coastal zones, 67

❏ Continue to fertilize epiphyllums with 2-10-10 or 1-10-10, 54

❏ Begin to fertilize avocado trees in coastal zones, 66

❏ Feed deciduous fruit trees, 69

❏ Fertilize roses, 71

❏ Begin to fertilize fuchsias, 73

❏ Spread manure over the roots of asparagus, bananas, cannas, ginger, and old clumps of geranium, 73

❏ Feed cineraria with 0-10-10 or 2-10-10 to promote bloom, 78

❏ Fertilize cool-season lawns, 83

❏ Fertilize raspberries and other cane berries when they begin to grow, 298

❏ Fertilize perennials, 79

Continued>>

Water

❏ Water all garden plants according to their individual needs; don't water succulents, 28–34 (195)

❏ Water roses, 71

❏ Keep bulbs well watered, 73

❏ Water cool-season lawns as required to keep them growing, 83

Control Pests, Diseases, and Weeds

❏ Continue to bait cymbidiums for slugs and snails, 55

❏ Control pests on citrus trees, 67

❏ Control pests on ash, alder, and sycamore trees, 69

❏ Bait clivia for slugs and snails, 71

❏ Protect roses from pests and diseases, 72

❏ Protect cineraria from leaf miners, aphids, and slugs and snails, 78

❏ Control crabgrass with preemergent herbicide, 58

❏ Hand-weed flowers and vegetables, 40

❏ Trap gophers, 283

❏ Protect celery from slugs, 91, 302

Also This Month

❏ Continue to harvest winter vegetables, 84

❏ Mulch young avocado trees, 67

❏ Make a compost pile, 76

❏ Mulch cool-season lawns, 83

❏ Aerate cool-season lawns if compaction has been a problem, 83

❏ Blanch celery a month prior to harvesting whole heads, 302

MARCH

The First Spring Planting Month

Our spring planting season begins on the first of March, so roll up your sleeves and pitch in. People who set aside extra time for gardening in spring and again in fall find that their gardens require less maintenance during the cool winter and hot summer months. Sometimes weeks go by when the landscape seems to get along all by itself with only an occasional boost from the gardener. At other times, especially in March and April and again during September and October, good gardeners often spend whole days working outdoors. These are the months when most of the planting is done.

During March you can plant most summer annuals and perennials, warm-season and cool-season lawns from seed, some cool-season and most warm-season vegetables, and almost all permanent garden plants, such as trees, shrubs, ground covers, and vines. (Wait a month or two to put in tropicals. They'll take off better in warmer weather.) If you've never gardened before you couldn't choose a better time to start, because you'll soon see results. One of the wonderful things about our sunny climate is how quickly it makes the garden grow. Gardeners with low-lying or mesa-top gardens should still be aware of cool temperatures at night and the possibility of frost until March 15, even late April in some foothill locations, but for most of us the weather has warmed up for sure. Winter is over; spring has arrived.

The Basic Landscape

Fertilize Permanent Plantings. Most ornamental trees, bushes, lawns, and ground covers respond well to fertilizer at this time. In good years abundant spring rains green up the hillsides and bring out wildflowers, gardeners don't have to water as much, and salts are leached out of our soils. But heavy rains also wash soluble nutrients, especially nitrogen, down to lower levels, sometimes out of reach of roots. So fertilize the basic landscape with a complete granulated fertilizer high in nitrogen. If you have a straggly ground cover that's never quite covered the ground, a sprinkling of granulated fertilizer in early March will do wonders. Water it in thoroughly or apply it when the weather forecaster says we're going to have rain.

This doesn't mean you should indiscriminately fertilize everything in sight. Many plants fall into the broad category of specialty plants because they require special handling. Some specialty plants, including cacti, succulents, and native plants, have little or no need for fertilizer. Others, such as camellias, azaleas, begonias, ferns, fuchsias, orchids, epiphyllums (orchid cacti), roses, fruit trees, and vegetables, have unique requirements. Follow the directions for them in this and other monthly chapters.

There are other exceptions, too. Old overgrown gardens in rich soil sometimes become virtual jungles feeding on their own refuse. To fertilize such a garden when there's no sign of nitrogen deficiency, such as stunted growth, yellow leaves, or disease, may simply contribute to more growth, requiring constant pruning. And

such invasive plants as blue gum eucalyptus (*Eucalyptus globulus*) and old stands of Algerian ivy (*Hedera canariensis*), once established, make one wish one had never planted them. Feeding them would make them more rampant.

Plant New Permanent Specimens. March is one of the two best times of year to plant almost anything we grow in the permanent landscape, such as trees, shrubs, vines, and ground covers. The other is October. Planting in fall is traditionally considered to be just a bit better than planting in spring, but after a year or two you'll never know the difference. Now through mid-June is the time to look your garden over, see its strengths and weaknesses, replace troublemakers you don't like, and add permanent specimens where needed. Choose drought-tolerant plants over heavy water users. Be sure to group plants according to their needs for water, for sun or shade, and for soil type. Before purchasing any plant, research its requirements and growth habit.

Frost Damage

If you have a cold, low-lying garden or live in an interior valley, beware: there's always the possibility of a late frost striking suddenly in early March. Keep a garden diary from year to year and listen to the evening news to help anticipate temperatures. Protect tender plants such as tomatoes with commercially available frost caps at night. Remove them during the day. If you grow tomatoes in cages, surround them with plastic. On cold nights throw a cover over the top.

Once all danger of frost has passed, take tender tropicals out from under eaves and the spreading trees where you sheltered them. At last you can cut off the unsightly frost-damaged portions of trees, shrubs, and vines. Control the urge to clean up too soon; damage may not be as bad as you think. As soon as leaves start showing, you can safely cut off dead portions without destroying more than necessary. With bougainvillea in particular, wait until you see growth resume; then cut back to it. (Follow up with food and water to hasten its regrowth.) Bougainvillea blooms on new wood, so spring pruning often results in more summer bloom.

Control of Snails and Slugs

Warm spring rains keep snails and slugs on the prowl. Our common garden snail is actually the edible European snail *Helix aspersa,* an important food source since ancient times. One can grow them in cages, purge them, and eat them. (Picart's book, *Escargots from Your Garden to Your Table,* and University of California Leaflet #2222, *Snails as Food: Escargots*, in the bibliography, tell how.) But if you're more interested in simply getting rid of them, strike back early and mount a multiflank attack. Here's a selection of controls:

- Go out at night with a flashlight and rubber gloves, handpick them, bag them, and dispose of them in the trash. (Look for them by day under leaves of amaryllis, agapanthus, agave, cannas, clivia, daylilies, and dracaena.)
- Wear rubber boots and squash them underfoot (though eggs may survive).
- Clean up the garden; get rid of undergrowth and other hiding places.
- Surround trunks of citrus trees with copper collars. Snails won't cross them. Cut off low-hanging leaves that brush the ground.
- Lay on the ground such traps as upside-down grapefruit rinds, loose lettuce leaves, upside-down flowerpots, and flat boards with 1½-inch wooden runners at each end to raise them off the ground. Next morning throw away the lettuce leaves and grapefruit rinds, pests and all. Lift the boards and flower pots daily and dispose of the slugs and snails lurking underneath.

- Fill yogurt cartons with 1½ inches of beer (or a solution of 1 cup water, 1 teaspoon sugar, and ¼ teaspoon baker's yeast). Make entry holes in the side. Sink the cartons upright in the ground up to the holes. (Slugs are attracted, become inebriated, and fall in and drown.)
- Keep ducks; they eat slugs and snails, though they also eat many garden plants. Chickens, guinea hens, jungle fowl, and bantams are also good at cleaning out slug and snail eggs, with varying appetites for plants. Other natural predators include ground beetles, skunks, snakes, starlings, frogs, toads, opossums, and—yes—rats. (If you live in an area free from snails, chances are it's infested with roof rats.)
- Introduce the African decollate snail, a carnivorous snail that eats young helix snails. (Their best use is in citrus groves rather than in home gardens since they damage new seedlings and transplants. They aren't legal in all counties.)
- Use baits. They come in spray, pellet, powdered, and thick liquid form. Products containing a high concentration of metaldehyde, such as Metro That's It, are highly effective but also most toxic and must not be used around edible crops. Liquid bait, such as Deadline, is effective and long lasting but may make animals sick if they step in it and lick it off. Prozap Agri-brand Snail & Slug AG pelleted bait attracts and kills snails and slugs through a uniquely designed pellet and low 2.5 percent concentration of metaldehyde.
  There's also a new snail bait called Sluggo,

🐌 Quick Tip

Make a Homemade Snail Jail. *To protect birds, wild animals, and pets from eating slug and snail bait, squash the sides of empty tin cans to leave a 1½-inch space—just enough room for snails to enter. Dampen the interiors and sprinkle in bait. Place the traps around the garden and tie them in orange trees. Fully enclosed, strong baits can be used safely.*

which contains no metaldehyde. The active ingredient in Sluggo is iron phosphate, an ingredient in fertilizers, which doesn't harm pets or wildlife and is safe to use around the vegetable garden. Currently Sluggo is the only iron phosphate snail bait on the market, though others may follow. It's more expensive than metaldehyde products but not if you compare the price to that of a trip to the vet with a dog or cat made sick by ingesting metaldehyde. Apply Sluggo in the evening at the rate of approximately 1 pound of bait to every 1,000 square feet of ground around plants. (Follow package directions.) Slugs and snails that ingest iron phosphate don't die immediately, but they stop eating, move slowly to a hiding place, and die in three to six days.

Metaldehyde works better in open areas because it works by paralyzing snails. If they're in the open the sun will kill them, but if they're in a moist shady area they'll hide and recover in a few days. Sprays are effective on ground covers, and they may harm birds less. All baits work better when you switch them from time to time. Products that contain a combination of carbaryl and metaldehyde can be used in the vegetable garden, and they kill sowbugs too, but they should not be allowed to come into contact with edible plant parts. The **Rule of Thumb** for all baits except liquid

types is: *When using snail and slug baits, bait once thoroughly; wait ten days or two weeks and bait again.* (The first treatment gets the parents; the second gets the offspring.)

Annual and Perennial Flowers

Plant Warm-Season Annual and Perennial Flowers. March is the first month to plant seeds or transplants of warm-season annual and perennial flowers outdoors. If you weren't able to take advantage of fall planting, fill all beds and pots with warm-season flowers now. If you planted last fall, however, most beds are full to overflowing with cool-season flowers. There's little if any room for planting more. The only planting to be done is to plant seeds in flats—for bedding plants to be set out later, to fill bare patches as they occur—and to plant pots and hanging baskets.

Continue to feed container-grown cool-season flowers with liquid fertilizer for growth and bloom. Fertilize cool-season flowerbeds with a granulated fertilizer if you see a slow-down of growth or flowering. Water it in well afterward. Deadhead flowers to keep them blooming.

Though nurseries are filled with such cool-season flowers as calendulas, Iceland poppies, nemesia, pansies, primroses, snapdragons, stock, and violas, wise gardeners remember that these are the flowers that should have been planted in fall. Planted now, cool-season flowers for the most part will give only a short season of bloom, especially inland. The height of their bloom season is April, though in coastal gardens some will last through May. Stock, snapdragons, calendulas, and Iceland poppies are particularly unhappy choices to plant now. Heat or disease knocks them down fast. Cyclamen, pansies, polyanthus primroses, and violas can be popped into blank spots, but don't fill whole beds. Polyanthus primroses and small-flowered cyclamen will bloom through June in cool coastal gardens, however, and can be kept alive to bloom another year. And newer varieties of small-flowered pansies are floriferous and heat tolerant. They may last into August.

If you're filling whole beds with annuals, prepare the ground thoroughly and choose mainly warm-season flowers. Good choices among annual flowers to plant now from pony packs for color in sunny spots all summer long include ageratum, cosmos, marigolds, nierembergia, petunias, salvia, sweet alyssum, and verbena. In semishade put in transplants of begonias, coleus, fuchsias, impatiens, and lobelia. (Bedding begonias and lobelia can take full sun along the coast when grown in the ground. Impatiens can take full sun only if they're in a cool breezy spot next to a lawn rather than hot pavement.)

A large number of warm-season flower species can be planted successfully now from seeds. They include achillea (yarrow), ageratum, anchusa, balsam, ornamental basil, browallia, calliopsis (*Coreopsis tinctoria),* celosia (plume flower), cleome (spider flower), coleus, cosmos, gaillardia, gazania, geranium, globe amaranth, Gloriosa daisy *(Rudbeckia hirta),* helipterum (everlasting), hollyhock, impatiens, lobelia, marigold, morning glory (be sure to nick morning glory seeds with a file, so they'll sprout), salvia, sanvitalia, sunflower, strawflower *(Bracteantha bracteata),* sweet alyssum, thunbergia, tithonia, and verbena. (Ageratum, coleus, impatiens, lobelia, and scarlet sage need light in order to germinate. Sprinkle seeds on top of prepared soil, and anchor them by pressing gently into the soil surface—don't cover them with earth. Keep them moist with frequent misting.)

Desert gardeners can plant Jerusalem cherry *(Solanum pseudocapsicum),* Madagascar periwinkle (vinca; *Catharanthus roseus),* nicotiana, portulaca, and zinnias from seeds, but the rest of us had better not plant them yet. These heat lovers can't stand cold feet. They'll do much better if we wait for warmer weather.

Choose and Plant Perennials. An incredible number of perennials can be put in now, including achillea (yarrow), agapanthus, basket-of-gold *(Aurinia saxatilis* or *Alyssum saxatile),* campanulas (bellflowers and cup-and-saucer plants), carnations, marguerites (Cobbitty daisy; *Argyranthemum frutescens),* columbine, coral bells, coreopsis, daylilies, delphiniums, dianthus, dusty miller, evergreen candytuft *(Iberis sempervirens),* gaillardia, geum, penstemon, perennial forget-me-nots *(Myosotis scorpioides),* Pride of Madeira *(Echium fastuosum),* Shasta daisies, and statice. Most of these have been grown in California since Victorian times, but in recent years a tidal wave of new perennials has swept into our gardens, and every year brings more. Botanical geraniums, salvias, and ornamental grasses have become so numerous they deserve separate treatment. (See pages 132, 188, and 238 for discussions of these.) It's an exciting time to be gardening, but also bewildering. Sometimes the only way to discover whether a new plant will work for you is to try it out. Here are a few facts about perennial gardening to keep in mind:

Technically, a perennial is a nonwoody plant that lives more than two years on the same roots, dies down in winter, and comes to life again in spring. In Southern California, however, this doesn't often happen. Many perennials that die to the ground in winter won't succeed in the mildest gardens along the coast. Other perennials turn into woody shrubs; some even flower year-round (making it difficult to decide just when to cut them back). Thus, the typical

Southern California perennial garden or border is a conglomeration of soft-tissued plants and flowering shrubs. It's usually tall and billowy and needs frequent pruning to keep the plants in line.

When choosing plants, try to find out their eventual size so you can space them properly. Planting a perennial bed correctly requires the gardener to place tiny plants so far apart that enormous gaps remain between each, to be filled for the first year with nothing but mulch and human patience. If yours is in short supply, fill in with annuals. Beware of plants that are too large for your garden. Cape mallow *(Anisodontea)* and *Westringea fruticosa,* for example, are dense shrubs that will grow inexorably to 6 feet tall and wide, crowding out smaller adjacent plants. For small spaces choose *W.* 'Morning Light'; it's finer textured with nice variegated foliage, a good substitute in small gardens for sprawling *Artemisia* 'Powis Castle'.

Allow the shapes, colors, and heights of plants to play against one another, just as you would in a flower arrangement. Even if space is limited, the tall, airy, purple-flowered stems of *Verbena bonariensis,* white *Gaura lindheimeri,* and the spikey *Salvia* 'Indigo Spires' are easily controlled and will add welcome relief to lower mounded plants like pink scabiosa *(Scabiosa africana* is difficult to find but the best kind) and white Santa Barbara daisy *(Erigeron karvinskianus; E. karvinskianus* 'Moerheimii' has larger flowers). Try to find plants that succeed for you and bloom over a long season or at a time when especially needed. Strive for a garden with its own distinct flavor and big drifts of color rather than a bit of this, a bit of that. The uncertainties involved in plant choice add to the fun of gardening; you can always move things that don't work out. When the garden does at last fill in and bathe itself in flowers, the sur-

prises and discoveries will increase your delight.

Once flowers fade, the need to deadhead takes over. Timely pruning and fertilizing plus replacement of plants as they die can keep a perennial garden going for many years. Left untended, a California perennial bed will soon become an overgrown tangle. By the end of March, for example, plants that bloom only in winter, such as yellow flax *(Reinwardtia indica),* need cutting back. Once it stops flowering, cut all the woody stems that have flowered down to the ground. Also, when you see new growth at ground level on blue lily turf *(Liriope muscari),* and variegated liriope *(L. muscari* 'Variegata'), and others—use sharp, one-hand lawn shears to cut off the faded foliage above the new growth, so the old leaves won't be mixed in with the new.

Roses

Water Roses Deeply. Give roses plenty of water this month so they can grow plenty of leaves, stalks, and buds for next month's flowers. In interior zones they may need as much as 2 inches of water per week at weekly intervals in fast-draining soil.

Fertilize Roses. Continue to fertilize your roses this month according to the system you've chosen. If you're feeding with a complete fertilizer recommended for roses, check your calendar to see when you did the job last month and fertilize one month later; once again mark the date on your calendar. (Fertilizing once every six weeks as recommended on many rose-food packages doesn't provide them with adequate nitrogen.)

If you're following the Rose-Pro Method of fertilizing (as summarized on page 308), give each rose 1 tablespoon of sulfate of potash (0-0-25) during the first week in March. (This is an annual application. Because potassium is longer lasting in soil than nitrogen, it needs to be added only once a year.) Also, this month start fertilizing each rose regularly—once a week—with 1 tablespoon of sulfate of ammonia (21-0-0). Simply toss these nutrients on the ground under each rose prior to a regular deep irrigation. Using this system, you can feed a great many roses in a relatively short amount of time. Try to stick to a schedule and fertilize your roses on the same day each week, but always make sure that the fertilizer is thoroughly watered into the ground.

Additionally, if you're using the Rose-Pro Method, start this month to give your roses micronutrients (trace elements) as a foliar spray. The easiest way to do this is to mix either Super K Gro or Miracle-Gro into the sprayer along with the fungicide or pesticide when you spray.

Control Pests and Diseases. If you prefer not to spray your roses with chemicals, control pests by handpicking, by spraying with Safer soap, and by introducing beneficial insects. Wash off aphids with the hose, or control them along with other sucking insects by using systemic pesticides in the soil (unless your roses are close to food plants). Disease control can be partially accomplished without spraying by growing disease-resistant roses exclusively and by spraying with the Cornell Fungicide Formula (see page 73) against mildew.

If you're growing roses for show or aiming for perfection, however, continue to spray at weekly intervals with Funginex to control fungal diseases. At midmonth start spraying also with Orthene to control pests. Measure the Orthene and Funginex at the rates per gallon given on their labels and combine them in the same quantity of water you would use for only one of them. To each gallon of mixed spray add a squirt of dishwashing detergent, to make your spray cling better. Also add the quantity of Miracle-Gro or Super K Gro recommended on the package, as mentioned above, to foliar-feed the roses with trace elements and acidify the spray. (Always wear protective clothing and follow all precautions when you spray.)

If you grow just a few roses, the above routines will take care of most pest problems, but if you grow many roses they're likely to be attacked by spider mites, a troublesome pest that's difficult to control without a miticide. If mites are a problem, substitute RosePride Orthenex Insect & Disease Control—Formula III for Orthene and Funginex. Nontoxic controls include spraying with SunSpray Ultra-Fine Spray Oil or using a water wand to squirt foliage with high pressure.

Begin Disbudding. If you're interested in growing roses for show or if you prefer your roses to bear only one large flower per stem, begin disbudding your hybrid tea and grandiflora roses early this month. To disbud a rose means to remove the secondary, or side, buds on the flower stem shortly after these appear. Secondary buds sap strength from the primary buds. By removing them you allow the center bud to grow to full size. (An exception is when roses send up new canes. In this case, allow them to "candelabra," to grow naturally without disbudding in order to get maximum height.)

In most cases there are only one or two side buds to remove, and some roses have none, but a few hybrid tea and grandiflora roses make so many secondary buds that none of the flowers can fully open. Nevertheless, most home gardeners never bother to disbud their roses. (Don't disbud roses that are naturally meant to grow in bunches, like floribundas or polyanthas.)

How to Grow Tuberous Begonias from Tubers

- Fill flats with damp peat moss. Roll the tubers in soil sulfur and sink them into the peat moss so that each one is barely covered, with the bumpy concave side up, the rounded bottom down.

- Place the flats in a warm, shaded spot with early morning sun or in a lath house or gazebo. Keep them damp but don't fertilize them yet.

- When growth is 2 or 3 inches high plant in well-drained acid soil in pots, hanging baskets, or the ground under an eave or noninvasive tree, preferably facing east. (Plant them with leaf points facing the front of the bed; the flowers will face the same direction.)

- Wait until growth is 3 or 4 inches high, then start feeding the plants regularly, every time you water; tuberous begonias are big eaters. Use an evenly balanced fertilizer such as 10-10-10, 8-8-8, or 20-20-20.

- Control mildew with a fungicide such as Funginex.

- Always allow plants to dry out a little between waterings. Begonias are far more drought resistant than they appear.

Bulbs

Spring-Flowering Bulbs. Unless rains are steady and frequent, continue to water spring-flowering bulbs. After they finish blooming, cut off the flower pods and feed the plants with a well-balanced fertilizer—it's an investment in next year's performance. Don't cut the leaves off until they go brown and die back. (If their floppy appearance bothers you, tie them in knots.)

Tigridias. Bulbs of tigridias, or tiger flowers, can be found at local nurseries now. Plant them 6 inches apart and 3 inches deep in full sun along the coast or where they'll get afternoon shade inland. Fertile loam or sandy soil is best. If you have clay soil, mix in plenty of soil amendment or plant in pots or raised beds. The colorful blooms appear in July and August. Each flower lasts only one day, but others follow on the same branch, so the bloom season is quite long.

Gladioli. Tie gladioli planted in February to stakes installed at planting time. Protect them from slugs and snails, and keep them well watered. Feed potted glads with liquid fertilizer. Continue to plant gladioli, though when planted now they will need more protection from thrips in summer.

Dahlias. Prepare planting holes for dahlias by mixing plenty of organic matter into the soil. Some aged chicken manure can be added to the soil now, along with premoistened peat moss, nitrolized wood shavings, or homemade compost, in preparation for planting in April. Dig the organics deeply into the ground—as much as a foot deep—and keep the soil damp.

Tuberous Begonias. Start tuberous begonias this month. If you kept some tubers from last year, take a look at them now to see whether they're showing signs of life. If so bring them out of hiding and start watering them. Buy new ones at local nurseries. Some tubers are slow to sprout, so choose those that already have a sprout or two.

Tuberous begonias aren't easy to grow, but if you have rich acid soil in an east-facing area, not too many snails, and a knack for growing begonias, they can be one of the most rewarding plants for summer color in semishade. Years ago they were considered suitable for coastal zones only. New heat-resistant varieties such as 'Non-Stop' have made it possible for gardeners in interior zones to try their hand at this most colorful and exotic-looking garden plant. If growing them from tubers sounds too involved, wait until summer and visit a "dig-your-own" nursery, such as Weidner's Begonia Gardens in Leucadia, San Diego County.

Herbaceous, or Softwood, Cuttings

March is the best month for rooting herbaceous cuttings, also called "softwood cuttings," to make more plants. Good candidates include 'African Blue' basil, cane and 'Richmondensis' begonias, chrysanthemum (*Dendranthema grandiflorum*), marguerite (Cobbitty daisy; *Argyranthemum frutescens*), euryops, pelargonium, russelia or coral fountain (*Russelia equisetiformis*), ornamental salvias, roses, and any perennial plant that has been cut back in winter and has new growth springing up close to the ground. To make softwood cuttings correctly, take them early in the day. For each cutting, clip 3 to 5 inches of succulent bendy growth from the tip of a branch. (It snaps when bent even though soft and flexible.) Remove the lower leaves of each cutting, leaving two or three leaves in place. (Russelia cuttings may have no leaves, but sections root easily.) Cuttings that are taken down low on the plant close to the roots contain more natural rooting hormone than others and root quickly. Some may even have root hairlets attached; leave these on. Dip the cut end in a rooting hormone, such as RooTone or Dip'N Grow, and plant in pots or flats of fast-draining potting mix to which you've added about 10 percent perlite. As soon as they're rooted, transplant them into pots or the ground. Feed them often. When they start to grow, pinch them back to make them bushy. Chrysanthemums root easily but then require more care than the others, including regular

feeding, pinching, pest control, and staking. Given this care, they can reward you with masses of old-fashioned color in fall.

Citrus and Avocado Trees

Now's a good time to plant citrus and avocado trees. They'll have all spring and summer to get established before winter's cooler temperatures slow their growth. Provide them with good drainage and choose varieties that are right for your area. If you wrapped the trunks of young trees last fall, unwrap them now.

In interior zones also begin fertilizing citrus and avocado trees this month (as described on pages 51 and 66). In coastal zones continue to fertilize them.

Macadamias

As with citrus and avocado trees, this is a good time to plant macadamias and to unwrap the trunks of young trees if you wrapped them for frost protection last fall.

Two species of macadamia are grown here, the smooth-shelled integrifolia (*Macadamia integrifolia*) and the rough-shelled tetraphylla (*M. tetraphylla);* both are from Australia. These trees are attractive, slow-growing evergreens with glossy green foliage and white flowers. The trees can survive drought well, but in order to bear a good crop they need about the same amount of water that avocado trees require. Overwatering is seldom a problem. Macadamias bear round nuts that are notoriously difficult to crack; a special nutcracker is a necessity. The kernels have a high oil content and delicious flavor; in stores they're a luxury item.

Fertilize Macadamias. The precise requirements of macadamias for fertilizer are not yet known;

overfertilization may actually harm the tree. When these trees are grown in fertile garden soil and given adequate water and full sun they'll increase in size and produce crops with no fertilizer whatsoever. However, if you're growing a macadamia tree in poor soil, or if it's stunted in size and bears poor crops, feed it very lightly every six weeks from now until June with a complete fertilizer containing no more than 10 percent nitrogen. The safest way to feed a macadamia is to apply a solution of fish emulsion over its roots twice monthly during any month of the year when the average minimum temperature is in excess of 50°F. Mix 5 tablespoons of fish emulsion into 5 gallons of water, and sprinkle the solution all over the ground under each tree.

Select and Plant Macadamias. When purchasing a macadamia tree, don't buy a seed-grown tree, which may or may not bear nuts. Be sure to choose a proven, grafted variety. Most varieties are hardy to 27°F, but all grow best in frost-free zones. Integrifolias and hybrids are more cold resistant than tetraphyllas. ('Cate' and 'Elimbah' are tetraphyllas, and 'Beaumont', a good backyard tree, is a hybrid between *M. tetraphylla* and *M. integrifolia*.) If gophers live in your vicinity, line the planting hole with a basket of chicken wire to protect the young roots from gopher damage.

Harvest Macadamias. The nuts on macadamia trees ripen at different times of year depending on variety. When the nuts are ripe, they usually fall off the tree over a period that may last several months—ninety days is common. The nuts from 'Cate', for example, ripen from September through mid-December, and those of 'Elimbah' ripen from December to April. 'Beaumont' is an exception to this rule; it hangs on to its crop long after the nuts are ripe, so you must pick them off. If you're growing a 'Beaumont', strip all the nuts from the tree during the first week in March. Unfortunately, most gardeners leave them hanging on the tree because they don't realize that the nuts on 'Beaumont' stick tight. Leaving the ripe nuts on the tree makes 'Beaumont' bloom throughout the year, eventually drop its yearly crop of nuts over about nine months—from October through June—and over several years will make the nuts successively smaller, until all you get are "peewees" (undersize nuts). But if you pick the nuts off by hand during the first week in March the tree will put all its energy into the new crop, and you'll get a good harvest of large nuts the following year. With all other varieties, wait until the nuts fall to the ground—don't ever pick them or shake them from the tree—and then gather them up at least once a week.

Some varieties of macadamia are self-husking—the husk, or outer covering of the nut, splits open when the nuts ripen. 'Cate' is somewhat self-husking, 'Beaumont' is reasonably self-husking, and 'Elimbah' and some integrifolias are less so. But with many varieties the gardener must manually remove the nuts from the husks.

Macadamia nuts require considerable processing. After harvesting and husking it's important to slowly dry macadamia nuts properly; otherwise they'll be sticky or gummy (see the accompanying box for directions).

Epidendrum

Epidendrum orchids are easy to grow in pots or the ground, are inexpensive, bloom almost year-round in frost-free zones, and are almost

How to Harvest, Husk, Dry, and Roast Macadamia Nuts

People who take the time to perform the following tasks can produce homegrown nuts that are every bit as good as those grown commercially. Because of the chemical makeup of macadamias, slow drying is essential for a good product.

- **Harvest Ripe Nuts.** If your tree is a 'Beaumont' variety, pick all the nuts from the tree during the first week in March. With all other varieties, you know that the nuts are approaching ripeness when they start falling from the tree. In the case of varieties other than 'Beaumont', the first few nuts that fall (during the first two weeks) may not be completely ripe. Open some up; if they're wrinkled or discolored, throw them out and wait until good nuts start falling. Once they do, rake them up every day or two and separate the nuts from the leaves. (The nuts are likely to spoil if left lying on the ground for more than a week.)

- **Husk the Nuts.** Use a large pair of pliers to remove the husks (the outer coverings of the nut that may or may not remain attached to the nuts). If your tree bears nuts that are difficult to husk, let the unhusked nuts sit several days in shade and then they'll be easier to remove. (It's best to husk the nuts from 'Beaumont' immediately.)

- **Air-Dry the Husked Nuts in Their Shells.** To do this, spread them in shallow, screen-bottomed trays and put the trays on a rack or other support in a dry, shady place. Leave them there for two or three weeks.

- **Finish Drying the Nuts in Their Shells over Low Heat.** Do this by placing them in a screen-bottomed container over a furnace register for three or four days. Or dry the nuts at 100° to 115°F for twelve to forty-eight hours, or more, in a shallow pan in the oven. (The lowest possible setting on an electric oven may dry the nuts in as little as twelve hours. The heat given off by the pilot light in an old-fashioned gas oven is ideal; it will dry the nuts in three or four days.) From time to time crack open one or two nuts to test their progress. When the shells are dry and brittle rather than bendy—even though still hard—and the nuts are loose in the shell and approaching crispness, they're done.

- **Store the Nuts in Their Shells.** Enclose the dried nuts in sealed heavyweight plastic bags to prevent them from absorbing moisture, and store them in a cool place.

- **Remove the Shells.** Crack open the hard nutshells with a special macadamia-nut cracker. These are available, for example, from the Gold Crown Macadamia Society, P.O. Box 235, Fallbrook, CA 92028, 760/728-4532.

- **Store the Nutmeats.** Store the nutmeats in tightly covered containers in the refrigerator or freezer. (Roasted nuts may also be stored this way.)

- **Roast the Nutmeats.** Shelled macadamia nuts are ready to eat or to use in cooking, or you can roast them. In a preheated conventional oven roast whole and half nuts for forty to fifty minutes at 250°F. (To avoid burning, don't roast broken pieces that are smaller than halves.) Watch them carefully, and stir them occasionally to prevent burning. Remove them from the oven as soon as you see them start to turn from white to light tan.

- To use a convection oven, first make a basket from folded quarter-inch hardware cloth. Fill it with shelled nuts of all sizes—whole, halves, and pieces—and roast at 300°F for twenty minutes.

immune to pests and disease. Grow them in full sun along the coast, part shade inland. They're spectacular in raised beds flanking swimming pools and worth hunting for in specialty nurseries.

Once an epidendrum stem has borne its clusters of cattleya-shaped flowers it won't bloom as well a second time. Cut it back to the second leaf joint from the ground. Stick the cuttings in the ground or in pots filled with potting soil and you'll soon have new plants. Feed them often with liquid fertilizer for growth and bloom.

Camellias

Improve the shape of camellia bushes now by judicious pruning, and bring the cut branches inside to enjoy, leaving on the flowers and leaves. Look at the structure of your camellias; cut where you want to increase bushiness. If you look closely at a branch you'll see the bump where last year's growth began. The new wood is a different color. Make your cut in this new wood just beyond the bump. This will produce branching and more flowers next year.

Azaleas

The more vigorous an azalea, the easier it is to grow. But some that are robust and easy to grow—Southern Indica azalea varieties such as 'Pride of Dorking', 'Formosa', and 'Phoenicia'; Rutherfordianas such as 'L. J. Bobbink'; and even some heat-resistant Brooks Hybrids—sometimes throw out extra growth in awkward places. Don't do allover pruning yet, but now's the time you can improve an azalea's shape by cutting out undesirable, crossing, or old woody branches that have ceased to bear well. These unwanted branches make lovely cut flowers to take into the house. Choose and plant azaleas while they're flowering, but don't feed them un-

til the bloom season is over. Overfeeding azaleas is a cardinal sin. It's possible to kill them with kindness as well as neglect. They also mustn't be overwatered, but never let an azalea dry out completely or it will die.

Fuchsias

Continue to feed and pinch back fuchsias. They bloom on new wood only. Every tip will produce flowers, so the idea is to make the plant produce as many tips as possible. As soon as each sprout grows three pairs of leaflets, pinch out the top pair. Take some of the bendy new unpinched growth for cuttings (see the box on page 102).

Hibiscus

Start to prune tropical hibiscus (*Hibiscus rosa-sinensis*). Hibiscus flowers only on new wood; if you never prune it, the flowers appear ever farther from the center until they're out of sight on top of a leggy shrub. Young plants need little or no pruning. Plants more than five years old should be pruned a little every month from now until August. Don't chop hibiscus all over like a hedge because that slices the large leaves in two. Here's what to do:

- Choose only three or four woody branches to remove now. For symmetry, they should be on opposite sides of the shrub. Reach into the hibiscus and prune out the whole branches, back to two or three growth buds from the center of the plant. This will encourage bushiness and regrowth from within. (With very vigorous varieties, such as 'Agnes Galt', prune harder now, taking out as much as one-third of the old, woody growth.)
- In a month or six weeks remove three or four

more old branches in the same way and proceed thus throughout summer. Note the schedule on your calendar. This progressive pruning will result in lots more growth and flowers. (Don't prune hibiscus in winter.)

- To keep hibiscus shaped as a screen or large hedge, head back one-third to one-fourth of the tip growth 1 or 2 feet into the shrub, here and there all over the sides and top of the hedge. Come back in a month and head back another third. Continue throughout summer. When you walk away, no one should be able to see you've pruned.
- Follow up with fertilizer and water.

Giant Whitefly

Be on the lookout for giant whitefly (*Aleurodicus dugesii* Cockerell), a native of Mexico that was first discovered in San Diego County in October 1992 and has spread throughout the Southland, mainly in coastal zones. Adults are approximately 3/16 inch long, slightly larger than other whiteflies. Look for infestations on aralia, avocado, begonia, bird of paradise, blue dawn flower (*Ipomoea acuminata),* citrus, eugenia, ginger, hibiscus, mulberry, orchid tree, xylosma, and all broad-leafed tropicals.

Giant whiteflies hide under leaves in large colonies. Females lay their eggs in a spiral pattern, usually on the bottom of leaves but sometimes on top. The eggs soon hatch into immature whiteflies, called "nymphs." Both nymphs and adults feed by inserting needlelike mouthparts into leaves and sucking on the plant's sap. The nymphs excrete sticky honeydew and exude long hairlike filaments of wax up to 4 inches in length that rapidly become a sticky and unsightly mass. Heavily infested plants are severely weakened and look as if they have been bearded or flocked.

Release Beneficials. To bring giant whitefly under control, entomologists are releasing legions of parasites and predators known to attack it, including two minute Mexican wasps *(Ideoporus affinis* and *Encarsiella noyesii). *Giant whiteflies are not a problem in Mexico because they coexist in balance with these and other beneficial creatures. Gardeners can help bring about a similar balance here by purchasing beneficial insect allies from nurseries and insectaries and by not spraying with broad-spectrum pesticides that can kill the beneficials. Beneficials you might start releasing now or next month against giant whitefly include Delphastus beetles *(Delphastus catalinae)* and, if available, nonstinging parasitic wasps of the genus *Entedononecremnus.* If you refrain from spraying with pesticides and if you also provide moisture in your garden and flowers for pollen, beneficials will settle down in your garden and increase year by year, thus helping to control the whiteflies (for more on beneficials, see page 37).

Wash Plants. Besides releasing beneficials, the best way to help keep this pest under control is to wash off the affected plants with strong jets of water at weekly intervals. (If you wait until summer, it may be necessary to knock down high levels of infestation by spraying with insecticidal soap or SunSpray Ultra-Fine Spray Oil a few days prior to releasing beneficials.) But water is the best and safest control. It is thought that spraying with pesticides against giant whitefly may be contributing to the return of eugenia psyllid, which was formerly almost totally under control by beneficials (see page 128). Birds also love to eat giant whitefly, especially on hibiscus, but they don't like all that sticky white stuff. To attract birds, first open up the shrub by pruning off heavily infested leaves and branches. (Bag the prunings and send them to

How to Start a Fuchsia from a Cutting

- Clip from an established fuchsia a soft, bendy growth tip with two or three pairs of leaves.
- Clip off the bottom pair of leaflets.
- Dip the cut end of the stem, including the node from which you have clipped off the leaves, in a rooting compound, such as RooTone or Dip'N Grow, and knock off the excess. (A node is the place on a plant stem from which one or more leaves grow.)
- With a chopstick make a hole in a 4-inch pot filled with fast-draining acid potting mix, such as Bandini #105.
- Take your first "pinch": clip off the top pair of leaves so the plant will begin to branch as soon as it begins to grow.
- Write the variety name on a plant label and stick it in the pot.
- Keep the plant moist in semishade. Begin feeding as soon as growth begins.
- As soon as the roots fill the container, pot the plant on—repot it in a container one size larger—and pinch it back to keep it bushy.

the dump.) Then squirt the white cottony material off with water. Birds, especially sparrows, will be encouraged to bathe in the water and feast on the pests. Once aware of the food source they'll return many times, especially if you keep the white filament down by frequently spraying with water.

Quince, Guava, and Cherimoya Trees

Quince, guava, and cherimoya not only are ornamental but also bear delicious fruit, and they grow well here. But even though they have many flowers, they don't always bear much fruit because we don't have the right insects here to pollinate them efficiently. You can help the local bees and ensure a larger crop by hand-pollinating. With quince and guava choose a warm, dry morning and simply dab the centers of the flowers with a small sable brush to distribute the pollen. If there are too many flowers for this, use a long-handled wool duster. Dust the pollen into the flowers all over the outside of the tree.

Pollinating cherimoya requires two steps because the flowers are both female and male. In the morning hours, when the flowers aren't fully opened, they're in the female stage. In the afternoon the flowers open fully and become male. First collect pollen, in the afternoon; hold a 35 mm film canister under each fully opened flower and brush the pollen and strawlike anthers into it with a small paintbrush. Close the container and keep it in a cool, dry place. The next morning find flowers in the female stage. Spread the petals with your fingers, dip the brush into the canister of fresh pollen, and apply it to the cone-like pistil with an even, swirling motion. It takes cherimoya fruit five months to mature, so if you pollinate ten or twenty blossoms once a week year-round you should have a far more abundant harvest, with fruit ripening throughout the year instead of only in November.

Bamboo

For thousands of years bamboo has been among mankind's most economically useful plants, but modern gardeners prize it most for its serene beauty and for the tropical or Oriental atmosphere it lends to the landscape. Nonhorticulturally minded people are often surprised to learn that bamboo is actually giant grass: like

How to Propagate Bamboo from Rhizomes

Bamboos grow from branching rhizomes that have joints on them, called "nodes," from which spring the fibrous roots and the bamboo stems or canes, called "culms." The rhizomes of running bamboos are elongated while those of clumping kinds are short and thick. The right time to separate bamboo is when new culms are just ready to sprout (when the underground buds have swelled but not yet begun to grow).

Starting now, from time to time dig down carefully with a trowel and see when buds are forming. Hardy bamboos (these are mainly the types with runners) usually begin to grow in early March, sometimes as early as late February along the coast. If the new shoots have already emerged from the ground it's too late; they will abort if you separate their rhizomes then. (If you're too late, try again next year.) Tropical bamboos (most clumping types are tropical) tend to sprout a little later. Divide the running and clumping types according to the methods given below.

Divide Running Bamboo. Look for a place where several mature culms emerge from the ground. They should be near each other.

- With a saw or long-handled loppers cut off a section of rhizome that contains at least two nodes and two to four existing culms (plus visible buds that are about to sprout).
- Dig up the rhizome with its roots.

- Cut back the culms by one-third to one-half of their height to compensate for the loss of roots.
- Plant the rhizome immediately in rich organic soil in a container or the ground, positioning it at the same depth at which you originally found it.
- Cover the roots with an inch or two of mulch; stake the culms, if necessary, to prevent them from being pushed over by wind; make a watering basin; and water thoroughly.
- Keep the roots moist until the new plant is well established.
- Beginning one month after planting, start fertilizing regularly with a lawn fertilizer.

Divide Clumping Bamboo. Look on the outside of the clump for a bulge of growth containing at least three or four culms and some rhizomes with buds on them. (This can be difficult since growth is often dense.)

- Slice down around the chosen bulge of growth with a sharp spade or cut through the rhizomes with a pruning saw to separate them from the parent plant. Then with a trowel or spade dig up the entire clump with the rhizomes and the roots attached.
- Proceed to cut back, plant, water, and fertilize the new plant as described above for running bamboos.

Bermuda grass, bluegrass, and wheat, bamboo is a member of the Poaceae (Gramineae) family. There are well over a thousand different species of bamboo (members of the *Bambuseae* tribe of grasses), and these are further divided into numerous genera, their actual number depending on which botanist you consult. Some bamboos grow 120 feet tall with individual stems (called "culms") a foot in diameter; some bamboos are low-growing ground covers—a foot or less tall; and there's every size between these extremes. Most bamboos are evergreen; some are hardy, and others are tropical.

There are two main types of bamboo: those that grow in a clump and those that send out long runners. The ones with runners can eventually spread all over your property, and they often invade your neighbor's garden, too. Control these invasive types by planting them above-ground in containers, or grow them in the ground but enclose them in drain tiles, bottomless containers, or a buried barrier of poured concrete or galvanized metal, or use Plantwell, the Bamboo Retainer System (818/350-8998). Another option is to grow them in a raised bed surrounded by a 1-foot-deep trench filled with fir bark; police the trench often to cut off escaping runners as they enter it.

Most bamboos are monocarpic: once they bloom and bear seeds they die. Some species flower at various times, and many of this type bloom without dying. But other species don't flower for many years, and when they do it's on a specific schedule—perhaps at intervals of 7, 15, 30, 60, or 120 years, possibly even several hundred years. (Some types have never been known to flower.) Amazingly, when members of many species flower, bear seeds, and die, they do so all at one time just as if they were one plant. Sometimes an entire species dies within a year or two all over the world. Eventually this bamboo species will come back from seed, and in some cases the rhizomes stay alive and put out new growth after a few years. This fascinating habit can be a tragedy if you're a giant panda bear and depend on a particular species of bamboo for food—or if you're a gardener and a species you grow reaches the end of its cycle.

Choose Unusual Bamboos and Feed Them Like Grass. A number of bamboos, including Mexican weeping bamboo (*Otatea acuminata aztecorum*), a graceful, drought-resistant variety that lives for thirty-five years, are well suited to Southern California gardens (consult the list and detailed discussion in the *Sunset Western Garden Book*), but only the most common ones can be found in most nurseries. Unusual bamboos

can best be found in specialty nurseries, such as Endangered Species in Perris (800/709-5568), at botanical-garden sales, or through the American Bamboo Society.

Most bamboos require good soil and plenty of water to look their best. They also appreciate a layer of mulch over their roots. Remember they are a type of grass, and feed them occasionally during their growing season—the warm months of the year—with a lawn fertilizer according to package directions.

Divide Bamboo in Spring. The easiest way to propagate bamboo is by separating rhizomes from the parent plant in spring just before the plants begin to grow. Bamboo can be propagated from seeds, but they aren't always viable. (See the accompanying box for directions on using rhizomes.)

Lawn Care

March is the time to feed all types of established lawns and to plant new ones from seed. You can also plant lawns from sod this month. First, though, decide whether it's lawn that you want.

Consider the Lawn-Free Landscape. Before putting in a lawn, consider the pros and cons of having one. Water shortages make large lawns inappropriate for modern needs, and you may have to let a lawn of any size go brown in a drought. But there's still a place for a small lawn, and there are several good reasons for wanting one. Nothing provides a cooler look, a better contrast for flowers, or a more comfortable play space for children and dogs. You can't play croquet on anything else. But if you don't have a good reason for planting a lawn, choose a landscape of patios, ground covers, flowers, trees, shrubs, and wandering paths. A cottage gardener

I know says, "Lawns take just as much care and water as flowers; I'd rather have flowers!"

Mow All Lawns. Warm-season grasses, such as Bermuda, St. Augustine, and zoysia, are waking up from winter dormancy in March. As soon as they start growing, begin mowing weekly with a reel mower to the correct height for each. Mow common Bermuda to 1 inch, hybrid Bermuda to ½ or ¾ inch, St. Augustine to between ¾ and 1¼ inches, and zoysia to ¾ to 1 inch in height. Cut 'Adalayd' or Excalibre grass with a rotary mower to between ¾ and 1 inch in height. Cool-season grasses, such as fescue, ryegrass, and bluegrass, are still growing fast; mow them weekly with a rotary mower to 1½ inches in height.

Feed Lawns. Feed all established lawns now with a complete lawn fertilizer—containing phosphorus and potassium as well as nitrogen—to get warm-season grasses off to a good start and keep cool-season grasses going longer. Fertilize lippia *(Phyla nodiflora)* lawns also to speed them out of dormancy. A healthy, well-fed lawn is better able to withstand pests and diseases and choke out weeds. While nitrogen gives your lawn top growth and a healthy green color you can see, phosphorus and potassium feed the roots and growth systems of the plant that are unseen but just as important. Phosphorus and potassium are longer lasting in soil than nitrogen, so one feeding a season with them is often adequate. After this complete feeding you can switch to a less-expensive, pure nitrogen fertilizer if desired, and feed warm-season grasses with it once a month for the rest of the growing season.

Feed most turf grasses at the rate of 1 pound of actual nitrogen per 1,000 square feet of turf. Feed the new tall, drought-resistant fescues at three-quarters strength. (The latter respond best to frequent but light applications of fertilizer.)

Apply fertilizer when the ground is damp and grass blades dry, and follow up by watering deeply; otherwise, you risk burning your lawn. If you're willing to pay the price, you can opt for coated slow-release fertilizers that will feed your lawn for as long as six months from a single application. These are fine to use on warm-season lawns now, but don't make the mistake of using a slow-release fertilizer on a cool-season lawn at this time of year. Cool-season grasses need little or no fertilizer during the warmer months of the year.

Try the Organic Way. The recommendations in this book regarding when to fertilize and how much nitrogen to give specific grasses are based on research done by experts using inorganic fertilizers, but today's gardeners often prefer to use organic fertilizers. Organic fertilizers don't tend to leach out of soils as rapidly as chemical fertilizers and are thus more environmentally friendly. They last longer in the ground, and they don't burn lawns or kill earthworms. On the other hand, they're more expensive than chemical fertilizers, and you need to apply a lot more of the product to get the same amount of nitrogen. Do your own experiment. Divide the lawn roughly in half; then for six months or a year feed one half with a chemical product, the other half with an organic product according to package directions. Keep notes on expense and lawn appearance; compare the results. Even if you decide on inorganic fertilizers, it may be possible to maintain a healthy and adequate-looking lawn with less nitrogen than the amounts recommended by experts. Some lawn authorities are now saying, "Feed your lawn just enough nitrogen so it looks as good as you want it to." So cut down on the recommended quantities if you wish, but keep an eye on the lawn to make sure it doesn't decline in health or appearance.

Water Lawns. Irrigate all lawns now, according to their individual needs, when rains aren't adequate.

Choose the Best Time to Plant. Both warm- and cool-season grasses may be bought as sod, and cool-season grasses can be planted from sod any month year-round. When planting from sod, ask for and file the names and proportions of the grass varieties in it so that you can duplicate the mix if you ever need to reseed a bare patch. Although you can plant both warm- and cool-season grasses from seed this month, wait if you possibly can to plant cool-season grasses. October is a better time to plant them because fall planting gives cool-season grasses planted from seed more time to establish a root system before summer heat arrives. When planting warm-season grasses, wait until the weather has warmed up in your area. (If you plan to plant zoysia, it's best to wait until June.)

Study Lawn Types Before Planting. How do you choose which grass is right for you? Begin by looking around your neighborhood. Talk to the owners of good-looking lawns. Don't just choose for appearance, though. Consider how much traffic your lawn will have to take and how willing you are to fuss over it. Also consult your Cooperative Extension Office and reference books on lawns to choose a grass that's right for your area and needs. Above all, consider drought resistance.

Weigh the Pros and Cons of Warm- and Cool-Season Grasses. If water were plentiful, the majority of gardeners would never choose to plant such warm-season grasses as Bermuda and zoysia because of their bad habits: they go brown in winter, and they invade borders. Most people prefer cool-season lawns because they stay green all year and look more like eastern lawns. But periodic droughts, dwindling water supplies, and forced cutbacks have made gardeners realize that it's totally unrealistic to expect a lawn to look like a golf green; the ideal lawn is one that can survive. Cool-season lawns aren't invasive, but they need more water than Bermuda or zoysia, which can look good on only 18 inches of irrigation a year, and you can cut that amount by two-thirds and still keep them alive. If you're forced to let them go brown in a drought, they'll pull in their horns and may live through it. The very characteristics that make Bermuda invasive and devilishly hard to get rid of are the same that help it live through tough times. (If you want to keep it from creeping into your flowerbeds, install a continuous concrete curb or install a product especially designed to stop roots from spreading, such as Biobarrier [see page 40].)

Seashore Paspalum. Seashore paspalum or 'Adalayd' grass (*Paspalum vaginatum*), sold here during the seventies and eighties, survives in some gardens. Its virtues are heat and drought resistance, the look of bluegrass, and remarkable salt resistance—it can thrive in ocean spray. But it turns brown in winter, it requires use of a reel mower, and its wiry stems can look unsightly after cutting. Currently there's a breeding program for seashore paspalum, so better varieties may soon emerge.

Tall and Dwarf Fescues. Among gardeners in coastal zones, cool-season lawns are still the favorite. The most popular choice today is one of the newer dwarf fescues. These grasses give you the look of a cool-season lawn but require less water and fuss than old-style cool-season grasses. They have fairly good shade tolerance, and they don't invade flowerbeds. Dwarf fescues make a thicker, better-looking lawn than the older tall fescues from which they were developed, though some of these are still around in seed mixes. (The original pasture fescues—'Kent', 'Alta', 'Fawn', and 'Gors'—were coarse and tall. These were followed by the so-called turf-type tall fescues with finer leaf blades and deeper green color; they're still included in good mixes because they have wearability and other virtues. Then in the seventies to mid-eighties came the dwarf varieties, which are somewhat shorter and finer bladed.

When planting from seed, choose a good named variety, such as 'Bonsai 2000', 'Jaguar II', or 'Finelawn', or a mix of good varieties; avoid generic brands. Read the small print on the package. Avoid the cheaper brands labeled VNS (variety not stated) or UCT (not certified); these may contain outmoded varieties and old stock. Also check the expiration date; don't buy a box that's been on the shelf too long. Plant your seed within a year of the germination test date given on the package.

Also pay attention to shade tolerance, wearability, self-healing, and other qualities of the grass you buy. For example, among tall fescue mixes, the original coarser-bladed Marathon actually fills in faster when damaged and is more shade tolerant than the finer-bladed, dwarfer Marathon II or Marathon III. The dwarfer and finer the fescue, the less shade tolerance, wearability, and ability to self-heal you get. (If you have a dog that spots the lawn, be sure to get a variety that's self-healing.)

Other Cool-Season Grasses. Among other cool-season grasses, perennial rye uses more water and is usually more subject to pests and diseases

than tall fescue. Nevertheless, people still plant lawns of perennial ryegrass mixes from sod or seed. Bent grass is thirsty, disease-prone, and ill adapted to our climate. Don't plant it. Kentucky bluegrass is often blended into ryegrass mixes to reduce fusarium wilt, but planted by itself Kentucky bluegrass, when grown here, is a troublemaker and a water hog.

Grasses for Special Needs. There are also some lesser-known warm- and cool-season grasses for meadows and informal lawns, and as gardeners' tastes change more may emerge. Among cool-season types, tall fescue (*Festuca arundinacea, F. elatior*) is sometimes used unmowed on banks for erosion control. Red fescue (*F. rubra*), also called Slope Saver or Slope Saver II, is a fine-textured, long-haired grass that looks like an evergreen waterfall on banks too steep to mow. It grows easily from seed and is also available as sod. Chewings fescue (*F. r. commutata*) is used the same way but looks clumpier. Among warm-season grasses, buffalo grass, which is the most drought resistant of all lawn grasses, and blue grama grass are often mixed together to make an extremely drought resistant and hardy lawn for interior and mountain zones.

Warm-Season Grasses. Common Bermuda grass, such as 'Mirage' or 'Jackpot', can be started from seed, but hybrid Bermudas and many other subtropical grasses are planted from rhizomes, sprigs, plugs, or stolons (sections of stem that creep along the surface and root into the ground). Many are also available as sod. A fine hybrid Bermuda grass such as 'Santa Ana', 'Tifway', or 'Tifway II', which are all very similar, mown short with a reel mower, will give you a good-looking lawn for most of the year. The newest varieties of common Bermuda, such as 'Mirage' or 'Jackpot', have improved early spring color compared to older varieties.

Newer varieties of zoysia, such as 'DeAnza' and 'Victoria', stay green year-round, thus making zoysia highly desirable. Hold off until June to plant zoysia if you are planting from plugs; it takes off much better in summer (see page 175). St. Augustine grass can take more shade than any other choice, but it needs a lot of water. Tests have shown that common Bermuda grass and Santa Ana hybrid Bermuda are the two most drought-resistant lawn grasses. You can keep them green with less water than it takes to keep many drought-resistant ground covers alive, including Australian saltbush (*Atriplex semibaccata*), coyote brush (*Baccharis pilularis*), and gazanias.

Plant New Lawns. Regardless of the type of grass and method of planting you choose, be sure to prepare the site thoroughly. If you're planting an invasive grass like Bermuda or an invasive variety of zoysia, first install concrete edging or Biobarrier to keep it from creeping into borders.

For all lawns, rototill deeply, add plenty of soil amendment, and level and lightly roll the ground. Sprinkle seeds evenly and cover them with mulch. Either roll stolons with a cleated roller to press them into the soil or partially cover them with topsoil. Keep your freshly planted lawn damp until established. Sprinkle it twice or three times daily, but avoid watering late in the day.

Mow your newly planted lawn for the first time when it has grown to one and a half times the normal cutting height of the grass variety you've chosen. Letting it grow longer before mowing will reduce the health of the lawn. Always follow the **Rule of Thumb** (mentioned in the box on page 81): *Never mow off more than one-third to one-half of the leaf length of your grass at any one time.* When you mow for the first time, be sure that the grass is dry and the blades on your mower are sharp.

Vegetable Gardening

Start planting summer vegetables now. If you've never before grown a vegetable garden, now is the best time to begin. The first week in March is the earliest time for putting in warm-season crops. The sooner you plant the sooner you'll have a harvest.

A wide range of crops can be put in now. Summer vegetables that can be planted in March include artichokes, chayote, corn, green beans, New Zealand spinach, and tomatoes. In coastal zones and warm, south-facing gardens cucumbers and both summer and winter squash can be planted by midmonth. If you have room there's still enough cool weather left to plant a few cool-season crops, such as broccoli, cabbage, head lettuce, kohlrabi, mesclun, and potatoes. And of course you can plant the crops that grow year-round, such as beets, carrots, chard, radishes, and turnips. Wait until April to put in the real heat lovers, such as eggplant, lima beans, melons, okra, peppers, and pumpkins.

Plant Herbs. Culinary herbs are the hallmark of a good potager, so plant some along with your vegetables. Herbs add beauty and atmosphere to the garden, health to surrounding plants, and pizzazz to summer dishes. But not all herbs are edible, and a few are dangerous to ingest (for more information, see page 302). Among edible herbs to put in now are basil, dill, marjoram, mint, oregano, parsley, rosemary, sage, summer savory, and thyme. Most of these can be interplanted with vegetables. Plant basil between tomatoes, for example, and dill next to cucumber. Or plant herbs separately in a raised bed or herb garden, in large ornamental pots, or as an edging surrounding the vegetables where you can reach them easily. Rosemary is not a good selection for interplanting because it soon grows large and woody. Grow it elsewhere in the garden. Mint can also be planted now, but it's invasive; confine it in a 5-gallon can or other container nestled near a hose so you can water it frequently. To keep pests at bay, release ladybugs and lacewings onto mint. Clip leaves often and fertilize it regularly.

Provide Adequate Light. Plant vegetables in full sun. Without it they'll succumb to disease and fail to flower, and you won't get a crop. Lay out your vegetable garden to make the best use of sunlight. The **Rule of Thumb** is: *Plant tall crops to the north and short crops to the south, and arrange your rows from north to south so the sun goes from side to side across them.*

If you're dying to grow vegetables but don't have full sun, try asparagus, lettuce, potatoes, and herbs—parsley, for example. In a pinch these choices will take partial shade. (For lettuce it's sometimes better.) Tomatoes will bear a crop with just four or five hours of midday sun in a warm, sheltered location, especially if it also provides reflected heat.

Provide Good Soil and Drainage. Vegetables need deep, fertile soil with adequate drainage. Sandy or decomposed-granite loam is best. But if you have red clay, adobe, or almost pure sand, don't despair. Good vegetables can be grown in heavy clay soils or highly sandy soils if plenty of organic soil amendment is added. Don't attempt to grow vegetables in areas clogged with tree roots, since they sap the water needed for healthy growth. If your soil is rock hard or drainage is nil, plant in raised beds that are filled with topsoil mixed with organic amendments. If

How Farmers Discovered That Legumes Need Inoculation

All legumes (plants such as peas and beans that have a pod shaped like a peapod) have the ability to take nitrogen out of the air. They do it by means of nodules on their roots and a symbiotic relationship with tiny bacteria called rhizobia. Centuries ago farmers noticed that certain patches of peas or beans produced better crops than others. They discovered that a handful of soil from one of these good patches mixed with the seed of legumes could improve growing conditions in less-productive areas. Unbeknown to themselves, they were actually inoculating their seed.

Modern inoculants are available by mail from seed companies and come with directions for their use. Most kinds can be applied by sprinkling them into the bottom of the furrow before planting seeds. When planting many seeds, mix them in a bowl with enough table syrup or honey to make them sticky. Then add inoculant and stir the seeds until each one is thoroughly coated. If you inoculate your seed, don't use nitrogen fertilizer; the plant will manufacture all the nitrogen it needs, and adding more will make the inoculant less effective.

roots are a problem, plant in large containers with paving stones underneath (see page 23).

Install a Drip System. Decide on a watering system. The furrow method is good, especially with heavy soils, but it wastes water. Overhead sprinkling can work early in the day, but it can be bad along the coast, where excess moisture on leaves, cool temperatures, and a moist atmosphere may encourage the growth of fungal diseases.

The best way for modern Southland gardeners to water vegetables is with a drip system. Most vegetables need the equivalent of an inch of rain per week for healthy growth. Drip systems use 40 to 60 percent less water by putting it

How to Grow Pole Beans

- Choose a spot 6 feet square in full sun.

- Dig up and loosen the soil to the depth of 1 foot, and cultivate a 4-inch layer of organic soil amendment (but not manure) into it.

- Sprinkle the ground with 2 pounds of commercial vegetable fertilizer (5-10-10 or 6-12-8, for example). Work this into the top 6 inches. Or, alternatively, you can work in 1 pound bone meal or 2 pounds 0-10-10 and provide nitrogen by inoculating your seed with nitrogen-fixing bacteria. (The accompanying box describes the origins of this technique.)

- Tie together at one end four 8-foot-long bamboo poles or green plastic-covered garden stakes. Set up your teepee with the legs spread about 4 feet apart and the ends shoved 3 to 4 inches into the ground.

- Plant five or six beans 3 inches apart, with the scar side down, around each pole. Plant 1 inch deep along the coast, 2 inches deep inland. Cover the seeds with commercial potting soil and pat it down gently.

- Water deeply after planting. Don't water again until the beans come up unless the soil begins to dry out. (Sometimes beans rot instead of coming up. If the problem is heavy soil, see the box for how best to plant in it. If the problem is cold soil—below 60°F—presprout the seed before planting it. See page 139.)

- Once the plants have emerged, keep them well watered and protect them from birds and snails.

- When the plants are 3 or 4 inches tall, thin to the best three on each pole. (Snip the others off with scissors.) Give the young plants a helping hand to start them winding around the poles. Once started, they'll keep going with no further help from you.

where roots are. Choose a system designed for row crops, such as nonclogging Drip-In ¼-inch soaker dripline, which can be buried under mulch. The time taken now to install a drip system will save untold hours later.

Plant for Successive Crops. When planting vegetables that mature all at the same time, like carrots and beets, don't plant the whole package at once. Plant quantities no bigger than your family can eat at one time, and save the rest of the seeds to plant at intervals for continued crops. The same goes for lettuce. If you continually harvest outside leaves you can lengthen the harvest, but if you plan to take out whole heads, plant at shorter intervals. With mesclun, cut sections with scissors to allow them to regrow (see page 85).

Make Space for Planting in Established Gardens. If you grow vegetables year-round in an established garden, begin now to make space for summer crops. When you plant winter vegetables in fall you can usually pull up just about everything and start out fresh. But when you plant summer vegetables in spring it's not quite that easy because the seasons for many crops overlap. It's often necessary to plant now among some winter vegetables that are still going strong and to pull out others—even if they aren't quite finished—in order to make enough room for summer vegetables.

The smaller the space the more important it is to schedule your fall planting so that your cole crops, such as cabbage, broccoli, and cauliflower, are finished by now. If they're still going, plant them earlier next year. Peas are often getting ratty-looking and mildewy by now, so pull

How to Plant Large Seeds in Heavy Soil

Heavy soils such as red clay or adobe often bake to a hard crust on top. Large seeds—beans or squash, for example—may not be able to break through. Take these precautions to avoid their rotting under the ground.

- Make a trench to the right planting depth. Soak the trench deeply, at least twice or three times, and let the water drain out.

- Place seeds in the bottom of the trench. (In the case of beans, place them with their scar side pointing down. The root will go straight down, and all your beans will come up at the same time.)

- Cover the seed with an inch of dry potting soil, in coastal zones, or with 2 inches of dry potting soil inland. Pat it down gently and don't water again until the beans pop through. The dry potting soil will act like a mulch and draw just the right amount of moisture to the seed for it to sprout.

them out and replace them with tomatoes and corn. Harvest the last of the fava beans and pull up celery, which by now is usually going to seed. Onions and garlic stay in the ground to mature as the days lengthen. Be sure to weed your onions often; their small root systems can't compete with the rapacious roots of weeds. Replace parsley now or next month. A good place for it is east of a row of trellised cucumbers, where it will get some shade on hot afternoons. By cleaning out most winter crops now and cultivating and amending the soil, you help prevent a carryover of pests and diseases.

Plant Green, Wax, and Purple Beans. Green beans are often called snap beans or string beans, though modern varieties are almost stringless.

🐦 Quick Tip

How to Protect Bean and Corn Sprouts from Birds. *Birds, especially mockingbirds, love young bean and sweet corn sprouts. Pop a green berry basket (the kind that strawberries and cherry tomatoes come in) over each planted seed. After sprouts have touched the top of the baskets, you can safely remove them; by then the birds will have lost interest.*

Wax beans are similar but turn yellow as they mature and usually have a milder flavor. Colorful varieties are available, including a delicious purple bean—'Royal Burgundy'—that turns green when it's cooked. All these beans do best when planted now.

For the earliest harvest plant bush beans—choose a good variety, such as 'Venture' from Park Seed or 'Pencil Pod', a wax bean. If you have limited space, plant pole beans. (See the accompanying box for directions.) You'll get a bigger and longer-lasting harvest and, in most cases, a better-tasting bean. Brown-seeded 'Kentucky Wonder' is one of the finest and easiest varieties for our area because it's resistant to rust. White-seeded 'Kentucky Wonder', also rust resistant, is actually a different strain and not quite as prolific. (Try both and compare.)

Plant Potatoes. Seed potatoes can be bought now at local nurseries. Plant them if you have room; they're fun and easy and delicious when homegrown. Cut seed potatoes in half so there are two or three eyes per section, roll them in RooTone or soil sulfur, and let them stand a day or two for the cuts to callus over before planting. Or, if you prefer, plant the seed potatoes whole. Tests indicate you may get a bigger harvest that way. (Potatoes can also be grown from seed, but until better varieties come along it isn't

Creating Visual Vegetable Excitement

Vegetables can be food for the eye as well as for the body, and designing the vegetable garden as much fun as picking the crops. Here are a few ways to spark up your potager.

- Separate your beds with geometric paths, edging these with low walls, hedges, clipped herbs, and dwarf espaliered fruit trees. (Meandering paths are an option but more difficult to use among vegetables.)

- Create vegetable parterres. Plant colorful crops, and crops with various textures, in patterns to be viewed from above. Cut a square bed into quarters, for example, edging the four pie-shaped triangles that result with basil 'Spicey Globe'. Then fill in two opposite triangles with chives or onions and the other two with colorful leaf lettuces. Many colorful vegetables can be planted this month, including 'Bright Lights' Swiss chard, red Swiss chard, 'Red Sails' lettuce, 'Green Zebra' tomato, and, from Renee's Garden, Cajun Hot Sauce Chiles, Rainbow Radishes, and Tricolor Pole Beans.

- Plant annual flowers, such as marigolds and nasturtiums, in sections of your vegetable garden or edge the vegetable garden with flowers. (Marigolds are reputed to have a beneficial effect on vegetables; nasturtiums are edible. Other edible flowers include bee balm, borage, calendula, chives, daylily, johnny-jump-up, scarlet clover, scarlet runner bean, scented geranium, society garlic, and violet.)

- Grow a few favorite vegetables, flowers, or herbs in ornamental pots, barrels, and other containers; use these as focal points among the vegetables or where paths intersect.

- Make ornamental plant supports of bamboo, willow branches, grape vine prunings, and other discarded plant materials. (Sculptural plants like the squash 'Zuchetta Rampicante', with 12- to 15-inch hanging fruits, from Shepherd's Garden Seeds, are dramatic hanging from overhead arches.)

- Add your own signature with tastefully selected birdbaths, statuary, and topiary.

🐌 Quick Tip

How to Keep Seeds Dry. *Fold over the openings of partially used seed packages, secure the fold with a paperclip, and place the envelopes in a dry screw-top jar. Add a homemade desiccant of 2 tablespoons dried skim milk powder wrapped in tissue and secured with a rubber band. Seal the jar tightly, and store it in the refrigerator or in a cool, dry place.*

worth the trouble.) Plant them 3 or 4 inches deep and 2 inches apart.

Potatoes grow best in fertile, sandy, slightly acid soil. Before planting them amend your soil with acid soil mix—for example, nitrolized redwood shavings or peat moss. Also apply a complete vegetable fertilizer according to package directions and work it into the top 6 inches of soil. As the plants grow, mound the soil up around their stems until you have formed a row that is mounded approximately 6 inches higher than the surrounding ground. Keep the ground moist by giving it an occasional deep watering.

Plant Artichokes to Grow as an Annual Vegetable. Globe artichokes (*Cynara scolymus*) are edible thistles that have been cultivated since the time of the ancient Romans. They grow well in Southern California, particularly close to the ocean. They're usually planted bare-root in fall to grow as a permanent plant that will produce a crop the following summer. (Bare-root plants

How to Plant and Grow Tomatoes

Tomatoes are the favorite vegetable for home growing. If you want to grow a special variety you can't find in nurseries—'Sweet Million', for example—you can sprout the seeds indoors (they germinate readily) and grow your own transplants. But it's easier and quicker to grow your tomatoes from transplants you buy at the nursery, so that's the method given here.

- Select a disease-resistant variety, such as 'Champion', 'Husky Red', 'Better Boy', 'Ace Hybrid', or 'Celebrity', that's appropriate for your needs and climate zone. For a quick harvest when planting in March, also plant an early variety—'Early Girl Improved', 'Fourth-of-July', or 'Enchantment', for example.

- Choose a spot in full sun, and prepare the soil by digging it deeply with a spade and adding soil amendment.

- Use either a vegetable fertilizer or one especially recommended for tomatoes.

- Plant transplants deeply. If they're leggy snip off the lower leaves, make a little trench with the trowel, lay the plant in sideways, and bend the stem up gently. Roots will form all along the buried stem.

- Choose a staking system (see the box on page 114).

- Water deeply and continue to irrigate so the soil stays evenly moist.

are the commercial variety 'Green Globe', which are the same kind you most frequently see for sale in your grocery store.) If you plant these in spring you can't be sure of a harvest the first year. Now, however, newer seed-grown varieties of artichoke, plus proper fertilization and care, can guarantee a harvest the same year, even if you plant as late as March. To plant now and grow artichokes as an annual, buy transplants already growing in pony packs or 4-inch containers. These are the seed-grown plants, and they'll produce a harvest as early as June. (If you live in a hot interior valley, wait until mid- to late summer to plant seed-grown plants for a late winter and spring harvest. Flower buds are woody if they mature during hot weather.)

Dig the soil deeply. To grow rapidly, artichokes need good drainage, plenty of fertilizer, and deep watering. Add a generous quantity of organic soil amendment and choose a good-quality vegetable fertilizer. Measure the dimensions of the ground to be fertilized and follow package directions. Cultivate the fertilizer into

the top 6 inches of soil. Space plants 4 feet apart—don't crowd them—and plant high to avoid crown rot. Cover the roots thoroughly with soil; then make a watering basin slightly deeper than the crown of the plant. As the plant grows, pile a little more soil around the main stalk to prevent irrigation water from touching it.

Water artichokes twice a week for the first two weeks and then deeply once a week, or use a drip system that provides ample water. (The ground must be constantly moist, so don't grow them during drought years.) Artichokes grow

🌱 Quick Tip

How to Foil Cutworms. *Save the cardboard tube from inside holiday wrapping paper. Cut it into 2-inch sections to make protective collars. When you plant tomatoes, first slip the leaves of each plant gently through a cardboard collar; then anchor the sleeve ½ inch into the soil around the transplant. Cutworms won't climb over.*

How to Stake Tomatoes

Don't let tomatoes sprawl on the ground; they'll rot, or pests will get them. Here are three staking methods. Each gives different results and requires different pruning and training. The third method is recommended only for coastal zones.

1. Bend a 6½-foot length of 5-foot-tall, 6-by-6 hardware cloth or cement-reinforcing wire to make a round cage 2 feet across. Place a cage over each plant. Stake it down firmly to withstand wind.
   Pruning and Training: Don't prune at all. The tomato will climb up inside the cage by itself and need no staking.
   Results: This method will give you the most fruit but the smallest.
   Areas for Which Recommended: Any zone, but especially those with hot, interior climates (because the fruit is well shaded).

2. Construct a trellis of 6- or 8-foot-tall hardware cloth or cement-reinforcing wire supported by three or four 8-foot stakes shoved a foot into the ground.
   Pruning and Training: Prune out most suckers but allow two or three main stems to grow. You don't need to tie up the vines; just weave them gently in and out as they grow. The trellis will support them.
   Results: The fruit will be bigger than by the cage-grown method and more numerous than by the single-stem method that follows.
   Areas for Which Recommended: All zones—either coastal or inland.

3. Support each tomato with a single 8-foot stake that you embed 1 or 2 feet in the ground.
   Pruning and Training: Tie up the tomato plant as it grows. Remove all suckers (side sprouts growing above leaves), allowing only one main trunk to grow.
   Results: This method takes more work but gives enormous fruit and an early harvest.
   Areas for Which Recommended: Coastal zones only (because fruit will sunburn inland).

A word of caution: If your tomatoes have ever been stricken with blight, a fungal disease that causes blackening of stems and rotting of fruit, do not remove the suckers from tomatoes. (Tomato blight diseases are discussed on page 138.)

quickly when watered and fed, and they tend to send up many offshoots or side shoots, sometimes called "suckers." Break them off as they occur. If you have room, stick them elsewhere in the garden; they'll grow. Or plant them in gallon containers to give to friends. (Artichoke plants in pots are amusing on a patio since they'll bear artichokes, though they'll be small in size.) Protect plants from snails, which love artichokes.

Purchase/Plant

❏ Plant drought-resistant plants, 32

❏ Plant asparagus from seeds, 86

❏ Don't plant tropicals, 89

❏ Plant trees, shrubs, vines, and ground covers, 90

❏ Plant flowerbeds with warm-season flowers, if you have space, 92

❏ Plant perennials, 93

❏ Plant tigridias, 96

❏ Continue to plant gladioli, 96

❏ Start tuberous begonias, 96

❏ Plant herbaceous, or softwood, cuttings, 97

❏ Plant citrus, avocado, and macadamia trees, 97

❏ Purchase epidendrums, 98

❏ Start fuchsias from cuttings, 102

❏ Plant lawns, 106

❏ Start planting summer vegetables. Plant more cool-season crops if desired, 108

❏ Replace parsley now or next month, 159

❏ Plant green beans, 111

❏ Plant potatoes, 111

❏ Plant artichokes from seed-grown transplants, 112

❏ Plant tomatoes, 113

❏ Plant culinary herbs, 108

❏ Plant edible flowers, 112

Trim, Prune, Mow, Divide

❏ In interior valleys prune begonias, cannas, ginger, ivy, pyracantha, and Sprenger fern, 75

❏ Dethatch warm-season lawns just after they begin to grow, 82

❏ Deadhead annual and perennial flowers, 94

❏ Start to disbud roses if you are growing roses for show, 95

❏ Tie floppy leaves of bulbs in knots (don't remove them before they go brown), 96

❏ Tie gladioli to stakes as they grow, 96

❏ Cut back epidendrum stems after bloom, 100

❏ Prune camellias, 100

❏ Take cut flowers from azaleas while they're in bloom, 100

❏ Pinch fuchsias to make them bushy, 100

❏ Start to prune tropical hibiscus, 100

❏ Propagate bamboo, 103

❏ Mow all grass lawns, 105

❏ Cut back blue hibiscus (*Alyogyne huegelii*) progressively from now until fall, 166

❏ Cut back clumps of *Festuca glauca* now or in fall, 240

Fertilize

❏ Begin to fertilize citrus trees in interior zones. Continue to fertilize citrus trees in coastal zones, 97

❏ Continue to fertilize epiphyllums with 0-10-10 or 2-10-10, 54

❏ Begin to fertilize avocado trees in interior zones. Continue to fertilize avocado trees in coastal zones, 97

❏ Fertilize fuchsias, 100

❏ Fertilize ornamental trees, bushes, lawns, and ground covers, 90

❏ Feed container-grown flowers with liquid or slow-release fertilizer, 92

❏ Fertilize cool-season flowers if growth or flowering slows, 92

❏ Fertilize roses, 94

❏ Begin to fertilize macadamia trees, 97

❏ Feed all lawns, 105

❏ Treat blue hydrangeas with aluminum sulfate, 232

Continued>>

Water

❏ When rains aren't adequate water all garden plants according to their individual needs, 54

❏ Keep fuchsias well watered, 169

❏ Water roses, 94

❏ Water spring-flowering bulbs when rains don't do the job for you, 96

❏ Don't let azaleas dry out, 100

Control Pests, Diseases, and Weeds

❏ Control slugs and snails, 91

❏ Control pests and diseases on roses, 95

❏ Protect gladioli from slugs and snails, 96

❏ Control cutworms, 113

❏ Pull weeds, 40

❏ Plant French marigolds (*Tagetes patula*) solidly and leave them for a full season of growth to control nematodes, 215

❏ Spray cycads for scale, 220

❏ Control giant whitefly, 101

Also This Month

❏ In interior zones protect tender plants until all danger of frost has passed, 90

❏ Once all frost danger is over, take out tender tropicals you sheltered during winter, 90

❏ When frost-damaged plants resume growth, cut off damaged portions, 91

❏ Prepare holes for planting dahlias next month, 96

❏ Unwrap trunks of young citrus and avocado trees, 97

❏ Harvest 'Beaumont' macadamia nuts and cure them correctly, 99

❏ Hand-pollinate quince, guava, and cherimoya, 102

❏ Install a drip system for irrigating vegetables, 109

❏ Continue to harvest winter vegetables, 111

❏ Inoculate legumes, 109

❏ Choose a staking method for tomatoes, 114

❏ Desert flowers begin to bloom in late March; see them now or next month, 93

❏ Make an herb garden, 108

APRIL

The Height-of-Bloom Month

April is a magic time, the height of spring in Southern California, and in the backcountry native plants deck the hillsides with color. So get out and take an observant walk around an old neighborhood, visit botanical gardens, go on garden tours sponsored by local clubs, and enjoy wildflowers in their moment of greatest glory. Take along a camera and notebook to record ideas. See native plants in bloom at such locations as Rancho Santa Ana Botanic Garden, 1500 North College, Claremont 91711 (909/625-8767); Torrey Pines Park, on the Coast Highway immediately south of Del Mar in San Diego County (858/755-2063); the Theodore Payne Foundation, 10459 Tuxford Street, Sun Valley 91352 (818/768-1802); and the Antelope Valley California Poppy Reserve, 15101 West Lancaster Road, Lancaster 93536

(go 15 miles west of Lancaster on Avenue 1, which becomes Lancaster Road) (805/774-1180; when not in service, phone the California Department of Parks and Recreation, 805/942-0662; San Joaquin Valley hotline, Jan.–May, 800/500-5376). For more ideas, purchase a copy of Bartel and Belt's *Guide to Botanical Resources of Southern California.* Or phone the Wildflower Information Hotline in Lancaster (805/948-1322) or the All-Southern California hotline (818/768-3533).

Southern California gardens are also in full bloom this month. We pride ourselves on year-round flowers, but we have more in April than at any other time of the year. Cool-season annuals planted in September and October reach their zenith early this month, and, by midmonth, countless permanent landscape plants are in full bloom. April is our second spring-planting month but less demanding than the first. If you did most of your spring planting in March, relax now and enjoy the fruits of your labor. If not, there's still time to catch up on jobs that went undone.

It's warm enough to sprout seeds quickly but not hot enough to scorch seedlings. Stormy days—often bringing heavy rains—alternate with sunny days, speeding growth and opening flowers. Pests also enjoy the warming trend. Cabbage butterflies, thrips, mites, and tobacco budworm speed up activities and need to be controlled. Despite this one negative note, April is a month to relish.

Valley and Desert Dwellers

If you live in a hot inland valley or desert area do your last planting this month before the onslaught of summer heat. This is the last moment for you to plant ground covers without risking development of ugly gaps, and it's not too late to plant tropicals and subtropicals—palms, for example. Local nurseries have assortments of heat-loving bedding plants that can go into the ground now, including balsam, Madagascar periwinkle (vinca; *Catharanthus roseus*), marigolds, petunias, portulaca, and zinnias. (In desert areas, plant petunias in fall.)

Mulch plants after setting them out, and protect them from the hot noonday sun until they're well started. A shot of well-diluted liquid fertilizer after planting can get plants off to a good start. Choose a fertilizer that has instructions for new plantings on the label.

Azaleas

April is the best month of the year in which to plant azaleas, though not the first possible. (Precise directions are given in January, page 52.) The largest number of azaleas are in bloom now, and while they're in bloom their roots are dormant so you can safely plant them. As soon as they finish blooming they'll take off and grow. Above ground they'll start putting out fresh leaves, and below ground they'll sprout tender young roots that shouldn't be disturbed.

Plant azaleas in tubs or the ground and in partial shade—a northern or eastern exposure is best. For easy care water with a drip system adjusted to keep roots evenly moist—neither soggy nor dry.

Wisteria

Choose wisteria vines now while they're in bloom. There are two main types: Chinese wisteria *(Wisteria sinensis),* which blooms all at once on bare branches, and Japanese wisteria *(Wisteria floribunda),* which has a longer period of bloom, more fragrance, and flowers that open from top to bottom as leaves appear. Besides the familiar violet-blue there are white, pink, and purple wisterias, some with 3-foot-long blooms. Always purchase named varieties or grafted plants. These have characteristics superior to those of chance seedlings.

Wisteria is one of our most satisfactory vines because, though it's easy to grow and highly drought resistant once established, its blooms are among the most romantic of flowers in color, shape, and fragrance. It's deciduous, so if you grow it on an arbor it can give you welcome shade in summer and sunshine in winter. And it flourishes anywhere from desert to beach. Plant the vines in full sun, provide strong support, and water and fertilize them often for the first year or two to get them started. Once a wisteria is well established you can subject it to benign neglect, but not before.

Epiphyllums

Epiphyllums, orchid cacti, are true members of the cactus family but native to open jungles rather than deserts. They like semishade, well-drained soil, and, because most are epiphytes or tree-dwelling plants (and because they're particularly delicious to snails), they do well in hanging baskets. There are more than nine thousand named varieties to choose from. Real fanciers fill entire backyards with these plants and have blooms year-round, but most gardeners grow them for a spectacular show beginning now and lasting through June. Begin looking for them in nurseries. Watch the newspaper for epiphyllum shows in May. Ask friends to save you a branch of this or that admired variety. They're easy to start from cuttings (the box on page 120 tells how).

For most of the year epiphyllums are the ugly ducklings of the garden. They can be kept tucked away in a semishady spot, watered once a week in dry weather, pruned of dead branches to encourage growth, and fed occasionally with a complete fertilizer such as 8-8-8 liquid or fish emulsion during the summer and with a high-bloom formula such as 0-10-10 or 2-10-10 from January until they flower. Now's the time to move plants to center stage and enjoy the exotic blooms. Make sure you face the plants in the same direction they're used to, or the flower buds may fall off.

Each flower lasts only a day or two, but more keep opening. For best appearance cut off the faded blossoms; otherwise their wilted petals will hang on for a long time. Mist "epis" frequently in dry weather, but don't overwater them. Though less drought resistant than almost all other cacti, epiphyllums use little water, especially if you irrigate them with a drip system instead of a hose. Test whether plants are ready for watering by sticking a finger an inch or two into the mix. If it feels damp don't water. If it feels dry turn on the drip system until you see water drain out the bottoms of the containers; then turn it off. During the rainy season don't water at all.

What's an Epiphyte?

An epiphyte is a plant that lives by attaching itself to another plant, typically to a tree, or in some cases to a rock. They often root in pockets of soil that gather in the crotches of trees and are fertilized by a regular sprinkling of bird droppings, dead insects, and the occasional dead animal. Unlike parasites, epiphytes don't take nourishment from the host plant. Most are native to humid tropical or subtropical regions. Many aroids, orchids, ferns, cacti, and bromeliads are epiphytic. They're good choices for our gardens because so many of them have developed built-in reservoirs, thickened leaves, or other devices to see them through drought.

All epiphytes prefer loose, acid, airy, well-drained soil. They're often grown in hanging baskets. Some are grown on slabs of bark, and all can be naturalized (made to grow and multiply as they would in the wild) on tree branches if kept moist with an automatic mist system.

Pruning

Cut Back Poinsettias. After poinsettia flowers have faded, sometime between now and the end of May, prune garden-grown plants back to two or three dormant buds. (These look like swellings or scars close to the bottoms of the branches.) Poinsettia (*Euphorbia pulcherrima*) is best known today as a Christmas potted plant, but old varieties like 'Hollywood' make easy-care garden plants, requiring only average watering in summer. (Among indoor varieties 'Annette Hegg' grows best outdoors.) Order

How to Start an Epiphyllum from a Cutting

- Cut off a branch from a plant you wish to propagate, making the cut at the narrow intersection where it joins another branch.

- Use a permanent broad-tip marker to write the variety name in block letters directly on one side of the cutting.

- If the cut branch is wide, trim off excess flesh to make a point. Dip the cut section in a rooting hormone such as Dip'N Grow or RooTone, knock off the excess, and allow the cutting to dry and "callus off" for a day or two.

- Plant in a 4-inch pot of dry—not wet—potting soil to a depth ½ inch above the two lowest areoles, or spine cushions. (On epiphyllums these are found in the notches on the stem.) Tamp the soil down firmly around the cutting; then stake the cutting with wood or bamboo and tie it securely.

- Mist the cutting daily, but take care not to water the soil until the cutting has rooted, in about a month. (You can check by pulling gently on the cutting; when roots have sprouted it will resist. Or you can tell by feeling the thickness of the cutting; when the roots begin to grow it will get plumper.) Once it has rooted, start regularly watering. Feed lightly when it has grown 2 or 3 inches tall. When roots fill the container, repot into a larger size.

- A good soil mix for epiphyllums is light and airy, drains well, and contains agricultural charcoal. The following works well: 1 gallon good-quality acid, commercial potting soil mix recommended for "jungle" plants, 1 cup perlite, and 1 cup agricultural charcoal.

garden varieties from nurseries or purchase them at plant sales. They grow easily from cuttings. Fifty years ago, before modern varieties and growing techniques made poinsettias so popular for Christmas, they were a staple of California gardens in frost-free zones, and they're still useful for hard-to-reach sunny spots, such as a south-facing garage wall.

Control Shrubs That Would Like to Be Trees.
Hedges and shrubs start fast growth now. Any green shrub that has an eventual size of over 6 feet needs frequent pruning during the warm months if you want to keep it as a shrub. (Remember to prune flowering shrubs that bloom for a specific season after rather than before bloom.) Many shrubs would like to shoot up and become trees; it's all right to let them—some make fine specimens—but when it happens by accident you end up with a crowded garden.

(A more sophisticated approach is to use dwarf plants that will always be the right size for the space.)

With shrubs in particular, work for a billowy, flowing form, wider below than above (so lower branches won't die from shade). There are three main ways to prune them:

1. Plants with small leaves can be clipped on the outside like a hedge, with shears or loppers.

2. Plants with large leaves are best cut from the inside, with branches cut out deep within to renew growth from inside out. This gives an informal look and is often necessary to keep heavy trunks from growing taller. (A saw or ratchet pruner can make this job easier; the built-in ratchet in particular increases your strength manyfold.)

3. Plants that grow from the ground in the shape of a fountain, such as oleander and heavenly bamboo (*Nandina domestica),* are best

pruned by taking out entire branches to ground level after bloom. Pittosporum, myoporum, and photinia are among the shrubs to prune beginning now.

- **Victorian Box** (*Pittosporum undulatum*). This is useful as a somewhat drought resistant, informal shrub in coastal zones. (It requires more water in interior regions.) It frequently starts as a volunteer. Victorian box rapidly becomes a 15-foot tree if allowed, then gradually grows to 30 or 40 feet in height and width—a nice-looking tree but drippy with leaves and sticky fruit. It can be kept as an informal hedge or screen indefinitely by cutting it back, mainly with loppers, beginning in spring and continuing occasionally throughout summer. A 9-foot hedge can be cut to 3 or 4 feet but will take a year or two to recover.

- **Tobira** (*P. tobira*). The standard variety of this pittosporum can grow slowly to tree height, but with shears and loppers it can easily be kept small or pruned into artistic shapes. 'Wheeler's Dwarf' is compact; it grows eventually to only 2 or 3 feet, with a mounded shape and no pruning necessary.

- **Myoporum** (*Myoporum laetum*). To keep this myoporum looking good as a shrub, windbreak, or informal hedge, control it from the beginning by cutting it back with loppers several times a year. Left to its own devices it shoots rapidly to 30 feet tall and 20 wide, and the bottom section eventually becomes bare and woody. A full-grown myoporum is an unattractive tree with only one virtue: it will grow in the teeth of the ocean wind, which stunts its size.

- **Photinia fraseri.** This plant naturally grows as a shrub—as tall as 10 feet if you don't cut it shorter—or you can prune it into a small tree while it's young by choosing a single trunk and cutting out all others. Prune it often with loppers to keep the size you choose and encourage fresh growth. New growth is red—dull when front-lit but exciting when planted on the west so that afternoon light shines through the leaves. If you are growing it as a shrub, don't let it get wide on top or the bottom section will become bare and ugly. If it gets too tall, cut it to the desired size this month. It will soon bounce back.

Deciduous Fruit Trees

Deciduous fruit trees that are overloaded with fruit always drop a lot of it later in the year, in a natural process called "June drop" (described on page 170). You can permit your fruit to grow larger with less June drop by starting to thin it now. Thin out the fruit lightly this month, removing one or two fruits from heavy clusters all over the tree. Thin the fruit again four to six weeks later. (Mark it on your calendar so you won't forget.)

Bulbs

Plant Dahlias. Dahlias are the best-kept secret in the garden. With just a little care they're easy to grow and so flamboyant they'll make any gardener look like an expert. Grown in rows they're unpleasantly stiff, so plant dwarf and bedding types in drifts among other flowers and tall ones at the backs of beds (see page 229).

Feed Irises. Fertilize irises with a low-nitrogen, high-phosphorus and high-potassium plant food—2-10-10 or 2-18-6, for example—to encourage bloom. Solid fertilizers are the easiest to use on plants growing in the ground. Use liquids in containers. Protect irises from slugs and snails, which will ruin the plants if allowed.

How to Plant Dahlias

- Choose a spot in full sun along the coast or afternoon shade inland, in rich, well-drained soil. Work in soil amendment if you didn't prepare planting holes in March.

- Dig holes 7 to 8 inches deep for large tubers or 5 to 6 inches deep for small tubers, and 1 to 3 feet apart according to size. Work into the bottom of each hole a handful of bone meal or 2 tablespoons of 2-10-10 or 2-18-8, or some other high-bloom fertilizer. (High nitrogen cuts down on bloom.) Cover this with 2 inches of fast-draining soil or sand.

- Place the tuber on top with the eye (the growth bud) up.

- Cover the tuber with 2 inches of soil. As the plant grows up through this soil, continually cover it with more.

- Stake tall varieties at planting time, with the stake next to the growth bud. Tie them up later. (Bedding varieties don't need it, but a stake will help you remember where the tubers are.)

- When plants are up 3 inches, begin to fertilize with diluted liquid fertilizer every two weeks or with a complete slow-release fertilizer according to package directions.

- When the plant has three sets of leaves, pinch off the top set to encourage branching. Some gardeners like to pinch again when plants are 1½ to 2 feet high. This will produce more but smaller blooms.

Tie Up Leaves of Spring-Flowering Bulbs after Bloom. Continue to water spring-flowering bulbs when rains aren't adequate. Feed those that have bloomed with a balanced liquid fertilizer or solid bulb food watered into the ground. This will help them flower better next year. Don't cut off the green leaves until they go completely yellow; tie them into knots to make them look neater, and plant summer flowers around them.

Roses

Control Pests and Diseases, Fertilize, and Irrigate. Continue to control pests and diseases on roses (as described on pages 72 and 95). If you've chosen to follow a regular spraying routine with chemical sprays, continue to spray with Orthene and Funginex or RosePride Orthenex Insect & Disease Control—Formula III if mites are a problem. If you prefer not to spray with chemicals, control caterpillars with BT (*Bacillus thuringiensis*) and other pests with SunSpray Ultra-Fine Spray Oil or insecticidal soap. Control mildew with Cornell Fungicide Formula (see page 73).

Fertilize your roses regularly. Either feed once this month with a commercial rose food or, if you're following the Rose-Pro Method, feed at weekly intervals with 1 tablespoon sulfate of ammonia per rose and foliar-feed with micronutrients (as described on pages 94 and 308).

In interior zones and fast-draining soils irrigate roses deeply with up to 1½ inches of water per application, and increase the frequency of irrigations now from once to twice a week. (One inch of water applied twice a week may be adequate in coastal climates and water-retentive soils.)

Prune Roses by Picking, Deadheading, and Disbudding. Roses start blooming in April, and when you pick them for cut flowers you're doing a kind of pruning. Roses naturally flower in flushes of bloom, but how you cut them affects both the lapse of time between consecutive flushes and the length of the stems they have. The longer the stems you cut, the more time it will take for the rose to rebloom, though the flowers will be good ones on long, strong stems. If you always cut your roses with short, stubby stems, the bush will bloom again much sooner, but with inferior flowers on short, weak stems.

So unless you're growing exhibition roses, choose the middle ground: cut neither down too far nor up too high.

The easiest way to encourage roses to put out strong, healthy growth while allowing them to bounce back into bloom within a few weeks is to follow this general **Rule of Thumb:** *Cut flowers from rose plants that are over one year old just above the first five-leaflet leaf that points away from the center of the plant.* (Leave more greenery on a first-year plant to make the bush stronger.) When flowers have been allowed to fade on the bush, deadhead them at the same point. This method of cutting roses quickly brings flowers back on long stems. (An exception should be made for varieties that naturally bear long-stemmed roses and are, in any case, more appropriately raised for their cut flowers than for their beauty in the landscape. You can cut these longer but always leave at least two leaves on the plant at the bottom of each stem. New growth will arise above them.)

For one-to-a-stem and show-quality roses, continue to disbud hybrid teas and grandifloras (as described on page 95).

Water Gardening

Fish and lily ponds are one of the most exciting yet tranquil elements of horticulture. Water can provide sound from fountains and waterfalls; movement from fish, birds, dragonflies, and sky reflections; a paradisiacal atmosphere; and colorful flowers. Ponds can be of any size or shape. You can grow a dwarf water lily or dwarf exotic lotus even in a half wine barrel.

Water lilies *(Nymphaea)* are among the most intriguing flowers we grow. There are two main kinds. Hardy water lilies, which are easy to grow, bloom during the daytime in summer and have flowers that float on the surface of the wa-

How to Keep Cut Roses Fresh

- **To Prevent Neck Droop of Cut Roses:** In early evening pick full buds that are beginning to open. Wrap them in a black plastic trash bag so no light can enter, and store them overnight in the refrigerator (between 6 and 12 hours). The next morning take out the roses and treat them as follows.

- **To Make Cut Roses Last Seven or Eight Days:** Immerse them in a sink filled with lukewarm water (100°F) for 20 or 30 minutes. Clip off the lower leaves (but not the thorns); then recut the stems underwater. Arrange the roses in a vase filled with either of these solutions: 1 quart water, 2 tablespoons fresh lemon juice, 1 tablespoon sugar, and ½ teaspoon bleach; or 1 pint regular 7-Up, 1 pint water, and ½ teaspoon bleach.

ter; tropical water lilies, which have a longer bloom season, carry their blossoms high above the water surface. Tropical lilies come in a rainbow of colors, including blue, with flowers often as big as dinner plates. Some are night blooming. Lotus *(Nelumbo),* an exotic plant sacred to the Hindu and Buddhist religions, requires much the same care as water lilies.

There are many other aquatic plants. Some grow like water lilies and lotus, with their roots in mud or soil and their foliage either floating on the surface of the water or standing above it. (Most aquatic plants that are rooted in soil are best grown in containers for ease of maintenance. See the accompanying box for guidelines on planting water lilies.) A second group of plants floats freely on the surface of the water, while a third type is completely submerged and adds oxygen to the pond.

The romance and beauty of water gardening, like all other types of gardening, has its practical

How to Plant a Water Lily

- Purchase a water lily planting tub from a mail-order company specializing in water gardening, or make your own from a plastic or cardboard plant container that is 14 or 18 inches in diameter and 6 to 12 inches deep. (Both are lightweight and hold up well underwater.) Plug the drainage holes with wads made of two layers of newspaper. Containers can also be made from plastic baskets like small laundry baskets. Line them with polyester quilt batting.

- Plant water lilies in rich garden soil; fertile loam is best. Make sure it contains no manure (which encourages growth of algae) and no peat moss, compost, commercial potting soil, perlite, wood shavings, or other lightweight soil amendment that might float to the surface of the pond. Or plant in Profile Aquatic Plant Soil according to package directions. (It will not foul pond water.)

- According to package directions, mix into the soil a complete, slow-release, granulated fertilizer that's recommended for aquatic plants and contains trace elements to enhance growth and flower color. Or choose a generic complete fertilizer such as 10-20-5, and mix ¼ cup of it into every 3 gallons of soil. Be sure the fertilizer you use contains trace elements but no herbicides or pesticides.

- Fill the container to 2 inches below the top with fertilized soil, and then water it so that it settles. Add more soil if necessary. Plant one lily at a time, keeping the others moist and in the shade. Don't let their roots dry out.

- In the case of hardy water lilies, plant them when the water temperature is 60°F or higher. Place the tuber with the bud facing up, and with the end that contains the bud pointing toward the center of the container and the other end of the tuber gently touching the inside of the container. Plant so that the crown or growth bud is ¼ inch below the surface of the ground and so

that the tuber slopes down at a 45-degree angle from the bud end to the place where the tuber touches the container.

- Cover the top of the container with a circle of ½-inch galvanized chicken wire that's cut 2 or 3 inches wider than the diameter of the container. Bend it down over the sides to keep out fish. The lily will grow up through the wire. Or, alternatively, cover the surface of the soil with a 1-inch layer of pebbles or sand.

- Immediately after planting, submerge the container in the pond so that the top of the soil is 6 inches underwater. When the plant is thoroughly established, lower it so the soil surface is 12 to 18 inches underwater. Use bricks or cement blocks under the container to adjust the height.

- Plant tropical water lilies when the water temperature is 70°F or higher. Place the round chestnutlike tuber of each tropical water lily upright in the center of the container with its roots buried and its crown, the place from which the foliage emerges, protruding slightly above the soil.

- If your tropical lily has foliage, make your circle of chicken wire 2 inches larger than for hardy lilies. Cut a hole 4 inches in diameter in the center. Then cut the circle of wire straight through the middle from side to side, dividing it into two equal halves. After planting the lily, fit the two halves over the surface of the soil so the plant is growing up through the middle, and tie the two halves together. Bend down the edges around the sides.

- Immediately after planting, carefully submerge the tropical lily in the pond with 4 to 6 inches of water above soil level. When the plant grows to 8 inches in diameter, lower the container so there are 12 inches to 18 inches of water above it.

side. First, the pool should be properly balanced, which means it should contain the right ingredients to prevent the water from becoming stagnant. The **Rule of Thumb** for balancing a pond is: *For each square yard of water you need two bunches of submerged oxygenating grasses, twelve water snails, two 5-inch-size goldfish or koi, and 1 medium-to-large water lily.* (In water barrels substitute several guppies or mosquito fish for the goldfish or koi.) Don't feed your fish. If you don't feed them they won't overproduce or grow too large. They'll get all they need from the pond and act as natural gardeners, helping to keep the water clean. In an ecologically balanced pond fish eat bugs, various organic materials floating on the top of the pond, submerged oxygenating grasses, and algae. Even though you don't feed your fish, they'll get to know you and they'll come to you when you approach the pond or touch the water.

Even if you've provided all the elements for balance, the water may turn green with algae, a diverse group of primitive flowerless plants, but it will eventually settle down and be clean and clear most of the time. There are two kinds of aquatic algae: filamentous, which attach themselves to walls and plants, and floating, which turn ponds green. Algae grow fast in unseasonably warm weather, and many balanced ponds go green for a while in spring. If this happens to your pond, don't worry; just wait. When the weather cools, or when the water is adequately shaded by lily or lotus leaves, it will clear up by itself. If your pond stays green throughout the warm months it may not be properly balanced, it may need more submerged oxygenating plants, or it may need more water lilies to shade the surface. Sixty to 70 percent of the water surface should be shaded by leaves during summer, less in winter.

Feed the Plants. For a pond this means getting in there bodily. You'll need to wear hip boots, protective clothing, and long rubber gloves for this job because some forms of algae can be absorbed through the skin and may produce allergic reactions. Fertilize water lilies and lotus in April. They're gluttons for food and won't bloom or grow well without adequate nourishment. Beginning now, feed one aquatic plant pellet (the 6-gram slow-release type—10-5-5, for example) to each container per month. Use a wooden dowel to shove each pellet deeply into the soil mix as close to the crown of the plant as possible. While you're about it, scoop up some of the muck from the bottom of the pond. (Some gardeners report good results from using this pond by-product as a fertilizer on roses and other plants. You can try this if you wish, but use it sparingly at first because it may contain harmful salts.) Don't be concerned about muddying the water as you work. It will clear again, and the fish won't come to harm.

If you don't have a pond, consider the several easy ways to add one to the landscape, including ready-made pond liners. Both shaped and flexible pond liners are available. Be sure to put your pond in full sun. For more information, order the magazinelike catalog from Van Ness Water Gardens, 2460 North Euclid Avenue, Upland, CA 91784-1199 (800/205-2425). Or refer to books on water gardening—for example, Sunset's *Garden Pools, Fountains and Waterfalls,* Paul and Rees' *The Water Garden,* or Hazel White's *Water Gardens.*

Pest Control

Spray for Caterpillars and Worms. This is the month when caterpillars and worms wake up and begin serious munching. In a shrub-surrounded garden with many beneficials, tree frogs, and birds in residence, it may not be necessary to spray. But if caterpillar and worm damage is out of control, spray with BT, the bacterial disease that affects certain caterpillars but no other pests or insects. It's sold as a liquid or powder under the Safer and Attack brands and such trade names as Dipel and Thuricide. (Read the labels to make sure it's BT you're getting.) When mixing powders into sprays, add a spreader-sticker, such as SunSpray Ultra-Fine Spray Oil. It will make mixing easier and increase the effectiveness of the spray.

Caterpillars are the immature stage, or larvae, of butterflies and moths. Butterflies are usually brightly colored and fly in the daytime; most moths fly at night and their wings are dull colored. In their mature stage butterflies and moths aren't harmful; some are even beneficial pollinators. But after mating, females lay their eggs singly or in groups on plants or other chosen food. When the eggs hatch, caterpillars emerge, and these are what do the damage. When the larvae of moths have grown to full size, they pupate within the plant or spin a silky cocoon in the soil or debris beneath it. When the caterpillars of butterflies pupate, they attach themselves to a branch or other support and form a protective shell called a chrysalis. After metamorphosing within the pupa for a few days or over winter, the mature butterfly or moth emerges, mates, and lays eggs.

Fortunately, most butterflies and moths are selective about where they lay their eggs, making it possible to choose between plants to spray with BT and those to leave unsprayed. Parsley, for example, is host to the larvae of swallowtail butterfly, milkweed to monarch butterfly, and passion vine to Gulf fritillary. Don't spray those plants. But obviously, when you see cabbage butterflies you need to spray your cabbages. And redhumped caterpillars, the larvae of a brown moth, always begin their attack on broom (*Genista*) in April. These yellow caterpillars have a red hump, a red head, and red stripes. Working in large numbers, they quickly devour all flowers and sections of foliage in repeated generations. So spray broom with BT weekly.

Control Budworms. Tobacco or geranium budworms also get going this month. Budworms drill a little round hole in the flowers of geraniums and bore out the inside, ruining the blossoms. They also munch on leaves. In order to control budworms with BT, you need to spray the plants before the budworms climb inside the flowers. This month you can time the treatment correctly because the night-flying moth that is the parent of the tobacco budworm usually makes its first egg-laying foray with the first full moon in April. So spray or dust all your geraniums with BT a day before the full moon and repeat the process three or four days after the full moon. This will cut down the population at the beginning of the season and catch the budworms before they are safely ensconced inside the flowers.

Control Fuchsia Gall Mites. Fuchsia gall mite (*Aculops fuchsiae*) attacks new growth on fuchsias, twisting and distorting the buds, foliage, and flowers and turning leaves red. Fortunately, predacious mites are keeping this pest under control in many areas. Sprays for controlling fuchsia gall mites are the same as those discussed in the section dealing with spider mites on the next page. The cautions and the information on beneficial predators given there also apply to fuchsia gall mite. If, nonetheless, you plan to spray your fuchsias, first cut off the infected parts 3 or 4 inches below the damage (or above it on hanging plants). Tie the trimmings in a plastic bag and dispose of them in the trash.

By far the best control for fuchsia gall mites is

to grow resistant varieties and take good care of the plants. Provide them with regular fertilizer (as discussed on page 168), the correct light (50 percent sunshine in coastal zones under lath or shade cloth), and daily irrigation by a drip system with mini-sprinklers concealed overhead to keep adequate moisture in the soil and the foliage washed off. In my garden I never spray my fuchsias. I start in early spring applying ladybugs and lacewing larvae to the foliage. I also release spiders onto them that I catch with damp facial tissue elsewhere in the garden or even in the house. I also concentrate on growing resistant varieties. Here are a few: 'Baby Chang', 'Chance Encounter', 'Cinnabarina', 'Dollar Princess', 'Englander', 'Golden West', 'Isis', 'Miniature Jewels', 'Mendocino Mini', 'Nonpareil', 'Ocean Mist', and 'Pink Marshmallow'. I've also had good luck with 'Lisa', 'Swingtime', and 'Voodoo'; a controversial variety, 'Voodoo' is susceptible to fuchsia gall mites in some areas and not in others.

Control Spider Mites. Now through summer watch carefully for spider mites; they're most active in warm weather. Spider mites are members of the arachnid family that live on pine needles and under the leaves of other favored plants, including roses, fuchsias, primroses, and cyclamen. They suck out plant juices and cause whitening, yellowing, stippling, and loss of color in the foliage that can sometimes mean death to the plant. If you think a plant has mites, place a white sheet of paper under the foliage and tap the branch. Look with a magnifying glass for tiny black or reddish spiderlike creatures scurrying around on the paper. Another telltale sign, which is easier to see, is fine, hairlike webbing—like spiderwebs but messier—around, over, and under leaves and twigs. Suspect spider mites on roses when their leaves

turn yellow and fall off. Rub a yellowing leaf on a white cloth; if a smudge results, mites are to blame.

Some plants, including fuchsias or moosehorn ferns (*Platycerium superbum*), can be so weakened by spider mites that they die. Roses won't die from them, but they can be set back. Healthy plants are less likely to suffer a bad mite attack. If you fertilize an affected moosehorn fern, for example, at the first sign of damage, it's quite likely to overcome mites without being sprayed. Well-fed and properly watered plants growing in a mixed landscape where beneficial mites have been encouraged to set up housekeeping will usually survive without spraying.

Beneficials that kill mites abound in our environment. These include brown and green lacewings, spider mite destroyer ladybeetle (*Stethorus picipes*), six-spotted thrips (*Scolothrips sexmaculatus*), and several predacious mites. Predacious mites are long-legged and colorless, more active and faster than pest mites, only stopping to feed. Look for them with a hand-held lens under plant leaves. Two of these mites—*Phytoseiulus persimilis* and *Metaseiulus occidentalis*—are commercially available, as are lacewings.

Attacking spider mites with chemical sprays can increase your problems. Mites quickly develop resistance to sprays, and, also, when you spray you destroy all their natural enemies. (If you've ever sprayed a plant with Sevin, an infestation of spider mites will result. Sevin kills a broad spectrum of pests, but it also kills all the beneficials that keep mites under control.) The best ways to control mites are by conserving their resident natural enemies, getting rid of ants, refraining from applying pesticides, and washing off plants to remove dust. Among pesticides registered for mites, Thiodan, contained in Cooke's Garden Insect Spray, is the strongest and most

🐞 Quick Tip

How to Encourage Ladybugs to Stay Put.
Before releasing ladybugs, chill them for an hour or two in the refrigerator; this lowers their metabolism. Release them at dusk. Place them low on plants so they can walk up. When the weather is dry, provide dishes of water on the ground at the base of plants; place a rock within each for ladybugs to land on. Remember, ladybugs can't swim, but they do need water to drink.

hazardous; it wipes out all the beneficials and doesn't break down in the environment. For roses, controls include Ortho Isotox Insect Killer—Formula IV, RosePride Orthenex Insect & Disease Control—Formula III, and Ortho Rose & Flower Insect Killer. Sulfur dust or spray can be used on some vegetables, but will burn cucurbits (members of the cucumber family, including, besides cucumbers, squashes, melons, gourds, and pumpkins). (When spraying with chemicals, follow package directions exactly and use only on listed plants.) If you feel you must spray, by far the safest and least harmful sprays to use are insecticidal soap, Safety Side or Sun-Spray Ultra-Fine Spray Oil, hot pepper wax (apply at the rate of 4 ounces to the gallon), or neem oil, contained in Green Light Rose Defense.

Control Eugenia Psyllid. For almost a hundred years eugenia (*Syzygium paniculatum*), also called Australian brush cherry, has been Southern California's most valuable hedge plant for frost-free zones; one can grow it to any needed height and clip it as narrowly as 1 foot. But sometime during the late 1980s the eugenia psyllid (*Trioza eugeniae*) was accidentally imported from Australia, and it has since rendered its namesake practically useless for new plantings. Eugenia psyllid is a small flying insect that lays eggs under new foliage on eugenia shrubs and trees. The larvae suck out the juices from fresh leaves, stunting, twisting, and distorting the foliage, but they don't kill the plants. Young plants show more damage than old ones.

The University of California has released beneficial insects to control eugenia psyllid, so don't cut down established eugenia hedges or trees. If you wish, you could try spraying them with Orthene once a month or with Mavrik at intervals of once every two months. But it's better not to spray because in the early spring the psyllid is active on new growth. Then, when the weather warms up slightly more, the beneficial becomes activated and wipes out the psyllid population. If you spray, you kill the psyllid but you also kill the beneficial so you don't have the long-lasting effect of the beneficial controlling the psyllid (see discussion on giant whitefly, page 101). Instead of spraying, hose off the plants now and put up with a little leaf damage, knowing that the plants will look much better as the year progresses. Or try Ace caps, a systemic pesticide—you drill a hole in the trunk and insert them. This systemic method has the advantage of not requiring you to go on a neighbor's property to spray. (Warn children not to eat the berries of sprayed or treated trees.) If you're planting a new hedge substitute another plant, like Carolina laurel cherry (*Prunus caroliniana*), *Podocarpus macrophyllus*, or yaupon (*Ilex vomitoria*). Yaupon is hardy and makes a fine smooth-textured hedge in coastal or interior zones, though it grows much wider than eugenia.

Release Beneficials and Encourage Animals.
Start releasing beneficial insects this month. Ladybugs are available at many nurseries now. Keep the packages damp with a few drops of water. Prior to releasing ladybugs, place them in their packages in the refrigerator for at least an

hour; this slows down their metabolism. Meanwhile, sprinkle the garden with water to provide an inviting environment. And then apply the insects by small spoonfuls here and there around the garden at dusk. Fewer fly away when prechilled and introduced into a moist garden in the cool evening hours. Put a few on each of your fuchsias. Also send away for other beneficials, including lacewings and predatory mites and wasps. Encourage birds—they eat many insects—and, though it may sound eccentric, also encourage bats, which eat night-flying moths whose larval forms, such as cutworms and budworms, are so destructive in the garden. (Much-needed homes for bats can be purchased from Bat Conservation International, Inc., P.O. Box 162603, Austin, TX 78716-2603, 512/327-9721.) Welcome spiders into the garden. Spiders, beneficial insects, and animals can help the gardener keep pests under control better than poisonous sprays. Try to interest your neighbors.

We have seen on a grand scale what beneficial creatures can accomplish. The ash whitefly has been almost eliminated, the pine tip moth and eucalyptus long-horn borer greatly reduced (though now another species of long-horn borer has arrived). These triumphs should give gardeners hope, but working with beneficials to control pests takes patience and the necessity of following a few rules. One rule is to get rid of ants; they kill the larvae of beneficial creatures while protecting and spreading aphids and other pests in order to milk them for their honeydew. To control ants, use COMBAT or MAX-FORCE baits. (If you have dogs, place bait containers inside tin cans bent partially closed, so dogs can't chew on them.) Also, don't spray with broad-spectrum pesticides. Beneficial creatures are easily killed by pesticides. If you eliminate all the pests, what will the beneficials eat? Instead, try to accomplish a landscape of

Plants That Attract Beneficials

Many beneficial insects feed on pollen and nectar, so to attract beneficials, grow old-fashioned annual and perennial flowers, wildflowers, and flowering herbs; these bear more pollen and nectar than modern hybrids. Plant carrots here and there in the garden and allow them to flower. When annual herbs like parsley, cilantro, and arugula start going to seed, don't pull them up; let them also flower. Do the same with a few cole crops, like mustard and broccoli. Here's a list of plants that are especially rich in nectar and pollen.

Achillea
Aster
Carrot
Chamomile
Cilantro
Cleome
Clover (white and scarlet)
Cosmos
Daisy (many kinds)
Daylily
Dill
Gypsophila (baby's breath)
Honeysuckle
Lantana
Lavender
Lemon balm
Nasturtium
Nepeta (catnip and catmint)
Parsley
Queen Anne's lace
Roses (with few or single petals)
Scented geraniums
Signet marigold
Silver sage
Sunflower (many kinds)
Sweet alyssum
Thyme
Valerian
Wild buckwheat (*Eriogonum* sp.)
Wildflowers
Zinnias

healthy plants within which pests and predators live side by side in balance with each other. Provide water in the garden for the beneficials to drink. A fish pond or a small garden fountain, an Indian grinding stone, or the top section of an old bird bath nestled down in the ground can do the trick. These work well because the sides are sloping so insects can reach the water. Finally, make sure there are pollen-bearing flowers, such as sweet alyssum or daisies, in the garden throughout the year, because when there aren't enough pests for them to eat, beneficial insects keep themselves alive by eating pollen and nectar. (See the box on page 129 for a list of pollen-bearing flowers.)

Annual and Perennial Flowers

A Word about Timing. April is an ideal month to plant warm-season annuals and perennials for summer color. In actual practice, however, most gardeners who planted cool-season flowers last fall have no room to plant in. All sunny beds are filled with flowers at the height of bloom now, at least until midmonth and typically until May. (Maintain these areas by deadheading, staking if necessary, and watering when rains aren't adequate.) The only beds bare of blooms now are those that were filled with cineraria or bulbs, now faded and ready to be replaced. If all your flowerbeds are bare of blooms in April, it's probably a sign that you didn't plant the right things at the right time. Don't despair; this fall you'll get another chance (see page 236).

For now, resist the urge to stock up on masses of spring flowers in bloom at the nursery, because they'll soon fade. It's very confusing to first-time local gardeners that in April nurseries are overflowing with cool-season flowers in full bloom. (The correct way to use

them is as fill-ins where something has died or faded. Or fill a pot or two for a party or special occasion.) Examples of items *not* to fill beds with now are calendulas, cineraria, dianthus, foxgloves, Iceland poppies, primroses, snapdragons, stock, violas, and pansies (except the newer heat-resistant varieties such as those in the Universal series).

Annual Flowers to Plant Now. Seeds of warm-season flowers to plant now include ageratum, anchusa, amaranth, calliopsis, cosmos, celosia, coleus, marigold, nicotiana, portulaca, scarlet sage, sweet alyssum, and verbena. (Except in the hottest areas wait until May to plant zinnias. They languish when planted in cold soil.) Save money by starting your own bedding plants from seeds that are easy to grow, such as ageratum, cosmos, marigolds, and scarlet sage, in flats of potting soil. Start them in semishade, cover them with a sheet of plastic, and keep them moist until germinated. As soon as they're up, remove the plastic, move them to sun, and water daily. When they've made two true leaves, start feeding for healthy growth. You'll have plenty of transplants to fill beds.

This is the best time of all to dress up patios with tubs and hanging baskets of warm-season annual flowers from nursery transplants. Annual flowers, and plants we treat as annuals, to put in now from pony packs and color packs include ageratum, globe amaranth, bedding begonias *(Begonia semperflorens)*, bellflowers (campanulas), dusty miller, gaillardia, impatiens, lobelia, Madagascar periwinkle (vinca; *Catharanthus roseus)*, marigolds, mealy-cup sage *(Salvia farinacea)*, nierembergia, petunia, and Swan River daisy *(Brachycome iberidifolia)*. Marguerites (Cobbitty daisy; *Argyranthemum frutescens)* can be planted now and will last until the end of June inland and up to three years in coastal zones, but they need watering every day. Euryops 'Green Gold' (*Euryops pectinatus* 'Viridis'), a permanent flowering shrub, is infinitely more drought resistant than marguerite. It's useful inland or along the coast. Some annual flowers, particularly daisy types such as cosmos, tend to shoot straight up on one stem and pop a bud on top. Pinch off this bud to encourage branching. It takes self-control to do this, because you destroy flowers, but it pays off with more bloom on bushier plants later.

Enjoy Your Perennials. As with annual flowers, perennial beds are usually filled to overflowing with color now. So place outdoor furniture strategically, on the grass if need be, so you and your friends can drink in the pleasures you've planted for. Also, pick bouquets of long-stemmed flowers to keep plants blooming and in bounds. If some of your alstroemerias are just a mass of foliage with many leafy, perhaps weak and droopy, stalks and few or no flower buds on them, it's time to shock the plant into blooming. Get down on your knees and yank off all those green leafy stalks. Don't clip them off. Take hold of each one low down on the stalk, give it a twist, and pull it off. Then water and fertilize the plant; almost immediately it will put out a mass of strong new stalks, each with flower buds on them. (Use this yanking method to deadhead or pick alstroemerias, instead of cutting off the stems, which will stop the plant from blooming.)

If you've just moved into a new house, or for some other reason have bare beds to fill, you'll find masses of perennials and flowering subshrubs in nurseries now, often in bloom. Even if you plant from 4-inch containers, they'll soon grow to larger sizes. Among plants in nurseries now are achillea (yarrow), alstroemeria, artemisia, 'African Blue' basil (a sterile hybrid that is a cross between *Ocimum* 'Dark Opal'

and African camphor basil *[O. canum],* courtesy of the bees in Athens, Ohio), bishop's weed (*Aegopodium podagraria;* plant it in shade), border penstemon (*Penstemon gloxinioides*), botanical geraniums, brachycome (*Brachycome multifida*), candytuft (*Iberis sempervirens*), Canterbury bell (*Campanula medium;* much beloved by children, it's also known as cup-and-saucer plant) and Italian bellflower (*C. isophylla),* catmint (*Nepeta faassenii),* columbine, convolvulus, coral bells, coreopsis, cranesbill (*Erodium*), crown pink (*Lychnis coronaria),* delphinium, dianthus, gaura, Jupiter's beard (*Centranthus ruber),* ladybells (*Adenephora liliifolia),* lavender (many kinds), licorice plant (*Helichrysum petiolare),* ornamental oreganos (*Origanum dictamnus* and others), pincushion flower (*Scabiosa*), rudbeckias, Santa Barbara daisy, scented geraniums (pelargoniums), star clusters (*Pentas lanceolata),* strawflower (*Bracteantha bracteatum),* thrift (*Armeria),* twinspur (*Diascia),* and wallflower. Another plant available now is New Zealand brass buttons (*Cotula squalida*), an easy plant to cover the ground under an open tree or cascade over a wall. It has spreading gray foliage with yellow button flowers that will spark up the garden through summer if not munched on by pests; bait cotula for slugs and snails and spray it with BT against caterpillars. Bellflowers (campanulas) also harbor snails and slugs. These and caterpillars are the main pests to watch for in the perennial garden this month. Unless you're vigilant, tiny caterpillars can vacuum all the petals off a mound of Santa Barbara daisies overnight.

Geraniums (and Erodiums)

What we commonly call a geranium is not a geranium at all—it's actually a pelargonium. *Geranium* is the botanical name of an entirely different group of plants. The flowers of true, or botanical, geraniums look symmetrical and have five separate overlapping petals. Pelargonium flowers also have five petals, but they are usually showier and have two petals pointing in one direction and three in another. Erodiums also look much like botanical geraniums, but they have only five stamens; geraniums have ten.

The botanical names for geraniums, erodiums, and pelargoniums came from the shapes of their fruits (seed containers), which were thought to resemble cranes, herons, and storks, respectively. The botanical name *Geranium* comes from the Greek word *geranos,* meaning crane; *Erodium* from *erodios,* meaning heron; and *Pelargonium* from *pelargos,* meaning stork. This is why geraniums are known as "cranesbills" and why erodiums are called "heronsbills." It's a shame pelargoniums didn't get the common name "storksbill" instead of "geranium," which has confused so many gardeners, especially now when dozens of geranium species and cultivars have been introduced to Southern California and several have become stalwart favorites. Here's a selection:

- *Geranium incanum*—The most popular true geranium, with a number of varieties and cultivars. It reseeds freely, spreads rapidly to about 4 feet and reaches about 18 inches high. Good in hanging baskets, it blooms year-round in coastal gardens. As it expands in size it flowers less freely; when that happens, cut it to the crown or dig it up and start over. It grows in full sun along the coast, needs some shade inland, goes dormant in frost.
- *G. 'Johnson's Blue'*—Good even in interior gardens because it can stand up to heat if given a little shade in summer. Goes dormant in winter but may be evergreen in some coastal gardens.
- Madeira Geranium *(G. maderense)*—An as-

tonishing plant in full bloom now, best in coastal zones. Biennial or occasionally perennial, it grows for the first two or three years as a foliage plant in full sun or part shade, creating a rosette of attractively shaped, fanlike leaves on strong stems splaying out from a central woody stalk. When the plant is ready to bloom, a massive inflorescence 3 or more feet in diameter and 4 feet tall emerges in March. Masses of purplish pink, 1½-foot flowers are displayed on sticky and hairy purple stems. Each flower lasts a day, but new ones constantly arise for a month to six weeks. The plant then dies, though offshoots may remain and many seedlings will spring up. (You can keep the flowers blooming for a special event in early May by deadheading the sticky little seed capsules daily.) Never prune off Madeira geranium's leaves or the plant will fall over. As the leaves fade, their stems bend down to support the plant.
- *G. riversleaianum* 'Mavis Simpson'—Mid-pink flowers blooming on annual flowering stems in a low mound; good in a large container or spilling over a wall; takes heat.
- *G. robustum*—Has the same cultural requirements as above but is larger and more vigorous than others; makes mound 2 to 3 feet tall and wide with slightly larger leaves, more substance, blue-gray foliage, and nonstop flowers. Good for embankments.
- *G. sanguineum striatum*—Mid-green leaves with white flowers irregularly splashed with violet-blue.

Pelargoniums (Garden Geraniums)

Begin spraying pelargoniums (geraniums) with BT for budworms in April (see page 126).

Pelargoniums are the plants most people call geraniums, thus creating a confusion between them and the true geranium (discussed above). Like their cousins the geraniums, pelargoniums are members of the geranium family (Geraniaceae). These tough, colorful, drought-resistant natives of South Africa are perfectly adapted to our climate. In cold-winter climates pelargoniums are the treasured aristocrats of the greenhouse, bought at precious price for the summer garden. Here they bloom year-round in frost-free zones, flowering happily on the edges of vacant lots or covering entire slopes in place of a lawn. There are many different kinds and four main categories:

- **Zonal geraniums** (*Pelargonium hortorum*) are the common upright garden variety, usually having double or single flowers in large, rounded clusters. Look closely to see a pattern or zonal marking on the leaves, hence the name. (More than fifty varieties of zonal geranium are grown, mainly for their colorful leaves in bright shades of pink, red, white, and yellow.) Zonal geraniums are outstanding in containers and window boxes and in pots on steps and balconies.
- **Ivy geraniums** (*P. peltatum*) are a largely disease-free and pest-resistant species with trailing stems and ivy-shaped leaves and a wide variety of flower shapes and colors. Excellent in hanging baskets, as ground covers in frost-free zones, and in flowerbeds. They need to be cut back and replanted occasionally, but their color display, peaking in spring and summer, is nearly year-round. There are also a number of crosses between zonal and ivy geraniums that combine the good qualities of each, are heat resistant, and stay compact in containers. 'Balcon' and 'Cascade' are among the best varieties for ground covers or in hanging baskets.

🌿 Quick Tip

Make an Easy Hanging Basket with a Continental Look. *In each 12-inch redwood basket or plastic container plant one 1-gallon-size, heat-resistant ivy geranium* (Pelargonium peltatum) *with tiny flowers, such as from the Balcon or Fischer Cascade series. (These are the ones seen spilling out of window boxes in Europe as far south as Italy.) Fill around them with good potting soil. Sprinkle the top of the soil with a few seeds of trailing blue lobelia, or, for a quicker start, add one transplant of lobelia from a pony pack to each corner of the container. Hang it in full sun or part shade, keep it damp, and feed it occasionally with a complete slow-release or liquid fertilizer (Peters 20-20-20 mixed half-strength or a similar formula).*

- **Martha Washingtons** or **Regals** (*P. domesticum*) are the geraniums gardeners most frequently refer to as pelargoniums. These have flowers reminiscent of azaleas. They're eye-catching in pots, beds, and borders and bloom mainly in spring and early summer, peaking in June.
- **Scented geraniums** are a group of over seventy separate species of pelargoniums with scented leaves, most of which are edible. Increasingly popular in recent years, scented geraniums are beloved for their charming appearance, fragrance, and usefulness as ground covers, in herb gardens, or as fillers in the perennial border. Several are good subjects for the drought-resistant landscape. Many are categorized as herbs because their leaves are used to flavor jellies and sauces and to decorate platters of food. Good landscape subjects include peppermint-scented geranium (*P. tomentosum*), an excellent ground cover spreading 2 to 4 feet wide in partial shade; rose geraniums (*P. graveolens*), a taller and rangier bush; lemon geranium (*P. crispum*), which

How to Grow Geraniums (Pelargoniums)

Here we discuss those plants that gardeners usually call "geraniums." Their correct botanical name is *Pelargonium* (as explained in the text).

- Plant pelargoniums in the ground or in containers in full sun along the coast, part shade inland. Most pelargoniums need at least four hours of sunlight every day with the exception of peppermint-scented geraniums and golden-leafed zonals, which can take light shade.

- Plant pelargoniums in well drained soil. (A mildly acid soil is ideal; at pH 5.5 and below poor growth will result.) When planting in clay soil, dig up the planting area and mix in a generous quantity of organic soil amendment. Then plant high, putting each plant on a slight mound so its crown is always dry. A good mix for pelargoniums in containers is 2 parts Supersoil to 1 part perlite.

- Provide irrigation when rains aren't adequate. Keep plants on the dry side; irrigate when the soil is dry to an inch or two from the surface.

- Fertilize once a month with a balanced, slow-release fertilizer, such as 14-14-14. Scented geraniums need little or no fertilizer unless you are growing them in containers; then feed half-strength. Martha Washingtons will flower better if fed before spring bloom.

- Control budworms with BT or a systemic such as Orthene. Begin spraying every year at the time of the first full moon in April (see page 126). Control rust with Daconil. (In coastal areas rust cannot be entirely eliminated.)

- Plant fresh, not old, cuttings of pelargoniums year-round. For optimum success, dip shears in alcohol prior to taking 2- to 3-inch tip cuttings. Dip the lower end of the cutting into rooting compound such as RooTone or Dip'N Grow, and plant in sterile soil mix in a sterile container.

- Prune pelargoniums according to their bloom schedule.

Zonals, ivy-leafed geraniums, and some species geraniums bloom year-round and thus should be pruned progressively year-round. Cut back a few ungainly stems each month by two-thirds of their length. With a ground-cover planting of ivy geraniums, shear all over when the plants grow lanky after heavy flowering. Martha Washington geraniums bloom in spring and summer. Cut these back progressively, beginning after bloom and stopping in November.

---

grows 2 to 3 feet tall; and nutmeg-scented geranium *(P. fragrans)*, which has small leaves and makes a mound 1 to 2 feet high. *P. sid-doides,* which comes in several colors including gray with burgundy, is much admired among perennials. Many others can be found in nurseries and the gardens of friends; in the latter case, ask for a cutting.

There are other groups of pelargoniums that are lesser known and less frequently grown. Some sport a weird, cactuslike appearance prized by collectors. Others are miniatures, and a few are best adapted for use as bonsai. For pelargonium culture, see the accompanying box.

Lawn Care

Feed, Water, Mow, and Plant. Feed all lawns this month, and water them thoroughly after feeding. Warm-season grasses are speeding up growth now and will need regular fertilizing throughout the warmer months. Water warm-season grasses deeply and infrequently to encourage deep rooting. Most cool-season grasses need more frequent and shallow watering.

All warm-season lawns can be planted from sod or stolons now, and common Bermuda can be planted from seed. Cool-season lawns can be put in from sod, although it's best to wait until October. (See page 157 for advice on lawn selection.)

How to Get a Huge Harvest of Sweet Corn

- Choose a good variety, such as the supersweet All American Award winner 'How Sweet It Is' or 'Kandy Korn'. Buy seeds for successive plantings of twelve to twenty plants at a time.

- Spade the ground deeply in a square area that gets full sun, north of shorter crops. (Corn is pollinated by wind. Pollen from the male flower must fall on the female silks, so plant in a block of several short rows rather than in one long, skinny row.) Mix organic soil amendment into the ground and cultivate a vegetable fertilizer (6-12-6, for example) into the top 6 inches according to package directions.

- Set up a drip system designed for row crops. Run the rows north to south, 3 feet apart (18 inches apart if space is at a premium). Mound the rows 4 inches high and 8 inches wide between furrows that are to be used as paths.

- Except in the hottest areas cover the entire area with black—not clear—plastic sheeting as mulch, to increase heat and yields.

- For supersweet varieties, presprout the seeds over bottom heat indoors. (The box on page 139 tells how.) Supersweet varieties have a "shrunken gene" that causes their seeds to be shriveled and difficult to germinate if soil is cool.

- As soon as the seeds sprout, plant them 2 inches deep and 12 to 18 inches apart in each row. (If the rows are only 18 inches apart, use the wider spacing within rows for a bigger harvest.) For each, use a razor blade to slit a 4-inch-square X in the plastic mulch, make a 2-inch-deep hole with your finger, and put the seed in with the root pointing down and the sprout pointing up. Press the soil gently back together. Fold the cut edges of plastic under and slip the lower edge of an upside-down berry basket into the slit area to protect seed from birds. (The berry basket will exactly fit the square space you have cut and be held firmly in place.)

- Water with a drip system—daily in sandy soil or twice or three times weekly in clay soil—until sprouts emerge. Gradually lengthen spacing between waterings until you're watering deeply and well about every three days in sandy soil, once a week in clay.

- When leaves reach the tops of the berry baskets, remove the baskets. Plant more corn in two weeks, and feed the first batch with fish emulsion.

- When the corn tassels out, give it extra water and feed it thoroughly with a balanced liquid fertilizer—for example, 2 tablespoons of Terr-O-Vite and 2 of 0-10-10 per gallon of water. Send this through the drip line, pour it around plants with a watering can, or, using a water wand attached to a siphon, soak the ground under the plastic with it. If you prefer to use granulated fertilizer, apply nitrogen fertilizer when the corn is 12 to 18 inches high and again when it is 24 to 30 inches high. Use 1 to 1½ pounds of actual nitrogen per 1,000 square feet of planted area.

- For full ears in a small plot, hand-pollinate: when tassels bloom with dusty pollen, break off sections and whip them on the silks at the tops of the ears. (So growth will be activated in every kernel, each silk needs one grain of pollen.)

Why Some Sweet Corn Varieties Must Be Isolated from Other Varieties

Because each kernel is individually pollinated by wind, corn easily crossbreeds when different varieties that mature at the same time are planted closely together. Sweet corn, popcorn, field corn, and ornamental varieties can all interbreed. For this reason, it's best to plant only one variety of sweet corn in staggered plantings or plant an early, a mid-season, and a late variety so that they will not produce pollen at the same time. Be particularly careful when planting SE and SH2 varieties. (See the accompanying box.) Also, when planting popcorn and ornamental corn, make sure maturity dates will be different from all other corn varieties. Pollination between two different types of corn will make your corn starchy and bland tasting.

Mow all lawns once a week to keep them at their proper height, as described on page 108.

Vegetable Gardening

Continue to Plant Summer Vegetables. Did you plant summer vegetables last month? If so you'll get an early harvest. If not, don't be discouraged; it's not too late. Many vegetables prefer being put in now. Among vegetables to plant now from seeds are green beans, beets, carrots, corn, endive, leaf (not head) lettuce, New Zealand spinach, pumpkins, radishes, salsify, squash, sunflowers, Swiss chard, and turnips. Put in transplants of cucumbers and tomatoes.

This is the last month to plant seed potatoes (as described on page 111; also see the section following on mounding and harvesting potatoes). In hot interior zones plant sweet potatoes beginning this month. This is the first month for

🐌 Quick Tip

How to Secure Plastic Mulch to the Ground. *With wire cutters cut the bent ends off wire coat hangers to make arched sections approximately 5 inches long. Shove them through the plastic down into the ground all around the edges and here and there on the paths (taking care not to spear drip lines). These can be used for several seasons.*

putting in the heat lovers: eggplant, peppers, okra, lima beans, cantaloupe, and watermelon. If you live in a fog bank, wait until May to plant cantaloupe. In this case, it usually isn't worthwhile to plant watermelons; they grow better inland.

Plant Herbs among Your Vegetables. Continue planting culinary herbs in April. Put in basil, oregano, parsley, rosemary, sage, summer savory, and thyme from nursery transplants. (You can also plant parsley and basil from seeds.) Cilantro and arugula can be grown throughout summer in semishade in some gardens, but they prefer cooler weather. Grow French tarragon (*Artemisia dracunculus*), horseradish, and mint in containers; they're invasive. (Don't be fooled into buying tasteless Russian tarragon *[Artemisia dracunculoides]* by mistake.)

Plant for Successive Crops. If you planted vegetables last month, continue to put in seeds now for additional crops. Many gardeners plant too much at one time; then it all matures at once, and they're swamped. A similar problem is planting too much of one crop; zucchini can easily overwhelm the unwary. Two or three plants are plenty for a family of four. A row will feed an army. Vegetables to plant successively are those that you harvest over a short period (a

Understanding Sweet Corn Varieties and High-Sugar Genes

Sweet corn varieties are available in white, yellow, or bicolor kernel colors and in tall or short sizes. They also come in varying maturities that are categorized as early (60 to 70 days), mid-season (70 to 80 days), or late season (90 or more days). Additionally, you can choose varieties for their genetic heritage. These are explained below.

- **Open-Pollinated Varieties**—Old sweet corn varieties like 'Gold Bantam', 'Early Gold Bantam', and 'Country Gentleman' are "open pollinated," meaning that the seed was derived from a natural pollination process, such as insects or (in the case of corn) wind, and that it will breed true, or nearly so. (Open-pollinated varieties change gradually as the years go by through natural or human selection.) You can save and plant seed from these.

- **SU, or Standard Varieties or "normals"**—The seeds of these modern F1 hybrids—including 'Silver Queen', 'Golden Midget', and 'Early Sunglow', are derived from a cross between two other varieties; thus they are the first generation (F1) after the cross. Hybrids have what is called "hybrid vigor." They provide the gardener with such characteristics as high yields, disease and pest resistance, sweetness, and dependable harvest.

- **SH2** or **Supersweet Hybrids**—This genetic type (SH2), including such varieties as 'Illini Extra Sweet', 'Early Extra Sweet', and 'How Sweet It Is', has sugar content twice as great as standard sweet corn at peak maturity. SH2 types are called "supersweet," "ultrasweet," or "extrasweet." The term "SH2" stands for "shrunken 2" because when the kernels dry their seed coats shrink, giving the seed a shriveled appearance. Supersweet varieties retain their sweet flavor longer than ordinary sweet corn both on the stalk and after harvest. But SH2 varieties must be isolated from other types of sweet corn, or else foreign pollen will make hard, ugly dented kernels on the SH2 ear. (See the accompanying box on isolation.)

- **Sugary Enhanced (SE) Hybrids**—Varieties in this class, including 'Kandy Korn', 'Earli Glow', and 'Snow Queen', are the result of a cross that produces a sweet flavor and tender texture. This genetic type (SE) contains genetically higher sugar levels, revolutionary in the flavor of sweet corn. The seed coat of this type is not shrunken like supersweet, so it sprouts more easily in the ground. It is also much sweeter than regular sweet corn and retains its flavor before and after harvest. SE hybrids must be isolated from SH2 hybrids but not from other SE varieties or SU varieties.

week or two), like corn and bush beans, or those in which individuals are harvested wholly, like carrots or beets. Lettuce can go either way; you can take just the outside leaves to extend the harvest or cut whole heads. When planting successively, use a quarter or a third of a package of seed at intervals of two to three weeks. Choose interesting varieties. Carrots, for example, come in many sizes, sweetness levels, and degrees of crunchiness. Grow several and taste-test them with your family.

Thin Those Rows. Don't forget to keep thinning your vegetable rows according to package directions. When you thin leafy vegetables like lettuce, transplant the extras into another row, but don't try this with carrots; they split when they're transplanted. Thinning seed rows—and flowerbeds, too—is a task too often neglected by first-time gardeners. People hate to do it because it seems so wasteful. Actually the reverse is true. You won't feel sad about thinning rows if you remember that overabundant plants have the

🐾 Quick Tip

Vegetable Space Saver. *For three crops in one space, interplant corn with pole or lima beans and one or two pumpkins or the kind of winter squash that grows on a sprawling vine, such as 'Sweet Mama'. The beans will climb up the corn and need no support. The squash or pumpkins will give you another crop on the ground (and incidentally will discourage raccoons from stealing your corn if these masked bandits live in your neighborhood).*

effect of weeds; by competing with one another they stunt your crops. This is especially true of plants like onions that have shallow roots.

Prune Tomatoes and Avoid Problems. You can train tomatoes several ways (as described on page 114). If you plan to grow them on stakes or a trellis prune each plant now to one or two major vines, by pinching off the suckers that grow as side branches above leaf joints. Check them weekly; they grow fast.

Occasionally gardeners complain of getting no fruit. This can happen if the plants are growing in shade. Sometimes plants have green growth but no flowers. This comes from too much nitrogen (treat the ground around the plants with liquid 0-10-10 to correct it). If plants flower but the blossoms drop off without fruiting, they may have been allowed to dry out completely. Other causes of bud drop are temperatures lower than 55°F or higher than 75°F at night or 105°F in the daytime. Desert dwellers should grow tomatoes during the fall, winter, and early spring months.

If low temperatures are the source of your problem, grow early varieties until the weather warms up, or try using a tomato blossom-set spray. Use it exactly according to directions: one slight burst of spray about 10 inches from each

bunch of flowers only three times, at intervals of ten days. Sometimes flowers drop off because they weren't pollinated. This can happen in wet weather or in greenhouses. Tomatoes have "perfect," or self-pollinating, flowers. The pollen has to go only a short distance within the flower, from the anthers onto the sticky stigma. Wind does the job more than bees, so if there's no wind there won't be any fruit. You can improve pollination of your tomatoes by rapping with a hammer on tomato stakes or cages in the middle of the day, when the weather's warm and dry.

Watch for Tomato Blights. Early blight and late blight are two major blights affecting tomatoes in foggy or rainy weather. Late blight causes downy mold on lower surfaces of leaves, drying and shriveling of leaves, water-soaked spots on stems, and grayish water-soaked spots on fruit. Rotting fruits have an offensive odor. Infected fruit is inedible. Early blight causes dark spots with light centers with concentric rings on leaves and stems, browning and dying back of lowest branches, and discoloration of fruit. Severe blight can cause almost complete defoliation, exposing fruit to sunscald. You can eat the fruit if you cut off the diseased portions. If your plants were infected with either of these blights last year, the spores may have endured in the soil; therefore, the following year, do not prune plants because infection can enter the plant through pruning cuts. Treat infected plants with Ortho Multi-Purpose Fungicide—Daconil 2787. Dusting with sulfur can also be helpful. (Refer to the *Ortho Problem Solver* for more information about tomato diseases.)

Mound and Harvest Potatoes. Until potato plants have grown 10 inches high, use a hoe to mound soil up around the stalks, but leave the leafy portion sticking out of the top. This in-

How to Presprout Seed for a Fast Start with No Rot

Some seeds, planted in the ground, may rot instead of growing. Examples are any beans planted in cold, wet soil, some varieties of sugar peas that have shriveled-looking seeds, and supersweet varieties of sweet corn that also have shriveled seeds caused by the "shrunken" gene that makes them so sweet. In these cases it's easy, timesaving, and worthwhile to sprout seeds indoors. Here's how:

- Wet a paper towel. Squeeze it out and spread it flat. Place a few more seeds than you need on half the towel, arranging them so they don't touch each other. Bend the other half over. Put the whole thing, flat, in a zip-locked plastic bag and seal it up.

- Place the plastic bag containing the paper towel and seeds over bottom heat at approximately 70°F. Possible heat sources include low-wattage lightbulbs; radiantly heated floors; antidampness bars used to keep closets, towels, and pianos dry;

heat vents; water heaters; or even the tops of TVs or VCRs. (If a lightbulb or heating bar is used, elevate the seeds on a cookie sheet or metal tray to diffuse the heat.)

- Check your seeds daily; add moisture if needed. Bean seeds sprout in about three days, corn and peas in four or five. As soon as they sprout, plant them in the garden. Handle them gently; don't break their roots.

- To plant, make a hole with your finger deep enough for the thin white root to go straight down; the thicker, yellowish sprout should point up. (In cool weather plant the seed only an inch deep. After the sprout comes up, you can mound the soil higher around it.) Press the soil gently but firmly from the sides to make good contact. If some sprouts fail to come up, presprout some more and replant to fill gaps in the row.

creases the harvest and keeps the potatoes cool and dark. (Potato skins turn green if they're exposed to light; all green portions of potatoes are poisonous, including stems, leaves, fruit, and sprouts.) If before mounding soil around the stems you first mix it with nitrolized wood shavings or homemade compost, harvesting becomes much easier. Stop mounding the soil when the mound is 5 or 6 inches high or when the plants begin to flower.

When flowers appear, some tubers have grown. You can then gently push the soft, amended soil aside and use a trowel to dig up just the number of small new potatoes you want for dinner. Replace the mound so the remaining potatoes will be protected from heat and sunlight. When the leaves begin to turn yellow with age, you can harvest as many full-grown new potatoes as desired. Leave smaller tubers in the

ground to continue growing. Once the tops of the plant have completely withered and died, harvest the remainder by digging up the whole row with a garden fork. Leave these mature potatoes on top of the earth to dry for two or three hours; then store them in a cool dark place at 40° to 45°F. If you store them at over 50°F, they'll sprout and eventually spoil.

Protect Lettuce against Pests. Bait lettuce against slugs and snails with a product recommended for the vegetable garden, or cut them off at the pass by baiting with a long-lasting snail bait, such as Deadline, around the entire perimeter of the garden. Watch for leafhoppers; they spread viral diseases. (Spray for them with insecticidal soap, or control them with diatomaceous earth if you feel it's absolutely necessary, but the latter will kill ladybugs and other beneficials, including spiders.)

Introduce beneficials, as discussed in the preceding section on pest control. Ladybugs, lacewings, trichogramma wasps, and other beneficials are especially important in the vegetable garden because most gardeners prefer not to spray vegetables with pesticides. Be sure to put ladybugs where you see whiteflies and aphids. Control caterpillars with BT.

Purchase/Plant

- ❏ Continue to plant drought-resistant plants, 32, 118
- ❏ Choose and plant azaleas while the greatest number of plants are in bloom, 118
- ❏ If you live in the desert or in a hot inland valley, finish all spring planting this month, 118
- ❏ Choose and plant wisteria while it is in bloom, 118
- ❏ Purchase epiphyllums, 119
- ❏ Plant dahlias, 121
- ❏ Plant water lilies, 124
- ❏ Plant warm-season flowers, 130
- ❏ Plant tubs and hanging baskets, 130
- ❏ Continue to plant summer vegetables, 136
- ❏ Plant corn, 136
- ❏ Plant herbs, 136
- ❏ Plant tropicals in inland valleys, 118
- ❏ Start perennials from seeds in interior zones, 173
- ❏ Purchase, plant, and transplant succulents, including cacti and euphorbias, 194
- ❏ Now through summer choose, plant, and naturalize bromeliads, 196
- ❏ Plant geraniums and erodiums, 131
- ❏ Plant pelargoniums, 132

Trim, Prune, Mow, Divide

- ❏ Break off suckers from artichokes, 114
- ❏ Remove suckers from tomatoes and tie up the vines, 138
- ❏ Take cuttings from epiphyllums, and root them to make new plants, 120
- ❏ Cut back poinsettias, 119
- ❏ Trim hedges and screens, including pittosporum, myoporum, and photinia, 120
- ❏ Thin out fruit on deciduous fruit trees, 121
- ❏ Prune roses by picking, deadheading, and disbudding, 122
- ❏ Mow lawns, 134
- ❏ Thin vegetable crops planted last month according to package directions (including beans), 137
- ❏ Stop pinching fuchsias when plants are well filled out and bushy. Remove seedpods often after flowers fall, 100
- ❏ Start to prune and train espaliers as they begin to grow, 211
- ❏ Propagate daylilies by planting their proliferates, 250
- ❏ Divide and plant dahlia tubers you lifted from the ground in December, 293

Fertilize

- ❏ Feed citrus trees, 50
- ❏ Feed avocado trees, 66
- ❏ Feed fuchsias, 168
- ❏ Feed tuberous begonias, 185
- ❏ Feed irises, 121
- ❏ Fertilize roses, 122
- ❏ Feed water lilies, 125
- ❏ Fertilize lawns, 134
- ❏ Fertilize peppers when flowers first show, 200
- ❏ Feed and water cycads, 220
- ❏ Treat blue hydrangeas with aluminum sulfate, 232
- ❏ Do not fertilize onions after they begin to make a bulb, 59

Continued>>

Water

❏ Water all garden plants according to need when rains are inadequate, 54

❏ Keep all vegetables well watered, particularly globe artichokes, 113

❏ Water roses, 122

❏ Water lawns, 134

❏ Don't let tomatoes dry out, 138, 200

Control Pests, Diseases, and Weeds

❏ Control crabgrass with a final treatment of preemergent herbicide, 58, 84

❏ Continue to control slugs and snails, particularly on irises and lettuce, 91, 139

❏ Control rose pests and diseases, 122

❏ Spray with BT against caterpillars if necessary, 125

❏ Control fuchsia gall mite, 126

❏ Control spider mites, 127

❏ Control eugenia psyllid, 128

❏ Release beneficials, 128

❏ Protect corn from raccoons, 138

❏ Control leafhoppers, 139

❏ Cultivate to remove weeds among shrubs and trees, 40

❏ Control weeds among vegetables and flowers by hand-pulling, 40

❏ Release ladybugs, 128

❏ Watch for tomato blights, 138

Also This Month

❏ Move tuberous begonias started in flats into pots or beds, 96

❏ Keep bamboo from running into your neighbor's garden, 103

❏ See spring flowers including wildflowers and native plants in full bloom, 117

❏ Continue to tie up leaves of bulbs that have bloomed, 122

❏ Treat cut roses to keep them fresh, 123

❏ Consider building a garden pond, 123

❏ Avoid problems with tomatoes, 138

❏ Begin to harvest potatoes, as needed, when blossoms show, 138

❏ Presprout hybrid corn if it won't germinate, 139

❏ Harvest vegetables while they're young and tender, 159, 201

❏ Save branches from pruning to use as pea stakes to support flowers, 259

MAY

The Fast-Growth Month

If you finished your spring planting in March or April, May is the month to watch everything grow. In good years, when seasonal rains have been generous, excess salts have been washed down into the ground and the entire landscape has been well watered. The gardener has helped things along by adding mulch and fertilizer in March. Now, as the weather gets warmer, all growth systems go full speed ahead. You can almost see some plants expand, especially the trees and bushes put in last fall.

May is also a month for catching up on neglected tasks. If you didn't finish spring planting in March and April, do it now. Heat-loving plants take off even better in May. If you live in an interior valley, waste no time getting your final planting done. Interior gardeners can safely expect occasional spells—two or three days long—of scorching heat this month.

While conventional landscape plants, most of which are imported, are beginning a season of fast growth, native plants are in a season of withdrawal. The chaparral is drying up and most wildflowers are going brown and setting seed. Many wild plants pull in their horns and let leaves fall as nature prepares for a long dry season. Those who live in interior valleys or near a canyon or wild hillside may sense a bit of nostalgia in the air this month similar to that in fall back East.

Deep Watering

From now until November the gardener's main task is to water deeply and appropriately for each plant, whenever available water supplies and local regulations allow it. In drought years, some plants may suffer during the late spring and summer from lack of adequate water. Observe which plants these are and consider replacing them with better choices. If you grow native plants, learn which ones can accept summer water and which cannot. All native plants need irrigation to get started. Some, such as monkey flower (*Mimulus* species and Verity hybrids), can be kept blooming longer by gradually replacing rainfall with some summer water. Others, including bush poppy (*Dendromecon rigida*) and woolly blue curls (*Trichostema lanatum*), may succumb to root rot if watered at all. Take the cue from nature and begin to taper off on watering these plants.

Because the price of water continually rises and domestic cutbacks occur whenever there's a drought, wise gardeners are thinking of ways to make the garden less thirsty. If you haven't already installed a drip system to water everything you otherwise would water with the hose, such as container-grown plants, now's a good time to do the job. Also, study your sprinkler system and see whether adjustments can be made to conserve water in the months ahead.

Irises

Bearded irises, those with a hairlike tuft on the falls, or lower petals, bloom this month. Whether or not you're growing them now, enjoy them in bloom, and consider planting some; the rhizomes can be found at nurseries in fall. They're among our best perennials—good in all zones, easy to grow, and not overly thirsty. See displays of them at botanical gardens and nurseries, and watch for newspaper announcements of shows.

Hybridizers have developed many kinds and heights of iris, but the tall bearded ones are the easiest to start with, and they're the most frequently grown. They prefer rich, humusy, well-drained soil but will accept almost any soil as long as they have full sun along the coast, six hours of sun inland, and moderate irrigation and protection from snails. If you have irises in your garden but they're not blooming, chances are they're growing in too much shade or need dividing (page 168 tells how).

Among other rhizomatous irises to consider growing are the spuria irises, which make tall clumps, bloom in June and July, and need little summer water, and in light shade the native Pacific Coast irises (*Iris douglasiana*), which are spring blooming, drought resistant, low growing, and good for naturalizing.

Cymbidiums

Now begins the main growing season for cymbidiums, terrestrial orchids that are usually grown in containers. The quality and number of flowers you get next winter partly depends on good summer care.

Although cymbidiums shouldn't be soggy, don't let them dry out. Move those that have finished blooming into less-conspicuous places for a season of growth. Through midsummer keep these Asian orchids in semishade, such as under an open tree; then in late summer (see page 183) bring them out into more light. Or keep them year-round under 50 percent shade cloth (35 percent in coastal zones).

As blossoms fade, cut off the bloom spikes and start feeding the cymbidiums with a complete fertilizer high in growth ingredients. An easy way to feed them is to sprinkle a small handful (2 or 3 tablespoons) of slow-release fertilizer, such as Osmocote or Acme 14-14-14, on top of the soil mix in each 5-gallon container once a month. The plant is then fed every time it's watered. Some gardeners prefer to apply liquid fertilizer—30-10-10, for example—once every two to four weeks. For this use a siphon attachment to draw fertilizer solution out of a bucket directly into the hose.

Transplant cymbidiums that have outgrown their containers no later than the end of June, in order not to destroy the next flowering cycle. They can flower well even when crowded, so wait until they're pushing against the sides of the container to repot them into the next size container. Don't be in a hurry to divide them. A huge plant with twenty bloom spikes can be a showstopper in a home garden. (A half whiskey barrel makes a fine container.) Divide them (see the box on page 146) when plants become too big to handle.

Camellias and Azaleas

Feed, Mulch, and Prune Camellias. Fertilize camellias after they finish blooming. Camellias aren't gluttons; they need only a light application three times a year. The **Rule of Thumb** is: *Feed camellias for the first time as soon as they've finished blooming, feed them again four to six weeks after that, and finally feed them six weeks later.* Mark these times on your calendar. Use an acid-type, preferably organic, commercial fertilizer especially recommended for camellias and azaleas, or make your own mix of 3 parts cottonseed meal to 1 part chelated iron, such as Tru-Green's organic chelate blend. Feed ⅙ cup of this mix to a young plant, ⅓ cup to mature plants, and 2 to 3 cups to large trees, per feeding. Sprinkle the fertilizer all over the ground under the branches but especially in a wide band under the drip line, and water it into the ground.

Never cultivate under camellias. Cover the ground with a fresh layer of mulch, such as fir bark or pine needles, to keep the roots cool and happy.

If you haven't yet pruned your camellias do the job now, to maintain the size you want, improve their shape, and increase bloom. Look closely at the tip of a branch. Notice the bump where last year's growth began and then the growth of the year before that. You can cut back into last year's growth or that of the year before and cause buds farther back on the branch to send out shoots. If this is done right after flowering there'll be no loss of flowers next year; in fact, there'll be more. You can even cut way back into smooth gray-barked wood to renew an old plant that's gotten out of hand, but in this case flowering won't resume for a year or two.

Feed, Mulch, and Prune Azaleas. Fertilize azaleas as soon as they've finished blooming. The **Rule of Thumb** is: *Azaleas need fertilizing only twice a year, once as soon as they've finished blooming and again in late September.* Some people feed them more often—and it's all right to give a lackluster plant a shot of Terr-O-Vite in midsummer—but many an azalea has been killed by overfeeding.

Feed with a dry pelletized or powdered commercial fertilizer especially recommended for camellias and azaleas and follow package directions, or use cottonseed meal and iron as recommended above for camellias. You'll need a yardstick to measure the height of plants as well as your plastic measuring cup marked "Garden." Sprinkle the fertilizer in a wide band under the drip line. You can, if you wish, work it down through the mulch with a gloved hand, but as with camellias, don't ever cultivate under an azalea, even with your fingers. Delicate feeder roots lie right under the surface and can easily be damaged.

It's also time to clean up and prune azaleas. Leaves may remain where they fall, but be sure to remove all dead blossoms to prevent blossom

How to Divide and Repot a Cymbidium

Cymbidium orchids need dividing when they overcrowd their containers or get too heavy to carry.

• Water plants well before dividing them.

• Use a can cutter or sharp knife to cut off the plastic container. If the plants are in a wooden tub, remove the old container with a hammer, and discard it.

• Use a large kitchen knife kept for gardening to cut between the pseudobulbs (the bulblike structures growing above ground) and down through the roots. Aim for at least three productive pseudobulbs and four or five back bulbs per division. (Back bulbs are fully grown pseudobulbs that once bore leaves and flower spikes but now are bare. They act as storage containers for the remainder of the plant.)

• Trim off all roots that are diseased, damaged, or simply messy. In all, you should remove about one-third of the roots.

• Optionally, soak the divisions in a solution of 1 quart bleach to 10 quarts water for ten minutes to kill any fungus or rot. Allow them to dry.

• To replant, choose plastic containers that have plenty of holes in the bottom and are the next size larger, or approximately 4 to 6 inches wider than the top of the root ball. (Oversize containers slow growth.)

• Hold the plant so that the bottom of the pseudobulbs is level with the top of the container. Fill around the roots all the way to the top of the container with a commercial soil mix recommended for cymbidiums or a homemade mix, such as 2 gallons pathway bark, 2 gallons ground nitrolized wood shavings, and 1 gallon commercial sterilized potting soil (Supersoil is one such brand). It's important to make sure the roots are completely covered with soil mix and the pseudobulbs totally above ground. (If the pseudobulbs are buried, they'll rot.)

• Water the cymbidiums thoroughly after planting, keep them in semishade, and wait two or three weeks before starting to fertilize.

blight from getting a foothold. Azaleas take well to pruning because the dormant buds that will respond to it are hidden under the bark all the way to the ground. Cut out old or ungainly branches and pinch back tips to promote bushiness. The easiest way to get a really professional look is to give azaleas a butch haircut now. Start by watering the plants deeply. Then, using hedge shears, shear off all the tip growth. Next year you'll have a solid blanket of flowers all over the top of the plant.

Roses

Continue to control rose pests and diseases and to water, fertilize, and prune them by picking flowers and disbudding. Follow the guidelines given in March (beginning on page 94) but, as in April, irrigate twice a week now, up to 1½ inches of water per irrigation (see page 122).

If you're fertilizing with commercial rose food, feed your roses with it four weeks after their last feeding. If you're following the Rose-Pro Method of fertilizing, switch now from sulfate of ammonia to urea and reduce the frequency of feedings. Now through July, feed 1 level tablespoon of urea (45-0-0) to each plant every other week. (Through the ages, up until the 1920s, the only food most roses ever got was animal manure over their roots plus extra nitrogen from human urine, a natural source of urea. Roses are gluttons for nitrogen and need a lot more of it than most home gardeners realize.) The reason for switching to urea now is that it's less acid than sulfate of ammonia, so by using it you avoid making the soil too acid for roses. Also, because it's based on an organic compound, it's more effective after the soil has warmed up. Don't use urea on dry soil, and always irrigate thoroughly after applying it; it's a strong source of nitrogen and could burn roots unless it's well diluted. (Continue to spray with micronutrients, as described on page 95.)

You can also plant canned roses this month. Prepare planting holes as for bare-root roses (as described on page 46), but omit building a mound on the bottom of the hole.

Tropicals

Late spring is an excellent time to put in tropicals of all kinds, including citrus and other tropical fruit trees, tropical flowering trees, palms, philodendrons, and flowering vines such as bougainvillea. (See page 159 for harvest times of dwarf citrus for year-round fruit and page 167 for instructions on planting bougainvilleas.) Tropicals are planted during their active growing season. If you live in a hot interior valley, April is an even better month to plant tropicals, because the weather can become scorching by late May and may burn your newly planted specimens.

Many tropicals don't actually have a built-in dormant season. In a warm climate and a jungle they grow year-round, sometimes in spurts to coincide with the alternating wet-dry seasons that last two or three months in their native habitat. Here in Southern California it's up to the gardener to get tropicals to grow fast during the warm months and rest from growth in winter—even though it's our rainy season. The way to do this is to feed and water your tropicals in spring and summer but withhold fertilizer in

early fall and water less when the weather cools down. Putting tropicals in the ground now in spring gives them a chance to get established all summer long, then slow down and harden off in fall so they can survive light frosts.

Ferns

Start feeding ferns once every two or three weeks now, and continue until fall. Native ferns that sprang to life with the first rain last fall, beneath toyons and on canyon walls, are dying down now and dropping fronds. They need no fertilizer. But most of the ferns we grow in our gardens and houses have awakened from winter torpor and are well into their season of fastest growth.

Ferns are ancient plants with poor plumbing systems. Most require shade, perfect drainage, and acid soil, and they have to be fed with care. Feed most ferns every three or four weeks during spring and summer with a well-diluted, complete, liquid fertilizer. (Feed staghorn ferns less frequently, as discussed below.) High nitrogen often spells "good-bye fern" if the fern is dry before you feed it. The safest food is fish emulsion, mixed according to package directions, because it's nonburning. Cottonseed meal is another good organic fertilizer for ferns. Or you can choose a complete formula recommended for houseplants or flowering plants, such as Spoonit 18-20-16, and apply it according to package directions, but take care that the soil is thoroughly moist before you fertilize. Ferns appreciate the high phosphorus and potassium plus trace elements that they can get from this or a similar formula. The humus-filled, acid soil mixes in which ferns are grown may contain little or none of these elements.

Now's the best time to transplant ferns that have outgrown their containers. When their

How to Renew a Hanging Squirrel's Foot or Bear's Foot Fern

- Using a keyhole saw, clippers, and long-handled loppers, saw and cut out the entire center of the root-filled basket.

- Rebuild the sides of the basket with fresh, damp sphagnum moss.

- Fill the cavity you've made with fresh, well-drained potting mix.

- Cut the growing tips from the removed portion of fern, dip them in a rooting compound such as RooTone or Dip'N Grow, knock off the excess, and plant them in the top of the basket. (Use leftover cuttings to start a new basket.)

- Attach a fresh set of wires or chains strong enough to hold up the plant.

- Keep the plant damp and in a shady, protected spot for two or three weeks until it's rooted; then feed it with diluted fish emulsion every week or two to speed its growth until it's well established.

roots fill their containers, repot 'Dallas' and 'Kimberly Queen' ferns to the next sizes, in fast-draining, acid soil mix. 'Dallas' and 'Kimberly Queen' are varieties of Boston fern (*Nephrolepis exaltata* 'Bostoniensis') that can flourish with less light than ordinary Boston ferns, and they grow more vigorously. (Repotting an ordinary Boston fern usually kills it unless it's growing in a greenhouse.)

Footed ferns, such as squirrel's foot fern (*Davallia trichomanoides*) and bear's foot fern (*Humata tyermannii),* are best adapted to growing in hanging baskets. Eventually the baskets become filled and covered with a solid mass of unproductive roots, and the plants begin to look distinctly ratty. Now's the time to renew them (see the accompanying box).

Collect Easy-Care Staghorn Ferns. Staghorn ferns (*Platycerium* sp.) are a group of about seventeen species of strikingly shaped, tropical, epiphytic ferns that are prized by plant collectors. (Certain of them are also called elkhorn, giant staghorn, or moosehorn ferns.) They attach themselves to the bark, branches, or crotches of trees by means of hairlike roots, and they grow two distinctly different kinds of fronds. The sterile fronds, which are at first green but go brown with age, are shaped like shields; they support the plant by accumulating organic matter and by wrapping themselves around the tree or branch on which the plant grows. The fertile fronds are green regardless of age and shaped like antlers; they jut out from the plant and bear spores on their undersides. (A spore is a microscopic, spherical, single-celled reproductive unit that's used in place of seeds by some primitive plants, including ferns, fungi, moss, and algae.)

The various common names of platycerium ferns match their striking shapes. The true staghorn fern (*P. bifurcatum)* has fertile fronds shaped like stags' antlers and is the easiest one to grow. (Individual specimens have withstood temperatures as low as 20°F when protected by a shade structure, and the species is widely grown as an ornamental patio plant in both coastal and inland gardens.) Elkhorn ferns (*P. hillii, P. veitchii,* and *P. willinckii)* are very similar in appearance to staghorn ferns but generally less hardy. Giant staghorn or moosehorn ferns— *P. grande* is the easiest one of these to grow—are highly decorative and well adapted to coastal gardens. Their 3- or 4-foot-long fertile fronds are shaped like moose's antlers, and they have majestic bright green, sterile fronds that often grow 4 or 5 feet wide. Moosehorn ferns are usually raised in greenhouses and adapt to gardens best when purchased and put outdoors now.

Keep all staghorns in bright, indirect light or

in filtered sunshine. Protect them from hot sun, winds, and cold weather. When you water them drench them thoroughly, but then allow the moss (or soil) to dry out before you water again. Platyceriums are much more drought resistant than their lush tropical appearance might lead you to think. In dry interior zones water staghorns thoroughly about twice a week during the summer and once a week in winter. Along the coast water them once a week in summer and once every two weeks in winter. (In any zone, a heat wave or a Santa Ana may make more frequent watering necessary, but feel with your finger to make sure. It's important not to overwater your staghorn ferns because they'll rot.)

Staghorns are easy-care plants. They need to be fed only once every two or three months, beginning in spring. Don't feed them during winter. The easiest way to fertilize staghorns is to drench them with a complete liquid fertilizer such as 18-20-16, mixed according to package directions.

Moosehorn ferns aren't easy to propagate, but you can do so with a combination of luck and patience. First, wait until one of the brown spore patches under the fertile fronds flakes off easily when you lightly rub it. This means those spores are ripe. Sterilize a clear plastic shoebox by washing it in a solution of 1 quart of water and 2 tablespoons of bleach. Allow the shoebox to air-dry, and then fill it with a 3-inch-deep layer of damp, sterilized peat moss. Hold the prepared shoebox directly under the spore patch, and with clean hands sprinkle some of the ripe spores—they're like fine, brown dust— onto the surface of the damp peat moss. Close up the box and keep it in bright light but out of direct sun and in a warm place (daytime temperatures of 72° to 80°F, and nighttime temperatures about 10 degrees cooler). Use distilled water to keep the contents damp, but never

Quick Tip

How to Sterilize Potting Soil or Peat Moss.
Thoroughly moisten 1 gallon of potting soil or peat moss. (Moisten peat moss by mixing it with 3 cups of boiling water.) Spoon the soil or peat moss into a plastic cooking bag; make a hole in the top of the bag, and place it in a baking pan. When using a conventional oven, bake at 350°F for fifteen minutes. When using a microwave oven, cook on high for three minutes per quart of soil. (Cooking times may vary depending on your oven, so watch over this process closely. When the soil or peat moss is steaming hot throughout, it's done.) Place the bag outdoors and allow the contents to cool to 70°F before you use it.

soggy, and in six months to a year you may be lucky enough to have some tiny 1-inch-wide platycerium ferns, big enough to plant in paper cups filled with light acid soil mix. Keep them warm and in filtered light, feed them lightly, and pot them on occasionally as they grow. Eventually you can mount them on boards as described in the accompanying box for the more common variety of staghorn fern.

Many staghorn and elkhorn ferns not only have spores but also make a great many offsets, called "pups." You can propagate these very easily by dividing them off at any time in spring after they reach the proper size (see the accompanying box).

Volunteers

Look around the garden now for plants that have seeded themselves in the wrong places, and weed them out. Admittedly, some plants are weedier by nature than others, but any plant can be a weed if it's growing where you don't want it. Even a native Torrey pine, live oak, or Washingtonia palm can be a weed if it seeds itself

How to Separate and Mount the Pups of Staghorn Ferns

Once the pups (offsets) of staghorn ferns have sprouted and grown to be at least 4 inches long, you can separate them from the parent plant to make new specimens.

- Soak some green sphagnum moss in a bucket of water while you prepare the planting base. To the back of an appropriately sized piece of wood or plywood (flat cork bark or a fern trunk can also be used) attach a plastic-covered wire for hanging. (Use screws or nails to fix it firmly in place.)

- Cover the front of this base with a 1- or 2-inch-deep layer of premoistened sphagnum moss, and hold it in place by winding nylon fishing twine around it, or, alternatively, cover the entire face of the sphagnum moss with a piece of Gardeneer Bird-X netting. Secure the netting by stapling the edges to the back of the base. Turn the base over and cut a horizontal slit 1 or 2 inches long in the center of the netting. (Wear rubber or surgical gloves when handling wet sphagnum moss; damp sphagnum moss harbors spores that can cause serious skin infections.)

- With your fingers, carefully pull off a clump of pups from the mother plant. For each new plant, use between one and four pups; each one must have a sterile frond as well as at least one fertile frond. (If possible, remove a small portion of the sterile frond of the mother plant to help hold the new plant together.)

- Wrap the roots of the pup (or pups) in damp sphagnum moss, and seat them in the center of the base you have made. Tie them in place with fishing twine, being careful to wrap the twine under but not over the face of the sterile fronds.

- Hang the new plant in a shady protected spot in bright light and keep it moist for two or three weeks until it's rooted. Then begin to feed it once every two weeks with diluted fish emulsion until it's well established.

- For even faster growth mist your young staghorn with water once or twice a week. Occasionally add diluted fish emulsion to the water you use for misting.

between the sun and your vegetable garden.

Develop the eye of an artist in regard to what to keep and what must go. If shade draws your sensibilities and your need is a forest retreat, you can achieve it easily by planting well-chosen trees, but don't let it happen by accident. If there's something you really don't want, grit your teeth and pull it up now, or you'll find yourself in a few years chopping it down at great expense to pocketbook and conscience.

Control of Mildew

Moderate temperatures combined with damp oceanic air make May the worst time for mildew. If you're still growing peas and you don't want to pull them out yet, try dusting the plants with sulfur at intervals of one week. Roses and tuberous begonias are particularly sensitive to mildew. Control it with RosePride Funginex Rose & Shrub Disease Control, which is registered for each of these plants. Remove badly diseased leaves from begonias and move the plants into more light. Antitranspirants, such as CloudCover, are also effective against mildew. (CloudCover can be ordered in bulk from agricultural supply stores and sprayed onto plants. Antitranspirants are designed to prevent wilting in dry weather. Their ability to prevent mildew is a serendipitous byproduct of this function.)

Pruning

Prune winter- and spring-flowering vines, bushes, trees, and ground covers after they finish blooming. A **Rule of Thumb** that applies in almost all cases is: *Prune flowering plants that bloom once a year after they bloom, not before they bloom, or you'll prevent them from flowering.* Refer to a pruning manual for additional directions by plant type; I especially recommend the *Sunset Pruning Handbook,* listed in the bibliography. Here are a few examples of plants to be pruned now.

- **Trailing African Daisy** (*Osteospermum fruticosum*). Give osteospermum a yearly haircut in early May after bloom to prevent the buildup of thatch, which could lead to death from summer fungus. Clean up the ground; remove clippings and dead leaves. Mulch with nitrolized wood shavings, and follow up with fertilizer. You'll get another show of bloom.
- **Geraldton Waxflower** (*Chamelaucium uncinatum*). One of our loveliest drought-resistant plants, this one responds well to heavy pruning after bloom. Cut back whole sprays—not all the way down to the ground but into the body of the plant and back to the trunk. If you have room, let it grow big like a small shaggy-barked tree, but if it has outgrown its space it can be chopped back to 2 feet high now. Fresh shoots will spring from apparently dry wood below the cuts, and you'll have a whole new plant by fall. (Don't ever give this plant manure. It hates the stuff.)
- **Polyanthum Jasmine** (*Jasminum polyanthum*). Lightly cut back this fragrant, winter-blooming vine after bloom to remove unsightly dead blossoms and produce a second wave of bloom. Then cut it back hard—almost to bare wood—to clean up the plant, prevent it from building up a tangled interior, and produce new wood to bloom next year.

- **Lady Banks' Rose** (*Rosa banksiae*). Cut this rose back hard after bloom to keep it in bounds; produce a second, lighter wave of bloom; and produce new wood to bloom next year.
- **New Zealand Tea Tree** (*Leptospermum scoparium*). Shape this large shrub or small tree during bloom by cutting sprays for cut flowers. After bloom you can further shape it by cutting out whole unwanted branches and by heading back tips of selected branches to increase bushiness and develop a natural billowy shape. Don't ever shear this plant like a ball—this practice ruins its growth habit and prevents proper flowering.
- **Wisteria.** Train young plants onto a strong support. Prevent long streamers from twining around each other, and tie them lightly where you want them. Once a vine has reached the size and shape you desire, begin in May to cut back all unwanted new growth to two or three buds from the main branch, to create bloom spurs that will flower for many years. (This spring and summer pruning will also stimulate sporadic summer bloom.)

Bulbs

Plant Tuberoses. If you're especially fond of fragrant plants, try planting tuberoses (*Polianthes tuberosa*)—known in Hawaii as lei flowers—in early May. Choose tubers with a green growth tip, and place them so that the tips are level with the soil surface, 6 inches apart, in acid, well-drained soil in pots or the ground. Choose a warm spot, in full sun along the coast or slightly shaded but with reflected heat inland. Water them and wait for a sprout to appear; then water often and well. Feed them monthly with an acid fertilizer for bloom and growth.

The heavily scented white flowers will appear

in August or September. After the plants die down, you can leave the tubers in the ground, though if you do sometimes they'll skip a year before repeating bloom. For surer results, lift them and store in perlite until next May.

Care for Spring-Flowering Bulbs as the Bloom Season Ends. Continue to keep spring-flowering bulbs well watered during and after bloom. If you grew some in pots and want to reuse the containers, slip the bulbs out carefully and plant them as clumps in a sheltered spot. A shot of complete liquid fertilizer after bloom will help your bulbs store up strength for next year. Don't cut off leaves before they go brown.

These instructions apply to bulbs grown in pots filled with potting soil. Bulbs that have been forced in pebbles and water should have been thrown out right after bloom; these will not bloom again.

Annual and Perennial Flowers

Clean Up and Replant Annual Flowers as They Finish Blooming. In Southern California we grow annual flowers year-round by planting with the seasons, twice a year. Beginning in September, but mainly in October, we plant cool-season annuals that bloom all winter and peak in April. This makes May the logical time to replace them with warm-season annuals for blooms all summer long. (If you planted ahead from seeds in flats, as suggested in March, you'll have plenty of homegrown transplants all ready to go in the ground.) So now's the time to pull out all cool-season annuals that have finished blooming, such as calendulas, cineraria, Iceland poppies, malacoides (fairy) primroses, snapdragons, and stock. As you clear the beds, also clean them up, add some mulch and fertilizer, and re-

plant the bare spaces with summer annuals, including cosmos, gomphrena (globe amaranth), marigolds, petunias, verbena, and zinnias, in full sun and begonias, impatiens, and lobelia in partial shade. (Semperflorens and 'Richmondensis' begonias can be planted in sun or shade in coastal zones.) Plant scarlet sage in partial shade inland, full sun along the coast. (For more, see the April flowerbed section beginning on page 130.)

Keep Plants That Are Still Going Strong. May border planting isn't like October's, when every summer annual can be pulled up by the roots to make way for cool-season flowers. Some of the seeds and transplants we put in during fall or early in spring, such as cosmos, Shasta daisies, and the new heat-resistant pansies and violas, will continue to bloom all summer long in most coastal and some inland zones. Clarkia, larkspur, lavatera, and many wildflowers will bloom through June and perhaps into July. Take care not to pull them up by mistake.

Many gardeners have become so dazzled by perennials that they've forgotten how easy and colorful annuals can be. The widespread dwarfing of bedding plants hasn't helped. To get the tall and showy varieties, grow them from seed. Try using them as fillers among your perennials or purposefully, as English gardeners do, to pep up their flowerbeds with added color and excitement. Annuals are actually much easier to grow than perennials; just plant, feed, water, and deadhead them or pick them for bouquets, and when they're ratty pull them out. Plant *Nicotiana sylvestris* next to a path or as an exclamation point among perennials; it's especially dramatic at night. It grows 5 feet tall with white, intensely fragrant flowers in tiers, and blooms for many months right into fall. (If you've failed with verbascum, a spiky perennial

A Foolproof Way to Plant and Grow Zinnias from Seed

- Choose a spot in full sun that is not hit by overhead sprinklers. Also choose a good variety. 'Yoga', from Shepherd's Garden Seeds, has giant flowers in bright colors and blooms in just sixty-five days. 'Profusion Orange' and 'Profusion Cherry' won the All-America Selections Gold Medal Flower Awards in 1999. They are compact and mildew resistant and need no deadheading.

- Dig the ground deeply and mix in a generous layer of organic soil amendment. Add a complete fertilizer recommended for annual flowers according to package directions, and mix it into the top 6 inches of soil.

- Use a garden hoe to make a dike of soil 3 or 4 inches high all the way around the seedbed; it will hold the water in when you irrigate. Rake the seedbed level inside this dike. Or first rake the seedbed level and then install a drip system that will water the bed at ground level. (Drip systems make water basins unnecessary.)

- Pour some seeds into the palm of your hand. Grasping them one by one, place each seed right where you want it to grow, in a continuous diamond pattern all over the bed or drift. (As for all bedding plants and ground covers, alternate the rows when planting so that the plants grow all over, evenly, rather than standing like soldiers in foursquare rows.) Follow the package directions on spacing. (Large varieties should be spaced about 12 inches apart, small varieties about 6 inches.)

- Cover the seeds very lightly with about ¼ inch of soil—zinnias need light in order to germinate—and pat it down gently. (If you're planting in clay soil, cover the seeds with potting mix rather than soil so they won't have to break through a hard crust.)

- Mist the seedbed thoroughly after planting. Continue to mist it twice daily (even more in interior zones) until the seeds germinate. (Covering the bed with a floating row cover, such as Reemay, can help keep seeds damp and speed germination in hot interior valleys. After seeds have germinated, take the row cover off.)

- Sprinkle the ground with granulated cutworm bait containing Sevin or diazinon. (If using a row cover, sprinkle on the bait before covering the bed.) Bait again a week or two later.

- Once the zinnias are up and firmly rooted, stop misting and start irrigating with the drip system or by putting the hose on the ground inside the dike. (Aim the hose into a sideways-set flowerpot to break the force of the water.) The **Rule of Thumb** for zinnias is: *Always water zinnias on the ground, never overhead, or you'll ruin the foliage.*

- When the plants are 3 or 4 inches high, start watering them more infrequently and deeply until you're applying 1 to 2 inches of water per week, depending on your soil and climate zone.

- To encourage branching, pinch out the first flower bud on each plant or pinch above the third set of leaves.

- Pick and deadhead zinnias throughout the summer. (Profusion series needs no deadheading; new growth hides faded flowers.)

that can be temperamental here, this makes a good substitute.)

Plant Heat-Lovers from Seed. At last it's time to plant heat-loving annuals, such as zinnias, from seeds. Modern hybrid zinnias bounce back quicker after transplanting than old varieties, but as a rule zinnias do best when planted from seeds right where you want them to grow. This allows you to choose varieties not usually found in nursery packs. If you've never grown anything from seeds and would like to try, zinnias are a good choice to start with (see the box on page 153). Other flowers you can plant now from seed include calliopsis, celosia (cockscomb or plume flower), Madagascar periwinkle (vinca; *Catharanthus roseus*), marigold, nicotiana, portulaca, scarlet sage, sunflower, sweet alyssum, verbena, and morning glory (see the Quick Tip on page 155).

If you live inland, do try growing cleome (spider flower). A tall old-fashioned flower and good cut flower that thrives on heat and neglect, it blooms in late summer and fall. Plant cleome from seed in the ground right where you want it to grow, at the backs of beds and outer edges of the garden. Seed racks offer all the colors in one packet called "Queen Mixed," plus the white one, 'Helen Campbell', and the old standby, 'Pink Queen'. ('Rose Queen' is more choice—a deep rose pink, but you may have to send for it.) Prior to planting, dig up the ground and work in plenty of organic soil amendment and some balanced fertilizer, raking the area smooth. Sprinkle the seeds on top of the ground and use the back of a hoe held upright to press them into contact with the ground; they need light in order to sprout, so don't cover them with soil. Keep the seeded area damp until established. Once cleome is up and growing, water deeply but infrequently; it detests wet soil and loves nothing better than sun and heat.

Use Nursery Transplants for Instant Color.
Pony packs of many summer annuals can be planted now; they'll soon fill out in size. Or, for instant flowerbeds and patio pots chock-full of plants, use the more expensive but larger-rooted "color packs." Arrange them in your shopping cart to see which color combinations look good together.

Years ago it was preferable to purchase flowers before they bloomed, but new varieties are made to bloom in the pack—even in tiny pony packs—and continue to perform spectacularly in the garden. The one thing the gardener must remember is to loosen up those roots when planting, or they'll just sit there for months thinking they're still in the container.

Deadhead, Cut Back, and Plant Perennials.
When those gorgeous spikes of bloom on Pride of Madeira *(Echium fastuosum)* are spent and begin to look unsightly, it's time to cut them off down to the plant's gray foliage. New growth will then sprout farther down on the stalks that have bloomed. In a month or two cut down to this new growth; the plant will branch and look better. If you have huge spaces to fill, you may prefer to wait until the seeds have gone brown and matured; then cut them off and shake them around for seedlings. However, seedlings are seldom as attractive as better selections with larger, deeper blue flowers.

Deadhead coral bells *(Heuchera)* after bloom and cut back columbine *(Aquilegia)*. If happy in their location, a stand of coral bells will last for many years, but columbine when grown here usually ignores the fact that it's perennial and soon dies from root rot. Be not dismayed; it's an efficient self-seeder. Unless you've deadheaded it with amazing regularity, you should find many progeny to dig up and move around in fall. Other plants that die after bloom—but for a different and more acceptable reason—are Canterbury bells *(Campanula medium)* and the ever-popular cup-and-saucer *(C. medium* 'Calycanthema'). These are biennials, so the end of their bloom season naturally signals their demise. They're prone to mildew and need cool temperatures, moist soil, and good drainage and thus are fussier, scarcer, and more expensive than foxglove, another biennial. But just for fun, why not try planting the variety 'Cup-and-

Saucer Mixed Colors' (available from Park Seeds) from seeds next fall? It grows 2½ feet high and may reseed itself after bloom next year.

Perennials aren't always what the name implies. Cast-iron plants like achillea, gaura, and Santa Barbara daisy settle down and live for years. Others, like lavender, live several years, then die. Clipping them back helps keep them going, but eventually you'll have to go out and buy others. Some gardeners can keep certain plants like coral bells alive year after year; others can't. And then there are the "perennials" that most gardeners here treat as annuals, never expecting them to last a second year—delphiniums, for example, or even strawflowers (*Bracteantha bracteata* 'Dargan Hill' and others). All bracteanthas were formerly classified as helichrysums, but by whatever name, I find it's best to buy new ones every year.

When tall varieties of Shasta daisy (*Leucanthemum maximum*) reach about 2 feet high, you can control their eventual height and make them more bushy by cutting them back by half in early May. (Use hedge shears.) If taller than 2 feet, cut them back about a foot; this will produce later bloom on a more compact plant. You can also shape them as you wish, cutting the front or the front and sides shorter than the back to create an illusion of depth. Your Shastas will bloom about a month later, in July instead of June; if you're going away in June you'll be home to enjoy them and do the deadheading too. Also stake plants now so they don't flop over later. Use English pea stakes (twiggy branches, minus the leaves, cut from shrubs) or commercial gridlike staking devices that plants grow up through. Circles of chicken wire or squares of hardware cloth can work the same way when supported horizontally above the plants on short bamboo stakes stuck down into

Quick Tip

How to Scarify Seed. *Some seeds with hard coats, like morning glory* (Ipomoea tricolor) *and lupine, have to be scarified (nicked) prior to planting or they won't sprout under garden conditions. To scarify a seed easily, grasp it with pliers and use a small three-cornered file to carefully file through the edge of the seed at any spot other than the "eye" from which it will sprout. Soak scarified morning glory seeds overnight in warm water before planting.*

the ground. (Bend the wire over to avoid sharp edges.)

These pruning and staking techniques can be used on most of the Compositae family, including asters, chrysanthemums, dahlias, daisies, echinacea, goldenrod, and many other plants, like phlox, with flower heads made up of many smaller flowers. Most well-established, multibranched perennials, including phlox, will branch more if you cut or pinch them back early in the season. But don't try this technique on nonbranching or spikey perennials whose flowers are born on single, long, straight stems, like those of astilbe, hosta, liatris, ligularia, or lisianthus; these won't flower if their terminal buds are removed.

Look for summer phlox (*Phlox paniculata*) among the many perennials for sale this month, though earlier in spring would be a better time to plant it. It languishes along the coast and suffers from mildew, but in interior gardens with well-amended clay it thrives in full sun or a little shade. The flowers of some varieties are 5 and 6 feet tall and continue into fall. (Many perennials are easier to grow in humusy clay soil than in sandy soil that dries out between waterings. If you have sandy soil, stick to drought-resistant perennials.)

Clematis Varieties for Southern California

Clematis armandii (evergreen clematis)—ivory white (March through April)

C. durandii—indigo blue flowers with gold stamens (July through September)

C. viticella 'Polish Spirit'—rich, deep purple; red center (summer)

'Asao'—pink with central white bar (summer)

'Duchess of Edinburgh'—white, double (late spring to early summer)

'Elsa Spath' (also sold as 'Xerxes')—lavender-blue flowers (June, September)

'General Sikorski'—medium-blue single with pale yellow anthers (abundant; early summer to early autumn)

'H. F. Young'—medium-blue single with faint pink bar when first open (late spring to early summer, early autumn)

'Marie Boisselot'—white single (early to late summer)

'Masquerade'—soft lavender single with dark reddish anthers (early summer)

'Nellie Moser'—mauve sepals, with dark red stripe in center of each (June and September)

'Niobe'—ruby red (summer)

'Proteus'—dusty purple-pink double (late spring to early summer; repeats in autumn)

'Star of India'—plum with deep pink bar on center of each sepal; anthers dusky brown (midsummer to early autumn)

'The President'—purple-blue single with pale yellow anthers (early spring into summer, late summer, or early autumn)

'Victoria'—lavender mauve single with yellow anthers (midsummer)

'William Kennett'—deep mid-blue with dark red anthers (early to midsummer and sometimes in early autumn)

Aster frikartii 'Mönch' and *A. frikartii* 'Wonder of Stafa', long cherished for ease of growing and long bloom season, are widely available now. *Aster ericoides* 'Monte Casino' (white) does well in coastal or inland gardens, blooming spring and fall with tall, airy spikes—a good substitute for boltonia, which won't grow here. Another cut flower is *Verbena rigida.* Drought resistant, it makes a spreading mat of growth with spikes of violet blooms 20 inches tall in summer and fall. And then there's *Hypoestes aristata* 'Lavender Cloud', which blooms in fall, but planting now gives it a chance to get established. (Perhaps you have a friend with seedlings.) Grow it from the beach to inland valleys, in sun or shade, and only ordinary care. Cut it back in winter and shape it in summer.

Clematis

Clematis is not a plant we think of as typically Southern Californian. You'll never get these deciduous vines to cover walls and trellises with sheets of color, as they do in summer at Roserie de l'Haie in Paris or Giverny, or to smother whole trees as they do in England, but you can achieve a fine, though more modest, display, especially in interior zones. Look for clematis this month at select nurseries and botanical-garden plant sales—the Los Angeles Arboretum offers them most years. Descanso Gardens has the display garden for the American Clematis Society. See the accompanying box for a list of varieties recommended by the Southern California Clematis Society, with additions by experienced growers (address: SCCS, P.O. Box 17085, Irvine, CA 92623).

Grow clematis vines as companion plants, climbing into shrubs, roses, trees, or other vines. Plant in rich, damp soil with excellent drainage, sunshine for the flowers, and a cool root run— "with their heads in the sun, their feet in the shade," as the saying goes. Their roots are easily broken, so tap them gently out of their containers and just place them into a well-amended hole, planting deeply—2 inches deeper than the surrounding soil. English gardeners place a large flat rock over the roots to shade them. In California, a large plant tub standing on a stepping-stone on the sunny side of the clematis might provide the adequate shade. Fertilize often during the growing season with organic fertilizer such as 5-5-5. Treat them like roses; they want to be fed.

Lawn Care

Plant Warm-Season Lawns and Dwarf Fescue. St. Augustine and Bermuda get off to a fast start when planted in May. (Hold off until June to plant zoysia; see page 175.) It's too late to plant most cool-season grasses from seed, but dwarf fescues can be planted from sod.

Lawns can be planted in several ways: from seeds, plugs grown in flats, or sod rolled out like an instant carpet. Bermuda and zoysia can also be planted from stolons (creeping stems with roots attached). Whichever method you use, be sure to prepare the ground properly. Before beginning, decide whether to plant a warm- or cool-season lawn (as discussed on page 106) and choose a variety appropriate for your area and needs.

Select the Best Variety for You. When you research grass types, be sure to consult with successful local gardeners and the nearest University of California Cooperative Extension Office. Consider these factors:

- St. Augustine is better adapted to shade than other lawn grasses but needs a lot of water.
- Dwarf fescue is now the most popular lawn grass in coastal regions. Good varieties, including 'Bonsai 2000', are disease resistant and more drought resistant than perennial ryegrass and a lot less troublesome.
- If you live close to a Bermuda golf course it will seed itself eventually into any ryegrass lawn, making it look ratty. To minimize this, plant a hybrid or selected strain of Bermuda for your own lawn in the first place. You might use 'Santa Ana', 'Tifway', or 'Tifway II'; all three are vigorous hybrids that make such a dense, fine-textured turf that common Bermuda usually cannot invade them. Another possibility is a newer variety with improved early spring color, such as 'Mirage' or 'Jackpot', which are not hybrids but seed selections from common Bermuda. (You'll need a reel mower, not a rotary one, for cutting Bermuda.)
- As mentioned earlier in this book, don't plant such troublemakers as bent grass or Kentucky bluegrass—they'll die in the first drought. Common Bermuda and 'Santa Ana' hybrid Bermuda grass are the two most drought-resistant choices.

Fertilize, Mow, and Water Lawns. Continue to feed warm-season grasses this month, and in coastal zones apply fertilizer to cool-season lawns once more this month at the same rate as that used during the winter. But in interior zones stop feeding cool-season lawns now, other than an occasional light application (one-fourth to one-half the normal dosage) applied only when necessary to maintain a healthy green color. Tests done by the University of California Division of Agriculture show that heavy feeding of cool-season grasses such as ryegrass, bluegrass,

How to Grow a Cantaloupe in a Tire

Gardeners in cool coastal areas often have problems growing cantaloupes. Here's a heat-increasing method that brings success.

- In early May plant a cantaloupe variety that will ripen at relatively cool temperatures, such as 'Ambrosia'.

- Dig a hole 2 feet wide and 1 foot deep in full sun. Mix together aged manure, compost, organic soil amendment, and some of the native soil from the hole to make a richly organic soil. Into this, mix 3 tablespoons of 6-12-6 or a similar vegetable fertilizer, and refill the hole.

- Lay an old auto tire over the hole, pack native soil into the sides of the tire with your hands, and fill the center up to the inside edge of the tire with more manure, compost, soil, and 2 tablespoons of fertilizer. Finish with a layer of potting soil and water deeply. (The bulging tire makes a perfect watering basin.)

- Plant five or six seeds, 1 inch deep; space them evenly around the top.

- Water deeply and daily until the seeds sprout. When the seedlings are up 4 inches, choose the strongest two. Clip off or pull out the others. For continued harvests plant other tires. Separate them from the first by 3 or 4 feet.

- Cover the ground all around the tires with a layer of black plastic mulch to raise the temperature of the melon patch. (Peg it down.) The vines will grow out over the plastic, which will keep the fruit clean.

- Once the plants are established, water deeply; lay the hose in the tire and let water soak in slowly. Do this twice a week when the plants are young, once a week when they're full grown. (If plants wilt, water them right away.)

- Water less as the fruit nears maturity. (Too much water then makes fruit less sweet.)

- Pick at "full slip," meaning there's a crack around the vine so that the melon slips off easily when it's lifted. Enjoy the sweetness and flavor.

and fescue during the warm season of the year subjects them to unnecessary stress.

Continue to mow and water all lawns.

Vegetable Gardening

Irrigate and Fertilize Summer Crops. Summer vegetables grow fast this month, and watering is the most important task. Vegetables aren't drought resistant—they need plenty of water but you can cut down on the water you use by installing drip irrigation. Plan the system now and switch to it before fall planting.

If any crop shows signs of slowing down, side-dress the row with vegetable fertilizer, following package directions. But don't overfertilize beans or tomatoes with nitrogen, or you'll risk encouraging leafy growth at the expense of harvest. (If you've already done that by mistake, soak the ground with 0-10-10 to stimulate flowering.) From time to time I recommend 0-10-10 liquid fertilizer for specific purposes. It's a good thing to have on hand, but don't run around feeding it to everything. Plants need nitrogen, and 0-10-10 has none (see page 26).

Continue to Plant. For continuous crops of vegetables, keep planting summer crops in whatever spaces you may have. By staggering plantings you'll get longer harvests and more manageable quantities. All the vegetables for summer plus the ones that can be planted year-round can be put in now, including beets, carrots, chayote, corn, cucumbers, eggplant, green

Harvest Times of Dwarf Citrus for Year-Round Fruit

Most citrus trees for home garden use are "dwarf." But there are no truly dwarf citrus varieties. When a citrus tree is called "dwarf," it simply means that a full-size variety has been grafted onto a dwarf rooting stock, such as trifoliate orange, *Poncirus trifoliata,* or Hiryu (Flying Dragon). Dwarf citrus trees are good choices for home gardens, and by selecting the right varieties according to their harvest times you can have year-round fruit.

Winter:
'Robertson' Navel Orange
Owari Satsuma and 'Clementine' Tangerines
Rangpur Lime

Winter and Spring:
'Ruby Pink' and 'Marsh' Seedless Grapefruits

Spring:
'Kinnow' Tangerine
'Sampson' Tangelo
'Shamouti' Orange

Late Spring:
Nagami Kumquat

Spring through Summer:
'Kara' Tangerine

Late Spring through Summer:
'Minneola' Tangelo

Summer:
'Summernavel' and 'Valencia' Oranges

All Year:
'Eureka', 'Lisbon', and 'Improved Meyer' Lemons
'Bearss Seedless' and 'Mexican' Limes
'Eustis' Limequat

beans, lima beans, leaf lettuce, melons, New Zealand spinach, peppers, pumpkins, radishes, summer squash, winter squash, Swiss chard, tomatoes, and turnips, as well as many herbs.

Harvest Regularly. Once beans and squash begin to bear, pick them daily to keep them coming. Picking vegetables is a type of pruning, like deadheading flowers to keep them blooming. Most crops, including root vegetables, should be harvested when young and tender. Hunt for zucchinis daily or you'll be tripping over giants as big as blimps. Eat the little ones flowers and all. Some oversized zucchini are good for nothing but laughs, but if you catch them in time they're delicious sliced, breaded, and fried, or in zucchini soup.

Pick herbs to keep them in bounds, and plant more to discourage pests. (There's little reliable research on the value of herbs as pest traps or pest repellents, but many home gardeners find

 Quick Tip

Why It's Okay to Plant Melons Next to Cucumbers or Squash. *Gardeners who watch bees visit flowers of a squash and then a melon sometimes fear that cross-pollination will affect the sweetness of the fruit, but it has no effect on it. The flesh of the melon will be just as sweet and the texture of the squash will be just as true as if they were self-pollinated. What will be affected is the seed. Do not save the seeds, as the next generation of plants from this mixed parentage will be totally unpredictable.*

that planting herbs among their vegetables provides a more pest-free garden.) Among herbs to plant or replace now is parsley. If you planted a row last year, it will probably go to seed now because it's biennial. Pull it up (don't throw away the roots; cook them in soup) and plant a new row in another spot. You may also want to leave a few plants in the ground, as I do, to go to

How to Grow a Giant Pumpkin

There's time to grow a giant pumpkin for Halloween if you plant now.

- Choose a giant variety, such as 'Big Max'. (It's actually a squash.)

- Dig a hole in full sun. Add the organic matter and fertilizer prescribed for cantaloupes on page 158. Include horse manure if it's available.

- Build a hill of amended soil that's 18 inches wide at the base and 4 or 6 inches high. Make a small watering basin on top for starting the seeds; also make a large watering basin in amended soil on the north side for watering the mature plant. (Later arrange the vines so they grow away from the basin.)

- Plant four to six seeds 1 inch deep on the top of the mound. Water them daily until sprouted. When the plants are up 4 inches, choose the best one and clip off the others. Start watering deeply in the basin.

- Allow many fruits to reach grapefruit size. Then choose the best one—the one closest to the roots and with the thickest stem and best color, size, and shape. Clip off all the others.

- Feed the pumpkin monthly with a high-nitrogen fertilizer. Fill the watering basin regularly so that total water is equal to an inch of rain per day.

- While you can still lift your pumpkin, slip a piece of plywood under it to keep the bottom dry and protect it from rot and pests.

- Here's an optional step, for even larger growth and contest-size fruit: Force-feed the pumpkin by means of a woollen wick that you enclose in a plastic tube. Insert one end into a gallon of milk, the other into the stem of the pumpkin. Replace milk bottles as necessary until the pumpkin stops growing (or perhaps until you hear a giant burp).

flower and eventually to seed. The flowers attract beneficial insects. The seeds often sprout and grow new plants.

Care for Tomatoes. Continue to tie up tomatoes growing on stakes and trellises (as described on page 114). Except on cage-grown plants pinch out the suckers to maintain one or two main trunks per plant, according to your preference. After indeterminate tomatoes (the ones that keep growing and bearing until they're cut down by cold weather) reach the top of 8-foot stakes, stop pinching out the suckers and tie bamboo or wooden stakes horizontally overhead between the vertical stakes, to hold up flopping vines. (Determinate varieties usually don't grow this tall because they're genetically programmed to grow only to a certain height, which differs according to variety.)

 Quick Tip

Enlist the Help of Scrub Jays. *Nail an empty tuna can on top of a tomato stake. Stock it with a few unshelled peanuts to attract scrub jays. They'll take the peanuts, notice the caterpillars, and come back for them.*

A word of caution about pruning: If your tomatoes have ever suffered from early or late blight, it is better to grow them in cages or on stakes or trellises without pruning out the suckers. The disease can enter the plant through the cuts you make when you prune. (Early and late blight are discussed in detail on page 138.)

Keep the soil evenly moist in order to avoid blossom-end rot (discussed on page 176). If you want plenty of evenly shaped, big tomatoes with many seeds in them, continue to hit tomato stakes and cages with a hammer at midday, or vibrate the individual flower clusters, to increase pollination. If you prefer meaty fruit with few seeds, you can stop this practice now, because warm temperatures, breezes, and insect activity will give you ample fruit anyway; if the fruit is not well pollinated it may be somewhat strangely shaped, but it will contain fewer seeds. For best flavor pick tomatoes when they're red and ripe.

Control Pests and Diseases. Continue to use organic methods to control pests and diseases on vegetables. Interplant with herbs to confuse the bugs. (A diverse collection of plants helps prevent pests from specializing, as they can do when only one crop is grown.) Introduce lady-bugs, green lacewings, and other beneficials. Handpick bugs and caterpillars, catch slugs and snails with raised boards (described on page 91), and go out at night with a flashlight and gather snails. (Just be sure to sing out a warning to any grub-digging skunks you might accidentally surprise.) If you feel you must spray, stick to a biodegradable insecticidal soap, such as Safer, and use BT against caterpillars.

Many diseases can be controlled by keeping the garden clean. Cut off any diseased leaves (dip the clippers in alcohol between cuts to disinfect them), keep the ground clean, and pick up rotting fruit. Don't pick beans when the dew is on them, in order not to spread rust. And always rotate your crops: when you harvest a row, plant something different in its place.

Purchase/Plant

- ❏ Plant irises, 144
- ❏ Plant canned roses, 147
- ❏ Plant tropicals, 147
- ❏ Plant tuberoses, 151
- ❏ Transplant potted bulbs into the ground, 152
- ❏ Replace cool-season bedding flowers with flowers to bloom in summer, 152
- ❏ Plant zinnias and other heat-loving flowers, 153
- ❏ Plant morning glories, 154
- ❏ Plant warm-season lawns, 157
- ❏ Continue to plant summer vegetables, 158
- ❏ Plant melons, 159
- ❏ Replace parsley, if you haven't already done so, 159
- ❏ Plant a giant pumpkin for Halloween, 160
- ❏ Start perennials from seed in interior zones, 173
- ❏ Purchase, plant, and transplant succulents, including cacti and euphorbias, 194
- ❏ Plant cleome and nicotiana, 154
- ❏ Plant perennials, 154
- ❏ Plant clematis, 156

Trim, Prune, Mow, Divide

- ❏ Stop pinching fuchsias if you did not do so last month, 100
- ❏ Mow all grass lawns, 157
- ❏ Thin out fruit on deciduous fruit trees, 121
- ❏ Pinch dahlias back when the plant has three sets of leaves; tie the plants up as they grow, 155
- ❏ Continue to pick and deadhead roses; disbud them if desired, 122
- ❏ Divide and repot cymbidiums that have outgrown their containers, 145
- ❏ Cut off bloom spikes from cymbidiums after flowers fade, 144
- ❏ Prune camellias if you have not already done so, 145
- ❏ Clean up and prune azaleas, 145
- ❏ Divide and mount staghorn ferns, 150
- ❏ Prune winter- and spring-flowering vines, shrubs, trees, and ground covers after they finish blooming, 151
- ❏ Continue to tie up tomatoes, 160
- ❏ Remove berries (seedpods) from fuchsias after flowers fall, 169
- ❏ Continue to prune and train espaliers, 211
- ❏ Propagate daylilies by planting their proliferates; cut off spent bloom stems, 250
- ❏ Remove the seedpods from white fortnight lilies, but leave the bloom stalks on the plant; they'll bloom again, 214
- ❏ Deadhead yellow fortnight lilies, by cutting down entire stalks after each one has finished blooming, 214
- ❏ Deadhead and cut back perennials, 154

Fertilize

- ❏ Feed citrus trees, 50
- ❏ Feed avocado trees, 66
- ❏ Feed fuchsias, 168
- ❏ Feed tuberous begonias, 185
- ❏ Feed water lilies, 125
- ❏ Fertilize corn, 135
- ❏ Feed cymbidiums that have finished blooming, for growth, 183
- ❏ Fertilize camellias after bloom, 145
- ❏ Feed azaleas after bloom, 145
- ❏ Feed roses, 146
- ❏ Feed ferns, 147
- ❏ Feed flowerbeds, 78
- ❏ Fertilize lawns, 157
- ❏ Side-dress vegetable rows with fertilizer, 158
- ❏ Feed all container-grown succulents with a well-diluted complete liquid fertilizer, 195
- ❏ Fertilize peppers when flowers first show, 200
- ❏ Feed and water cycads, 220

Water

❏ As the weather becomes drier, water all garden plants regularly, 143

❏ Taper off watering those California native plants that do not accept summer water, 144

❏ Water cymbidiums, 144

❏ Water roses, 146

❏ Water vegetables, 158

❏ Do not water succulents, 195

Control Pests, Diseases, and Weeds

❏ Control rose pests and diseases, 146

❏ Control mildew, 150

❏ Control pests on vegetables, 161

❏ Control weeds among permanent plants by mulching or cultivating, 145

❏ Control weeds among vegetables and flowers by hand-pulling, 40

❏ Control gophers before planting lawns, or trap them, 261, 283

Also This Month

❏ Keep bamboo from running into your neighbor's garden, 103

❏ Keep cymbidiums in semishade, but where they will get some sun, 144

❏ Mulch camellias and azaleas, 145

❏ Renew overgrown fern baskets, 148

❏ Remove volunteers that are growing where they aren't wanted, 149

❏ Pull out cool-season annuals that have finished blooming, 152

❏ Harvest vegetables regularly, 159

❏ Harvest bananas whenever they are ready, according to type, 219

❏ Begin to harvest short-day onions to slice and eat raw, 285

❏ Harvest citrus, 159

JUNE

The Easygoing Month

June is the month when we're most aware of our proximity to the ocean. As the continental air mass warms in early summer, it has a tendency to rise and pull cool oceanic air inland. There's always a chance that the year may be different, but if the weather behaves in a normal manner damp ocean air now often extends inland beyond the first range of hills, well into Zones 20 and 21. The weather forecaster's familiar "night and morning fog along the coast" often lasts all day, and even gardeners in the interior may experience some overcast.

It's an easygoing month in the garden. Most of the spring planting should be done by now, and the hot, dry days of summer haven't yet arrived. Gardeners in interior valleys face the onset of scorching heat by month's end, but early in June, except for an occasional hot spell of two or three days in the hundreds, it's still pleasant enough to garden in the middle of the day.

June Bloom

In Southern California, it's possible to have color year-round from permanent plants. If your garden lacks color now, notice what's in bloom in local gardens, botanical gardens, and nurseries. Consider adding one or two of the following plants that bloom during June:

- **Lemon Bottlebrush** (*Callistemon citrinus*). Among our finest drought-resistant small trees or shrubs, lemon bottlebrush grows slowly to 25 feet. Named cultivars have the best color and largest flowers.
- **Chinese Fringe Tree** (*Chionanthus retusus*). White flowers shaped rather like lilac blossoms cover the entire tree in June.
- **Fuchsia, Hydrangea, and Lantana.** All these are at the height of bloom in June. Fuchsias need regular water but adapt well to drip systems. Hydrangeas also need plenty of water, but they make good container plants or

choices for moist canyons with damp but well-drained soil. Lantana is one of the easiest full-sun, drought-resistant plants to grow and is a great bank cover.

- **Jacaranda with Agapanthus.** Jacaranda is a spectacular tree. Try planting white agapanthus, also in bloom now, at its feet. Or use blue agapanthus for a mirror effect—blue on the tree and on the ground as well.
- *Puya berteroniana.* This spiky accent plant, drought resistant once established, has flower stalks like huge asparagus, 3 to 6 feet tall, that open to red, lavender, turquoise, and white flowers. Use puya to complement areas of cacti and succulents, in a spot where they can get slightly more water.
- **Vines.** All of the following bloom in summer and can be purchased and planted now:

  Bower vine *(Pandorea jasminoides)* is pink ('Rosea') or white ('Alba'). Protect it from wind.

  Mandevilla 'Alice du Pont' is bright pink and a good choice to espalier on an east wall.

  Violet trumpet vine *(Clytostoma callistegioides)* is easy, disease resistant, and gorgeous in its late-spring, early-summer bloom.

  Blood-red trumpet vine *(Distictis buccinatoria)* does best near the sea but can be grown in the interior, though it will suffer frost damage.

  Royal trumpet vine *(D. 'Rivers')* is a strong grower, disease resistant, with flowers ranging from mauve to royal purple.

  Vanilla trumpet vine *(D. laxiflora)* is violet fading through lavender to white.

Tropicals and Subtropicals

Fertilize tropical and subtropical plants, according to their individual needs, during summer while they're growing. Continue to plant them except in interior valleys, where scorching days may burn their foliage if they're planted this late. Tropicals and subtropicals give us our distinctively Southern California atmosphere, and not all are great water users—some are drought resistant.

Among the numerous tropical and subtropical plants that like to be planted in June (in all but the hottest interior zones) are bougainvillea, gardenia, ginger, hibiscus, Natal plum, palms, tree ferns, and many flowering trees, such as cassias, coral trees, crape myrtle *(Lagerstroemia indica),* floss silk tree *(Chorisia speciosa),* golden trumpet tree *(Tabebuia chrysotricha),* and orchid trees *(Bauhinia).*

Also plant blue hibiscus *(Alyogyne huegelii),* a splendid dry-climate shrub from Australia with eye-catching bright blue flowers that bloom on and off year-round in full sun. Plant it in your hottest spot or it won't bloom. It's widely available either in its natural shrub form or as a standard, with a 3- to 4-foot trunk. The only fault of blue hibiscus is that it's rangy and open and doesn't branch freely. You can remedy this and also keep the plant blooming if once a month from spring to fall you cut back two or three of its longest branches by half or two-thirds their length.

Other choices to plant now include tropical fruit trees, such as avocado, banana, cherimoya, citrus, pineapple guava, and white sapote. (As mentioned in other chapters, some of these species can be planted happily at other times as well.) In most areas—other than the warmest interior valleys—the early summer weather stimulates growth but isn't yet hot enough to dry them out. Keep them well watered until established.

How to Plant a Bougainvillea and Get It Growing

Bougainvilleas are drought resistant, free from pests and disease, romantic, glowingly colorful, and easy to grow—but not easy to plant or get started. Use them as large ground covers on banks and have them pouring over walls, roofs, fences, and arbors. Here's how to plant them.

- Choose plants with the color, eventual size, and growth habit you desire. Some are vines and some shrubs. Some are more vigorous than others. Five-gallon sizes make a faster start in the ground than l-gallon sizes do.

- Choose a spot in full sun, preferably where the root run—the area where the roots grow—is also hit by full sun. (In the desert and hot interior valleys bougainvilleas will bloom in light shade.)

- Dig a hole twice as wide as the container and the same depth as the container. Loosen the soil in the bottom of the hole, and work in 2 or 3 cupfuls of bone meal. (If the soil is heavy clay, also work in gypsum.) Cover this with enough soil so that, when you set in the plant, the top of the root ball will be level with the surrounding ground. Add slow-release fertilizer tablets according to package directions, around the bottom of the hole.

- Bougainvilleas are fragile when young and often killed when they're planted because their roots and crown are broken. Turn the plant on its side. With sharp pruning shears, cut around the bottom of the container and look to see whether it's well rooted. If it is, slip the plant out sideways by pushing from the bottom. Lower it carefully into the hole while supporting the roots with your hands. Backfill with native soil.

- If the plant is not well rooted, slit the sides of the container from the bottom up in several places; then tape it back together with masking tape. Lower the plant into the hole with the taped container holding the roots in place. Loosen the tape and slide the bottom out. Slip out the cut pieces from the sides as you backfill the hole with native soil.

- Press the soil down around the plant with your hands. The top of the root ball should be even with the surrounding ground.

- Make a watering basin, and water deeply right away. Then, in fast-draining soils, water once a day for three days; for the next two weeks water three times a week; and for the following month water twice a week. Thereafter, for the first three years, water once a week. In clay soils you should water enough to keep the root ball damp but not soggy for the first three weeks to a month. Thereafter water deeply after the ground dries out. (Bougainvilleas are drought resistant not because they don't need water, but because their roots extend into the ground until they find an underground water source. When young they take all the water they can get, as long as drainage is adequate.)

- For the first three years after planting, fertilize bougainvilleas once a month between April and August. After three to five years you can stop fertilizing in summer, stop watering in winter, and reduce the frequency of summer watering to once a month or every six weeks—or perhaps never, depending on placement and variety. (Container-grown vines will always need regular fertilizer and water.)

Morning Glories

Perennial morning glory, more correctly called blue dawn flower *(Ipomoea acuminata),* gets started rapidly when planted now. Grow this vine in full sun and in ordinary or poor soil, with no nitrogen fertilizer added. Water regularly to get the plants started; then irrigate occasionally thereafter. These vines are invasive, drought resistant, and permanent once established. Use morning glories for an old-fashioned, colorful,

How to Divide Irises

- With a garden fork dig up an entire clump, shake off excess soil from the roots, and then squirt it with the hose to wash all soil from the rhizomes. (A rhizome is a thickened stem that grows horizontally underground or on the surface of the ground.)

- Using a sharp knife, from the outside of the clump cut vigorous, healthy divisions. Each division for planting should have one fan of leaves, a section of young, healthy rhizome approximately 2 to 6 inches long, and some roots coming out the bottom. It may also have one or two new growth buds, or eyes, bulging out on the sides.

- Discard the following: the old, woody center of the clump that has no leaves, anything that is diseased or rotted or has been attacked by pests, any thin or spindly growth, and all immature rhizomes with no leaves.

- Cut off the tops of the fans at a neat right angle, with the center point 4 inches higher and the sides 2 to 3 inches higher than the rhizome.

- Cut back the roots by about one-third; dip the cut ends of the rhizomes in a fungicide, such as captan; and allow them to dry in the sun for two or three hours.

- Dig up the bed or prepare individual planting areas, in full sun along the coast or where there's six hours of sun inland. Work in compost and bone meal.

- Replant the rhizomes on the same day, three to a clump, with the leaves pointing out from the center. Irises keep growing in the direction of each fan of leaves. On hillsides plant them with the bare rhizomes pointing downhill and the part with the leaves pointing uphill.

- For each rhizome use a trowel or a small spade to dig a hole approximately 4 inches deep and 8 inches wide. Make an elongated mound in the planting hole. Arrange the roots over the mound with the rhizome resting on top so that the top of the rhizome is level with the surrounding soil. If the roots bend on the bottom, dig the hole deeper. Cover the roots with soil and press it down firmly with your hands. When you're finished, the top of the rhizome should still be level with the surface of the soil.

- Water the bed thoroughly after planting and keep it damp, but not soggy, until the plants are rooted.

countrified look and to camouflage chain-link fences. They're not for formal gardens but can be an eye-catching ornament in the right spot and in old neighborhoods, sometimes clambering into trees and covering neglected hedges.

Bearded Irises

If your irises don't bloom, they're either growing in too much shade or they need dividing. (They need full sun along the coast and six hours of sun daily in the interior.) After bearded irises have been in the ground for three or four years, they become crowded. Their roots inter-

twine, the clumps rise ever higher out of the ground, and if they're not divided they'll stop blooming. In coastal zones divide irises as soon as flowering is finished, in June. If you don't finish the job in June, you can continue into July in most areas. In the hottest interior valleys wait until October. Sometimes, in old gardens, irises have been neglected for years and it's a big job to divide them.

Fuchsias

Fuchsias should be covered with a blanket of bloom this month. Feed them often with a balanced fertilizer that's high in nitrogen as well as bloom ingredients, such as 14-14-14. When the individual flowers of most fuchsia varieties fade they fall off the plant, but they leave their seed-pods still attached to the branch. Pinch off these seedpods—or berries, as they're often called—daily if possible, after the flowers fall. This keeps the plants blooming. If you don't have time for removing seedpods, grow single varieties, which are self-cleaning, such as 'Ballerina Blau', 'Belle of Salem', 'Display', 'Gartenmeister Bonstedt', 'Nonpareil', 'Orange Drops', or 'Red Spider' rather than double varieties. (The top four, often upward curving, petal-like parts of fuchsias are called the "sepals." The true petals hang down in the center and are called the "corolla." Varieties with five or six petals in the corolla are considered single. Flowers with big, fluffy, many-petaled corollas are double.)

Water fuchsias regularly to prevent them from drying out, but don't overwater. Soggy soil can lead to root rot, fuchsias' worst bugaboo. Be on the lookout for pests, and spray if necessary with BT for cabbage loopers.

In my garden I control all other pests on fuchsias by beginning in spring to place garden spiders, ladybugs, and lacewings onto them. People often ask me why my fuchsias don't have whiteflies. The answer is that I release beneficial insects, locate them in places with the right light for fuchsias, and provide adequate fertilizer and daily automatic watering with a drip system leading to a mini–spray head hidden over each basket. Spraying against whiteflies is a two-edged sword. You kill the beneficials and don't control the whiteflies (see the detailed discussion on page 173).

Visit nurseries to pick out new fuchsia varieties this month, and you'll have a whole summer and fall to enjoy them. Choose them according to the environment you'll provide. White and pastel colors usually need more shade. Reds, purples, and small single varieties usually can take more sun. No fuchsia can bloom in solid shade; all need partial sun, such as under lath, shade cloth, or an open tree. In interior zones concentrate on growing heat-resistant varieties such as 'Angel's Earrings', 'Bonanza', 'California', 'Carnival', 'Checker-board', 'Display', 'Papoose', and 'Swingtime'. Such upright varieties as 'Gartenmeister Bon-stedt' are best in the ground or tubs. Trailers, such as 'Lisa' and 'Pink Galore', are best in hanging baskets. Some, like 'Swingtime', one of the easiest fuchsias to grow, can go either way.

Epiphyllums

Some epiphyllums (orchid cacti) are still in bloom, so it's not too late to choose these unde-manding and dramatic plants at nurseries. After they finish blooming, prune off diseased and desiccated branches and feed them occasionally with a weak balanced formula, such as 8-8-8 or fish emulsion. Keep them in semishade.

Prune off ungainly branches and root them to make new plants (see directions in the box on page 120). For a faster start, root four cuttings of the same variety in one 6-inch plastic container. (Never mix two varieties in the same container. The more vigorous one will soon crowd out the other, and you'll lose a prized color.) Pruning stimulates growth more than fertilizer alone, so if you desire to hasten growth of a sluggish vari-ety, cut off all unsightly branches and feed it of-ten. If you want to keep plants the same size, however, don't prune them too much and never overfeed with nitrogen.

Gardenias

Gardenias are among our most-grown and least-understood plants. They're often put in the wrong spots, such as small, shady patios, where they invariably get whiteflies. Wrong locations can also cause bud drop, especially in warm coastal zones. Gardenias need acid soil, good drainage, adequate moisture, full sun along the coast or part shade inland, protection from thrips, and also regular fertilizing for growth and flowering with an acid-type product that contains trace elements to prevent chlorosis. However, you can meet all these requirements and still have gardenias that drop buds instead of blooming. The reason is that if night temperatures get over 60° to 62°F, the buds won't develop. They'll stay on the plant but won't grow. Then if suddenly a few cool nights occur, they'll all drop off. So don't grow gardenias where they'll be subjected to warm night temperatures—for example, on patios or porches or close to house walls. Put them where temperatures are colder at night—away from the house and out under the open sky; with the daily temperature spread they'll bloom.

Deciduous Fruit Trees

Do the last thinning on deciduous fruit trees after June drop has occurred. June drop is nature's way of getting rid of an overload of fruit. It may occur at any time between early May and July but is most likely to happen around the first of June. One day you visit your apple, peach, or apricot tree and find a circle of immature fruit lying on the ground under the branches. These trees often set more than double the amount of fruit they could possibly ripen properly, so they simply drop off part of it.

If you followed the advice for April and thinned out the fruit on your trees then and again four to six weeks later, you enabled the remaining fruit to grow larger and thus less fruit will drop off now. Nevertheless, you may need to remove even more fruit than naturally drops in order to space your crop evenly down the branches. Inspect other deciduous fruit trees that are less subject to June drop—plums, for instance—and thin out their fruits also.

Clean up the fallen fruit under the tree before it has time to rot and spread disease. If it's healthy, chop it and add it to the compost pile (cover it with earth to protect against flies and rodents). Also water deciduous fruit trees well in June and July.

Roses

Continue pruning, spraying, irrigating, and fertilizing roses as you did during the month of May (follow the chart on page 308 and explanations on pages 71 and 94).

You can plant canned roses now, but be sure to purchase them from a reputable nursery. Canned roses may harbor rose pests whose larvae live in the soil under the rose. The safest way to buy roses is bare-root.

Shrub Daisies

Two groups of shrub daisies, marguerite (now often called Cobbitty daisy) and euryops, are often sold side by side in nurseries. Because of their similarities, these plants are frequently confused, but they actually have different characteristics and needs. To further confound the issue, we now have many new varieties of marguerite, a new botanical name for all of them, and several new common names.

Marguerites. For many years gardeners have grown and loved marguerite daisies, a flowering shrub native to the Canary Islands and Madeira, in the Atlantic Ocean. Because marguerites differed from other members of the chrysanthemum genus, their former botanical name of *Chrysanthemum frutescens* has now been changed to *Argyranthemum frutescens.* Meanwhile, breeding programs, mainly in Australia, produced new hybrids and selections that were so different from the old marguerites that growers gave them new common names as well. The name Cobbitty daisy was chosen for the town in Australia where the University of Sydney has its research center, and Elfland daisy, for a group of dwarf varieties.

Cobbitty daisies and other new types of marguerites *(Argyranthemum frutescens)* are more compact, easier to grow, more durable, longer lived, and longer blooming than old-fashioned marguerites. Plants range in height from 6 inches to 3 feet and are equally wide, with single, double, semidouble, or anemone-shaped flowers in shades of white, yellow, pink, lavender, rose red, and deep burgundy. Like the old-fashioned marguerites, they make good pot plants and fillers in the garden. Given good care, they'll live several years.

Water marguerites regularly and fertilize them occasionally with a balanced formula. Most new types will continue to bloom even if you don't deadhead them, but they'll look better if you remove faded flowers. If many flowers die all at once, as may happen now in June, give them a butch haircut. Use hedge shears to shear off all the dead flowers and some of the buds along with an inch or two of foliage. Follow up with fertilizer and water, and they'll soon bounce back. Cobbitty daisies survive cutting back better than old varieties did, but remember they're still marguerites. They don't have dormant buds hidden under bare woody bark, so don't cut them back into old bare wood or they'll die. Always leave some foliage on the plant.

Euryops. Euryops are yellow shrub daisies native to South Africa. They're more drought resistant than marguerites, including the new Cobbitty daisies. Also, euryops have dormant buds hidden under their bark all the way to the ground. This means you can, if you wish, prune them hard, into old bare wood, and they'll grow back, though it's always best to leave a bit of foliage on each branch. Follow up with water and fertilizer. Two euryops cultivars are widely grown in Southern California. Both can withstand drought but need some irrigation for best appearance. One has gray foliage and bright lemon yellow flowers with narrow petals *(Euryops pectinatus),* and it blooms mainly in fall, winter, and spring. Cut back this type in June after bloom. Shear the plants all over with hedge shears. Remove dead flowers and 3 or 4 inches of tip growth to shape and renew the plant.

The other most commonly grown cultivar is green-gold euryops (*E. pectinatus* 'Viridis'). This has golden yellow flowers, wider petals, and dark green foliage. It blooms year-round but a little less in summer than in the cooler months. It can be pruned, if necessary, at any time of year, but now's the best time to shear and shape it.

Annual and Perennial Flowers

Annuals. It's a little late for planting seed for summer annuals, but there's no rule against it. You'll simply get a shorter season of color than if you'd planted earlier. Seeds will sprout fast now. So if you've just moved into a new home with oceans of bedding space to fill but no money for transplants, planting from seeds is the way to go. Just don't skimp on soil prep.

Annuals that can be planted from seeds now include anchusa, coleus, cosmos, lobelia, marigold, portulaca, sunflower, sweet alyssum, and zinnia. For the fastest and easiest results choose zinnias and marigolds, perhaps with an edging of sweet alyssum. Dwarf sunflowers are equally easy and even faster to grow, though the splash of color they give you is soon gone. They're worth growing simply because people find them so amusing. (Pull the plants out after their flowers fade or they'll ruin the look of your border.) In semishade, sprinkle seeds of impatiens onto well-prepared ground and blue lobelia along the edge. Don't cover them with soil. Press them into the ground with the back of your hoe. They need light in order to germinate. Keep the ground damp.

For quicker results and to fill empty spots in existing beds purchase nursery transplants. Madagascar periwinkle (vinca; *Catharanthus roseus*) is a good choice for filling bare spaces in the hottest spots in full sun. It's easy to grow and mixes well with other flowers. Cosmos is good for the backs of beds. It blooms into fall and, in coastal zones, often seeds itself so new plants bloom through winter.

Deadhead and pick summer annuals to keep them going. Keep an eye out for stem borers on zinnias. These worms enter the stem and cause the top of the plant to die and sometimes fall over. Open the stem and find and squash the worm. If the plant is high enough, it will branch and continue to bloom.

Perennials. Be on the alert for interesting summer-blooming perennials at your nursery. More are for sale in June than at almost any other time of year because many perennials bloom in June. Some of the best are sold only when flowers are on the plant, so now's your chance to find some treasures. Be wary of buying plants that are not right for your climate zone or the conditions in your garden. Among a multitude of perennials that thrive here and should be easy to find now are Italian bellflower (*Campanula isophylla*), purple coneflower (*Echinacea purpurea*), *Scaevola* 'Blue Wonder' (best in coastal zones), *Verbena bonariensis,* and *Rudbeckia fulgida* 'Goldsturm', a superior garden variety of black-eyed Susan. *R. laciniata* 'Hortensia' (golden glow) is difficult to find but especially useful for hot interior gardens. Its yellow flowers with yellow centers continue to bloom right through October. *Gaillardia grandiflora* 'Yellow Queen' also isn't easy to find but worth hunting for; it blooms into September and is excellent in the interior. For shade, try the graceful meadow rue (*Thalictrum*) and *Bergenia ciliata,* but bait them for snails. 'Victoria Falls' iris is a fine repeat bloomer with tall flowers. Add charm to the garden by creating little lawns in flat areas and filling small spaces between rocks or stepping stones with chamomile, creeping oregano (*Origanum laevigatum* and *O. vulgare* 'Compactum'), creeping thyme, pennyroyal, and *Dymondia margaretae,* a dwarf, matlike relative of zinnias.

You probably fertilized all your perennials in early spring. Now it's time to clean up, deadhead, and lightly cut back those plants that have bloomed or grown floppy, fertilizing them again to encourage summer flowers (refer to the suggestions on page 154). *Hypoestes aristata* 'Lavender Cloud' doesn't bloom till fall but needs some shaping during the year; prune lightly and pinch back its tips to promote bushiness. Continue to pick flowers to keep them blooming. (This plant is rare but worthy of a hunt at botanical-garden sales and specialty nurseries.) Deadhead coreopsis by grabbing handfuls of faded flowers and shearing them off with one-hand grass shears. For large clumps, use hedge shears. (A few buds will bite the dust, too.) Follow up with water and fertilizer; coreopsis will bounce right back with another wave of bloom. Shear off faded flowers of dianthus.

Cut back perennials that bloom in winter and early spring—for example, *Euphorbia characias wulfenii.* A good plant for gardens in which the soil goes dry between irrigations, it has blue-green foliage delightfully complemented by chartreuse flowers. Flowers are followed by long-lasting seedpods. When the pods fade and begin to look ratty with yellow stems, cut them down to the base, but leave the basal foliage—the new shoots you should see sprouting below—these will bloom with chartreuse flowers next year. Look for young euphorbia plants in nurseries now through fall, usually among the succulents.

June is the best month to start perennials from seeds in coastal zones. (Gardeners in the interior can start a month or two earlier.) Warmer temperatures help seeds sprout faster. This is an enthralling undertaking that can save money and give your green thumb the acid test, but it takes perseverance—almost a whole year of it.

First choose and purchase seeds, taking care to select plants that are recommended for your climate zone. Fill flats or peat pots with sterilized soil and plant the seeds according to package directions. (Some are easy to germinate, others not.) Mist the flats to moisten them, cover them with glass or plastic, and keep them in semishade. As soon as seeds sprout, remove the cover and replace it with bird netting, to protect the seedlings from birds and cats. Water regularly, and after the plants form two true leaves, start fertilizing with a weak solution of complete fertilizer or fish emulsion. As the seedlings grow, gradually move them into more light, protect them from pests and disease, trans-plant them into 4-inch individual containers, and pot them on throughout the year. If all goes well, by next spring or summer you'll have sturdy, gallon-size plants to go into the ground.

Pest Control

Many pests are active in June. Spider mites, caterpillars, slugs, and snails are just a few of the usual pests that you are continuing to watch for now. But among the pests that seem to rear their ugly heads most avariciously this month are thrips and whiteflies. If your garden suffers from an infestation of whiteflies, you probably know it already because they're highly visible; but if it's inhabited by a large population of thrips, you may be aware of the damage they're causing but not know which culprit you should blame.

Thrips. Thrips are small, slender, black, rasping insects that often step up activities in June. They're difficult to see, so be on the alert for signs of their damage—distorted flowers on marguerites, roses, and gardenias and scratched stems and leaves on gladioli and beans.

If you feel you must use a chemical control use systemics in the ground, but only on ornamentals. (Spray with systemics only as a last resort.) In the vegetable garden diazinon and carbaryl (Sevin) sprays can be used. The best solution is to use organic controls that don't upset the balance of nature. These include insecticidal soaps and SunSpray Ultra-Fine Spray Oil as well as keeping a clean garden, destroying weeds, growing resistant plants, and rotating crops. Continue to introduce beneficial insects to your garden and neighborhood to control pests.

Whiteflies. Of all the pests that plague gardeners, greenhouse whiteflies *(Trialeurodes vaporariorum)* seem the most maddening. These

Pest Management in New Gardens

Gardens on freshly bulldozed land usually have few problems during the first year other than with soil type, drainage, and possibly wireworms (click beetles) left over from chaparral. The ground hasn't yet built up a resident population of pests and diseases.

Get rid of wireworms with diazinon granules. Be careful not to import pests. Inspect gift and nursery plants carefully. Introduce beneficial insects, and try to interest your neighbors in integrated pest management (as discussed on page 37). Develop a healthy garden from the beginning with a well-balanced population of pests and beneficials.

tiny—1/16 inch—winged insects skulk under the leaves of favored plants and fly out in an embarrassing cloud every time someone brushes past the foliage. (The giant whitefly is different and is discussed on page 101.) Lift a leaf gently and you can see them hiding underneath. It's actually not the flying insect but microscopic larvae that do the damage, sucking plant juices, weakening plants, and excreting a sticky honeydew that's attractive to ants. Some of whiteflies' favorite plants are tomatoes, cucumbers, mint, fuchsias, and neglected patio plants such as ferns and gardenias that grow in too much shade.

Whiteflies are difficult to get rid of because they multiply rapidly and quickly develop new generations with resistance to pesticides. That's what happened with common, generic malathion, which once was an effective control. Also, whiteflies go through five different stages of growth between egg and adult, each of which is susceptible to a different pesticide or to none at all. Thus, if you spray with a pesticide and are successful in killing those in one stage, those in

🐞 Quick Tip

Control Whiteflies with Ladybugs and Spiders. *In the evening, prechill ladybugs for one hour in the refrigerator; then put small teaspoonfuls of ladybugs on premoistened foliage. (Adults may fly away but leave eggs to hatch into beneficial larvae that eat the larvae of whiteflies.) Catch spiders without harming them. Either use a commercial spider catching device or drop a damp facial tissue over each spider and close the tissue gently under it. (Spiders escape from dry tissues but climb up inside wet ones.) Place your captured spiders on such plants as hanging-basket fuchsias.*

other stages remain to proliferate. Only repeated spraying works.

The best defense against whiteflies is keeping a clean garden of healthy, well-fed plants that's well stocked with beneficial insects, tree frogs, and spiders and that is free from ants. (In my garden I don't spray against whiteflies, preferring to control them by the method described in the accompanying tip.) *Encarsia formosa* is a tiny parasitic wasp that specializes in killing whiteflies and can be purchased in quantity from some garden supply houses. Ladybugs, lacewing larvae, Delphastus beetles, and spiders can be effective when placed on plants early in the season. Sticky yellow traps are effective in greenhouses and enclosed spaces such as patios. Whiteflies are attracted to the bright yellow color, which they interpret as young foliage, and they stick tight. Purchase these traps ready-made, from nurseries, or make your own. (To make your own, first spray bright yellow paint—the same shade as that on a container of Prestone antifreeze—on strips of cardboard or on empty food cans. Then cover the painted surfaces with a sticky substance such as Vaseline or Tangle-Trap Insect Trap Coating, and hang the traps among infested plants.)

If you must spray, use insecticidal soaps and light summer oil. Chemical controls include Cooke's Garden Insect Spray, containing Thiodan, and Isotox. Because these kill beneficials along with pests I don't recommend their use except in badly infested small patios and condo gardens where all else has failed. You'll need to spray more than once. Follow package directions.

Lawn Care

Cool-Season Grasses. It's time to reset the cutting height of your lawn mower. Cool-season lawns such as ryegrass, bluegrass, bent grass, fescue, or a mix of cool-season grasses should be allowed to grow longer during the summer. Longer leaves give them more resistance to hot weather. So set the blades of your lawn mower to 2 inches. If your lawn is an improved tall fescue, such as Marathon I, II, or III, set the mower to its top setting of between 2 and 3 inches and be sure to keep the blades sharp. The **Rule of Thumb** is: *Never cut off more than one-third of your lawn's height at one time. (This rule applies to all lawns, but it's particularly important for tall fescue.)*

Keep cool-season lawns well watered according to the needs of each type. From now until fall feed them lightly at the rate of a half pound of nitrogen per 1,000 square feet, when and if needed, to maintain color.

Warm-Season Grasses. If your lawn is a warm-season grass, such as Bermuda, zoysia, or St. Augustine, start now to mow it as short as possible. Set the mower blades lower in order to cut common Bermuda to 1 inch. Hybrid Bermudas like 'Tifway', 'Tifway II', and 'Santa Ana' can be cut even shorter, to ½ or ¾ inch. ('Tifgreen', more often used for golf greens than home lawns, can be cut as short as ⅛ inch.) Cut zoysia

and St. Augustine to between ¾ inch and 1 inch, and cut kikuyu to ½ inch. Feed all warm-season grasses regularly during their growing season except for 'Adalayd' grass (*Paspalum vaginatum*; called Excalibre in sod form), which can be fed in June and July but, during the heat of August and early September, only lightly if at all. Kikuyu grass is another exception; because of its invasive qualities, don't feed it unless you notice poor color or stunted growth. Continue to water warm-season lawns deeply and as infrequently as possible while still maintaining good appearance.

Zoysia. Late spring or early summer is the best time to plant zoysia from plugs or stolons in Southern California. Tests done by the University of California have shown that when you plant from stolons or plugs in June, zoysia grass will take off faster and have less competition from weeds than when it is planted at any other time of year. (For fast coverage, plant stolons at the rate of 12 bushels per 1,000 square feet, double the commercial rate, or plugs spaced on 9-inch centers.)

Zoysia makes a tough, good-looking turf that's tolerant of drought, heat, salinity, and heavy foot traffic. It has few, if any, pest problems and is largely disease free, especially when grown in hot, dry interior zones. Once established it's practically immune to weeds. Despite these virtues it hasn't been much grown, because of its slow rate of establishment, tendency to produce thatch, and long dormant period. But now zoysia is greatly improved. Newer varieties, such as 'De Anza' and 'Victoria', have finer leaf blades, faster rate of coverage, a nice springy texture underfoot without building up thatch, and, best of all, stay green year-round.

As zoysia fills in, water it regularly for fast growth, and keep weeds pulled. Feed mature zoysia grass at the rate of 2 to 3 pounds of nitrogen (37-0-0) per 1,000 square feet at intervals of six to eight weeks. (What you want is a deep green color. Feed it when its color declines.) Water well after fertilizing. Mow zoysia regularly to a height of ⅝ inch with a reel mower.

Vegetable Gardening

By now the summer vegetable garden should be in full swing. Harvest root and leaf crops regularly, while they're still young and tender. Pick the outside leaves of lettuce as needed. Pick beans and summer squash daily while they're still small, but pick tomatoes when fully ripe.

As crops reach the midpoint in their growing seasons, if you didn't do the job last month, side-dress the rows with fertilizer to keep them going. Most crops need additional nitrogen at some point during the growing season. Beans are an exception; don't fertilize them unless they show signs of nitrogen deficiency (slow or stunted growth), because too much nitrogen can prevent them from bearing. Beans that were inoculated at planting time need no fertilizer. Corn needs additional nitrogen and plenty of water when it starts to tassel out. The best time to side-dress tomatoes with additional nitrogen is when they start to bloom.

Water regularly and deeply. Overhead watering is all right inland but must be done early in the day. Ground-level soaking or subterranean irrigation with a drip system is best in all areas. Most vegetables require the equivalent of 1 inch of rain per week. It's especially important not to let cucumbers or tomatoes dry out. Thirsty cucumbers turn bitter. Watering tomatoes unevenly can cause blossom-end rot, a black discoloration on the bottom of fruits. Overwatering tomatoes can cause root rot and wet, rotting fruit.

It's not too late to put in seeds, either to fill in for continued harvests or to plant a whole garden. As with annual flowers you'll simply get later results. Seeds that can be planted now run the gamut of summer vegetables, including corn, cucumbers, green beans, lima beans, leaf lettuce, okra, peppers, pumpkins, New Zealand spinach, summer squash, and winter squash; melons; and also the vegetables we plant year-round, such as beets, carrots, Swiss chard, radishes, and turnips. Heat lovers such as eggplant and peppers do well and grow rapidly when put in from transplants this month. For a fall crop of tomatoes, plant seeds now or put in transplants next month.

Rotate Crops. Crop rotation is important, not only because it prevents soil depletion, but also because it cuts down on pest damage. If you plant the same thing in the same place time after time, pests and fungus organisms and other diseases build up in the soil. Wireworms (the larvae of click beetles), for example, like onions and carrots, and they'll settle down and multiply in rows where these crops are repeatedly planted. If you clear out two rows at the same time, crop rotation is easy; just switch when you replant. When you clear only one row look for the next item that's likely to be harvested and replant with that, or with something totally new and different. Branch out and try exotic vegetables you haven't tried before.

Control Vegetable Pests and Diseases. As in the ornamental garden, concentrate on keeping the garden clean and keeping an eye out for pests and disease. Also continue to introduce beneficial insects and arachnids (spiders and beneficial mites), still our best and most enlightened defense against pests. Release Delphastus beetles, lacewing larvae, and ladybugs in the vegetable garden. Resist the temptation to spray, which can upset the balance of nature. Now is a great time to observe all the fascinating wild insects and spiders that are helping you. To identify them, use a book like Starcher's *Good Bugs for Your Garden.*

Don't pick beans early in the day when plants are wet with dew, because doing so can spread rust and mildew. Wait until midday or late afternoon when the vines are dry. Wash off aphids with soapy water. Handpick large bugs and beetles. If caterpillars are a problem, spray with BT or introduce beneficial wasps. Mint, basil, and dill are said to protect tomatoes from hornworm. (Confine mint to 1-gallon cans; don't let it loose in the garden. Like horseradish it will take over.) Attract scrub jays (see the Quick Tip on page 160).

Leafhoppers on tomatoes, beans, and cucumbers spread mosaic virus diseases. Spray with insecticidal soaps or homemade sprays of onion or garlic. Personally, I never spray with chemicals in the vegetable garden and seldom, if ever, in the ornamental garden, but if you feel you must go this route diazinon, carbaryl, or malathion will control leafhoppers. (Always follow package directions to the letter and only spray affected plants, or you risk killing more beneficials than necessary.)

Mix vegetables as much as possible and interplant them with herbs and marigolds to muddle and confuse insects. Solid plantings of anything, whether ornamental or vegetable, always get hit more severely by pest and disease problems than plants grown in a mixed landscape.

Help Strawberries Bear More Fruit. Strawberries tend to grow vegetatively in June, by sending out runners instead of blooming and bearing fruit. Clip off the runners as they occur. A shot of 0-10-10 fertilizer now will help prolong the harvest.

Unless you're growing strawberries on plastic, keep the ground deeply mulched with pine needles or straw. Sprinkle bait underneath organic and plastic mulches against sowbugs, snails, and slugs. Don't let the plants go dry now, or fruiting will stop.

Purchase/Plant

- ❏ Continue to plant drought-resistant plants, 32, 166
- ❏ Continue to plant melons, 176
- ❏ Plant tropical and subtropical plants, 166
- ❏ Plant bougainvilleas, 167
- ❏ Plant perennial morning glories, 167
- ❏ Purchase fuchsias, 168
- ❏ Continue to purchase epiphyllums, 169
- ❏ Plant seeds of heat-loving annuals, 172
- ❏ Use bedding plants for quick color, 172
- ❏ Purchase perennials in bloom now at nurseries, 172
- ❏ Start perennials from seeds in coastal zones, 173
- ❏ Plant zoysia grass, 175
- ❏ Continue to plant summer vegetables, 176
- ❏ Plant exotic vegetables, 176
- ❏ Purchase, plant, and transplant succulents, including cacti and euphorbias, 194
- ❏ Purchase alstroemerias throughout summer while they are in bloom, 214
- ❏ Plant papayas and bananas, 218
- ❏ Plant and transplant palms, 219

Trim, Prune, Mow, Divide

- ❏ Continue to pick and deadhead roses, 95, 122
- ❏ Pinch back chrysanthemums to make them bushy, 155
- ❏ Divide and repot cymbidiums that have outgrown their containers, 145
- ❏ Remove berries (seedpods) from fuchsias after flowers fall, 169
- ❏ Divide bearded irises if necessary (but wait until October in hot interior valleys), 168
- ❏ Prune epiphyllums, 169
- ❏ Thin out deciduous fruit trees after June drop, 170
- ❏ Give marguerites (Cobbitty daisies) a "butch" haircut, 171
- ❏ Cut back euryops, 171
- ❏ Deadhead and pick summer flowers to keep them going, 172
- ❏ Mow cool-season lawns longer, 175
- ❏ Mow warm-season grasses short, 175
- ❏ Clip runners off strawberries, 177
- ❏ Prune climbing roses that bloom once a year in spring, but wait until flowers fade, 183
- ❏ Divide English primroses after bloom, or wait until September, 236
- ❏ Continue to prune and train espaliers, 211
- ❏ Continue to remove spent bloom stems from daylilies and to propagate the types that make proliferates, 213
- ❏ Deadhead alstroemerias often by pulling off the stalks with a sharp tug, 214
- ❏ Clean up, deadhead, and cut back perennials, 172

Fertilize

- ❏ Feed citrus trees, 50
- ❏ Look for yellow leaves and green veins indicating chlorosis in citrus, gardenias, azaleas, and others; treat it with chelated iron, 193
- ❏ Feed avocado trees, 66
- ❏ Feed fuchsias, 168
- ❏ Feed tuberous begonias, 185
- ❏ Feed bamboo with a slow-release fertilizer, 104
- ❏ Feed water lilies, 125
- ❏ Fertilize corn, 135
- ❏ Fertilize cymbidiums with high nitrogen for growth, 183
- ❏ Give camellias their second feeding for the year, 145
- ❏ Fertilize roses, 94
- ❏ Feed ferns, 147
- ❏ Fertilize tropicals, 166
- ❏ Feed epiphyllums, 54
- ❏ Fertilize marguerites (Cobbitty daisies) after pruning, 171
- ❏ Feed container-grown annuals and perennials with a complete fertilizer, 26
- ❏ Fertilize cool-season lawns lightly, 175
- ❏ Fertilize warm-season lawns, according to type, 175
- ❏ Side-dress vegetable rows if you didn't do it last month, 176
- ❏ Give strawberries a shot of 0-10-10 to prolong the harvest, 177
- ❏ Feed all succulents growing in containers with a well-diluted complete liquid fertilizer, 195
- ❏ If peppers look yellow despite adequate nitrogen, spray them with Epsom salts, 200
- ❏ Feed cycads, 220
- ❏ Fertilize perennials, 80

Water

❏ Water all plants except some well-established drought-resistant plants and some native plants, 144

❏ Water cool-season lawns more often and shallowly, 175

❏ Water warm-season lawns deeply and infrequently, 175

❏ Water corn well as it tassels out, 176

❏ Water vegetables, 176

❏ Don't let strawberries dry out, 177

❏ Water cyclamen occasionally, though they are semidormant now, 229

❏ Most succulents growing in the ground need no water this month, 195

Control Pests, Diseases, and Weeds

❏ Control slugs and snails, 91

❏ Watch chrysanthemums for pests, 173

❏ Control rose pests and diseases, 72

❏ Control pests on fuchsias, 169

❏ Watch for stem borers on zinnias, 172

❏ Control thrips and whiteflies, 173

❏ Manage pests in new gardens, 174

❏ Control pests and diseases on vegetables, 176

❏ Protect strawberries from slugs and snails, 177

❏ Control weeds in the vegetable garden and flowerbeds by hand-pulling, 40

❏ Control weeds among permanent plants by mulching or cultivating, 145

❏ Spray tuberous begonias against mildew, 185

❏ Protect English primroses from caterpillars and slugs and snails, 194

❏ Control corn earworm if you can't live with it, 222

Also This Month

❏ Hand-pollinate corn growing in small plots, 135

❏ Prevent bud drop from gardenias, 170

❏ Reset mower blades for cool-season lawns, 175

❏ Harvest vegetables regularly, 176

❏ Practice crop rotation, 176

❏ Put bloomed-out cyclamen and English primroses in a shady spot for the summer, 194

❏ When the tops of globe onions fall over, stop watering them; allow them to cure, and then harvest, eat, and store them, 284

JULY

The First Real Summer Month

In July the weather starts getting hot even along the coast, and we like to spend as much time as possible outdoors. In hot interior valleys the early morning and evening hours are the best ones for sitting, playing, or working outdoors, but in coastal areas outdoor living is comfortable all day long if we've taken steps to make it so. Because we're in the open air so much this month, it's a good time to notice whether our landscape is as attractive and useful as we want it to be. We may find garden improvements taking root in our minds. July is not a particularly good month for planting—spring and fall are much better—but it's a great time for planning ahead. Do you need to plant another shade tree? Except in the hottest areas, tropical and subtropical plants can still be planted early this month, as well as in June. Perhaps you have space for a romantic vine-covered arbor or pergola or an additional patio. Think about these options now when you can see just where shade and comfort are most needed. (For detailed advice on shade planting, consult this chapter's section on shade plants.)

Hot, dry weather makes regular watering the most important task now through September.

And because there are right and wrong ways to water, summer is a good time to plan as well for water conservation. It's the prime time of year to benefit from a basic landscape of drought-resistant plants that's irrigated by a drip system. Plants that are heavy water users can be limited to small areas close to the house and to containers that can be phased out in times of drought.

Watering

Except for some California native plants and a few well-established drought-resistant plants from other parts of the world, all plants need regular watering now. Water large trees deeply but infrequently, to encourage deep and healthy roots. Allow the soil to dry out somewhat between irrigations, to permit air to enter the soil pores and provide the oxygen that roots need. When drought is inevitable, trees with deep, healthy root systems are better able to survive it. The best, most water-saving time to do regular watering is early in the day.

Mist systems that pulse on briefly throughout the day in shady areas enhance the environment for some plants. Many shade plants, including bromeliads, orchids, ferns, epiphyllums, and fuchsias, either absorb water through their foliage or appreciate the cooling evaporation of a fine spray of water.

Mulch Bare Ground

Look around the garden for areas of bare soil and cover these with a 2- or 3-inch-thick layer of organic mulch. Organic mulch keeps the ground cool, conserves water, keeps many weeds from growing, and adds valuable organic matter to the soil. Mulching is one of the easiest ways to gradually improve your garden's soil. In general, stick to smooth-textured mulches in flowerbeds and vegetable gardens because these decompose fairly quickly and can be safely dug into the ground when replanting. Rough-textured mulches are longer lasting and thus work well under permanent shrubs, trees, and vines and on pathways. Be alert to slugs and snails, which can find hiding places in some rough-textured mulches. (For more on mulch and a list of organic materials, see page 24.)

Citrus and Avocado Trees

Don't let citrus and avocados dry out in July or August or a great deal of fruit may fall off. This doesn't mean you should keep the trees in a boggy condition. They don't like that either. Established trees in most soils need deep watering every two or three weeks depending on soil type and weather conditions. Newly planted trees usually need deep watering once a week. (The best way to know when trees need water is to use a soil auger or a tensiometer; see page 31.)

Citrus need water in a broad band starting one-third of the distance from the trunk to the drip line and extending an equal distance beyond the drip line. This is where their feeder roots are, not next to the trunk. Put the hose on the ground and let it run slowly, filling a well-placed watering basin. The bark of citrus trees must be kept dry to prevent the fungal disease gummosis, which can infect their trunks.

Avocados need water all over the ground under their branches, up to a foot or two from the trunk. The best way to water them is slowly, with a sprinkler. Avocados are highly prone to phytophthora root rot (a fungal disease that's spread by infected plants and favored by wet or poorly drained soil), but they're not susceptible to gummosis.

Cymbidiums

This is the time of year when cymbidiums are growing new leaves and pseudobulbs. Continue to feed for growth with a product such as 30-10-10 liquid or 14-14-14 slow-release pellets. Keep them in filtered shade for the summer, and don't let the roots dry out. In interior gardens a drip system is ideal. Misting the foliage can be beneficial in the dry interior, but it's not necessary in coastal regions. Along the coast watering once or twice a week suffices. Overhead sprinklers are fine, but don't allow them to run for a long time—and avoid overwatering in general—since these practices can cause fungal problems, especially when the irrigation is done late in the day.

Sometimes cymbidiums are kept in too much shade, such as under a dense tree—a frequent mistake in home gardens. Black marks on the leaves and pseudobulbs are signs of fungal problems. The plants don't die, but they won't bloom as well. It's probably best to get rid of stricken plants so they don't spread the disease to healthy specimens. Some varieties seem more resistant to disease than others. Stick with those, and grow plants in a coarse, fibrous potting soil that drains well and in appropriately sized plastic containers. Don't put a cymbidium in a container that's too large for its roots or you'll drown it with soggy soil.

Roses

Continue to control rose pests and diseases and to water, fertilize, and prune the plants by picking the flowers, but stop disbudding them now. Follow the basic guidelines given in March (page 94) and expanded in April and May (pages 122 and 146). In hot interior zones step up the frequency of irrigations now to three times per week at the rate of 1½ inches of water per irriga- tion. (In coastal zones, twice a week may be sufficient.) Keep the ground around the plants well mulched.

Prune Climbing Roses That Bloom Only Once a Year. Most modern climbing roses bloom continuously from April to January. These should be pruned along with your other roses in January. But some roses still grown in Southern California bloom only once in spring. The **Rule of Thumb** is: *Established climbing roses, over three years old, that bloom only once in spring or early summer should be pruned after bloom.* These roses bear their flowers on wood that grew during the previous year. If you wait until winter you risk cutting off new canes that will bear next year. There are several kinds of spring-blooming climbers, among which are the following:

- **Ramblers.** Rambling roses have thin, bendy canes and massive clusters of small, flattish flowers no bigger than 2 inches in diameter. Older types bloom magnificently but only once, in spring or early summer. Newer types bloom several times during the year. Where there's room, ramblers can be allowed to sprawl over the support of mature trees, large shrubs, or house or shed roofs, and they'll continue to grow larger and bloom massively without ever being pruned. (If they've been allowed to mound and climb for many years, clean out as much as possible of the dead interior after bloom.)

If you want to control the size of old-fashioned rambling roses, prune them immediately after their bloom finishes by cutting out old (gray) wood and canes that have bloomed this year. But don't cut out any fresh green canes. You have a choice of options: you can cut all the way to the ground, or you can keep a structure of main canes over a support and cut back the laterals that have bloomed to two buds, or eyes.

New growth starts now, in summer. Tie up the abundant new canes as they grow, but cut off weak, twiggy ones at ground level. All new canes will bloom the following year.

- **Spring-Blooming, Large-Flowered Climbers.** Large-flowered climbers have thicker canes than ramblers and larger flowers, with fewer per cluster. Some old types flower once in spring; many repeat the bloom once again in summer. Several, such as 'America', 'Don Juan', and 'Handel', three of the best, bloom continuously from April through December.

Don't prune young plants. Prune established plants that bloom only once, right after the bloom finishes, by cutting out old woody canes more than three years old but leaving all younger canes and as many succulent ones that grew this year as you have room for. (Two- and three-year-old canes bloom best.) Cut back laterals on canes that have flowered to two or three buds each. These will bloom next year. Rearrange them and retie them onto their supports. Remove any suckers that sprout from below the bud union.

- **Spring-Blooming Species Roses.** These old-fashioned roses were originally found in the wild, though some selections, such as the Chinese species known as Lady Banks' rose (*Rosa banksiae*), have been cultivated for centuries. In some areas Lady Banks' rose continues to bloom through June. In early July, or as soon as blooming stops, cut back the outsides of established plants hard, to shape and control them, and to encourage lots of new growth that will bloom next year. Follow up with a balanced fertilizer, and water deeply.

🐌 Quick Tip

Instant Shade for a Hanging Basket. *Fuchsias, begonias, and other shade plants are often burned by afternoon sun when hung from west-facing shade structures or porches. For these, spray a Japanese parasol with clear plastic, to weatherize it, and shove the handle into the soil at a low angle to provide shade.*

Shade Plants

How to Garden in Shade. Every garden is bound to include a certain amount of shade, and now's a good time to study these areas while their relative coolness is most appreciated. Well-designed and properly planted shade gardens are the most refreshing parts of any landscape, but you can't plant them properly unless you understand the characteristics of shade.

How Shade Occurs. Many homeowners start out with mostly full sun but then either plant too many trees or let volunteers grow wherever they plant themselves. After a few years on this course, a sunny garden can become a shady or even gloomy one. It takes real courage to cut down mature trees, but sometimes this is the only way to reclaim the sun. In some cases you can lace trees out (remove twiggy branches and interior growth) to let adequate light through. The best shade is that which you create yourself, either by building a shade structure or by planting an appropriate number of well-chosen trees in the right places. The most difficult shade is that which you can't control—solid shadows of buildings or walls, sometimes alternating with an hour or two of burning hot sun.

How Shade Moves and Differs in Degree. Shadows don't stand still; every day they move from west to east as the sun moves across the sky from east to west. They also lengthen north-ward as the sun moves south during fall and winter, and then they gradually shorten again as the sun moves north in winter and spring. These factors make gardening in the shade a lot trickier than gardening in full sun. So if you're interested in shade gardening, begin by observing and understanding the shadows in your own garden; notice where they occur, how dense they are, and their duration.

Not all semishade or even dense shade is alike. It differs widely according to what causes it and its exposure (the direction it faces). So before you plant, it's important to learn how to distinguish between these various degrees and exposures of shade and to learn which plants are most likely to succeed in each of them. Shade plants vary greatly in shade tolerance. Most shade plants, particularly flowering ones, need semishade, which by definition means part sun. Only a small number of plants will grow with no sun at all; yet many gardeners have to contend with total unmitigated shade in some areas. (See the accompanying box for a list of the main types and exposures.)

How to Create a Restful Atmosphere. A peaceful shade garden can remind you of a cool forest glade even if you've housed it in lath or covered it with manmade shade cloth. So when you design your shade garden, work for a natural and informal feeling. Accent your plantings with rocks, driftwood, and stepping-stones—perhaps surrounded by moss or baby's tears. Pools and waterfalls lend a cooling atmosphere, and in some cases they use less water than heavily irrigated plants. The sight and sound of a splashing fountain can make a hot day seem cooler. Create charm and interest by adding rustic seats and wandering paths, and use pastels and color tones from the cool half of the spectrum; they're more restful than bright colors.

🦋 Quick Tip

Keep New Guinea Impatiens from Wilting in Hot Weather. *Place shallow saucers under 8- and 10-inch plastic containers of New Guinea impatiens. Water the plants daily with enough water to flow out the drainage hole and fill the saucer to overflowing. During the day, roots will take an extra drink as needed, and the saucer will be dry by nightfall. (Don't try this on other plants—they'd die from root rot.)*

Tuberous Begonias. If you planted tuberous begonias in March they'll be in full bloom now. They're heavy feeders, so feed them regularly with balanced liquid fertilizer, such as 8-8-8, every week, or use slow-release 14-14-14. Don't overwater. Let them dry out between waterings. Always remove spent blossoms but leave the stems on the plant. They'll fall off in a few days and can then be removed.

Control mildew with a chemical product, for example Funginex, or try an organic control such as the antitranspirant Wilt-Pruf. (It cleans up mildew as a by-product of its labeled uses; however, it may be difficult to find here except at floral supply stores or at Christmas-tree lots in December.) Order it in bulk from agricultural supply companies. Also, dot the ground around the base of your tuberous begonias with Deadline to protect them from snails and slugs. If you didn't raise these flamboyant flowers yourself, you can find them in bloom now at some specialty and dig-your-own nurseries.

Impatiens. Impatiens fill dappled shade with color faster than any other flower. For the most color and easiest care choose the regular single variety. New Guinea impatiens have colorful leaves as well as flowers. They need more light than other types, and plenty of water. Water

The Kinds of Shade and Some Plants to Grow in Them

Some shade plants are adapted to several of the areas described below, others to only one or two. So use the following list as a starting point rather than as a set of immutable rules. You can learn more by experimenting with the shade in your own garden.

- **Full Shade.** This occurs under thick evergreen trees and north-facing overhangs and in some patios, atriums, and covered porches.

  Characteristics: Virtually no sunshine hits full shade, at any time of year. This is the most difficult kind of shade to cope with, since few plants survive in dark places. (If these areas get some reflected light they're easier to plant.) The ground in full shade is cold and often poorly prepared. When it gets wet it stays wet, unless it contains tree roots. Yet if it's under an overhang it's often neglected, and in that case it's watered too seldom.

  Special Tips: Prepare the soil by first removing some of it. Then dig up the ground deeply and replace the removed soil with large quantities of acid soil amendments (most shade plants are acid loving). Add 1 to 3 pounds of soil sulfur per 100 square feet. Check the soil often to make sure it's moist but not soggy. Cover bare ground with a smooth-textured mulch or cloak it with a ground cover. Accent gloomy areas by digging holes in the mulch or ground cover and slipping in potted, seasonal plants already in color or bloom, including caladiums, calceolarias, chrysanthemums, cymbidiums, cineraria, and cyclamen. Rely heavily on design elements, like bromeliads mounted on driftwood, stepping stones, and fountains. Illuminate at night with soft light.

  Plants That Grow in Full Shade: Paradise palm *(Howea fosterana);* Japanese aralia *(Fatsia japonica);* fatshedera *(Fatshedera lizei);* Japanese aucuba *(Aucuba japonica),* including gold dust plant *(A. japonica* 'Variegata'); monstera; many houseplants, including philodendron, dracaena *(Dracaena fragrans),* Swedish ivy *(Plectranthus australis),* aspidistra (one of the best for difficult, dark shade, including windy exposures); ferns, including leatherleaf fern *(Rumohra adiantiformis),* sword fern *(Nephrolepis exaltata), N. exaltata* 'Dallas', and *N. obliterata* 'Kimberley Queen'; liriopes and ophiopogons, including mondo grass; baby's tears *(Soleirolia soleirolii);* small-leafed ivy, including 'Needlepoint'; cryptanthus; and—where there's plenty of reflected light—clivia.

- **Filtered Shade.** This occurs—though rarely—as dappled shade under an open-branched tree. More often it's found inside a structure built especially for shade plants and covered with wooden lath or shade cloth.

  Characteristics: From morning to night at all times of year small shadows move from west to east over the plants. This is the ideal situation for most shade plants because it cuts the intensity of the sun, which otherwise could burn leaves or flowers. Plants stay cool and comfortable, but they get plenty of sunshine for growth and bloom.

  Special Tips: Shade houses are best built in areas that were originally in full sun. When using wooden lath, always arrange it so the individual slats run north and south. When using shade cloth, choose its degree of shade according to your climate zone and the plants you wish to grow under it. In general, use cloth that casts 25 to 30 percent shade in coastal zones and 50 to 75 percent shade inland.

  Plants That Grow in Filtered Shade: All shade plants without exception. Some plants that are especially well adapted to filtered shade include camellias; azaleas; bromeliads; all ferns, including staghorn ferns; fuchsias; impatiens; epiphyllums; all orchids that can grow outdoors in your climate zone; tuberous begonias; and shade-loving annuals, particularly coleus.

- **East-Facing Partial Shade.** This occurs on an east-facing porch, under an east-facing overhang, or to the east of a house, wall, or tree.

Characteristics: This is one of the finest kinds of shade to plant in. Cool morning sun shines into these areas, but they're protected from the burning hot sun of midday and afternoon hours.

Special Tips: Grow plants that must have sunlight in order to bloom but can't stand the burning rays of hot midday or afternoon sun. Plants that need partial shade inland but full sun along the coast will usually do well in eastern exposures. Hanging-basket plants such as fuchsias will be one-sided. Don't attempt to turn them, since that would deprive them of necessary light.

Plants That Grow in East-Facing Partial Shade: Tree ferns; mahonia (*Mahonia bealei* and *M. lomariifolia);* Tobira pittosporum (*Pittosporum tobira* 'Wheeler's Dwarf'); Japanese privet (*Ligustrum japonicum);* euonymus; abutilon; acanthus (*Acanthus mollis);* daylilies; agapanthus; snowbush (breynia); bergenia; fuchsia; impatiens; cymbidiums; epiphyllums; begonias, including tuberous begonias; coleus; geraniums (pelargoniums); calla lilies; hydrangeas; so-called sun azaleas; and all shade-loving annuals and perennials.

- **West-Facing Partial Shade.** This occurs to the west of a house, wall, or tree or under a west-facing overhang.

Characteristics: Plants are totally shaded throughout the morning and hot noonday sun, and then suddenly in the afternoon the sun strikes them in all its fury. When this condition is combined with a heat wave or Santa Ana, all west-facing plants get fried. (The problem is at its worst in inland areas.)

Special Tips: Unless you live near the coast, don't even try to grow shade plants in unprotected western exposures. Instead choose plants that are capable of growing in either sun or shade. Cut the force of the afternoon sun by planting open trees and shrubs or by building a patio overhang, view garden, or shade structure that will allow you to grow a wider selection of plants.

Plants That Grow in West-Facing Partial Shade: Pittosporum; India hawthorn (*Rhaphiolepis indica);* nandina; breynia; aeoniums and other succulents; Madeira geranium (*Geranium maderense*) (coastal zones only); daylilies; euryops; fortnight lilies (*Dietes, Moraea);* agapanthus; geraniums (pelargoniums); abutilon; 'Richmondensis' begonias; semperflorens begonias; 'Gartenmeister Bonstedt' fuchsia; and any plant that's described in the *Sunset Western Garden Book* as being suitable for planting in either sun or shade in your climate zone.

- **North-Facing Partial Shade.** This occurs to the north of a house, wall, or tree but not directly beneath a north-facing overhang, porch cover, or tree. (These areas are in full shade.)

Characteristics: North-facing shade changes with the seasons. In winter such areas enjoy full bright shade under the open sky, sometimes called "skyshine." Unless shaded from the side, they get full sun for a month or two in late spring and early summer, when the sun reaches its northernmost position. The shadows to the north of houses and trees will be shortest at the summer solstice (June 21 or 22).

Special Tips: Make sure these areas get adequate water in summer while they're exposed to more sunshine. If shade plants get burned by summer sun, install removable panels of lath or shade cloth. Provide more shade in summer for a north-facing backyard by building a freestanding shade structure or pergola, and growing a deciduous vine, such as wisteria, over it.

Annual flowers and vegetables can be grown in north-facing flowerbeds that are shaded in winter but sunny in summer. In fall plant them with winter-blooming flowers for shade; in summer switch them to sun-loving flowers or vegetables, like zinnias or tomatoes. You can also plant bulbs if you plant them where sun will hit them when it's time for them to bloom. Raised beds can increase the speed of the returning sun by lifting plants above the shadow of the house.

Plants That Grow in North-Facing Partial Shade: Camellias; azaleas; clivia; many ferns, especially tree ferns; Japanese maple (*Acer palmatum);* leopard plant (*Ligularia tussilaginea*

187

'Aureo-maculata'); billbergia; bergenia; cineraria (plant in October for late-winter bloom); bulbs, including daffodils and prechilled hyacinths and tulips (also for fall planting); and annual flowers and vegetables as described above. (For a discussion of a north-facing perennial bed, see page 187.)

- **South-Facing Partial Shade.** This occurs under a deep, south-facing overhang, under a south-facing porch cover, or under the branches of a south-facing tree. (Areas to the south of a wall, a tree, or your house that are open to the sky or under a very narrow overhang—1 to 3 feet—are in full sun.)

  Characteristics: South-facing shade exists in summer but not in winter. In winter the area under the branches of a large, dense, south-facing tree or under a deep south-facing overhang, solid-roofed patio, or porch will be flooded with sun in the middle of the day. In summer these same areas will be in total shade in the middle of the day.

Thus the comfort level for people in south-facing shade is first-rate, but plant choice is difficult.

Special Tips: In general, south-facing shade is a prime place for a patio or porch. Pave these areas wherever possible and you'll have an ideal spot for sitting comfortably outdoors in both winter and summer. Decorate south-facing covered patios and porches with containers that can be moved or replanted according to the seasons.

Plants for South-Facing Shade: Winter-blooming annuals for full sun or partial shade, including primroses, violas, pansies, and snapdragons, can be switched in summer to such houseplants as Swedish ivy *(Plectranthus australis)* and African violets—those that like extremely bright light but no direct sun. Or grow succulents year-round. They like sun in winter and don't mind shade in summer, and many, such as *Kalanchoe blossfeldiana,* have the added attraction of winter or spring bloom.

🐌 Quick Tip

Keep Impatiens from Getting Leggy by Progressive Pruning. *Each time you feed impatiens, select the two longest shoots on opposite sides of the plant. Cut off two-thirds of their length. The plants will remain full, well branched, and bushy at all*

impatiens daily now, especially when growing them in containers. They like loose acid soil but aren't as fussy about drainage as other plants. You can buy small bedding sizes of impatiens to transplant into tubs or the ground, or purchase them in hanging baskets and keep them in the containers they came in. Feed regularly but lightly for growth and bloom. Prune progressively (see accompanying Quick Tip).

Salvias

Tough, ornamental, easy, sometimes fragrant, often drought tolerant, and seldom bothered by pests, the members of the *Salvia* genus, commonly called sages, have been beloved by local gardeners for years. Recognize them by two-lipped flowers in almost any color of the rainbow, arranged in whorls evenly spaced or in tightly massed spikes on single or branching stems. Some salvias are shrubs; some are native plants; others are annual bedding plants, culinary herbs, or good subjects for the perennial garden. Many are old garden favorites. Now dozens of new ones from South America, Mexico, Asia, Europe, and Africa are lending an air of relaxed sophistication to every garden in which they're grown. Here are some good choices, both old and new, for local gardens:

- **Autumn Sage** *(Salvia greggii).* Usually red blooms, occasionally yellow or purple. Needs full sun, good drainage; very drought resistant, it needs no water along the coast once established.

- **Cleveland Sage** (*S. clevelandii* 'Pozo Blue', 'Aromas', and the compact 'Allen Chickering' and 'Winifred Gillman'). California native that can take some garden water without dying.
- **Pitcher Sage** (*S. spathacea*). Another native; forms a dense mat; can take some shade and attracts hummingbirds.
- **Purple Sage** (*S. leucophylla* 'Point Sal Spreader', 'Figueroa', or 'Mrs. Beard'). A good bank cover and native that needs no summer water once established.
- *S.* **'Indigo Spires'.** Not a species but a hybrid with excellent color and long bloom. Needs staking; alternatively, let it twine into other plants or flop on the ground to form a sheet of blue.
- *S. chiapensis.* Attractive, airy upright plant to 1 to 2 feet with bright fuchsia, nonstop-blooming flowers. Needs moist, well-amended soil with good drainage; responds well to organic fertilizer. Reseeds.
- *S. confertiflora.* Richly colored, foot-long, velvety orange spikes on a 6-foot shrub for large gardens. Prune after spring bloom and tie to pea stakes to support heavy fall bloom.
- *S. involucrata*. Hot pink flowers late summer and fall; a good combination with 'Indigo Spires' in large gardens; dense velvety foliage on a shrub 5 feet tall.
- *S. patens* **'Oxford Blue'.** Does well in inland or coastal regions; 2 to 3 feet tall.
- **White Sage** (*S. apiana*). Native with flat leaves; good for making smudges.

Annual and Perennial Flowers

Plant Annuals. You can still plant annuals this month, especially in coastal zones. You'll just

Quick Tip

How to Revive a Wilted Impatiens. *When an impatiens wilts from too much heat, sun, or dryness, don't despair. Plunge the entire container up to the stems of the plant in a bucket of water. Come back in half an hour; the plant will have recovered.*

get a shorter season of bloom. The best choices are the heat lovers, such as Madagascar periwinkle (vinca; *Catharanthus roseus*), marigolds, portulaca, zinnias, and, early in the month, celosias. (If you plant the last too late, it won't make a proper head.)

Care for Coleus. We grow coleus for its colorful leaves and not for its flowers. Once considered a Victorian plant, it is coming back into favor thanks to new varieties with brighter colors and interesting characteristics. You can have success with this potentially fine annual if you give it what it needs.

Coleus sickens in full shade and burns in too much sun, so grow it in filtered sunshine. Plant it in porous, slightly acidic soil, either in containers or in beds, away from the roots of invasive trees and protected from snails. Keep the soil damp but not soggy; too much water will cause the leaves to drop off. When the flowers appear pinch them off; they sap the plant's strength. Feed coleus lightly with fish emulsion or a complete fertilizer mixed half-strength. (Don't overfeed it or you'll get all stalk instead of leaves.) Coleus is almost always sold in mixed packs, but it looks especially attractive when, instead of mixed colors, only one color is grown solidly in a drift among other shade plants of contrasting colors.

🐌 Quick Tip

A Timesaving Way to Grow Foxgloves from Seed. *Sprinkle seeds on any warm, semishaded section of bare ground kept continually moist by a drip system, such as the top of a hanging basket under a mister or a vegetable row between stalks of a tall crop, like tomatoes. Dig up and transplant the resulting seedlings in late summer or early fall.*

Start Biennials. Now's the time to start biennials from seed. These are plants that take two years to bloom, such as foxgloves *(Digitalis),* sweet William *(Dianthus barbatus),* and Canterbury bell *(Campanula medium).* Foxgloves are well worth growing from seed because tall varieties aren't always available in nurseries, especially in fall when you most want to plant them. (Dwarf foxgloves, such as 'Foxy', bloom soon after fall planting instead of waiting until spring, and the bloom usually doesn't last long.) Tall varieties take up no more space than short ones and give you a bigger display for the same amount of effort. Take these steps to grow them from seed:

- Provide rich, fertile, well-dug soil. Alternatively, use a flat filled with damp, sterilized potting soil that contains a high percentage of milled peat moss.
- The seeds are tiny, so mix them with a little sand and sprinkle them on the surface of the soil. Press them gently into the soil surface with a flat piece of wood. Don't cover them with soil; they need light to germinate. Mist them with water.
- Put flats in a warm, shady spot. Cover them with a plastic sheet to keep them moist until the seed germinates. Once they sprout, remove the cover.
- After the plants have developed two real leaves, start feeding them with a well-diluted solution of fish emulsion. Transplant them to the garden in late August or September.

Deadhead and Water Perennials. Continue to deadhead perennials. Keep them well watered now and cut back spring bloomers that stopped blooming at the arrival of hot weather.

Border penstemons *(Penstemon gloxinioides)* are bloomed out by now, so cut back the stems that have bloomed, leaving two green leaves at the bottom of each. Leave any basal foliage in place. (With plants like penstemon that don't go woody, you shouldn't cut their stems all the way to the ground.) Penstemon will then flower again on side branches in late summer.

When gaura has its midsummer "downtime," shear off all the dead flowers and a bit of foliage, so plants stand 12 to 15 inches tall; in a month or less it will be back in bloom.

Artemisia doesn't take well to shearing, so when it spreads too much, lift the top branches and cut off the older lower ones, as close to the crown as you can reach.

Deadhead pentas (star clusters; *Pentas lanceolata);* if you do, its white, pink, lilac, or red flowers will bloom for months. Grow pentas in full sun, cover its roots with mulch, and give it frequent fertilizer, regular water, and good drainage. It doesn't do well in sandy soil that dries out between waterings or where tree roots are a problem. Strengthen and shape lavender shrubs by shearing them after bloom. Licorice plant *(Helichrysum petiolare)* looks good spilling over the hard edges of a path; pinch it back to keep it from sprawling too far.

Control of Bark Beetles on Conifers

Most vigorous and healthy conifers, such as cypress and pine trees, can withstand numerous attacks from bark beetles. But trees such as Monterey cypress and Monterey pine, if they are already stressed from lack of care, may suddenly die in summer, or at least portions of them. If a tree's looking sick, inspect the trunk. Look for drill holes, "frass" (boring dust), or "pitch tubes" of frass and sap mixed together. Peel back the bark around a drill hole, and you may see galleries excavated by beetles right under the bark, where they live and reproduce. Once damage has girdled the trunk, the tree will die. Preventive measures and solutions include the following:

- Maintain healthy trees: Don't plant pines and other conifers in wet, poorly drained areas; do fertilize with nitrogen; and irrigate the trees adequately and deeply from early spring to late fall, particularly in hot, dry weather.

- Once beetle damage is noticeable, don't expect sprays to cure the problem, especially in a weakened tree. However, professional spraying with the appropriate product may help protect a healthy tree.

- Remove badly infested or dying trees promptly. Don't pile the wood or tree trimmings near conifers, or the beetles may spread to healthy specimens. (If you want to save the wood for your fireplace, remove its bark so it will dry quickly; this will prevent the larvae from maturing.)

- Valuable trees may be worth spraying for protection from attack. Call your University of California Cooperative Extension office and ask for pamphlets on the control of bark beetles.

- Wait until cool weather (November through February) to prune conifers. Warm-weather pruning increases beetle activity and stresses the trees. For more detailed information on bark beetles, consult the *Ortho Problem Solver*.

Control of Pine Pitch Canker and Cypress Canker

Monterey pines on the Monterey Peninsula have recently been attacked by a relatively new disease, pine pitch canker. This disease causes sunken areas on branches, branch dieback, a tremendous amount of dripping sap, and eventual death of the tree. Unfortunately, the canker is not restricted to Monterey pines but has been found on virtually every other pine species we grow in California, including the Torrey pine. Another canker disease, cypress canker, has for many years infected Monterey cypress trees and sometimes juniper.

Unfortunately, there is no known cure for pine pitch canker or cypress canker. Your only options are to remove and destroy infected branches to slow the disease, cut down trees that are dead or dying, and avoid planting species that are poorly adapted for local conditions. Until a solution is found for pine pitch canker, do not plant pine trees in California. Meanwhile, maintain the health of your pine and cypress trees. Well-fertilized and watered trees can better withstand diseases. Don't let pines or cypress trees go dry in summer, and don't prune them now; wait until winter.

Even in winter, cleaning out the debris-filled crown of a very old, previously unpruned Monterey cypress tree means almost sure death to the tree. With such specimens, remove outer dead branches and tip-prune only.

Don't Kill All the Butterflies

Caterpillars, loopers, and worms—especially green loopers, tomato hornworms, and cabbage worms—are the bane of many gardeners. If necessary, control them with BT. But butterflies, with the possible exception of white cabbage butterflies, are the floating flowers of the

How to Make Cut Hibiscus Flowers Stay Open at Night

Most hibiscus flowers close up at night. You can keep them open this way.

- Pick blossoms just as they're barely open at 9 or 10 A.M., and slip each one into an empty Sno-Cone cup to protect it. (Pick them right under the flower rather than at the base of the stem in order not to tear the bark.)

- Put the Sno-Cone cups containing the flowers in a plastic bag and place them in the refrigerator for the day.

- Take the flowers out in the evening. They'll soon open fully and then stay open all night without water. (Some new varieties will stay open for three days.)

- Since water isn't needed, you can use these methods to arrange them: Spear the blossoms on toothpicks, and stick the toothpicks into arrangements. Or, to use the flowers in vases, spear them on long bamboo barbecue skewers and arrange the skewers. Or instead of the stiff bamboo skewers, substitute the center veins of fronds cut from a pigmy date palm (*Phoenix roebelenii*). Cut off the individual leaflets from each vein to bare stem and then spear a flower with its sharp tip. Your hibiscus will be transformed into cut flowers with long, graceful, arching stems.

garden. So why kill them all? In fact, why not encourage them? Gardeners who plant meadows filled with wildflowers often provide perfect habitats and never notice the depredations of the attendant caterpillars, a necessary stage before you get butterflies.

If you like swallowtail butterflies, grow parsley and common fennel (*Foeniculum vulgare*)—plenty of it, for both you and them. The caterpillars are attractively striped and not overly voracious. They do, however, like willow trees, poplars, and sycamores. If you grow these trees, you're likely to have a resident population already.

Monarch butterflies can be attracted by growing butterfly weed (*Asclepias tuberosa*). Large-flowered passion vine will attract Gulf fritillary, a red-orange butterfly with black-to-brown markings and silver spots under the wings. The fuzzy black caterpillars will decimate leaves of passion vine but not touch much else in the garden. The mourning cloak butterfly is attracted to newly mown lawns and is often fearless enough to sit on a gardener's moist outstretched palm. For more about attracting butterflies, see Sedenko's *The Butterfly Garden*.

Hydrangeas

Once hydrangea flowers have faded to brown or green, cut back each stalk that has bloomed, leaving only two buds or leaf scars, from which new wood will grow to bloom next spring. (Cut back young plants lightly.) Don't cut off green stems that haven't yet bloomed because they'll bear flowers next year—or later this year if the plant has a north-facing exposure. (Hydrangeas perform best facing east.) Feed for growth.

Hibiscus

Continue to prune, water, and fertilize hibiscus. Continue also to release beneficials onto them and wash the plants off with water to control giant whitefly. (For a full discussion of this pest, see page 101.) Now's a good time to plant these showy garden shrubs. There are about thirty varieties available in a wide range of shapes, sizes, and vibrant colors. Fancy-flowered varieties are less vigorous, lankier in growth, and need more protection from frost than common garden varieties. Grow them for their flowers, prune them

Chick Eglee's and Ninkey Dalton's Pacific Palisades patio has a sense of place. One glance at
the orange tangerines, red cannas, yellow
daylilies, flickering koi, brightly painted house,
and fountain made from a vintage Bauer pot,
and you know you're in Southern California.
(Design by Rob Steiner.)

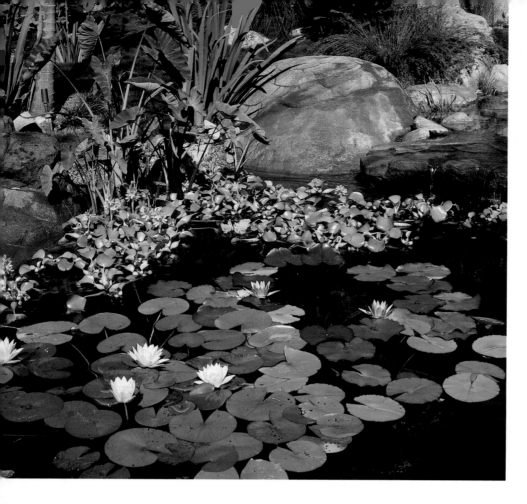

Ponds (discussed on page 123) add magic to gardens, reflecting the sky and attracting birds, frogs, and dragonflies. A water feature can be as simple as a tub garden or as elaborate as this elegant Santa Barbara lily pond complete with waterfall. (Design by Pat Brodie.)

Tucked into the Hollywood hills, an informal landscape of largely drought-resistant plants, including weeping bottlebrush, fortnight lilies, lamb's ears, santolina, woolly thyme, rosemary, lavender, convolvulus, and roses, softens the edges of a lap pool that doubles as a reflecting pond. (Design by Griffith and Steiner.)

A tipu tree (Tipuana tipu), *fish pond, and pergola provide a peaceful spot for meditation in a corner of my daughter, Francesca Filanc's, former garden in Olivenhain.*

Drifts of blue agapanthus and old-fashioned montbretia (Coscosmia crocosmiiflora, [Tritonia]) bloom in midsummer on the banks of a little stream in Lani Freymiller's Rancho Santa Fe garden. Eucalyptus trees loom in the background.

Over sixty years ago my friend and mentor, the late Manchester Boddy, cleaned out a grove of native oaks growing on his land and planted a forest of camellias and azaleas in their shade. Now the results of Boddy's vision inspire all who visit Descanso Gardens.

Fields of ranunculus bloom every spring in Carlsbad. To create your own display, plant corms in fall in pots or in drifts among other flowers (as described on page 278). No other bulb gives so much for so little.

Top: In spring, the pink rose 'Carefree Wonder' sets my garden's mood, surrounded by easy-care Santa Barbara and paludosum daisies, daylilies, pelargoniums, and Madeira geraniums (Geranium maderense).

Bottom: Last fall I sprinkled seeds of annual toadflax (Linaria maroccana) onto prepared soil around the edges of my vegetable garden. I raked them into the ground and kept them moist. In spring, here's the result. You can do it too. (See the fall chapters for advice.)

Top: Spring-blooming wildflowers I planted from seeds in fall include baby blue eyes (Nemophila menziesii), orange calendulas, and pink linaria. Paludosum daisies (below the wall) seed themselves; where I don't want them, I weed them out.

Bottom: Camellias and azaleas are among our best plants for semi-shade. Given the right care (advice begins in January) they'll reward you with a lifetime of spectacular winter and spring bloom. (Design by Descanso Gardens.)

*My youngest grandchild, Rachel Woolf, loves
New Zealand Brass Buttons (*Cotula squalida*).
Year-round it's a pleasant carpet of ferny, gray-
green foliage dotted with a few flowers, but in
spring just look what fun this plant can be!*

Last winter I added this arbor at the bottom of my garden; now with 'Sally Holmes' on one side and 'Cécile Brunner' on the other, it's a favorite spot. In front are Shirley poppies, planted from seed last fall; at my feet Madeira geraniums (discussed on page 132), which plant themselves.

*Vines add romance to a garden. Here blue dawn
flower (*Ipomoea acuminata, *discussed on page 167),
frames the front door of Chick Eglee's and Ninkey
Dalton's Pacific Palisades house opposite a spectacular
angel's trumpet (*Brugmansia candida), *very fragrant
at night. (Design by Griffith and Steiner.)*

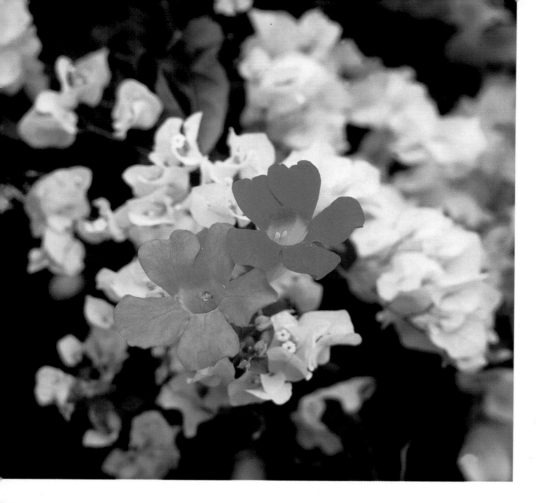

Some vines intertwine pleasantly, making a happy marriage, as with this royal trumpet vine (Distictus 'Rivers') and a vigorous white bougainvillea, lightly tinged with pink in Diane Uke's Del Mar garden. (Design by Sharon Drusch.)

White bougainvillea cascades over a trellis-topped wall surrounding the Uke garden; at its feet a streetside planting of westringea, bulbine, rosemary, lavender, and lantana gives pleasure to passersby. (Design by Sharon Drusch.)

Flanking Marilyn Herlihy's Spanish-style entranceway in Fallbrook is the old alba rose 'Grusse en Aachen', a garden treasure which tolerates partial shade; across from it the colorful bougainvillea, 'Camarillo Festival'.

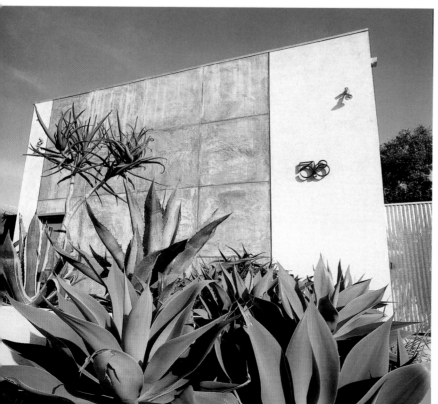

Top: When carefully chosen, well grown, and skillfully arranged, cacti and euphorbias (discussed on page 194) can create a stunning landscape, as this Pasadena garden amply demonstrates. (Design by California Cactus Center and EPT Landscape Design.)

Bottom: In a front yard in Venice, statuesque agaves native to America and aloes from Africa complement each other and the industrial architecture.

In a Pasadena garden, the fantastic shapes of cacti, euphorbia, and pachypodium, softened with vines and a lawn, create a delightful marriage of architecture and landscape. (Design by EPT Landscape Design.)

Top: Ornamental grasses (discussed on page 238) add a new dimension to gardens, as in this pleasing combination in a Santa Barbara garden of Muhlenbergia capillaris *with blue* Trachealeum caeruleum *and gray-foliaged nepeta. (Design by Pat Brodie.)*

Bottom: Like a pink cloud floating over the plant, the blooms of Muhlenbergia are stunning when highlighted by the magic of the setting sun.

Top: For best effect plant ornamental grasses, such as moor grass (Deschampsia sp.*), where the flowers can catch the rays of morning or evening sun.*

Bottom: Miscanthus sinensis 'Morning Light' has a finer texture than other varieties of maiden grass and features a white streak in the center of each blade. (Design by Pat Brodie.)

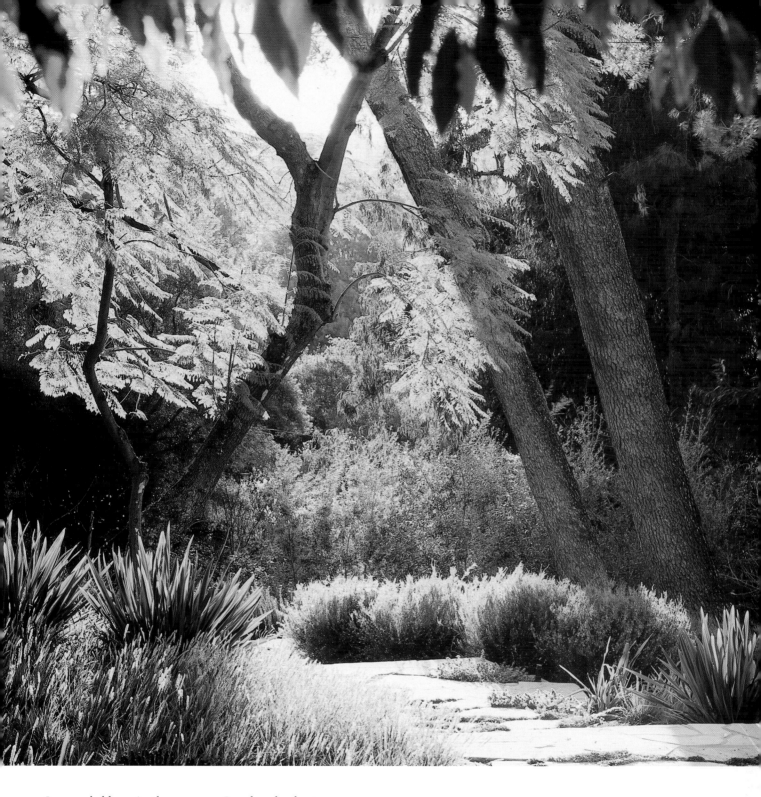

*Surrounded by a simple, easy-care, Pasadena landscape
well-adapted to our Mediterranean climate, New
Zealand flax (Phormium tenax 'Maori Queen') glows
with color in the early morning sun, as if illuminated
from within.*

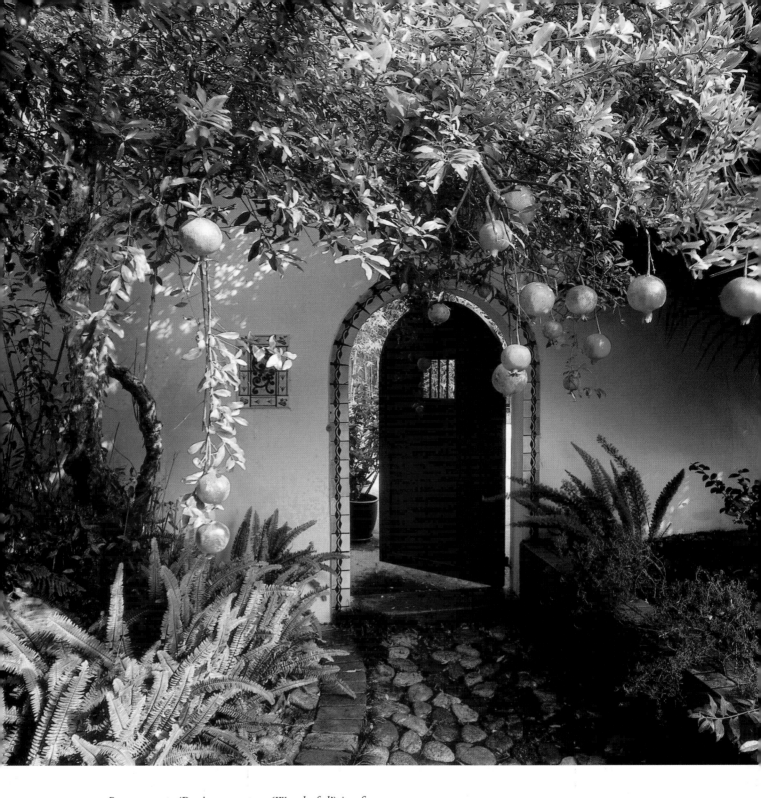

Pomegranate (Punica granatum 'Wonderful') is a fine drought resistant shrub or small tree. Best where it can get summer heat, as in this Pasadena garden, it's as ornamental as it is useful and typically Southern California with a long heritage here.

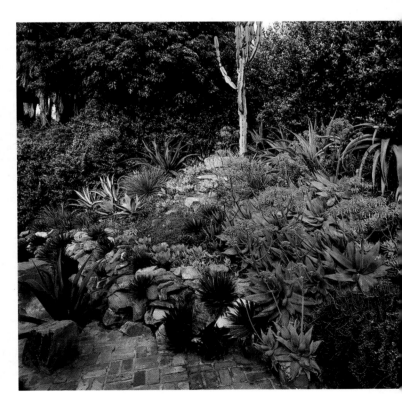

Top: A Mediterranean look is achieved here with plants from similar climates around the world, including New Zealand flax, ornamental grasses, and Verbena bonariensis *with splashes of scarlet sage* (Salvia splendens).

Bottom: In Montecito, a man-made streambed furnished with bog plants is the focal point for a lush Xeriscape of aloes, agaves, ornamental grasses, and yuccas.

Top: On Stone Canyon Road, treacherously spined, blue-green foliage of century plant (Agave americana) *creates a striking background for a roadside planting of Mexican sage* (Salvia leucantha).

Bottom: Aloes make a colorful addition to this Hollywood succulent garden, blooming spectacularly in winter.

Top: Old roses and English roses abound in Marilyn Herlihy's Fallbrook garden. This bed includes David Austin's cup-shaped 'Heritage' and the antique Hybrid Perpetuals, 'Baronne Prévoste', 'Candeur Lyonnaise', and 'Reine des Violettes'.

Bottom: The tall stalks and floating flowers of Verbena bonariensis *make it a perfect companion for fuchsia-colored, fragrant Damask 'Rose de Rescht'.*

Opposite: On a hilltop in Fallbrook Marilyn Herlihy has created a dreamlike Mediterranean garden with formal terraces, a classic urn, clipped hedges surrounding a rose-planted parterre, and Italian cypresses here catching the last glints of the evening sun. (In the distance, a field of leptospermums grown for cut flowers; foreground; Austin roses 'Prospero' and 'English Garden'.

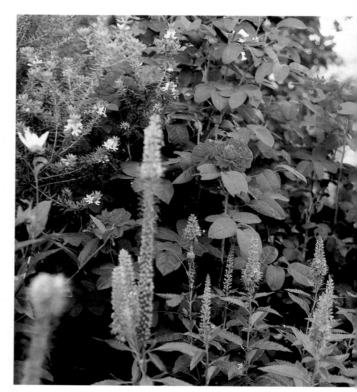

Top: In Patty Daniels's Olivenhain garden, against a background of delphiniums and Shasta daisies, Grandiflora 'Tournament of Roses' puts on a summer show.

Bottom: In the San Fernando Valley, a single rosebud catches the morning light.

Top: Pure white, fragrant rose 'Iceberg' twines through a section of old iron gate, creating the illusion of age in a fairly new garden. (Design by Marilyn Herlihy.)

Bottom: Gray-foliaged westringea and veronica make pleasant companions for David Austin's very fragrant English rose 'Othello'.

Despite the presence of cats, Patty Daniels's Zone 23 garden resounds with the songs of birds invited there by plentiful feeders, birdhouses, birdbaths, flowering perennials, and trees. (On the arbor, the single-flowered, red climbing rose 'Altissimo'.)

Top: At the end of a hot summer day, birdsong fills the air, open trees provide a canopy of shade, and Trachealeum caeruleum *planted at the feet of a gray-foliaged butterfly bush creates a symphony in blue.*

Bottom: Delphiniums bloom in partial shade in this hot summer garden. In full sun at the back of the bed, cleome 'Pink Queen' was planted from seeds in May (see page 154 for how to grow).

*On a plateau on the eastern edge of Olivenhain,
it's summer in Patty Daniels's garden; agapanthus,
alstroemeria, and a pink Austin rose called 'Mary
Rose' are in full bloom.*

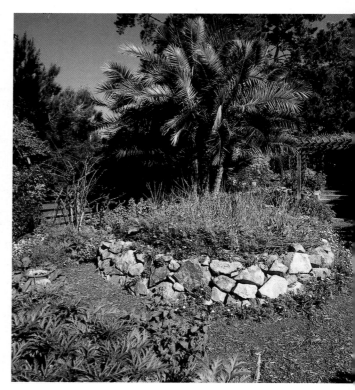

Top: Standing on stepping-stones arranged between drip lines, I sprinkle wildflower seeds onto prepared ground, then rake them shallowly into the soil. (The red plant in the background is Russelia equisetiformis.)

Bottom: Helped by a friend, Lucy Warren, I cover the pea stakes with bird netting to keep out marauding birds and weight the netting to the ground with beach rocks.

Top: The next step is to push English "pea stakes" (twiggy branches cut from pittosperum and other shrubbery) into the ground between the drip lines.

Bottom: In January, when bloom begins, I take off the netting and wrap the edges of the bed with long bendy rose canes to keep out skunks.

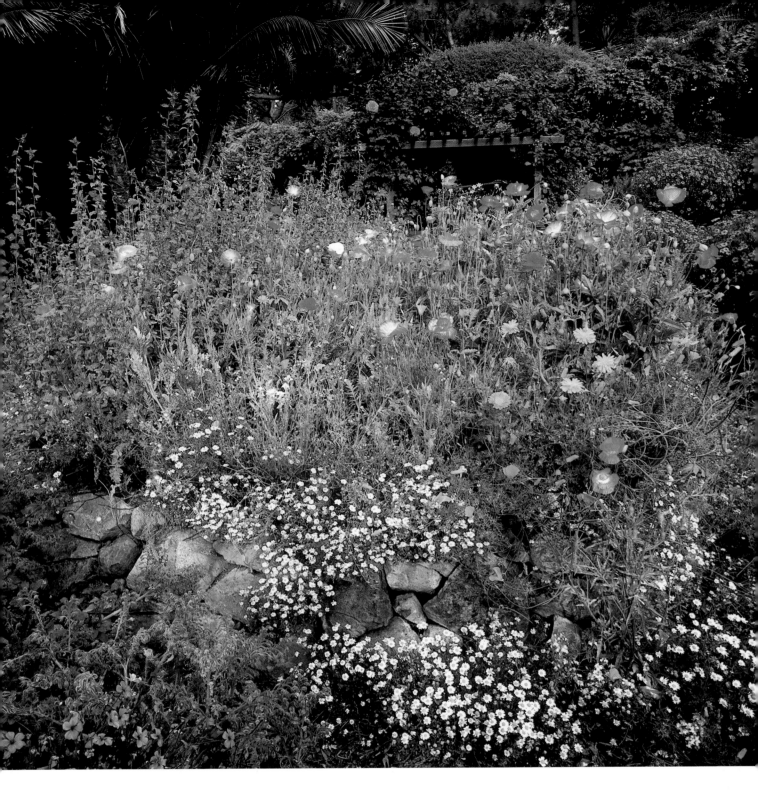

And here's the result in spring! On the left is Clarkia un-guiculata *'Rocky Mountain Improved', and in the center* California poppies, Shirley poppies, Linaria moroccana, *baby blue eyes, scarlet flax, and paludosum daisies. Every year it's slightly different, but always a joy. Flowers continue until June, when I replace with zinnias from seed. (Left foreground and right background,* Geranium maderense. *On the arbor is climbing rose 'America'.)*

Top: In a garden of rooms, many are ornamented by collections of old tools, such as these galvanized watering cans. (Design by Lani Freymiller.)

Bottom: A box of vintage flowerpots, when not in use, adds decoration to a rustic patio.

Top: Five rusty garden trowels hanging for use on a wicker stand exude what the Japanese call wabi-sabi, *meaning "the patina of age."*

Bottom: Above a twiggy wreath, a mask of Bacchus peers from a weathered wall hanging, adding a touch of mystery to a cascade of white roses.

A room in Lani Freymiller's country garden is
skillfully arranged and yet so nonchalant with its
lavender-surrounded birdbath, soft shavings underfoot, comfortably worn furniture, and bits of
picket fence.

A secluded pond filled with tadpoles, frogs, and fish creates an enchanted world in Lani Freymiller's garden of many rooms.

*Found objects and simple plantings—a worn
bench, an old watering can, a pot or two of
chives—give this cottage garden the illusion
of age. (Design by Lani Freymiller.)*

Top: In a protected corner of Evonne Kane's oceanfront garden in South Laguna, a statue provides the focal point for foxgloves, nasturtiums, begonias, forget-me-nots, violas, and tibouchina.

Bottom: In a garden in Woodland Hills, Canary Island sage (Salvia canariensis) grows six feet tall and bears flowers all summer, lasting in bouquets when stems are recut underwater. (See page 188 for more on salvias.)

Top: A pond and waterfall in Malibu Park, densely surrounded by brugmansia, Mexican weeping bamboo, tree fuchsias, Mexican lobelia (Lobelia laxiflora), alstroemeria, and blue lily bells (Adenophora lilifolia). (Design by Teresa Reyes of Garden Culture Landscape Design.)

Bottom: Once common, now seldom seen, long-blooming knotweed (Polygonum capitatum) makes a tough but pretty groundcover for containers or spilling over a wall.

Cosmos 'Dazzler' is easy to grow. Plant seeds of
this and other warm-season annuals in spring
and you'll have color all summer long. (See the
spring and fall chapters for which annuals to
plant and when.)

In Malibu, a simple planting of drought-resistant Mexi-
can evening primrose (Oenothera berlandieri), *Cleve-*
land sage (Salvia clevelandii), *and melaleuca* (Melaleuca
nesophila) *creates a stunning look with this country-style*
house. (Design by Burton/Spitz.)

Layer Camellias and Azaleas to Make New Plants

Treasured varieties of camellia and azalea that you cannot find commercially, plus many other woody ornamental plants, can be propagated now. To layer them (bury an attached branch in the ground to allow it to root, so it can be cut off as a plant in its own right), follow these steps:

- Choose a low-lying branch. (If none is low enough to bend to ground level, place a pot filled with damp potting soil under a suitable branch.)

- With a sharp knife carefully cut halfway through the chosen branch, making your cut several joints from the tip of the branch.

- Brush the cut with a powdered rooting compound, such as RooTone or Dip'N Grow.

- Insert a sliver of wood or a small pebble into the cut section to hold it open.

- Bury the cut section in damp soil. Firmly peg the branch down on both sides—"elbows" cut from

coat hangers work well—and place a brick on the ground over the cut section to hold it down. Keep the soil damp throughout the summer.

- Check the branch in fall. When it's thoroughly rooted, sever the new plant from the parent branch, dig it up, and plant it in a suitably sized container (unless you already rooted it in a container of the right size).

Note: Air-layering is a method of propagation similar to layering, but it's done above ground. For this method first wrap a section cut as above in damp sphagnum moss. Then cover the moss with plastic sheeting, and wind tape around the plastic and the branch both above and below the cut section to keep the moss damp. In a few weeks, after roots grow, sever the branch below the cut. This system is very easy to use on some houseplants, especially corn plant (*Dracaena fragrans*).

lightly, train them as espaliers, or grow them as large perennials at the backs of beds.

Camellias and Azaleas

Feed camellias for the third and last time approximately one month or six weeks after their last feeding. (Feeding is discussed on page 145.) Use an acid fertilizer that's recommended for camellias and azaleas, and follow package directions exactly. Avoid overfeeding camellias; neither they nor azaleas are heavy eaters. Keep the roots damp but not soggy. Check to see that soil is not collecting around the trunk.

Give azaleas that bloomed through June their first feeding of the year immediately after blooming stops. Don't feed them again until late September unless one or two fail to respond. If this should occur, treat these sluggish growers

once or twice with Terr-O-Vite. If you can't find it at nurseries, try agricultural supply stores. The manufacturer is Security.

Check all your camellias and azaleas for signs of chlorosis (a deficiency in iron evidenced by yellow leaves with dark green veins). Treat the soil around chlorotic plants with a chelating product that contains iron, manganese, and zinc. Liquid formulas can also be sprayed on leaves. (Terr-O-Vite contains trace elements, so when you treat sluggish growers with it you also correct chlorosis, especially when you spray it on the foliage as well as pour it around the roots.) To start new plants, layer camellias and azaleas (see the accompanying box).

Primroses and Cyclamen

Cyclamen and certain primroses, including

A Good Soil Mix for Succulents and Cacti

Choose a commercial mix especially formulated for succulents and cacti, or make your own by combining these ingredients.

- 6 to 7 parts pumice
- 2 parts commercial potting soil (such as Uni-grow)
- 1 part sterilized oak leaf mold

English, or polyanthus, primroses, are perennials often grown as cool-season annuals. When they've finished flowering at the end of June you can, if you wish, just toss them out. But many gardeners, especially in coastal zones, keep them from year to year (reviving them in September; see page 236). After polyanthus primroses stop blooming, leave them in their pots, or, if they're in conspicuous beds, dig them up, divide the plants, throw out the woody centers, and plant healthy offshoots in 6-inch plastic pots. Put them in a shady, out-of-the-way spot for the summer. Water the primroses about once a week to keep them damp, feed them occasionally with fish emulsion, and protect them from slugs, snails, mites, and caterpillars.

Cyclamen can be summered-over in one of two ways. One way is to allow a plant to become completely dormant by removing it from the pot and drying the entire root mass in the sun. Once it is dry, slip the root and tuber back into the pot and store it on its side in a cool, dry place. This method is best for gardeners in hot, dry interior regions, although a few tubers may be lost to rot during the summer.

Coastal gardeners will have more luck allowing cyclamen to go into semidormancy. Put the plants in a shady, out-of-the-way spot—a hanging basket under a tree is ideal. Keep them on the dry side, watering occasionally. Most leaves will fall off but a few will be retained. Don't fertilize. You can keep cyclamen flowering, especially plants with small blooms, by fertilizing them for growth and bloom year-round in cool gardens. However, forcing semidormancy will give you a better winter display.

Succulents and Cacti

Succulents and cacti are such a basic part of the Southern California landscape that almost all gardens contain at least one or two. But despite our familiarity with them, many people don't know the difference between a succulent and a cactus. The difference is simple: All plants that store water in their leaves or stems are called "succulents," while "cactus" actually is the name of just one large family of plants within the succulent group. All cacti have spine cushions, called "areoles," out of which spines arise, but many succulents—crassulas from Africa and echeverias from the Americas, for example—have no spines at all.

Euphorbias are another large group of mostly succulent plants that are often confused with cacti because, at first glance, there's considerable resemblance. But whereas many euphorbias have spines, none of them have spine cushions. Other differences are that cacti are nonpoisonous and their sap is clear, while euphorbias are usually poisonous and their sap is white and cloudy. Also, all but a few cacti are native to the Americas, and most euphorbias are from Africa or Madagascar. Many of the vast number of tender succulents we're fortunate to be able to grow outdoors are houseplants in the rest of the country.

Choose Succulents for Widely Varying Conditions. Succulents have playful shapes, lovely flowers, undemanding and drought-tolerant natures, plenty of variety to keep one interested, and the ability to draw enthusiastic comments from anyone who sees them. If you live in a place where it's difficult to garden they're ideal plants. They're also perfect for collecting—they make good hobby plants. One plus to growing succulents in containers is their portability. If you move take them with you. Or for the easiest care grow them in the ground.

Your garden needn't look like a desert scene for succulents to fit in. Many have a lush, green look; some make good accent plants; and others can be used as ground covers. They're good choices for rock gardens, and they mix well with other drought-resistant plants.

Clean Up, Feed, and Water Succulents. Choose and plant succulents year-round. Some take full sun; others need semishade. Most container-grown specimens do best in partial shade. They're perfect for dressing up a balcony or a condo patio—places where hot sun alternating with solid shade makes survival difficult or impossible for almost all other plants.

The colorful blooms of succulents occur mostly in winter and spring. After plants have finished flowering, cut off the spent blooms and seedpods if they are unsightly. This applies also to cacti—epiphyllums, for example—unless you wish to propagate the seeds or eat the fruit. (The fruit of some cacti and both the young leaves and fruit of prickly pear cactus [*Opuntia ficus-indica*] are edible. But remember: All parts of African euphorbias are poisonous.) Clean up all succulents by pruning off diseased or desiccated portions.

Feed all cacti and euphorbias in July with a complete product such as Greenworld Fertilizer 8-8-8 or Liquinox Grow 10-10-5. Mix it in a

🐛 Quick Tip

How to Remove Cactus Spines from Your Skin. *Some cactus spines are easy to see and remove with tweezers. But fine, almost invisible, hairlike spines, called "glochids," have hooks on their tips and are painfully irritating when embedded in human flesh. To remove them, glob on rubber cement and let it dry. Then rub it off, spines and all.*

watering can according to package directions and pour it around their roots. If you grow succulents of any type in containers, feed them at the rate of 1 tablespoon per gallon once a month during the growing season or, alternatively, ⅓ tablespoon per gallon every time you water, or three times out of four. (Many succulents, other than cacti and euphorbias, need little or no fertilizer when they grow in the ground.)

Most succulents growing in the ground need no irrigation during the winter. Those in containers need water only during dry spells. The **Rule of Thumb** for watering container-grown succulents, including cacti and euphorbias, is: *If the soil is dry 1 inch below the surface, it's time to water.* But all begin to need irrigation this month. Depending on the weather and your climate zone, water them every one to three weeks throughout summer and fall. The exception to this rule is lithops, or "living rocks." More lithops die from overwatering than from any other cause. (If you've ever killed lithops, now you know why.) Water lithops from March 1 to July 1 and withhold water in July and August. Resume watering September 1 and continue until they finish blooming in mid-November. Allow lithops to go dry in winter, putting them under cover so they don't get rained on. Allow plants to dry out slightly between waterings. Good drainage is important.

195

How to Transplant Cacti and Spiny Euphorbias

Most spiny succulents can be safely handled with leather gloves, but all cacti and a few euphorbias have spines that are either sharp enough to penetrate leather or, in the case of some cacti, are barbed so they can permanently attach themselves to it. To avoid ensnarement, try this method:

- Hold tiny plants gently with barbecue tongs. To grasp a small plant, roll a sheet of newspaper in the shape of a tube, flatten it, and wrap it around the cactus. The jutting ends of the newspaper provide a handle. Grasp large plants with rolled burlap. Tie the burlap ends together with twine. Use these handles to securely hold and support the plant as you dig up its roots and lift it out of the ground or container. (More than one handle may be necessary for large specimens.)

- Transplant the cactus into loose, well-drained soil mix appropriate for cactus and other succulents. Use a chopstick to work the soil mix down around the roots.

- Cover the roots completely with soil mix up to the original soil level. Tamp gently but firmly with a blunt stick. Stake and tie tall specimens.

- Cover the soil mix with a layer of ornamental gravel or volcanic rock. Water thoroughly. Keep potted plants in semishade for a month.

Bromeliads

Like cacti, bromeliads are native to the Western Hemisphere, except for a lone adventurer found in Africa. The bromeliad family includes such widely differing plants as the pineapple and Spanish moss, but most family members share the basic shape of a rosette of leathery leaves, sometimes plain and at other times strikingly variegated. They can be brilliantly colored, striped, or mottled. Often these leaves are arranged in a cone that forms a natural reservoir to collect rainwater and see the plant through drought. Flowers either are hidden in the cone or arise from it on straight or cascading stems. Often the inflorescences are bizarre, exciting, and spectacularly colored.

Queen's tears (*Billbergia nutans*) was the first bromeliad to be widely grown in California gardens; it thrives on neglect. In the 1970s silver vase plant (*Aechmea fasciata*) took its place as the most popular bromeliad. Most bromeliads are experts at survival, and they thrive outdoors in Southern California, even naturalizing in some gardens.

Propagate Bromeliads. All bromeliads except one are monocarpic—they bloom but once and then die. But in the process they leave many progeny in the form of seeds and offshoots called "pups," which sprout from the mother's stalk. With proper care you can have plants for life. Now's a good time to propagate bromeliads by separating the pups from their parents to make new plants (see the accompanying box).

Give Them Proper Care. Bromeliads need good air circulation, fast-draining acid soil mix, and occasional watering. In interior zones hook up a mist system to keep their foliage and the air around them moist in hot, dry weather. It's not necessary along the coast. Most bromeliads need bright light—up to 50 percent sunshine in coastal zones, 25 percent inland. Once in a while let their center cups go dry. Flush them out occasionally to prevent mosquitoes from setting up housekeeping. But if tree frogs live in them, as they do in mine, you'll have no mosquitoes.

Feed and Flush Bromeliads. Feed bromeliads lightly with a close-to-equally-balanced fertilizer, such as 20-20-20, mixed one-third to half-strength. (Spoonit, Miracle-Gro, Peters,

How to Repot Fragile Donkey Tails

When donkey tails *(Sedum morganianum)* out-grow their small hanging pots, replant them in large baskets. When grown this way the plants can attain stunning beauty and spectacular size—often growing to 5 feet or more in length.

- Paint an 18-inch wire basket with rust-resistant gutter paint. Allow it to dry. Attach chains strong enough to support approximately 75 pounds. Hang the basket briefly to test the chains' length and make sure it hangs level.

- Presoak sphagnum moss. Wearing gloves, shove moss tightly between the two top wires of the basket. Trim this with grass shears into a neat circle to make a finished lip all around. (Shape it like the fat inner tube of a child's bicycle.)

- Line the basket with a thick layer of premoist-ened sphagnum moss.

- Another way to line a basket is to purchase pre-cut palm fiber liners made for this purpose.

- Fill the lined basket with loose, fast-draining potting soil. Make a hole in the middle.

- Gently place the plant, pot and all, into the hole, carefully spreading the long stems over the edge of the basket. (This may take two or three people.)

- Carefully break the pot in several places with a hammer. Pull out the shards. (If the pot is plastic, reach between the stems and cut it apart with strong clippers. Then remove it.) Fill in the gaps with more soil.

- Dip the ends of broken branches in RooTone and plant these too. Hang the basket on a stout hook in semishade. Protect it from wind and birds. Keep it moist and feed occasionally.

Greenworld Fertilizer, and Liquinox Gro are a few of the fertilizers that have been found to work well. For bromeliads, dilute any one of these so it becomes one-third or half the strength of the recommended solution for most other plants.) Some hobbyists feed their bromeliads only three or four times a year, with fine results. Others fertilize once every two or three weeks in the summer months, which brings even better results. Pour some of the diluted fertilizer around the roots and a little into the cup. Mist tillandsias (air-plant bromeliads) with the solution. (Foliar-feeding benefits all bromeliads regardless of type.)

Lawn Care

Cool-Season Grasses. As in June, cool-season lawns such as perennial ryegrass, bluegrass, and fescue are growing slowly now, so don't mow them short. Cut ryegrass and bluegrass 2 inches high now. Tall fescues should be left even taller—between 2 and 3 inches after cutting. (Use the top setting of your mower.) Mow tall fescues often, never cut off more than one-third of their total height, and always use a sharp mower.

Extend the time between irrigations of tall fescue now, and water it deeply to encourage deep roots. Almost all other cool-season grasses need shallower and more frequent watering than warm-season grasses do. In hot weather most cool-season grasses need to be watered twice or three times a week in interior zones, and at least once a week along the coast. Early morning—any time between midnight and dawn—is the best time to irrigate both for water conservation and for lawn health except in the desert, where evenings are acceptable.

Don't fertilize cool-season grasses now in interior zones. Along the coast fertilize very lightly—one-half the normal amount.

How to Divide and Multiply Bromeliads

When you propagate bromeliads, remember that spines from prickly varieties can enter your flesh and fester, so wear leather gloves when handling them. (If you get a spine in your flesh, see page 195.) You can divide a plant when the pup is at least a third or half the size of the mother or has formed roots of its own. Here are two methods.

• Depending on what will work with the size and type of plant you're propagating, stick a serrated knife, keyhole saw, sharp hunting knife, or blade-type pruning shears down into the soil and cut off the pup as close to the mother plant as possible. Continue with the directions for pot planting that follow immediately, or skip to the last item.

• Place one 5-gram tablet of slow-release fertilizer, such as 14-4-6, in the bottom of a 4- or 6-inch plastic container, and fill it with premoistened fast-draining potting soil.

• Dip the cut section of the bromeliad pup in a rooting hormone, such as Dip'N Grow or RooTone, and knock off the excess. Make a hole in the planter mix. Insert the plant and press the damp soil mix around it.

• Water the bromeliad occasionally, and keep it in semishade.

• Most tillandsias are grown on a piece of wood or bark, with no soil at all. Vase-type bromeliads can also be grown without soil. To mount them this way, first cover the base of the bromeliad with a handful of damp sphagnum moss. Then place the plant upright on a branch or in the crotch of a tree or on a large piece of driftwood, and attach it firmly in place by winding clear fishing twine around the branch or driftwood, the moss, and the plant base. The bromeliads will soon develop aerial roots. (Mature Australian tea trees [*Leptospermum laevigatum*] make particularly attractive settings for bromeliads because their branches are often at eye level and they have interesting, twisted shapes.)

Warm-Season Grasses. Warm-season lawns such as Bermuda, zoysia, kikuyu, 'Adalayd' grass, and St. Augustine thrive in summer and are growing at their fastest now. As in June, cut common Bermuda short, to 1 inch, and cut improved Bermuda even shorter, to ½ or ¾ inch. Cut zoysia to between ¾ inch and 1 inch and kikuyu as short as ½ inch, to keep it in bounds. (Slice down through and pull out escaped kikuyu stolons often, to thwart their tendency to creep into flowerbeds.) St. Augustine grows fast, so cut it often to ¾ or 1 inch at least once a week.

All warm-season grasses should be watered deeply and infrequently to encourage deep rooting, rather than shallowly and often. St. Augustine needs the most water; it can die if allowed to go dry. Water it at least once a week—more often in sandy soils. Bermuda, zoysia, and kikuyu can often go as long as two weeks between waterings, depending on the weather and your climate zone. Water deeply, and extend the time between irrigations as much as possible while still maintaining good appearance.

Feed most warm-season grasses every four to six weeks during the growing season. Feed 'Adalayd' half-strength, early in the month. (Too much fertilizer in hot weather can stress it.) If kikuyu is growing well, don't feed it at all. Too much fertilizer can turn it into a monster. If you want to get rid of kikuyu or Bermuda as weeds, kill them now, with glyphosate (Roundup), and pull them out by the roots, but be aware that they may come back from seeds.

Lippia as Lawn. *Lippia repens (Phyla nodiflora)* is a useful and attractive lawn substitute for interior and desert regions. It's tough, evergreen, and drought tolerant, and once established it withstands foot traffic. It creates a thick mat that blooms in early summer and fall with pink flowers that are pretty to look at and attractive to bees. To protect children and dogs from bee stings, mow the flowers off now. Follow up with lawn fertilizer and deep water.

Vegetable Gardening

As early summer vegetables are harvested, clean up the rows, add soil amendment and organic fertilizer, and then plant more crops. All summer vegetables can be planted now, but they'll have a shorter growing season. If you need the space in September for winter vegetables, don't plant crops now that won't bear until fall. (Read the seed packages and count the days to harvest.)

Where Are All the Bees? Perhaps you've noticed in recent years how few bees there are in your garden. If so, your fruit trees are probably bearing smaller crops than they used to and you're probably picking fewer peppers, cucumbers, and squash. No bees, no food, or a lot less. The fact is, about a third of the food on our tables comes to us as a result of the pollinating abilities of the lowly little honeybee. Any reduction in their numbers amounts to an environmental disaster, and unfortunately that's just what happened.

During the late 1980s two species of predatory mites, the varroa mite and the tracheal mite, which attack and kill honeybees, were accidentally introduced into California, destroying feral hives. Meanwhile, changes in the tax laws together with the expense of controlling varroa mites in managed hives forced many commercial beekeepers out of business. Now the African-

The Apple Trick to Make a Bromeliad Bloom

An event occurring sometime during the first third of the twentieth century altered the history of bromeliads in cultivation. As the story goes, smoke from a wood-burning heater accidentally escaped overnight into a greenhouse filled with bromeliads, including some species that had been there for years without blooming. Within six weeks to two months most of the plants—including those that had never bloomed—suddenly sprouted inflorescences. The smoke was analyzed and found to contain ethylene gas. This discovery enabled growers to make pineapples bear fruit year-round.

In our climate most well-grown bromeliads will naturally cycle into bloom at the right time of year for each species. But if desired, mature plants, particularly any recalcitrant ones that have never bloomed, can often be "gassed" to stimulate bloom on demand. One way to do so is to place a full-grown plant into a large plastic bag and drop in a whole 'Red Delicious' apple (a better source of ethylene gas than 'Golden Delicious'). Tie the bag closed and keep it in cool solid shade for one week. Then take the bromeliad out and care for it as usual. Another method is to spray the plant and the interior of the cup with Florel, which produces ethylene gas, or pour into the bromeliad's center cup a solution of ¼ ounce calcium carbide in 1 quart water.

ized honeybee, which is less susceptible to the varroa mite, has arrived in California and is interbreeding with the European honeybee in commercial hives, creating even more work and expense for beekeepers. The offspring swarm more frequently and defend their nests more aggressively than pure-blooded European honeybees. Also, the queens in all commercial hives must now be replaced annually by certified European bee queens. See the boxes on pages 202

Quick Tip

How to Keep Seed Rows from Drying Out in Hot Weather. *Cover a seeded row with a 4-inch-wide strip of burlap. Sprinkle it thoroughly to soak the row every morning. Pick up the edge of the burlap daily to check progress; remove it as soon as the seeds sprout. Floating row covers also work well for sprouting seeds.*

and 204 for ways in which you can protect yourself from Africanized bees and increase the number of beneficial native bees in your garden.

Crops You Can Still Plant. The best things to plant now are the heat lovers, such as corn, cucumbers, eggplant, peppers (in coastal zones only; see the accompanying box), and summer squash. Tomatoes and chard can also be planted. Continue to put in beets, carrots, and radishes in small quantities for successive crops. Green beans can be planted now but will be less vigorous and have more insect problems than those planted in March. It's too late to plant melons along the coast. Inland you can plant cantaloupe, pumpkins, and Crenshaw and honeydew melons early in the month, if you know from experience there'll be enough hot weather to ripen them in October. (Planting this late is much riskier than planting in May or June.) It's too late to put in winter squash and be sure of a harvest. For all these crops keep the seed rows damp. It's often necessary to mist them more than once daily (see accompanying Quick Tip).

Fending Off Problems. Watering and either cultivating or mulching (as well as harvesting) are the most important tasks in the July vegetable garden. There's no use in kidding ourselves—vegetables aren't drought resistant; they need a steady supply of water. If a cucumber plant goes

How to Have Success with Peppers

Peppers are classed as hot-weather vegetables, but they perform best within a precise range of temperatures. The fruit sets best when night temperatures are between 60° and 75°F. Daytime temperatures near 75°F are best—when they top 90°F, they can cause blossom drop.

Feed peppers lightly with a balanced liquid fertilizer as soon as you see the first blossoms open, and keep the ground evenly moist. A lack of dark green leaf color despite adequate nitrogen may come from lack of magnesium. In this case spray the leaves with a solution of 1 teaspoon Epsom salts to a pint of lukewarm water.

dry the cucumbers will be bitter. If tomatoes go dry they'll drop flowers or get blossom-end rot (as discussed on page 176). (Tomatoes growing in heavy soil can go a long time between waterings if their roots are deep in the ground but not if they're shallow rooted, in very sandy soil, or in containers.) If drought forces the shutdown of your vegetable garden, or part of it, don't be discouraged. Work for solutions to our water problems, keep up your hopes, and plant again in fall. Drip irrigation is the most water-wise method for keeping row crops happy.

Continue to side-dress rows with fertilizer halfway through the vegetables' growing seasons. If you're an organic gardener, use cottonseed meal and blood meal to provide extra nitrogen if crops show signs of nitrogen deficiency, such as yellowing foliage or a slowdown in growth. Excellent vegetables can be grown without the addition of commercial fertilizer if the soil has been deeply dug up and turned and is rich in organic matter, and if the plants have plenty of sunlight and water.

All gardeners need to watch for pest problems now. Handpick caterpillars, get birds to help, or use BT. Continue to release beneficials.

When and How to Harvest Summer Vegetables. Pick summer vegetables when they're young and tender—it's half the fun of growing your own. They grow so fast that many crops need checking daily. Whenever possible, eat them the day you pick them.

- **Beets.** Harvest at any size, but they're best between tiny and golf-ball size.
- **Cantaloupe.** Pick at "full slip," when a crack forms around the stem next to the fruit and the fruit falls off in your hand with no pulling.
- **Carrots.** Ready to eat when finger sized. In sandy soils pull them up by the leafy crown. In clay soils loosen them first with a garden fork or trowel. (Be careful not to disturb others left in the ground.)
- **Corn.** When the tips of the silks go crispy brown and the ears are filled out, pierce a kernel with your thumbnail. If the juice is milky the ear is just right; if clear it's not yet ready; if dry or pasty you've waited too long.
- **Cucumbers.** Harvest at any size, but mature fruit with small seeds, dark green skin, and crisp texture taste best. Harvest often to keep the vines bearing.
- **Eggplant.** The fruit should be glossy, filled out, and big enough to eat. The flesh should not spring back when you press it with your thumb. If the seeds or skin are brown the eggplant has gone too far. Pick often; the more you pick the more you get.
- **Green Beans.** Pick often and pick young—as soon as immature seeds fill the pod but before the pods get bumpy, and while the outside's still slightly velvety. Wait until the leaves are dry before walking among the plants to pick beans. (Picking when the leaves are wet from dew can spread rust.)

Beware of Sleepy Bumblebees

Pole beans, dahlias, and zinnias are bedrooms for bumblebees. Watch for them when picking flowers and vegetables in the late afternoon or evening. These gentle creatures don't want to sting you, but they will if you grab them.

- **Lima Beans.** Don't pick these too soon. Leave the full-grown pod on the plant until it fills with beans and you can clearly feel them inside.
- **Peppers.** Pick as soon as the fruit are well formed and full sized, with crisp, thick skins and seeds that are almost mature. Leave a few fruits on the plant to go red if desired, but not all, because the plants have a built-in fruit load. Once they reach their limit they'll stop blooming unless you pick some.
- **Radishes.** Plant often and pull daily in small quantities, as soon as they mature but before they split. (These tend to get very hot to the taste during summer.)
- **Summer Squash.** Pick while the skin can be easily pierced with your thumbnail. Try picking tiny ones with the blossom still on the plant and cooking them blossom and all. If crops get too overwhelming, slow them down by picking both male and female blossoms to batter-fry or add to ratatouille.
- **Tomatoes.** For the best flavor leave these on the vine until they're fully red and ripe, unless birds, animals, or caterpillars are getting them first.
- **Watermelon.** Harvest when the skin under the melon turns from pure white to a creamy color and the tendril on the stem starts to dry up. Thumping doesn't help. (When the sound changes from a sharp tap to a dull thud the melon is usually overripe.) Also count the

Good Bees for Your Garden

Bees are one of the most important and necessary of all the insects. Bees pollinate most flowers and over a hundred food crops and also produce honey and beeswax. Unfortunately, some people think of bees as enemies, and the arrival of the Africanized honeybee has not helped. But bees only sting in self-defense or when they sense their hive is threatened. Stinging is serious business to the honeybee because the process of stinging means death to the bee. Each honeybee can sting only once, and then it dies. So protect yourself from the Africanized honeybee (see the accompanying box), but also take steps to protect our precious bees of all species.

Fortunately, many types of native bees help with pollination. The ground-dwelling squash and gourd bee, for example, came to California along with these crops and starts pollinating early in the morning when the flowers open. Many native bees get going earlier in the mornings than honeybees and even pollinate flowers in winter. Provide homes for native bees; purchase special houses from catalogs or make your own. Leave some bare ground in your garden—some moist and some dry—for ground-dwelling bees to nest in, perhaps between stepping stones, where you can watch them come and go. Do not spray with pesticides, and don't use diazinon in the soil. Remember: Every time you get rid of a pest, you're also killing bees. Keep some flowers blooming in your garden year-round to provide pollen for the bees and other beneficials. (See the list of pollen-producing flowers on page 129.) Here are a few beneficial bees to protect, enjoy, and encourage:

- **European Honeybee.** True bees of the Apidae family, these highly social creatures live in large colonies. They are our best pollinators; pollen from flowers clings to the special branched hairs that cover their legs and bodies and then gets brushed off onto other flowers. They also collect pollen in special sacs on their back legs and carry it from flower to flower while gathering nectar, from which they make honey.

- **Bumblebee.** Four local species of true bees, up to an inch long, also of the Apidae family, marked with furry black-and-yellow stripes. Excellent pollinators for all vegetables, bumblebees are actually better than honeybees at pollinating tomatoes and eggplants. They nest in small colonies in the ground or in tree hollows, or even—as happened at my house last summer—in an empty birdhouse. Catalogs carry ready-made bumblebee houses with built-in observation panels. Many flowers attract bumblebees, especially zinnias.

- **Carpenter Bee.** These large—almost 1-inch-long—black or dark blue, shiny creatures of the Anthophoridae family are also good pollinators, especially of tomatoes. Like bumblebees, they will sometimes hit you with their bodies without stinging in order to move you a little farther away from their nest. (Tell them you're just gardening; it calms them down.) The less-numerous males are spectacularly covered with golden hairs. The females nest solitarily, drilling round holes into soft wood. (The one that's nesting in my redwood patio table is apparently unconcerned that her progeny are covered by a tablecloth during mealtimes.) To increase pollination in your garden, you can purchase carpenter bee larvae and blocks of wood in which these amusing bees can nest. Wisteria attracts them.

- **Mason Bee.** Small, ⅜- to ½-inch bees of the Megachilid family, with long black hair and black legs, that are better pollinators than honeybees for orchards and pollinate during winter when European bees are all buzzing inside their hives trying to keep warm. Mason bees are gentle and don't sting unless swatted. You can buy houses for them, wooden nesting blocks with holes drilled in them, and also their live larvae, which are shipped in winter, from several catalogs. (One source is Entomo-Logic, 9807 N.E. 140th Street, Bothell, WA 98011-5132; 425/820-8037.) Install these bees in your garden, and you'll get more apples and other fruits from your trees that bloom in winter.

- **Metallic Sweat Bee.** Bright green, shiny, housefly-sized bees that nest in the ground and are a good pollinator of melons, these sting if swatted but not as painfully as honeybees.

- **Leaf-Cutter Bee.** Several species of bees of the Megachilid family. Good pollinators, about half an inch long, and hairy in colors of brown, gold, or black, they cut round pieces out of leaves to construct a nest. These bees will also make their nests in nesting boxes you can buy from catalogs. (Some catalogs may also carry larvae.)

days since planting. Small varieties may ripen in late July; large varieties, maybe not until August.

Stop Removing Runners from Strawberries. Summer heat shuts down fruit production, so stop pinching off runners early in July. In fall you'll be able to use the runners that have grown to make new plants. Fertilize them to encourage growth. If you're growing strawberries on plastic mulch, remove it now so runners can root in the soil.

How to Live with the Africanized Honeybee

To an untrained observer, Africanized honeybees look exactly like their European cousins, and, if you are stung only once, their sting is identical. The problem is that Africanized honeybees anger more quickly and defend their hives more aggressively than European honeybees. When aroused, large swarms of Africanized bees pursue intruders up to half a mile from their nest. They also nest in more places, forming smaller colonies, storing less honey, and moving more frequently. Africanized honeybees are good pollinators and are no more prone to sting when you are working in your garden than European honeybees. You can safely work in the garden in close proximity to them. They are dangerous, however, if you come too close to a nest.

Inspect your property. Bee-proof your home by removing possible nesting sites; seal openings larger than ⅛ inch with cork, foam, or stucco patch. Be alert to bees entering or leaving a particular location. Close openings to cavelike places under roofs or porches with ⅛-inch hardware cloth. If you find a nest, hire a professional to remove it.

If attacked by a swarm, cover your face—Africanized bees will go for your face first—and run for the closest shelter in a house or car; do not jump into water because the swarm will wait until you come up for air. (However, one woman who was attacked by bees and denied entrance to a house survived the attack by holding a hose over her head and body with the water running full-force until help arrived.) Use a credit card or flat-edged object to scrape stingers out; do not squeeze them. Wash the stung area with soap and water and apply ice packs. Seek medical attention if you have been stung numerous times. If you are a member of the 1 percent of the population that is extremely allergic to bee stings, carry a bee-sting kit with you.

For more information about the Africanized honeybee and how to live with it, call your local University of California Cooperative Extension Farm and Home Advisor's office. Ask for the brochure "Bee Alert: Africanized Honeybee Facts."

Purchase/Plant

❏ Continue to plant tropicals in coastal zones, 166

❏ Purchase tuberous begonias already in bloom, 96

❏ Continue to plant summer annuals, 189

❏ Start biennials from seeds, 190

❏ Choose and plant hibiscus, 192

❏ Choose and plant succulents, 194

❏ Transplant succulents, including cacti and euphorbias, 196

❏ Continue to fill in vegetable rows with summer crops, 200

❏ Continue to plant papayas, bananas, and palms, 166

❏ Transplant palms, 166

❏ Select and plant salvias, 188

Trim, Prune, Mow, Divide

❏ Continue to pinch back chrysanthemums, 155

❏ Continue to pick and deadhead roses, but stop disbudding them now, 122, 183

❏ Remove berries (seedpods) from fuchsias, 169

❏ Deadhead flowers, 190

❏ Prune climbing roses that bloom only once a year, 183

❏ Prune impatiens, 188

❏ Pinch flowers off coleus, 189

❏ Cut back hydrangeas, 192

❏ Pick hibiscus blossoms, 192

❏ Divide English primroses, or wait until fall, 194

❏ Clean up succulents by pruning off diseased and dessicated portions and removing unsightly spent blooms and seedpods, 195

❏ Propagate bromeliads by dividing the offshoots from parent plants, 196

❏ Mow cool-season lawns long and warm-season lawns short, 197, 198

❏ Mow off the flowers from lippia lawns, 199

❏ Stop removing runners from strawberries, 203

❏ Continue to prune and train espaliers, 211

❏ Continue to propagate and clean up daylilies, 213

❏ When Martha Washington geraniums stop blooming, clip off their faded flowers and begin to cut them back progressively, 251

❏ Cut back penstemon, artemisia, and pentas, 190

Fertilize

❏ Feed fuchsias, 168

❏ Feed water lilies, 125

❏ Feed cymbidiums with a high-nitrogen fertilizer for growth, 183

❏ Fertilize roses, 94

❏ Feed ferns, 147

❏ Fertilize tropicals according to need during the summer months, 166

❏ Feed tuberous begonias, 186

❏ Fertilize impatiens, 185

❏ Feed coleus lightly, 189

❏ Fertilize azaleas that bloomed through June, 193

❏ Check camellias and azaleas for chlorosis; treat if necessary, 193

❏ Give camellias their third and final feeding for the year, 193

❏ If an azalea fails to respond to spring feeding, treat it with humic acid, 193

❏ Fertilize cacti and euphorbias that are growing in the ground, 195

❏ Fertilize bromeliads, 196

❏ Fertilize cool-season lawns lightly along the coast; do not fertilize them inland, 197

❏ Feed warm-season lawns according to type, 198

❏ Feed and water lippia after mowing, 198

❏ Continue to side-dress vegetable rows with additional fertilizer according to need, 200

❏ Treat pepper plants that lack good green leaves with Epsom salts, 200

❏ Feed and water cycads, 220

Continued>>

Water

❏ Water all bougainvilleas that are under three years old, paying particular attention to newly planted ones, 167

❏ With the exception of certain California natives, water all garden plants according to their individual needs. Don't neglect to water young drought-resistant plants, 182

❏ Water citrus and avocado trees, 182

❏ Water cymbidiums, 183

❏ Increase water for roses to as much as 1½ inches three times a week in fast-draining soils, 183

❏ Give plants in north-facing shade extra water now while sun hits them, 187

❏ Water impatiens daily, 188

❏ Begin to water succulents growing in the ground once every two or three weeks, 195

❏ Water lawns according to their specific requirements, 197

❏ Keep newly planted seed rows damp, 200

❏ Continue to water vegetables regularly; don't let tomatoes or cucumbers go dry, 200

❏ Keep transplanted palms well watered, 220

❏ Do not water lithops in July or August, 195

Control Pests, Diseases, and Weeds

❏ Control weeds by cultivating, mulching, or hand-pulling, 40

❏ Continue to control rose pests and diseases, 72

❏ Control mildew and slugs and snails on tuberous begonias, 185

❏ Control bark beetles on conifers, 190

❏ Don't kill all the butterflies, 191

❏ Kill unwanted kikuyu or Bermuda grass with glyphosate, 198

❏ Continue to control pests on vegetables, 176

❏ Control corn earworm if desired, 222

❏ Control pine pitch canker, 191

❏ Protect yourself from Africanized honeybees, 204

❏ Attract good bees to your garden, 202

Also This Month

❏ Spread mulch to cool the ground and conserve moisture, 182

❏ Study the shady areas in your garden with an eye to improving them, 184

❏ Create additional shade where it's needed, 185

❏ Replace plants that are dying or doing badly in full shade with better choices for dark places, 186

❏ Replace plants in west-facing shade with better choices if they are being burned by sun or wilting in the afternoon, 187

❏ Protect fuchsias from burning rays of sun, 169

❏ Propagate camellias, azaleas, and other woody plants by layering, 193

❏ Move cyclamen and English primroses to a shady spot for the summer, 194

❏ Replant donkey tails, 197

❏ Flush out bromeliads occasionally to prevent mosquitoes from breeding, and allow the cups to dry out from time to time, 196

❏ Harvest summer vegetables according to special techniques for each, 201

❏ Beware of bumblebees as you harvest vegetables and pick summer flowers, 201

AUGUST

The Height-of-Summer Month

August may not always be the hottest and driest month of the year, since September sometimes shoves the thermometer higher, but August usually attacks the job with more persistence. Along the coast the weather's almost always sunny this month, with oceanic breezes to keep temperatures cool and comfortable, albeit drier than in early summer. Every few years, however, if you live along the coast, you can experience a disappointing August—either overcast skies or a blanket of fog. Thirty or forty years ago in interior zones there was seldom, if ever, a cool or moist August day and almost never a cloud in the sky. But in recent years, a reliable number of tropical storms have been wheeling up from the South Pacific and hitting various portions of Southern California. Sometimes these storms bring humid weather; at other times they simply bring clouds that have a cooling effect. Usually they don't bring a measurable amount of rain, so watering is still the major task in the garden, and pest control comes next.

Other than in coastal zones it's too hot to

plant most permanent additions to the land-scape, but it's a good time to start seeds. In the vegetable garden harvesting is important. For the most part August is a time to enjoy life, take it easy, and maintain what you've got. Go to the beach. And if you want, bring home a bag of seaweed to add to the compost pile or work directly into garden soil.

Watering

When the weather's hot and dry and there's no measurable rain, even the most inept gardeners are aware that most plants won't survive without regular irrigation. Unfortunately, one response is to stand with hose in hand and squirt water on the plants or on the surface of the ground around them. This doesn't do much but dig up the soil. Wise gardeners give their plants the amount of water each one needs in ways that save time, effort, and water.

Use the Right Equipment. Much water can be saved in summer by using the irrigation method appropriate to each part of the garden. Briefly, hand-sprinkling is fine for sprouting seeds, but all other watering should be done with conventional irrigation systems or drip systems. In general, conventional irrigation systems work best for most of the basic landscape, including lawns, while drip systems work best for plants in containers and vegetable gardens. Reserve watering by hose for filling furrows and basins around trees and bushes, when these are not equipped with bubblers. (When you water this way, put the hose right down on the ground, and let the water sink in slowly.)

How Often Should You Water Now? For most plants it's best to irrigate deeply once a week or every ten days—even less for many plants, de-pending on your climate zone and soil. Lawns—with the exception of Bermuda and zoysia—vegetables, certain annual flowers, and some perennial shade flowers are the thirstiest plants in the garden. Water these as frequently as necessary to prevent wilting. Some plants, such as fuchsias and impatiens, need water daily when growing in containers. Some drought-resistant native and exotic plants need little summer water or none at all. (In general, native plants that are summer deciduous should never be watered during the hot summer months, or they'll die from root rot. Some native plants that don't drop their leaves in summer, including flannel bush *[Fremontodendron]*, should be watered only if they show severe wilting and, even then, sparingly if in clay soils.)

Other plants recommended for their resistance to drought—Mexican fan palms *(Washingtonia robusta)*, Torrey pines, and Aleppo pines are good examples—will look better if they are watered deeply at least once during August. Water all pine trees deeply as needed—usually once every three weeks—to prevent stress in hot weather, which invites attack from bark beetles. Subtropical trees—including coral trees *(Erythrina)* and floss silk trees *(Chorisia speciosa)*—should be watered deeply, early in the month. Allowing chorisia to go on the dry side in late August often contributes to more spectacular fall bloom.

Remember to look for signs of stress and think of each plant as an individual; water accordingly. With deep, infrequent waterings, teach them to send their roots far into the ground, so when there's a drought they'll survive.

Check for Malfunctioning Sprinklers and Drip Emitters. The easiest way to supply plants with the water they need is with an automatic system controlled by a clock, but once it's installed you can't just walk away and forget it. Automatic irrigation isn't entirely trouble-free; when it malfunctions, it can cause havoc. Broken sprinklers and buried drip hoses with holes in them waste water. Clogged sprinklers and drip emitters can kill plants. If you go away on a trip, be sure to ask a responsible person to watch your garden, and leave the phone number of an irrigation repair person in case something goes wrong.

Now's a good time to check out your irrigation system. Begin by installing a new backup battery in your timer. Then flush the filters and the header lines of drip systems. Also, check all the drip emitters and clean out or replace those that are either flooding plants or failing to give them adequate water.

Run each section of your conventional sprinkler system on the manual setting; look for broken or clogged sprinklers or bubblers, and replace or repair the culprits. If your sprinklers don't adequately reach all parts of the lawn, you may get brown spots, especially after fertilizing. Sometimes gardeners don't realize how little water is actually penetrating the top layer of soil. In lawns, insufficient penetration may be caused by thatch (discussed on page 81). Or the problem may be that sprinkling is done too often and not long enough at one time. Set out empty juice cans to see how much water your sprinklers deliver in the amount of time you let them run. Adjust the timer to deliver water sufficient to sink deeply into the ground.

Another possible problem is that the soil has gotten so dry it won't absorb water. (Dry sandy soils often shed water.) Check now by digging down to take a look. If this is the problem, treat the soil with a surfactant such as Aqua-Gro Soil Wetting Agent to increase water penetration.

Improve Soil's Water Retention and Permeability. One way to keep the soil in containers

How to Keep Water from Pouring Off a Bank

When sloping ground is irrigated, water often runs off and pours down the street. It may run off because the ground is hard and dry or simply because it has insufficient time to sink in. Here are some solutions.

- Apply a layer of mulch over the roots of plants growing on the slope to catch and hold moisture and increase water penetration. (Be sure to irrigate enough that water enters the ground as well as the mulch.)

- Install a time-lapse control clock that pulses water onto the area in brief bursts; the water sinks into the ground during the shut-off periods. (Check the instructions for your existing timer; it may already have this option.)

- Install low-volume sprinklers and set them to run for a longer time.

- If the slope is planted with lawn, aerate it in fall and follow up with mulch.

- If all else fails, terrace the area by installing retaining walls or Gardenblock mortarless garden wall (a patented concrete block used to create miniature terraces in which to grow plants on a bank).

from drying out is to work a water-saving polymer, such as Broadleaf P4 (a nontoxic chemical product designed to reduce plant watering frequency), into the potting mix. Polymer crystals can aid aeration as they expand and contract. They catch and store up to 200 times their weight in water and release 95 percent of it to plants as they need it. The crystals remain effective for more than two years. Polymers work best when you place them under the roots of plants at planting time; mix a few granules into the soil in the bottom of each 6- to 8-inch-diameter planting hole. (Don't use polymer crystals in clay soil.)

Profile Professional Soil Conditioner is a natural mineral that has been kiln fired, creating ceramic chips that have thousands of internal and external pore spaces for holding air, water, and nutrients. When mixed into sandy soils, it makes them hold water and nutrients better. Profile Professional Clay Soil Conditioner is for mixing into heavy clay soil; when enough is added, it can turn heavy, compacted clay into a loose growing medium containing adequate water and oxygen.

Large quantities of Profile are required for instant results, but you can achieve gradual improvement in a vegetable garden or flowerbed by mixing in one bag of Profile twice a year along with your regular additions of organic amendments. The ideal is to eventually achieve a level of between 15 and 20 percent Profile in the soil. In potted plants, hanging baskets, and containers, use 1 part Profile to 3 parts potting soil. For flower and vegetable gardens pour Profile out of the bag, rake it evenly to a depth of approximately ½ inch, and turn it into the soil with a spade or tiller to an average depth of 4 to 6 inches. One 40-pound bag covers approximately 15 to 20 square feet.

Renew Watering Basins and Terraces. Creating a basin of soil to hold water around the roots of bushes and trees is a typical way to provide efficient irrigation in the Southwest, particularly on sloping ground, and the basin can be made into a decorative feature. Loose rocks can be used to hold the mounded soil in place. (Early Californians used abalone shells.) In some gardens a permanent system of wooden, concrete, or rock walls can convert steep slopes into usable garden space.

If no rock or cement is used to hold the soil, eventually it will erode away. Now's a good time to check watering basins and rebuild them if

necessary. (Get the children involved. Shaping the walls of the basins can be fun, especially if it's wet and muddy.) Sometimes it's best to haul in unwanted clay soil from somewhere else in the garden, if you have some, instead of digging into the soil on a slope and creating more erosion.

Be sure to make tree basins big enough. Water standing around the trunk can cause crown rot and will never reach the roots, which aren't near the trunk but out farther, under the drip line. If the walls of the basin are made high enough, the center can be filled with mulch to hold moisture and improve the soil.

Give Special Care to Plants in Containers. Plants in containers often suffer at this time of year. Water them frequently. (A drip system can save time plus all the water that's wasted when you go from plant to plant with a hose.) In interior zones containers often dry out as soon as they're watered. It's not only the heat; dry air literally pulls moisture out of the soil right through the sides of terra-cotta pots.

Terra-cotta containers add charm to gardens and patios, but, surprisingly, most plants actually grow better in plastic. The idea that plants are helped by a pot that "breathes" is a mistaken one. The soil mix itself should breathe. It should be light and airy, which can be accomplished by adding perlite, sponge rock (a natural volcanic product that holds air), or an inorganic soil modifier such as Profile Professional Soil Conditioner, as described above. In containers that breathe, roots follow the water as it escapes through the sides of the pot, forming a solid mat that clings to the inside of the pot, dries out daily, and causes the plant to wilt. When plants are grown in plastic, roots tend to form more evenly throughout the mix. (Eventually they congregate at the bottom and wind around the sides, but then it's time to repot them to the next size of container.) Before planting in porous containers, seal the insides with a double coat of black waterproofing tar to help prevent escape of moisture.

Deciduous Fruit Trees

Don't feed deciduous fruit trees now even if you happen to read a newspaper column advocating this practice. Such columns are syndicated for the country at large, and the advice doesn't apply here. It's difficult enough for us to get our fruit trees into dormancy in this area without stimulating growth so late in the season.

Prune Unwanted Sprouts. Water sprouts are tall shoots that grow in summer straight up from the trunk and branches in the centers of mature deciduous fruit trees. Their growth is so sudden and rapid they soon look like buggy whips. Spot this growth as it begins and cut it out flush with the bark. A tree in which water sprouts have been allowed to persist and take over is a sorry mess. They eventually thicken and bear branches just like miniature trees within a tree, taking energy from the parent and ruining its shape. Some deciduous fruit trees also send up suckers from the base of the trunk and from roots. Cut these off now too, so they don't sap the strength of the tree.

Water These Trees Infrequently. Water deeply and infrequently to encourage deep rooting, but don't subject your trees to absolute drought unless it's unavoidable. The **Rule of Thumb** is: *Mature deciduous fruit trees growing in hot interior valleys need two or three deep irrigations per month throughout the growing season in order to grow well and bear good fruit. Full-grown trees along the coast should be watered deeply once or twice a month.* Trees in sandy soil need

Double-Potting Beats the Heat

Hot sun hitting dark-colored containers can burn roots and damage or kill plants. Use double-potting to grow plants in plastic containers, enjoy the artistic look of terra-cotta pots, and keep plant roots cool.

- Plant any item you wish to grow in an appropriately sized plastic container, or, when roots aren't crowded, leave it right in the nursery can.

- Sink the planted container into a terra-cotta pot large enough to hide it. (Spherical Mexican pots are ideal; they hide planted containers best.)

- Where tree roots are a problem, place the outer pot onto a large stepping stone. This will prevent roots from entering from below.

more water. Young trees require more frequent water to get established.

Train Fruit Tree Espaliers. Throughout the growing season train the whippy new growth that you want to save into the shape you want, while it's still soft and pliable. Tie it gently but firmly into place. (Refer to pruning manuals such as Tanner's *Living Fences: A Gardener's Guide to Hedges, Vines and Espaliers* for detailed instructions.) While the branches are still flexible, try tying bamboo poles onto them to train them in straight lines. This method can be especially helpful if you're training your espalier onto a wire framework, because wire bends but bamboo is rigid. Remove the poles when the wood has hardened. Also cut off unwanted water sprouts, flush with the bark, from espaliered trees now.

On trees that bear on spurs, such as apples, apricots, and pears, cut new growth back to two or three buds to stimulate production of fruiting spurs. (Apricots aren't ideal for espalier. After several years, when their old wood no longer bears as well as formerly, retain some well-placed fresh growth to replace it. Then, during winter dormancy, cut out the old wood; start training the new growth to take its place.)

Pool Planting

Replace or trim vines and trees that drop leaves, fruit, or petals near swimming pools. Tidy vines such as Carolina jessamine *(Gelsemium sempervirens)*, Madagascar jasmine *(Stephanotis floribunda),* and star jasmine *(Trachelospermum jasminoides)* do well in the special microclimate near pools, and they add fragrance. If a tall accent is needed, choose a tree that has a tendency to hang onto its foliage until it is trimmed, such as Mediterranean fan palm *(Chamaerops humilis),* Spanish dagger *(Yucca gloriosa),* giant bird of paradise *(Strelitzia nicolai)*, or firewheel tree *(Stenocarpus sinuatus).* For color try epidendrum, succulents, hibiscus, canna lilies, kangaroo paw *(Anigozanthos),* gazania, and verbena. Fill large tubs, watered daily with a drip system, with 'Richmondensis' begonias surrounded by *Scaevola* 'Blue Wonder'. These plants aren't messy, and they can stand the reflected glare at poolside. Kahili ginger *(Hedychium gardneranum)* does well if given rich soil, plenty of water, and protection from burning hot sun.

Fuchsias

Most fuchsias look bedraggled and bloomed out in August. Cut them back lightly and pinch the tips for a week or two; you'll have a second flush of bloom that will last until cold weather. Continue to feed them regularly and remove berries (seedpods).

Cuttings root quickly now. (Use the method described on page 102.) Take your cuttings from the fresh, succulent growth that results from pruning. Root them in small pots filled with the same potting soil that you grow your fuchsias in and the plants won't suffer root shock when they're repotted.

Watch for pest problems. If possible, avoid spraying with anything other than a soap spray, like Safer soap, in order to preserve beneficials. Well-fed plants that are free from ants and have an adequate supply of beneficials may never need spraying. However, if you feel you absolutely must spray, the recommended products are BT against certain caterpillars, specific miticides against mites, insecticidal soaps against whiteflies, SunSpray Ultra-Fine Spray Oil, for giant whitefly, and Sevin against fuchsia gall mite. (Always mix Sevin with a miticide to prevent an outbreak of spider mites.) Systemics, such as Orthene, get rid of caterpillars and mites plus many other insects, both pests and beneficials. Sevin is also a broad-spectrum spray. Don't spray everything in the garden, or you'll kill all the good guys.

Ferns

Keep ferns well watered during August and September. Protect them from drying winds, which can turn fronds brown and subject the plants to disease. Most ferns like an atmosphere comparable to the floor of a Northern California redwood forest—shady, damp, and thick with acid mulch. The closer you come to it, in an atrium, shady entryway, or some other protected spot, the happier your ferns will be. Leatherleaf fern *(Rumohra adiantiformis)* and southern sword fern *(Nephrolepis cordifolia)* are valuable exceptions to the rule. They're drought resistant, unfussy, and easy. (Sword fern is invasive but is a good filler in narrow, awkward beds.)

Many ferns are sold mainly as houseplants, but few of them can actually survive long inside most homes. ('Dallas' fern [*Nephrolepis exaltata* 'Dallas'] and 'Kimberley Queen' [*N. obliterata* 'Kimberley Queen'] are exceptions; they can withstand lower light than most ferns.) The common type of Boston fern (*N. e.* 'Bostoniensis') is among the most often bought and quickly killed of all houseplants. Indoors they die within a few months, but they thrive outdoors in semishade in coastal zones (see the Quick Tip at right). One way to have success with houseplant ferns is to grow them outdoors but cycle them into the house for a week at a time.

Roses

Continue to feed, fertilize, water, and control rose pests and diseases. If you're following the Rose-Pro Method, omit urea this month; instead, give one application of 2 tablespoons of Epsom salts and ½ cup of Milorganite to each plant. Sprinkle both over the top of the soil above the roots and water them into the ground. Milorganite will provide slow-acting nitrogen in organic form. The Epsom salts provide magnesium. (Continue foliar-feeding as described on page 95.)

Prune Lightly. Roses usually take a rest during the heat of August while they gather strength for a great burst of bloom in fall. You can cooperate by cutting them back lightly now to stimulate fall flowering. Remove dead twigs, spent flowers, and hips (the fruits of roses, which contain the seeds). Cut down a little farther than usual to make new growth for fall bloom. Remove thin, lanky growth back to a promising bud. Cut off suckers sprouting from below the bud union.

🐚 Quick Tip

How to Keep a Difficult Boston Fern Alive.
When you leave for work in the morning, take the fern out and hang it under a tree (like putting out the dog). Take it in when you return. One Southern California gardener used this method to keep her houseplant fern alive for seven years.

Daylilies and Agapanthus

Clean up daylilies (*Hemerocallis*) and agapanthus now by removing stems that have bloomed. On most daylilies the stems go brown after flowering; simply yank these off. But many varieties, especially the newer everblooming ones, have stems that never go brown. Instead they stay green and continue to grow; don't try to pull them off or you'll uproot the plant. After these green stems finish flowering, they sprout leaves and form plantlets, "proliferates," on the stem. As soon as the proliferates have formed one or two short roots, cut the stems off the mother plant, so they don't sap its strength. Gently snap off the pups and plant them elsewhere in the garden, or give them to friends.

Agapanthus stems have to be cut off. Some gardeners hang them upside-down to dry and then use them in flower arrangements or dip them in glue and glitter for holiday decorations.

Fortnight Lily

Fortnight Lily (*Dietes vegeta* or *D. iridioides, Moraea*) has white blossoms with orange blotches on them. It's good near swimming pools and is drought resistant, easy to grow, and one of our commonest plants—some people think it's much too common. There's also a yellow type (*D. bicolor*). Both have clumps of upright narrow, pointed leaves and bear their flowers in flushes every two weeks or so, spring through fall, sometimes year-round. Keep them looking their best by feeding them lightly now and watering them well. After flowers fade from the yellow species, cut off the flower stalk at the base. Remove the seedpods of white fortnight lily to clean up the plants and promote continued flowering, but don't remove the stalks; they'll bloom for several years.

Alstroemeria

Peruvian lilies, or alstroemerias (*Alstroemeria aurea, A. aurantiaca, A. psittacina, A. ligtu,* and hybrids) are members of the lily family whose azalealike blossoms and many virtues have captivated the hearts of local gardeners in recent years. The plants are considerably drought resistant; the blooms have sturdy stems, and their cut flowers last two weeks. The craze for alstroemerias began when a photograph of the Berkeley Botanical Gardens' massive display of peach, orange, and gold ligtu hybrids was published on the cover of *Sunset* magazine. But ligtu hybrids have some drawbacks; it takes at least three years to get them going, and once established they're almost impossible to eradicate or transplant. Their tall flowers make a magnificent display, but they do so only once a year in June and July.

Alstroemeria seeds are widely available though difficult to germinate. You can order the plants of ligtu hybrids from mail-order houses, including B & D Lilies, P.O. Box 2007, 330 P Street, Port Townsend, WA 98368; 360/385-1738. Flowers & Greens is developing improved alstroemerias (catalog $2). Contact the company at P.O. Box 1802, Davis, CA 95617 (530/756-9238).

Meyer hybrids are more heat resistant, easier to grow, and less invasive than the ligtu types. They also bloom longer and can be transplanted, divided, or moved in fall. They come in many shades of white, lavender, maroon, rose, and pink with stems ranging in height from 1½ to 2½ feet. They're available at nurseries throughout Southern California. If you let them go dry in summer they won't die, though they will stop blooming, but if you water, feed, and deadhead them regularly, many of them will bloom on and off year-round.

Look for Meyer hybrid alstroemerias in summer and plant them in fall in loose, well-drained soil with plenty of organic matter worked in. After a few years divide and transplant the clumps, handling the tubers gently to preserve their delicate roots. After the flowers fade, remove each spent stalk by giving it a sharp tug. By pulling off the stems singly you remove them cleanly and safely from the tubers, and this stimulates the plant to produce more bloom spikes. (Cutting off stems makes the plant stop blooming.) Follow up each wave of bloom with an application of complete fertilizer, and water it thoroughly into the ground.

Wisteria

Wisteria sends out long twining stems in summer. If your plant is young, continue to train the vines where you want them to go, and tie them loosely in place. Catch them before they get twisted around each other. They'll eventually become a structure of thick vines from which the flower spurs will spring. If your vine is mature, keep only those stems on the outer edges where you have more space for wisteria to cover. Cut all unwanted new stems back to two buds to encourage the growth of more flower spurs.

Water and feed young vines for growth. Give mature vines one deep watering in August.

Trees for August Bloom

Crape myrtle (*Lagerstroemia indica*) is an elegant, drought-resistant tree for small gardens in interior valleys. (It gets mildew along the coast.) It blooms in white and electric shades of pink and red from July through August. Its lovely gray-brown bark peels off yearly to soft pink. Look for the plants while they're in bloom. (People either love or hate some of the colors.)

The gold medallion tree (*Cassia leptophylla*) is the most dramatic of the cassias that can be grown here. It's best in a warm, sheltered spot and when watered deeply and infrequently, but it will grow in lawns if it has excellent drainage.

Along the coast the flame eucalyptus (red-flowering gum; *Eucalyptus ficifolia*) can grow in the teeth of the wind and still bloom magnificently. This is the time you may be able to pick out the color you want. (Young ones often won't bloom in the can.) The orangey red is gorgeous viewed against the sea. Grow it with a single trunk, or, if desired, cut it back to make a huge, multibranched shrub. It blooms on and off all year. The eucalyptus beetle prefers blue gum eucalyptus (*E. globulus*) and usually doesn't attack this species unless it's under stress from drought.

Control of Nematodes

Nematodes are especially active in warm weather. These are microscopic worms that bore into roots of susceptible plants, causing galls and knots and weakening the plants. Here are two ways to significantly reduce large populations of nematodes.

Solarize the Soil. Solarization—using the effects of the sun's rays—is the method to use only when nematode and fungal problems are acute and unbearable. It kills useful organisms, including worms and beneficial fungi, along with the bad ones. (This method works best where summer days are hot—90°F—and skies are clear.)

- If nematodes and fungus have rendered a vegetable or flower area unusable, sacrifice the plants now. Pull them out roots and all. (Don't compost the roots; destroy them.)
- Thoroughly soak the soil with water.
- Cover the area with clear (not black) polyethylene plastic that's 1 to 4 millimeters thick. Peg it down around the outside, and bury the loose edges. (A few round rocks in the middle will hold it down in case of strong wind.) Tests at University of California, Davis show even better results with two layers of clear 1-millimeter polyethylene film separated by a 6-centimeter air space. (Prop up the top layer here and there with wire hoops or bamboo frame.)
- Leave the plastic in place for six to eight weeks of hot, sunny weather. Test plots under a single plastic layer in the San Joaquin Valley reached 140°F at a depth of 2 inches and 102°F as far down as 18 inches. Almost all traces of harmful disease organisms were destroyed, including fungi.

Plant Marigolds. Many people think marigolds repel nematodes, but the truth is they attract them. Root knot nematodes entering marigold roots are killed by a natural plant chemical before they have a chance to reproduce. Planting a single row of marigolds among vegetables won't get rid of nematodes, however. Marigolds can be used to rid the ground of these pests, but you have to start earlier in the planting season. Consider this method for next year.

- In March solidly plant the area to be treated with French marigolds (*Tagetes patula*). Space the plants in a 7-by-7-inch pattern all over the bed.
- Leave the marigolds in place for a full 120-day season of growth.

- Systematically remove all weeds at their earliest appearance.

After this treatment the ground can be planted with any desired crop. Nematodes will gradually return, but they'll be discouraged if you regularly add organic soil amendment. They don't like humusy soil.

Harmful nematodes can also be controlled by releasing beneficial nematodes into the ground. Beneficial nematodes can be purchased from catalogs (see page 38 for list). Beneficial nematodes, unlike the harmful types, need moist soil to survive.

Control of Fireblight

Fireblight is a bacterial disease of the rose family (Rosaceae) that infects such common garden plants as apples, pears, evergreen pear *(Pyrus kawakamii)*, pyracantha, cotoneaster, California holly (or toyon; *Heteromeles arbutifolia*), plum, cherry, quince, and loquat (though some varieties are resistant to fireblight; see the *Ortho Problem Solver* for a list). Fireblight first wilts the fresh green growth, then shrivels and blackens it as well as twigs, branches, berries, and fruit, making the victim look as if it had been caught in a flash fire. Birds and insects carry the bacteria from tree to tree during the bloom period. Remove disfigured twigs and branches now to reduce the sources of infection. Cut out infected branches 8 to 15 inches below any visible damage, and destroy them. (Dip the pruning shears in rubbing alcohol after making each cut to avoid spreading the infection.)

Oleander Leaf Scorch

Since 1994 oleanders *(Nerium oleander)*, particularly in interior valleys, have been stricken with a bacterial disease called oleander leaf scorch, caused by a new strain of *Xylella fastidiosa*, which in the late 1800s wiped out vineyards in Southern California. *Xylella* is a disease spread by glassy-winged sharpshooters, leaf-sucking insects native to the southeastern United States. Once a plant is infected, its leaf edges go brown, then whole branches die and finally the entire plant. At the present time there's no known cure for leaf scorch. Until a solution is found, maintain good plant health by watering and fertilizing regularly. Destroy infected branches and dying plants and don't plant oleanders. Boston ivy *(Parthenocissus tricuspidata)*, Virginia creeper *(P. quinquefolia)*, crape myrtle *(Lagerstroemia indica)*, and periwinkle *(Vinca)* are potential hosts of sharpshooters and leaf scorch bacteria, so don't plant these near oleanders. (Be careful handling oleanders; all parts are extremely poisonous.)

Annual and Perennial Flowers

Plant Cool-Season Annuals from Seeds. Gardeners who want to grow their own transplants of winter flowers, particularly tall rather than dwarf varieties or single colors rather than mixed, should plant seeds of cool-season annuals now. Plant in flats, small pots, or peat pots. If you can't find the seeds you want locally, kick off your shoes, relax in the shade, study the seed catalogs, and send away for seeds. A few varieties may be sold out but most are still available, and service now is swift.

Seeds of such flowers as calendulas, cineraria, delphiniums, dianthus (pinks), Iceland poppies, nemesia, pansies, primroses, snapdragons, stock (discussed in detail below), and violas, planted in August, can give great numbers of transplants with which to fill beds in October.

Plant Stock. Growing tall varieties of stock (*Matthiola incana*) is particularly worthwhile from seed, since you can be assured of disease-free transplants. (Stock is susceptible to stem and root rots, so don't plant them in the same place two years in a row.)

To grow stock, disinfect flats and fill them with sterilized potting soil. Place the seeds on top of the soil, carefully spacing them where you want them; press them down gently. (Stock needs light to germinate.) Keep them moist and in semishade. Cover the flats with plastic until the seeds germinate. Then take off the plastic, protect the sprouts with netting, and move the flats in stages—over a period of two or three weeks—into increasing light, eventually into full sun. Start to feed the plants lightly when each has two real leaves. Transplant seedlings into beds when they are 3 to 4 inches tall. The sooner you get stock in the ground the better, because early planting enables the plants to build big, strong root systems and hefty stalks. You'll reap a long-lasting and dramatic display.

Try to find seeds of the brand-new variety called 'Vintage', which may revolutionize stock for home gardeners and perhaps the floral trade. 'Vintage' produces large branching plants with three to four shoots, each as strong and as full of flowers as the main stem. Your color display will be much greater and last longer. Mixed-color seed packets of 'Vintage' include copper, a new color for stock.

The real problem with stock is disease, and yellowing leaves are the first symptom. To make stock more resistant, feed it when you plant it and treat it with Roots, a product containing humic acid. Fertilize often with any general fertilizer. If you plant stock in September, you will have color in December. It's one of the best winter-color plants.

Pick Summer-Blooming Annuals. Continue picking or deadheading warm-season annual flowers and feed and water them regularly. Tall varieties of zinnia and cosmos will bloom through September if you give them this care.

Maintain Perennials. In interior zones August is far from the best time to plant perennials. Continue to pick flowers, deadhead, and clean up as needed. Renew mulch. Water in the early morning hours. When summer phlox (*Phlox paniculata*) begins to look tired and bloomed out, cut off its main terminal flower heads. This will force the side branches to produce blooms that will flower into September. Continue to deadhead pentas. Every time you cut off a faded flower, two more pop out, but it can't do so without regular fertilizer and water.

Along the coast, gardeners will find many interesting and often new perennials in bloom in nurseries. Big blue lilyturf (*Liriope muscari*) is far from new but is a fine shade plant that blooms now. The benefit of finding plants now is that you know that they will bloom at this time every year. Some gardeners take their finds home but keep them in the containers for fall planting. Personally, I find it harder to keep a plant in good shape in a nursery container than in the ground.

In all zones you might find *Crassula falcata* now among the succulents or ask for cuttings from a friend. A super plant for a tub, a bank, or well-drained bed, its bright scarlet blossoms against blue-green foliage will light up a patio or delight the sunbathers next to a swimming pool in late summer.

Fire Protection

There's no sure way to protect your home from a raging fire, but there are some things you can do to minimize risk. If you live next to native brush or chaparral—near a canyon, for example—take these steps to protect your property:

- Keep the landscape close to your home well watered. Don't grow such flammable plants as pine trees close to your home or allow them to overhang your roof. (Shrubs and trees with lush green leaves, like pittosporum, are recommended for greenbelts.)
- Don't mound shrubbery close to your house. Shrubs should be spaced apart from each other and kept low. For safety from fire when houses are close together, it's best to have no shrubbery between them.
- Create a buffer zone. A well-watered green area of low-growing plants can act as a fire-break between you and the chaparral. The buffer zone should be at least 30 feet wide on flat ground and progressively wider as slopes get steeper. Walls, rocks, patios, rustic seats, and wandering paths can be part of the land-scaping. Use plant materials that have proven their ability to withstand some fires, such as succulents and cacti. Coarse *Carpobrotus* ice plant is not recommended, but rosea ice plant *(Drosanthemum floribundum)* is. (Ask your local UC Cooperative Extension office or the California Department of Forestry for additional information and plant lists.)
- Manage the existing brush. Go right down into the chaparral and remove the fuel load from inside. (Be on the lookout for poison oak, rattlesnakes, and sudden drop-offs in the terrain.) The buildup of dead leaves, twigs, branches, and weeds in the understory is what makes the hottest fires. You may have to use a chain saw. (Keep a fire extinguisher and a shovel close at hand in case of sparks.) Cut out and haul away or chip and compost all the dead stuff that builds up inside native shrubs. Leave all the green growth, on the outside.

When you're finished, you'll have a wonder-land of usable space for birds and the other wildlife that inhabit our precious chaparral.

Tropicals

It's somewhat late for planting most tropicals this month, except in coastal zones. Among tropicals that can be planted along the coast now (or during any summer month) are papayas, bananas, and palms.

Plant Papayas and Bananas. Papayas *(Carica papaya)* and bananas *(Musa, Ensete)* will grow and bear fruit in all frost-free zones, but they do best near the coast and thrive on sheltered, south-facing hillsides. Papayas are tall, single-trunked, succulent trees with a palmlike cluster of leaves on top. It's a common misconception that bananas, like papayas, grow on trees; they actually grow on a large, green, herbaceous, perennial plant. The apparent trunk of a banana plant is actually a group of leaf stalks. Surprisingly, the fruits themselves are technically berries.

Plant Papayas from Seed or Plants. If you compost papaya skins and seeds, many papaya plants will come up here and there during the summer. Look for these seedlings now and plant a group of three to five of them in full sun, 4 to 6 feet apart. (You need both male and female plants to get fruit.) Feed your papayas for growth and provide them with good drainage and plenty of water. Or start papaya seeds in flats. For the quickest germination, gently rub a handful of seeds on a piece of screen under running water to remove the aril (protective seed covering). Sprout the seeds in the kitchen on a plate that's covered with a wet paper towel and zipped into a plastic bag. As soon as the seeds sprout, carefully plant them in a premoistened flat of fast-draining potting soil. Keep them damp in bright—not dark—shade; a warm shady spot with an hour of morning sun is ideal.

You can also purchase papaya plants at nurseries specializing in rare and tropical fruits, such as Papaya Tree Farms in Granada Hills, Exotica Seed Company in Vista, or Pacific Tree Farms in Chula Vista. The babaco papaya *(Carica heilbornii)* is a popular type because, though expensive, it's hardy to 28°F, and the plant is small enough to grow in a half whiskey barrel. Babaco papayas bear fruit when young, often while they're still in a 5-gallon can, and you need only one plant to get fruit. The fruit is large—sometimes a foot long—and equal to other papayas in its health-giving properties, but it tastes more like a melon than an ordinary papaya. The fruit starts to ripen between now and fall. Pick it when it's yellow and gives slightly to the touch.

Start Bananas from Plants You Buy at a Nursery. Begin with a good variety, such as 'Ice Cream' or 'Enano Gigante'. (The plants are small, but the fruit is giant.) Fertilize often with a complete fertilizer, such as 16-16-16. Bananas are big eaters; they're also thirsty, so water them well. You can keep them barely alive with less water and fertilizer in drought years, but their growth will slow down and they won't bear fruit.

As suckers, or pups, form around the main trunk, use a sharp spade to slice off all but one, and plant them elsewhere in the garden. The one pup you leave will remain to replace the mature stalk after it has borne fruit. (Each stalk of a banana plant is monocarpic and won't bear fruit again.) At thirteen to fifteen months after planting you should have a scape covered with fruit.

Transplant Palms. Summer is a good time to

How to Tell When Homegrown Bananas Are Ripe

Some varieties ripen on the plant. When the fruit of these begins to turn yellow, reach up with a long-handled fruit picker or pruning hook, and pick one banana. If it's creamy yellow inside and soft textured and sweet, it's ready. To harvest, cut off individual hands of fruit as they ripen or, if they're too far out of reach, cut the whole trunk down as described below.

Most varieties don't ripen on the plant. Pick their fruit when they've lost their sharp edges and indented sides; wait until they lose their angularity. When the fruit is still green but has become rounded, filled out, and fat looking, it's ready to pick. (You will know if you have this type of plant because the fruit will not turn yellow on the plant.)

Once ready, cut the whole plant down by nicking the underside of the trunk with a sharp knife or giving it a single whack with a machete. It will fall of its own weight. Ask someone to stand below and catch the fruit as it falls. Cut off the entire fruit stalk (scape) and hang it in a shady place to ripen, such as your front porch or patio overhang. When individual bananas go yellow, they're ready to eat.

Chop up the remains of the stalk that's borne fruit; use it to mulch the rest of your bananas, or bury it and let it rot. Plant your next banana there.

plant or transplant palms because they take off well when planted in warm soil. Before transplanting any palm, be sure it's a species that can be transplanted successfully. Most can; a few cannot. Trim off all faded fronds and cut back the remaining fronds by one-third to make up for the loss of roots. Bend these upright and tie them together on top with stout twine to protect the meristem layer (the area of actively dividing cells at the bud of the plant). Each

Protect Canary Island Date Palms from Fungus

Before having Canary Island date palms *(Phoenix canariensis)* pruned, insist that the tree pruners sterilize all pruning tools by soaking the blades for 15 minutes in a solution of 1 part household bleach to 1 part water. (Request that a saw with a reciprocating blade be used—not a chain saw, which cannot be effectively disinfected.) Pruning with unsterilized saws causes healthy date palms to fall prey to fungal attacks, because it allows spores carried from infected palms to enter fresh cuts. As an additional precaution, remove only dead and dying fronds, not fresh green growth.

single-trunked palm has only one bud; if it's damaged, the tree will die. After transplanting, leave the fronds tied for a month or two to shade the bud. (Be sure to water palms well after planting and keep them well watered for at least a year, until established.)

Palms can lend a tropical atmosphere to any garden, and not all are heavy water users; some are drought resistant. They're incredibly interesting and varied, so before choosing a palm, study the options and your requirements. Notice that some palms have fronds (leaves) shaped like feathers and others have fronds shaped like fans. Some palms form a clump while others are solitary. Some palms are self-cleaning—the fronds fall off without pruning. The fronds of others cling to the trunk after they're dead and need to be pruned off, or in some cases the old fronds look best left on the tree. Among those with persistent fronds, some have trunks that are easily cleaned off by pruning, while others have leaf bases that tend to stay on the trunk for many years. An important factor to consider if you have children is that some palms are armed with formidable spikes; others are unarmed.

Cycads

Dating from the age of dinosaurs, cycads (Cycadaceae) are among the most ancient plants on Earth. They're also one of nature's first attempts at making seeds. Male plants bear prominent cones that give off pollen, while female plants develop a sporophyll (a brushlike spore-bearing organ) that can produce seeds if fertilized (though this is a rare occurrence in gardens). In appearance cycads look like ferns or palms, but they're not even closely related to either. The best known and most commonly grown cycad is often mistaken for a palm and even bears the confusing name of sago palm *(Cycas revoluta)*. In gardens cycads are long lived and slow growing. They grow well outdoors in most of Southern California if provided with some shade.

Water cycads well now; don't let their roots dry out. When cycads are neglected, their leaves may turn brown, pale, whitish, or yellow in color. Brown tips on leaves usually come from salt burn (sago palms are particularly sensitive to salts in the soil); drench the ground to leach out salts. Pale or brown patches on the leaves can come from sunburn; in this case, consider digging up the plant and transplanting it into more shade. All-over yellowing or loss of color most likely means lack of nitrogen or trace elements; pour a complete liquid fertilizer such as Terr-O-Vite around the roots of the plant at intervals of two or three weeks throughout the growing season, and provide it with ample water. (Cycads also respond well to foliar applications of fertilizer.)

Yellowing and loss of color may also result from insect attack. Scale is the worst offender. Look under the fronds for small, round, brown bumps—these are scale insects. The safest way to get rid of them now is to painstakingly scrub them off with a brush or sponge dipped in soapy solution; they come off easily. Oil sprays kill scale, so you could spray with SunSpray Ultra-Fine Spray Oil. (Other oil sprays will damage foliage in hot weather.)

Malathion is recommended against scale insects, but it works best in spring while the insects are in their crawling stage. (Spray several times in early spring at intervals of a week or two.)

Lawn Care

This is the time of year when warm-season lawns, such as Bermuda, zoysia, and St. Augustine, are looking their best, but cool-season lawns, such as Kentucky bluegrass, perennial ryegrass, and tall fescue are at their worst. Water warm-season lawns deeply and infrequently, feed them every month to six weeks, and mow them as short as possible. Don't feed kikuyu or 'Adalayd' (Excalibre) in August. Continue to water cool-season lawns regularly, cut them high, and feed them lightly, if at all. (Overfeeding cool-season lawns now can stress them. See page 197 for basic guidelines on summer care for lawns.)

Control Crabgrass When It Turns Red. Now, in August, you have yet another chance to control crabgrass, when it goes red in color but before it sets seed. Use an herbicide labeled for postemergent crabgrass control in actively growing lawns, such as calcium acid methanearsonate. Be sure to follow the directions on the package and not to use these products in the middle of a hot day. Water deeply the day before use, and then avoid watering again as long as possible. For best results, pull out the clumps after they die. (Another possible control is to spot-treat with glyphosate [Roundup], but it will kill anything it touches.)

Control Pests and Diseases on Cool-Season Lawns. Dead or brown patches often disfigure cool-season lawns now even if you water and feed lightly. Take hold of a tuft of grass in one of the bad patches and yank up on it. If the patch is circular and grass blades pull off at the roots but the roots stay in the ground, the problem may be brown-patch fungus. Some other fungal diseases cause variously shaped brown patches; with these the grass sticks tight when you pull on it. In some cases there's a dark green or grayish green line or circle around the damaged patch. (Consult the *Ortho Problem Solver* at your local nursery for pictures and descriptions.)

Treat affected grass with fungicide. Always read the entire label and follow all directions and precautions carefully. Unless you use a product that already contains fertilizer, follow up with light application of it. Water early in the morning, not late in the day. Aerate the ground to improve water penetration.

If you've noticed large numbers of moths fluttering in a zigzag pattern over the lawn in the evening and the grass blades are chewed off at ground level, look among the roots for silky white tubes with brown or gray black–spotted grubs in them. These are signs of sod webworm. For this treat the lawn with a spray or granular product recommended for controlling webworms.

If the grass is loose and comes up like a mat, roots and all, the problem is white grubs. Roll the turf back and look for curled white grubs living under the turf and eating the roots. (In our area these are not grubs of the Japanese beetle, as is the case in the East and Middle West, but of several other beetles.) Treat with a product recommended for the control of white grubs, such as diazinon. They're easiest to kill when young, but you may have to treat more than once.

Vegetable Gardening

The main jobs in the vegetable garden this month are watering, harvesting, and pest control. All summer vegetables can be planted now, especially the heat lovers, but most gardeners prefer to wait this month out and start planting winter crops in mid-September. Most vegetable gardens in interior zones get pretty well burned up by the end of August.

Start Seeds for Cool-Season Crops. By mid-month seeds of bedding plants can be started in flats or peat pots for fall planting. (Keep them in semishade.) Good candidates are celery and all members of the cabbage family, including broccoli, Brussels sprouts, cauliflower, and cabbage. Homegrown transplants will be ready to put out in the garden in late September or October. If you need only a few it's much less trouble to buy transplants at the nursery.

Unfortunately, these plants bought at nurseries are usually labeled generically rather than by variety. Learn about good varieties for your zone, and ask your nursery to carry them as transplants. Patronize companies that grow "gourmet varieties." They're more expensive, but there's a good reason: the seeds cost more. If enough gardeners become informed buyers, bedding-plant growers and nurseries will gladly give them what they want.

Control Corn Earworm. If your corn is badly attacked by corn earworm now and you're not an organic gardener, try dusting the silks with Sevin. (Treat when the silks first emerge and continue to treat every three to five days until the silks turn brown.) Mineral oil on the silk has been tried with varying success by organic gardeners. In my garden I don't even try to combat this pest, since the worms usually don't do more than disfigure the tops of the ears. If yours are being rendered inedible, perhaps you're waiting too long to pick. (Directions for when to harvest corn are given on page 201.)

Corn needs lots of water while it's forming ears. Once you've picked them, cook the fresh corn no more than three minutes after the second boil.

Continue to Harvest, and Take Stock for Next Year. This is the time of year when people who love to can and freeze are happily stashing away jars and bags of produce for winter use, and those of us who don't are giving away armloads of vegetables and perhaps vowing to plant less next year. By now first-time gardeners have learned that they don't need a whole row of zucchini to feed a family of four—three plants are plenty—but you never can plant enough corn—it goes fast.

Purchase/Plant

❏ Continue to plant tropicals in coastal zones, 166

❏ Transplant biennials you started from seed in July, when they are 2 or 3 inches high, into the garden, 190

❏ In coastal zones continue to purchase, plant, and transplant succulents, including cacti and euphorbias, 194

❏ Replace untidy plants growing near swimming pools with better choices, 212

❏ Choose crape myrtles in interior zones, 215

❏ Purchase cassias and pick out flame eucalyptus to plant in coastal zones, 215

❏ Grow your own transplants by planting seeds of cool-season flowers, 236

❏ Plant buffer zones between your home and native chaparral, 218

❏ Plant papayas, bananas, and palms, 218

❏ Transplant palms, 219

❏ If you want to grow your own vegetable transplants, start seeds of cool-season vegetables now, 222

❏ Plant stock from seed, 217

❏ Plant perennials in coastal zones, 217

Trim, Prune, Mow, Divide

❏ Stop pinching chrysanthemums, 155

❏ Cut off water sprouts and suckers from deciduous fruit trees, 211

❏ Prune and train espaliers throughout the growing season, 211

❏ Trim untidy trees and vines growing near swimming pools, 212

❏ Give fuchsias a light midsummer pruning, 212

❏ Give roses a light midsummer pruning; remove suckers, 213

❏ Clean up daylilies and agapanthus by removing stems that have bloomed, 213

❏ Propagate daylilies by planting the proliferates, 213

❏ Cut off bloom stalks from yellow fortnight lilies; take off seedpods only from white fortnight lilies, 214

❏ Prune and train wisteria, 214

❏ Clean out native brush; clear buffer zones, 218

❏ Remove only dead and dying foliage from date palms; use sterilized tools, 220

❏ Pull out dead crabgrass if you have previously treated it with weed killer, 221

❏ Maintain perennials, 217

❏ Cut back any unsightly cool-season ornamental grasses to two-thirds height, 239

Fertilize

❏ Feed fuchsias, 212

❏ Feed tuberous begonias, 185, 96

❏ Feed water lilies, 125

❏ Feed cymbidiums with a high-nitrogen fertilizer for growth, 183

❏ Feed ferns, 147

❏ Feed tropicals, 147

❏ Fertilize warm-season grasses with the exception of 'Adalayd' and kikuyu, 221

❏ If cool-season lawns show signs of nitrogen deficiency (yellow leaves, stunted growth), fertilize lightly; otherwise not at all, 197

❏ Fertilize biennials started from seed in July with fish emulsion at weekly intervals, 190

❏ Feed all container-grown succulents with a well-diluted complete liquid fertilizer, 195

❏ Don't fertilize deciduous fruit trees now, 211

❏ Fertilize roses, 213

❏ Feed fortnight lilies lightly; follow up with water, 213

❏ Feed and water cycads, 220

Continued>>

Water

❏ Reduce irrigation of cantaloupes when melons start to ripen, 201

❏ Water succulents, 195

❏ Water plants adequately during hot, dry weather, 208

❏ Don't water summer-deciduous native plants, 208

❏ Water drought-resistant plants, including Mexican fan palms and Aleppo pines, 208

❏ Water floss silk trees and coral trees early in the month, 208

❏ Study your irrigation system to see if it can be more efficient, 208

❏ Check for malfunctioning sprinklers and drip emitters, 208

❏ Install a new backup battery in your irrigation timer, 209

❏ Flush filters and headers of drip systems, 209

❏ If lawns develop brown areas, find out what's causing the problem and solve it, 221

❏ Renew watering basins, 210

❏ Make watering basins for large trees out under the drip line, not next to the trunk, 210

❏ Water plants in containers, 210

❏ Water deciduous fruit trees in accordance with their age and your soil and climate zone, 211

❏ Water roses with up to 1½ inches of water 3 times a week, 183

❏ Keep ferns well watered and protect them from dry winds, 212

❏ Give mature wisteria vines at least one deep watering, 214

❏ Keep transplanted palms well watered, 220

❏ Water warm-season lawns deeply at least once a week in most zones; water cool-season lawns more shallowly and frequently, 221

❏ Water vegetables, 222

❏ Don't water lithops, 195

Control Pests, Diseases, and Weeds

❏ Continue to control weeds by mulching, cultivating, and hand-pulling, 40

❏ Control rose pests and diseases, 72

❏ Control pests on fuchsias, 212

❏ Control serious nematode and fungal problems with soil solarization, 215

❏ Control fireblight by removing disfigured branches and twigs, 216

❏ Protect Canary island date palms from fungus, 220

❏ Check cycads for scale, 220

❏ Control crabgrass after it goes red with a selective crabgrass killer, if desired, 221

❏ Control pests and diseases that cause dead brown patches on cool-season lawns, 221

❏ Look for signs of sod webworm on lawns, particularly cool-season lawns; treat if necessary, 221

❏ Control white grubs on cool-season lawns, 221

❏ Control corn earworm if desired, 222

❏ Release beneficial nematodes, 216

❏ Control oleander leaf scorch, 216

Also This Month

❏ Watch cantaloupes for signs of ripening; pick them at "full slip," 201

❏ Continue to harvest summer vegetables, 201

❏ Before planting in porous containers, seal the insides with a coat of tar, 211

❏ Use double-potting to keep roots of container-grown plants cool, 211

❏ Keep indoor ferns, including Boston ferns, alive in coastal zones by giving them equal time outdoors, 213

❏ Order seeds and supplies for fall planting from mail-order catalogs, 214

❏ If you live next to native chaparral, consider ways to minimize risk of fires, 218

❏ Harvest bananas when they are ready, according to type, 219

❏ Untie the fronds of palms transplanted in June, 220

SEPTEMBER

The First Fall Planting Month

September marks the beginning of the fall planting season, one of the busiest times of year in the garden. This is when we switch gears in preparation for winter—and winter is a great time to garden here! Beginning now, we switch from summer-blooming to winter- and spring-blooming annual flowers and from warm-season to cool-season vegetable crops. Spring-flowering bulbs fill nursery shelves, some of which can be planted in September. It is also the best time for planting perennials and a good time for giving perennial beds an overhaul. Warm-season lawns can still be planted now, and cool-season lawns can be planted along the coast. In addition, most bushes, shrubs, trees, and ground covers, other than tropicals, do best when planted in fall before the winter rains.

This great flurry of activity doesn't happen all at once. Start now to clean out faded flowers and vegetables, but leave good ones in place to enjoy as long as they're still going. Prepare the ground, begin to plant—but keep in mind that October, the best planting month of the year, is still ahead.

Meanwhile, continue to water deeply and according to the individual needs of plants. Though nights may begin to cool off along the coast and shadows are noticeably lengthening, early September is largely a continuation of summer weather. Sunny, warm days are the norm. More often than not we get a blast of extremely hot weather and Santa Ana winds before midmonth. If this happens, water early in the day or in the evening. Also, check drought-resistant plants, other than summer-dormant natives, for signs of stress. One deep watering now can sometimes save the life of a tree or bush that's hanging on the brink of extinction and tide it over to the winter rains. Many mature trees, like Torrey (*Pinus torreyana*) and Aleppo (*P. halepensis*) pines, could be saved from beetle attack and other horrors if only people would realize they need to be watered at least once now. Put a sprinkler under the canopy to the drip line and let it run for several hours, without runoff. When water supplies are curtailed because of drought, use the precious water you have to irrigate mature shrubs, trees, and vines. Let your lawn and petunias die if you must, but save your valuable old plants—especially trees.

Bulbs

One of September's most important and exciting jobs is to start buying and planting spring-flowering bulbs. Bulbs are easy plants to grow. They have a mystique bordering on the miraculous, but growing them here in Southern California is different from growing them in the East or Middle West. Many bulbs need to undergo a cold winter in order to bloom. Some will bloom without cold weather but tend to rot during our hot, dry summers. Others can be grown here after being prechilled in the refrigerator, but in many cases they won't naturalize (come back year after year, bloom, and multiply). Countering these drawbacks, we're able to grow a huge number of charming and fascinating bulbs that are little known and rarely grown back East. Many of these naturalize readily, are drought resistant, and are almost unbelievably easy to grow.

Buy Bulbs Now to Plant Later. Begin purchasing spring-flowering bulbs in mid-September. They soon get picked over and sometimes put back in the wrong bins. A reliable local nursery is the best source of varieties that will do well in your climate zone, though some rare varieties can only be bought from catalogs. Choose the largest and fattest bulbs, because they produce the biggest blooms.

Among hardy bulbs (the kind grown in cold-winter climates), the best choices for Southern California are daffodils (*Narcissus*), hyacinths, Dutch irises (*Iris xiphium* hybrids), and tulips. In inland gardens add grape hyacinths (*Muscari*). (*M. armeniacum* is best adapted to our climate.) Crocuses are difficult to grow in Southern California, though Dutch crocus (*Crocus vernus*) may succeed in inland valleys. Italian species crocuses, such as *C. niveus,* are rare but can naturalize in some gardens. Most trumpet and large-cupped narcissus have to be replaced yearly, although several varieties, including 'February Gold' and 'Fortune', will often naturalize and eventually form large clumps.

Look for daffodils with three or more divisions. Don't pull them apart. If they're still attached, each point will produce a bloom. Feel them gently to make sure they're firm to the touch; softness means rot. Hyacinths perform best and give the most bloom if you buy large bulbs. Tulips have to be bought yearly. (You could dig them in fall and rechill them, but those who try this find that, though the bulbs can attain great size, their flowers are tiny and on short stems because of our hot summer weather.) Don't buy "naked" tulip bulbs, ones that have lost their tunics (the brown papery skin)—they might be dried out.

Take anemones, crocuses, daffodils, grape hyacinths, hyacinths, ranunculus, and tulips home, but don't plant the bulbs yet. Getting them in the ground too early is a big mistake. Keep them cool and dry. The garage is usually a good place. Crocuses, hyacinths, and tulips need to be chilled beginning next month or in November for six to eight weeks prior to planting. You don't have to put them in the refrigerator just yet. Exceptions to this rule are the species tulips (wild tulips), including candia tulip *(T. saxatilis),* Florentine tulip *(T. sylvestris),* and lady tulip *(Tulipa clusiana),* which can be planted straight into the ground or in pots now. These will multiply and come back year after year. Grape hyacinths don't need prechilling, but as noted earlier, they usually don't grow well in coastal gardens. In interior zones grape hyacinth often comes back year after year. Anemones, daffodils, Dutch irises, and ranunculus need no prechilling.

Buy Bulbs to Plant Now. Some bulbs can and should be planted in September as soon as you buy them. Among these are some superb choices from the daffodil *(Narcissus)* tribe that naturalize readily and often spread over large areas. These are known as the Tazetta and Tazetta hybrids, and they include paper whites, 'Grand Soleil d'Or', 'Cragford', Chinese sacred lilies, and 'Geranium'. Save some for forcing in pebbles later (page 277). They're popular and sell out early.

Most important to purchase and plant now are the many captivating drought-resistant bulbs that are well adapted to our climate—so well they'll often naturalize even in areas that receive little or no summer water. Among these are various oxalis from the Western Hemisphere and many bulbs and corms from South Africa, such as babiana (baboon flower), *Chasmanthe aethiopica,* crocosmia, freesia, ixia (African corn lily), lapeirousia, sparaxis (harlequin flower; *Sparaxis tricolor*); streptanthera *(S. elegans),* tritonia (montbretia), and watsonia. Most can take summer water if drainage is good. Some actually need it—for example, *Crocosmia masoniorum* 'Lucifer', an excellent variety for June bloom. (You may have to order it by mail.) Chasmanthe *(Chasmanthe aethiopica),* often incorrectly called crocosmia, tritonia, or montbretia, with tall, straplike leaves and orange flowers, is so

drought resistant it naturalizes even under invasive eucalyptus. *Ornithogalum arabicum* has long-lasting white flowers with unique, shiny, black, beadlike centers that bloom later than other spring-flowering bulbs. Chincherinchee *(O. thyrsoides)* has white blooms on 2-foot stems. Both thrive in flowerbeds. Spring star flower *(Ipheion uniflorum)* is great for planting around the edges of beds. Once you get it going, it multiplies rapidly, comes back every year, and blooms for several months in winter and spring.

When purchasing your bulbs, jot down the planting directions for depth and spacing. A general **Rule of Thumb** is: *Plant large bulbs at a depth that equals twice their height and small bulbs a little deeper than twice their height.* There are exceptions to this rule, so to be sure of correct depths and other care, refer to a bulb handbook. One of the best is Bryan's *Manual of Bulbs.*

Consider the Lilies. Lilies are dramatic plants in the garden, but, while some gardeners swear by them, they have a reputation of being difficult to grow here. They need excellent soil, good drainage, and constant moisture—they're not good choices for drought years. There are many complicated differences among them. They're classified under nine divisions, within which are hundreds of varieties and species. In general new varieties are easier to grow than old ones. Some may do well in one zone but not in another. The best way to find kinds adapted to your garden is through trial and error and by purchasing your bulbs at a local nursery that has a good reputation for carrying the right things. If you live inland, grow early varieties for June bloom. My own experience is that Mid-Century hybrids and the Imperial Series, classified under Division 7 (Oriental Hybrids), are the easiest. (Try growing 'Imperial Pink'; it often succeeds where others

When Is a Bulb Not a Bulb?

Many of the plants we call bulbs aren't bulbs at all. It's become common to lump together under this term not only true bulbs but all plants that grow from a thickened or bulbous storage organ. (Plants like clivia, daylilies, and iris are in a shady area between bulbs and perennials, so you find them discussed in books on bulbs and also in books on perennials.) Here's how bulbs differ, so you can tell them apart:

- **True Bulb.** A modified subterranean leaf bud, the true bulb has a basal plate, above which are food-storing scales (rudimentary leaves) surrounding a bud that contains the magic makings of a plant. Some bulbs, like onions, tulips, and daffodils, are tunicate—they're covered with a papery skin. Others, like lilies, are imbricate—they have overlapping scales.

- **Corm.** A thickened subterranean stem that produces a plant. The inside is just a solid piece of tissue. The buds are on top. After bloom the old corm is used up, but new ones have grown on top or at the sides to take its place. Gladioli, sparaxis, and freesia grow from corms.

- **Rhizome.** A thickened stem or branch that grows on the surface of the ground or horizontally underground. Bearded irises and calla lilies grow from rhizomes.

- **Tuber.** A thickened stem that serves as a storage chamber but is usually shorter, thicker, and rounder than a rhizome. It grows totally or partially underground. Tuberous begonias, cyclamen, and potatoes grow from tubers.

- **Tuberous Root.** Growing underground, thus differing from a tuber in that it's a swollen root rather than a thickened stem. Tuberous roots have growth buds on top in the old stem portion, from which spring the plants. Dahlias and sweet potatoes grow from tuberous roots.

fail.) I've also seen regal lilies (*Lilium regale*, a species discovered by the plant explorer "Chinese" Wilson and favored by Gertrude Jekyll) with flower stems 6 feet tall. They were thriving in a semishaded bed in Altadena, and the gardener claimed they were easy to grow.

Plant lilies as soon as you get them home. They never go completely dormant and must never be allowed to dry out. All lilies need loose, humusy, well-drained, moist soil (sandy loam is best) with plenty of bone meal worked in beneath the roots. Plant them at twice the depth of the bulb, unless instructions that come with the bulb say otherwise. (Madonna lily *[Lilium candidum]* should be planted near the surface.) Feed them with 2-10-10 fertilizer when the first sprouts show. Almost all lilies like to have their heads in the sun, their feet in the shade, a cool root run, and no wind. If you can provide these conditions plus protection from snails and slugs, in pots or the ground, perhaps lilies will do well for you.

Divide Irises. If irises aren't divided every three or four years they'll stop blooming. If yours need it and you didn't divide them last summer after bloom, now, in mid-September through mid-October, is the time to tackle the job. Gardeners in hot interior valleys have no choice. It's do it now or wait another whole year (see page 168 for directions).

If your irises don't need dividing this year, clean up the bed now. Pull or cut off damaged leaves, clean up the ground, and mulch the bed. Bait for slugs and snails.

Purchase Cyclamen. In most of the country cyclamen are grown only as houseplants, but here

How to Make Bulb Plantings Look Informal and Natural

Don't plant bulbs in rows; instead, plant them in drifts (the gracefully shaped areas that flow from back to front and from side to side in a flowerbed and are planted solidly with one flower). Do as nature does; put many bulbs of one kind or one color together in a single drift, and then mix one or two of another kind or color in with them. To arrange a drift, mark the outline with gypsum and toss the bulbs onto the ground. Plant them where they fall.

they're one of our most aristocratic plants for cool-season bloom outdoors. Begin purchasing them now, either as tubers or as plants already in bloom. Grow them in pots, hanging baskets, or the ground.

When buying cyclamen tubers, look for those that are already beginning to sprout—they're the easiest to start—and plant them so the top half of the tuber protrudes above the surface of the soil. Put them in moist, humus-rich soil and keep them damp until the tubers are well rooted. Keep the plants in semishade; they prefer a cool spot, away from reflected heat. Once they're well rooted and leaves have begun to grow, begin feeding regularly with a complete fertilizer.

Don't overwater cyclamen. Wait until the leaves slightly wilt and the plant looks as if it's dry; then water it. Cyclamen plants also wilt from overwatering. You can tell if wilting results from over- or underwatering by the condition of the plant's stems. If your cyclamen's stems are soft and wet you've overwatered it, but if the stems are dry, crisp, and firm—though wilted—you've underwatered it. Also, don't clip off the faded blooms; this too can lead to rot. Pull them off with a quick downward yank.

🦟 Quick Tip

Use Bulb Covers to Mark and Shade the Ground over Bulbs. *When planting bulbs, plant low-profile cool-season flowers over them. The bulbs will grow up through them and the ground will be ornamented while you wait. Nemesia, pansies, primroses, schizanthus (poor man's orchid; S. pinnatus), dwarf snapdragons, sweet alyssum, and violas, including johnny-jump-ups, make good bulb covers.*

Wake Up the Cyclamen That You Summered Over. If you summered-over some cyclamen, it's time to get their tubers to wake up and grow again. Start feeding them every two weeks with a balanced fertilizer for growth and bloom. (If you feed only nitrogen you'll get lots of leaves and no flowers.) Meanwhile, protect the plants from slugs and snails. Colorless leaves that are twisted out of shape are caused by cyclamen mite. Spray with a specific miticide. You may have to treat them more than once.

If the roots of some of your cyclamen are crowded and you think they need repotting, wait until the plants start to grow again; then move them into pots one size larger—don't drown them in soil. Often they'll stay in the same container for several years and will flower better when they're a little rootbound.

Tropicals and Subtropicals

This is the last month of the growing season for tropicals, so it's also the last month when they can be fertilized, if necessary, in most zones. (If you live in an interior valley it's better not to fertilize them this late in the season.) Tropicals need to slow down in October and then harden off for winter during November. If you live in a largely frost-free zone you can give them a final feeding of fast-acting fertilizer, such as Terr-O-Vite, early in the month to help them increase strength during this warm month and to eliminate any signs of nitrogen deficiency. But don't fertilize with a slow-release product. The idea is to strengthen the plants without triggering soft growth later in fall, when it could be nipped by frost.

In coastal zones this is also the last month for planting tropicals, such as bougainvillea, hibiscus, lantana, Natal plum *(Carissa macrocarpa),* philodendron, and tropical flowering trees. In the interior it's best to wait until spring to plant tropicals, because fall planting will make them more subject to frost. But regardless of this, many fall-blooming subtropical trees are in nurseries now, and it will be impossible to choose the colors you prefer at any other time, when the trees aren't in bloom. Trees you can find now include Chinese flame tree *(Koelreuteria bipinnata* or *K. elegans),* floss silk tree *(Chorisia speciosa),* and Hong Kong orchid tree *(Bauhinia blakeana).* Floss silk tree is one of our most spectacular large trees and reasonably drought resistant. The whole top of the tree turns vivid pink, magenta, or burgundy in fall. (There's also a white species, *C. insignis.)* The trunks are green and bear prominent, weirdly wonderful spines, but if you're planting in areas where children or animals might be endangered, choose a grafted kind without spines. Chinese flame tree is good near houses, is noninvasive, doesn't grow too large, and is quite drought tolerant. The display of salmon-colored pods in fall looks as if a bougainvillea got accidentally tangled in the top of the tree. (There's no choice of color with this tree, so you can wait if you wish and plant one next spring.)

Don't let fall-planted tropicals dry out in the almost-inevitable September heat wave; inland, hose off the area around them twice a day to raise the humidity during these spells. And come winter, remember that it's important to protect them from frost.

Don't prune hibiscus this month. But in frost-free zones several other heat-loving plants that bloom all summer, such as bougainvilleas, Cape plumbago *(P. auriculata),* and oleanders, can be pruned now after bloom. They'll regrow during winter for a big burst of bloom next spring and summer. (Pruning in spring instead of fall can cut down on spring bloom, but it's necessary in areas that suffer hard frosts.) Prune oleanders by taking out whole stalks that have bloomed—down to the ground. Take off several a year to renew the plants. Don't chop off the tops like a hedge. This fails to renew the plant with fresh growth from the ground and destroys all the flowers. (You could choose a much better green hedge, if that's all you want.) Don't prune New Zealand tea tree *(Leptospermum scoparium)* now, or you'll get no winter flowers.

Citrus and Avocado Trees

Make sure citrus trees are adequately and evenly watered during September. If their roots go dry now, the result can be fruit that splits. (Fluctuations in fertilizer levels can also cause fruit to split. Varieties with thin skins are more prone to the problem than those with thick skins.)

Continue Picking 'Valencia' Oranges. If you haven't eaten all your 'Valencia' oranges by now, you can continue picking them. 'Valencia' will turn green again in fall in a process called "regreening," but it won't affect its flavor or sweetness. You can continue harvesting and eating 'Valencia' until navel oranges are ready to pick in winter. But do check over the trees now for old corky fruit that may have hung on the tree for a year or two. Clip these off and eat or juice the good ones (see page 159).

Treat Lemon Trees for Brown Rot. Commercial growers pick lemons all at once, but most home gardeners leave lemons hanging on the tree until needed. If you do this, you'll have fresh ones year-round whenever you want them. The only problem is that fruit left hanging on the tree after it's turned golden-ripe sometimes develops brown blotches or turns brown all over. Brown skins can be caused by leaving the fruit on the tree so long that it becomes overmature. If the tree looks generally healthy and the brown fruits occur here and there all over the tree, then discoloration is most likely caused by leaving fruit on the tree too long. Pick the overripe fruit and leave the rest on the tree.

But brown blotches on the rinds of lemons (or fruit that turns brown all over) may also result from a condition called brown rot, which is caused by several fungi that live in the soil under the tree. You can tell if fungus is the culprit because, in this case, fruit of all sizes will be affected but the discoloration will occur primarily on fruit that's closest to the ground. Sometimes a white mold will appear on the fruit, and sap may ooze from the trunk of the tree, near the ground. Branches may also die back. Brown rot is at its worst in wet weather, when the fungi splash up onto the tree from the ground.

If your fruit has ever been affected this way, you have a chance to clear up the problem by spraying now with a garden fungicide, such as captan. Unfortunately, you have to pick all the ripe fruit before spraying. Then clean up the ground under the tree and prune off any tips of branches that are brushing the earth. It's a good idea to cut out any diseased or dead growth while you're about it, and make sure there aren't any mummified fruits hanging around in the tree. Then spray the fungicide all over the ground under the tree and up into the branches, paying particular attention to the lowest 3 feet

How Cymbidiums Came to California

Cymbidiums are largely terrestrial orchids native to cool tropical jungles, from the Himalayas eastward through southern Asia. For at least two hundred years they were hybridized and grown in cool greenhouses by English collectors. During the Second World War a great many varieties were sent to Santa Barbara to save them from the bombs. It soon became clear that cymbidiums flourish outdoors in Southern California. They multiplied so rapidly that when the loaned varieties were sent home after the war, many more plants were left here, to continue to grow in our gardens. They've since become one of our best plants for winter and spring bloom.

of growth. Spray in the early morning or evening to prevent burn, and use a spreader-sticker or a few drops of SunSpray to help spread the spray. (Water the trees well before spraying; oil can cause leaf drop on trees that are under water stress.)

Cymbidiums

Not all cymbidiums bloom every year. (You need three plants to be assured of annual bloom.) But some gardeners complain that none of their cymbidiums ever bloom. These plants are remarkably easy to grow, but they do have certain requirements. Here's how to make them bloom.

Switch Fertilizers in September. Beginning on the first of September switch fertilizers from a high-nitrogen formula for growth to a formula higher in bloom ingredients, such as 15-30-15 or 10-30-10. (If you're feeding with high-nitrogen slow-release tablets continue their use, but once

How to Stop Blue Hydrangeas from Turning Pink

- Start with a hydrangea that was blue when you bought it. Some kinds never turn blue. White varieties always stay white. Some pinks turn purple instead of blue.

- Plant and grow blue hydrangeas in acid soil mix. When planting in containers, use a commercial soil mix designed for camellias and azaleas. When planting in the ground, amend the native soil in the planting hole with camellia and azalea mix according to package directions, or use two-thirds premoistened peat moss. Mulch with leaf mold or redwood.

- Check the root run of established plants to make sure the soil is acid. Use a soil test kit to test the pH of the soil. A pH of 4.5 to 5.0 yields blue flowers, a pH of 5.5 to 6.5 yields mauve, and a pH of 7.0 to 7.5 yields pink.

- Maintain the desired pH with aluminum sulfate. Use 1 tablespoon aluminum sulfate per foot of plant height, or ¼ teaspoon per potted plant. Mix this in water and apply it as a drench several times in spring and fall, beginning in September.

- Never use fertilizer that contains phosphorus. Phosphorus is alkaline, so the use of it will raise the pH of the soil and turn blue hydrangeas pink.

every two or three weeks treat the plants additionally with 0-10-10 or 2-10-10 liquid.) Cymbidiums continue to grow year-round so they always need some nitrogen, but a higher percentage of phosphorus and potassium now will encourage development of bloom spikes.

Keep Cymbidiums in Bright Light. Don't keep cymbidiums in too much shade. If you've sheltered yours from hot sun under a tree, during the summer, bring them out into more light now. Along the coast they can take full sun, though they'll need protection during the Santa Ana or sudden heat wave that almost always strikes sometime in September. Inland they need protection from the burning rays of midday sun—under 50 percent shade cloth or in a lath house is ideal. They often can take more sun than we give them. If your cymbidiums have dark green leaves, chances are you're keeping them in too much shade. Give them enough light to turn the leaves a yellowish color. Spread the plants apart, and allow sunshine to hit those pseudobulbs. Crowded plants won't bloom as well because the leaves shade the bulbs. (Trim off dead leaves and brown tips, but don't cut off or shorten healthy leaves. Cymbidiums need all their leaves to nourish the pseudobulbs.)

Provide a Wide Range of Temperatures. Large-flowered cymbidiums need a daily temperature range of at least 20 degrees during the hottest time of the year in order to trigger bloom. What they like best is nights that drop to 45° or 55°F and daytime temperatures of 80° or 90°F. Our gardens provide adequately warm days and cool nights, but our patios or porches often do not. They're too warm and sheltered at night. So situate your cymbidiums away from protective house walls and don't keep them indoors, or they'll never bloom.

Recent advances in hybridizing have broken the size barriers and expanded the bloom seasons of cymbidiums. Standard or large varieties usually don't bloom until they're 4 feet tall. Miniatures, on the other hand, will bloom in 4-inch pots when they're only a foot tall and may produce two to four spikes of twelve to twenty-four flowers on each. (Plants with flowers less than 3 inches across are classed as miniatures.) Miniatures tolerate hot weather better—up to 115°F—and will bloom when night temperatures in summer are as high as 65°F—higher than standard cymbidiums require to trigger bloom. Miniatures come into bloom in November and continue into March, while standards bloom from January to mid-May. So, if you have had problems getting cymbidiums to bloom in your climate zone or on your patio or porch, try the small-flowered varieties. They bloom more readily both inland and along the coast, and the bonus is that some of their flowers are highly fragrant.

Meanwhile, water cymbidiums enough to keep the pseudobulbs from drying out and shriveling. Water should always drain right through. Cymbidium roots can't survive in a puddle. As the spikes grow, stake them so they don't get broken, and protect the plants from slugs and snails.

Camellias

Keep camellias well watered this month. Letting them go dry now will make the buds go brown and drop off later, so you won't have any bloom this winter or next spring. Don't confuse this with natural bud drop. Some varieties form a great many more buds than they can open, and they always drop a lot of them of their own accord. These naturally dropped buds will be green, not brown. (Bud drop can also be caused by growing a variety that needs winter chill in a mild coastal zone where the buds can't open.)

Disbud Camellias. For the largest blooms start disbudding camellias now, by removing all but one flower bud from each tip or joint. Twist off all but one flower bud from each cluster, being careful not to remove the growth bud. (The flower buds are round and fat. The growth bud is thin and pointed.) Drop the buds in a plastic bag and dispose of them in the trash. Some gar-

deners don't disbud camellias because they have too many of them or simply can't be bothered. When plants are as tall as trees it's almost impossible to disbud them. But all plants look better when they've been disbudded; the flowers become not only larger but better shaped and less prone to blossom blight.

It's a good idea to retain some forward-facing but mainly downward-facing buds, especially when plants are tall or light colored. On tall plants downward-facing flowers will be seen better. On light-colored plants they'll be less prone to sun damage. In all cases they'll last longer; when it rains, water will pour off their backs instead of soaking into the center and causing rot.

Azaleas

The time-honored method for feeding azaleas requires you to fertilize them only twice a year, once immediately after they finish flowering and again in late September. So give azaleas their second and last meal of the year during the last third of this month. (Some growers feed azaleas once a month with liquid fertilizer during the growing season. But it's possible to kill azaleas with too much kindness.) The easiest way is to use an organic fertilizer especially formulated for azaleas or camellias, following package directions exactly, or to feed with cottonseed meal or a complete organic fertilizer such as Gro Power. If the plant shows signs of chlorosis (yellow leaves, green veins), use a chelating fertilizer (containing iron) to correct this deficiency.

Roses

Continue to water roses with up to 1½ inches of water each time you irrigate, but reduce the number of irrigations from three times a week

How to Grow Thanksgiving, Christmas, and Easter Cacti

- Grow these cacti indoors or out. (They can grow as big as 3 feet across.)

- Start by buying small ones of the same color. Plant three or four cacti in a 6-inch container in good, porous potting soil, such as Jungle Growth, to each gallon of which you add 1 cup of agricultural charcoal and 3 cups of perlite. Pot them on as necessary.

- Keep the cacti in bright but not burning light. Filtered sun is okay, but hot rays through south or west windows are not. Keep them in natural light (away from electric lights at night) for the two months prior to bloom. (During bloom, flowers last longer when plants are kept cool.)

- Fertilize the plants year-round once every two to three weeks or with a well-diluted solution every time you water. Feed with 8-8-8 most of the year. Switch to 0-10-10 two months prior to bloom.

- Water regularly throughout the year. Keep the cacti slightly drier for a month or six weeks after bloom, but don't ever let the roots shrivel. In general, water well in summer, less in fall. (Some experts withhold water for one month after the weather cools in fall; others water year-round.) Always maintain good drainage— no soggy soil allowed.

to twice a week. Continue to fertilize roses once a month with the commercial or organic rose food of your choice, or, if you're following the Rose-Pro Method, fertilize your rose plants with 1 tablespoon of urea every week. (By giving more nitrogen now you prepare roses for a spurt of growth and flowering in fall.) Continue to control rose pests and diseases with Orthene and Funginex or by using other methods of your choice. If you are following the Rose-Pro Method, stop mixing micronutrients (Miracle-

Gro or Super K Gro) into your spray this month. Pick or deadhead the flowers according to your custom, but there's no need to disbud now.

Along with other fall planting, you can plant roses from nursery containers, if desired, from now through October.

Thanksgiving and Christmas Cacti

Zygocactus, or crab cactus (*Schlumbergera truncata*), is an epiphyte with "leaves" (actually thickened stems) shaped like crab claws. It's often sold as Christmas cactus, but it really should be called Thanksgiving cactus because it blooms at Thanksgiving, sometimes staying in bloom until March. The true Christmas cactus (*S. bridgesii*) has smooth "leaves." The flowers usually open on Christmas day. (There's also an Easter cactus [*Rhipsalidopsis gaertneri* or *S. gaertneri*], which blooms in April and May and often again in fall.)

These cacti can be so gratifying that people fall in love with them. Nevertheless, because of one characteristic they all share, they sometimes don't bloom: they are all "photoperiodic" (they respond to the length of the daylight hours). If you keep the plants indoors they often won't bloom, because house lights at night extend their days to a length that isn't right to stimulate flowering. So put your Thanksgiving and Christmas cacti outdoors now for six weeks or two months, in a shady place where night lighting won't strike them. Meanwhile, feed them with 0-10-10 to stimulate bloom. (See the accompanying box for year-round directions.)

Plant Sweet Peas for Christmas Bloom

- **Choose the Right Variety.** Look for the words "early flowering." ("Spring-flowering" or "summer-flowering" types won't bloom until days are more than twelve hours long.) Among tall varieties that flower early are a winter-flowering mix—if planted in September, these start to bloom between Thanksgiving and Christmas when the plants are only 2 to 4 feet tall—and 'Winter Elegance', which grows 6 feet tall with heavily blooming, very fragrant, strong-stemmed flowers. (The Territorial Seed Company catalog carries mixed packages of both varieties; buy both and compare. Park Seed's flowers and vegetables catalog carries 'Winter Elegance' in a mix or as seven individual colors, including 'Scarlet Improved' and white, the Christmas colors. See page 307 for addresses and phone numbers.) On seed racks, look for these names as well as 'Early Spencer', 'Early-Flowering Multiflora', 'Early Multiflora', and 'Mammoth'. Do not buy heat-resistant varieties; they will not bloom in winter. Among short varieties that require no staking are 'Snoopea', 'Supersnoop', and 'Jet Set'. 'Bijou' is a compact bush that flowers early. Short varieties are good in hanging baskets and patio containers.

- **Dig a North-South Trench in Full Sun.** Make your trench 1½ feet deep and 6 or 8 inches wide. (For bush types prepare the whole bed.)

- **Provide Rich Soil.** Fill the bottom of the trench with one sack of manure per 8 to 10 feet of trench. Fork it in well. Then mix the soil from the trench with one-third nitrolized ground bark or compost and a low-nitrogen fertilizer according to package directions. Backfill to 1 or 2 inches from the top. Soak this with water, and let it settle overnight.

- **Provide Strong Support.** Tall varieties need some kind of trellis to grow on. Shove metal posts or several 8-foot-tall metal plant stakes into the ground, and wire to them either hardware cloth or chicken wire. Or, alternatively, create an artistic support out of natural materials such as willow, Cape plumbago, or bamboo. Be sure to anchor your trellises and arbors firmly into the ground (use a crowbar to make holes for the posts); also lash them tightly together so they will not be toppled by strong winds.

- **Soak the Seeds in Water Overnight.** Put the seeds in a jar and pour lukewarm water over them. Leave them overnight. Plant the next day.

- **Plant the Seeds an Inch Deep.** After you sow the seeds 2 inches apart, cover them with 1 inch of potting soil—sweet pea seeds need darkness to sprout. Pat it down gently. Sprinkle daily to keep the seeds damp until they sprout. Then water regularly. Or bury a drip tube under the row prior to planting.

- **Protect Sprouts from Birds and Snails.** Cover the row with bird netting or bent aviary wire. Once the sprouts are up 6 inches, remove it; the birds won't kill larger plants. Bait regularly for slugs and snails.

- **Thin and Pinch Seedlings.** When the plants are up 6 inches, thin them to 6 inches apart. Pinch their tips to force branching.

- **Add String If Necessary.** Sweet peas have tendrils and are often better at hanging onto their supports than edible peas, but if winds and rains are strong, tie twine around the row to hold up your vines.

- **Pick Frequently.** Once sweet peas begin to bloom, pick frequently to keep them flowering.

SEPTEMBER

Annual and Perennial Flowers

If you were in Southern California last April, you know how delightful our spring gardens can be. If you want to achieve flowerbeds brimming with color—beds like those you noticed in the best gardens last spring—now's the time to plant for it. Don't wait until April and either regret not planting or try to plant then. That's one of the worst mistakes in local gardening. Start now; you have plenty of time—three whole months in most areas.

Plant Beds with Cool-Season Flowers. September is the first month when you can plant cool-season annual and perennial flowers. The earlier you get them into the ground, the more likely you are to get them to bloom before Christmas. It's a race between you and the weather. Get them blooming in early December, and they'll stay in bloom all winter and spring. Otherwise, you'll have to wait until February or even March for flowers.

If you're a good gardener, even early October will not be too late, so you have a choice. If the summer garden is still looking presentable, you can keep it going through September by removing faded flowers, grooming plants, and feeding them with fertilizer high in bloom ingredients; or if the flowerbeds look ratty, you can tear out summer annuals now, dig up the beds, add soil amendment, and replant in mid-September with winter and spring flowers.

When planting in large tubs, replace about one-third of the planting medium with fresh soil mix. When planting in small containers, or those that are chock-full of roots, replace all earth with fresh mix. Throw the old stuff in the compost. (Remember to place a piece of broken crockery over the drainage hole in the pot before refilling with potting soil.)

Among good choices to plant from pony packs now are calendula, candytuft (*Iberis*), foxglove, Iceland poppy (the smaller the better), nemesia, pansy, English primrose, malacoides or fairy primrose, obconica primrose, snapdragon, stock, sweet alyssum, sweet William (*Dianthus barbatus*), and viola. Plant seeds of annual African daisy (*Dimorphotheca sinuata*), calendula, cineraria, snapdragon, stock, sweet alyssum, johnny-jump-up and other violas, and wildflowers. (See page 258 for how to plant wildflowers.) Sweet peas are another good choice for planting from seeds now. You can have armloads of sweet peas (*Lathyrus odoratus*) in December if you plant them now, choose the right varieties, and do the job right (see the accompanying box).

A word of warning: The last of the year's summer flowers, such as French and African marigolds and petunias, are sometimes on sale now. There's nothing to be gained by buying them since they'll soon be out of bloom. Petunias will live through winter in frost-free zones (without flowers) and do better than ever next summer, but marigolds will die in October. However, September is one of the best times to plant euryops and marguerites (Cobbitty daisies; *Argyranthemum frutescens*) because they bloom mostly in fall, winter, and spring. Plant them in full sun; they'll take off well in September's warm weather, and you'll enjoy their flowers throughout the cool months.

Wake Up Primroses. Did you summer-over your English primroses (*Primula polyantha*)? As with cyclamen, which is also a member of the primrose (Primulaceae) family, it's time to awaken these plants and get them growing again. Clean up the plants; also separate, divide, and replant them if necessary. Primroses will often go for a couple of years in large pots without needing to be repotted or divided, but old plants eventually grow thick, tuberlike stalks and appear to push themselves up out of the ground or soil mix. If this happens, repot—or replant—them in fresh soil; place the roots an inch or two deeper, but don't bury the crown.

Feed English primroses with a high-nitrogen fertilizer, such as blood meal or cottonseed meal, to stimulate growth now, and then switch to a complete fertilizer for growth and bloom when buds show. (I like to give mine a shot of Roots to get them growing.) The bigger you can get English primroses to grow now, the bigger the flowers you'll achieve later. Spray them against caterpillars with BT, if necessary, and protect the plants from slugs and snails. Colorless leaves are most likely caused by spider mites. Spray with a specific miticide; you may have to treat the plants more than once. Washing them off with insecticidal soap can also help destroy the mites and their webs. However, a regular routine of fertilizing combined with appropriate light (bright semishade now and full or partial sun in winter) will often give English primroses enough vigor to fight off mites without additional assistance.

Plant Perennials. As with so many other plants, fall is the traditional time for choosing and planting perennials. However, the reality is that one finds perennials throughout the year when they're in bloom because that's when nurseries stock them. Thus, most gardeners plant year-round. Nevertheless, there are many perennials available now in nurseries, and if you're just starting out there could not be a better time to plant, except for the fact that some of the plants that go totally dormant and die to their roots in winter get better established here when they are actively growing in spring.

Many shade-loving perennials, some of which we think of as East Coast or Northern California plants, like astilbe, botanical geraniums, wild ginger (*Asarum caudatum*), hosta, hydrangeas, lady's mantle (*Alchemilla mollis*), Oriental lilies, summer phlox, scillas, Solomon's seal (*Polygonatum*), sweet William (*Dianthus barbatus*), and tiarella, will thrive here, especially in interior zones and north-facing beds, if they're given moist, humusy, acid soil. Humusy clay soil or loam is better for these plants than sand because it holds moisture. Azaleas, camellias, clematis, coral bells, lilac, and rhododendrons are other acid-loving plants that need humus-filled acid soil.

Balance Soil for Acid-Loving Plants. If you're installing a shady bed of acid-loving perennials for the first time, you now have a unique opportunity to use soil sulfur to correct the pH, something Southern Californians seldom think about. Soil sulfur has to be actively dug into the ground in order to work. It doesn't migrate in soil, so sprinkling it on top of the ground won't accomplish anything and may be harmful.

Begin by testing your soil with a soil-test kit (see page 18 for instructions). A score of 7 on the pH scale is neutral. If the soil in your shady bed registers a pH of 7.5 or more, try to knock it down to a pH of 6.5 or less by adding soil sulfur and compost. (A pH of 6.5 is actually ten times more acid than 7.5, since pH is a logarithmic scale.) Evenly spread soil sulfur (not wettable sulfur) over the ground at the rate of 1 to 3 pounds per 100 square feet. (Wear gloves and goggles; be careful not to get sulfur in your eyes, and don't breath the dust.) Dig the sulfur thoroughly into the ground. The particles will stay where you put them and will last longer in clay soil. Sulfur takes a long time to work, so wait a year before testing the soil again to see how much you've changed the pH. If necessary, you can then add another dose of soil sulfur and thus gradually, by degrees, make the soil more acid and more inviting for acid-loving plants.

Maintain Perennials. Meanwhile, maintain the perennials already growing in your garden. Cut back and clean out acanthus, removing those unsightly old leaves down to the ground. Almost immediately, new growth will leap up to replace them. Clean up the ground, treat for snails and slugs, renew mulch, and fertilize. Enjoy Michaelmas daisy hybrids, New England aster *(Aster novae-angliae),* and New York aster *(A. novi-belgii)* while they're in bloom. These are fun to grow but best in moist, fertile, well-drained soil. Even with these advantages, you'll seldom see them perform as spectacularly here as they do in Oregon or England. *A. frikartii* 'Mönch' and *A. frikartii* 'Wonder of Stafa' grow better here and bloom on and off from May to October. Now is the easiest time to find these plants in most nurseries. 'Monte Casino' is worth a hunt. A choice aster that looks like boltonia, it thrives here (boltonia doesn't) and blooms spring and fall with masses of tiny, white, yellow-centered flowers on 3-foot-tall stalks.

Another plant that will be in bloom in your garden this month if you already have it is the perennial sedum *Sedum spectabile.* The light green foliage is pretty in the garden year-round and the flower colors gorgeous as long as they last. 'Autumn Joy', the most popular nationwide, starts out pale pink, then turns rose, and ends up deep terra-cotta. 'Meteor' is bright magenta. 'Brilliant' is rose colored. 'Carmine', soft pink, is most frequently grown here. Find it in bloom now in nurseries.

Ornamental Grasses, Sedges, and Rushes

The latest arrivals, as a group, onto our vast horticultural palette are the ornamental grasses, sedges, and rushes. True grasses are members of the Poaceae (Gramineae) family and are "monocots." (Unlike most plants, which are "dicots"—that is, they produce two cotyledons, or seed leaves—the seeds of monocots produce only one seed leaf and their mature leaves have closely parallel veins.) The stems of grasses, which in some species are only visible when they flower, are usually round and are hollow with solid joints or nodes. Most sedges, on the other hand, have triangular stems filled solidly with pith, while most rushes have round, pith-filled stems. Sedges and rushes prefer boggy soil, and many are highly invasive.

How to Use Them. The statuesque shapes, varied colors and textures, long-lasting inflorescences, and subtle qualities of ornamental grasses allow ample scope for creativity. Use them as focal points or foils for other plants, structural accents and screens, or major themes for entire gardens. Ornamental grasses have the reputation of being drought resistant, but many of the most attractive types actually prefer well-amended soil and look best when provided with occasional fertilizer and regular irrigation. Given these conditions, most grasses are easy to establish, easy to grow, and largely pest-free.

Know How They Grow. Almost all ornamental grasses need to be cut back annually, but first you need to know how they grow. Like lawn grasses, ornamental grasses can be divided into cool-season and warm-season types. Cool-season species grow vigorously in winter, bloom in late winter or spring, and go dormant or grow slowly in summer. Warm-season species grow vigorously in warm weather, bloom in spring or summer, and go dormant or grow slowly in winter. As anyone who has ever mown a lawn knows, you can cut back grasses, and they'll continue to grow. (This is because the growth center of grasses is close to the ground, thus allowing them to survive grazing.)

When to Cut Back. Cut back warm-season grasses that go dormant in winter, including the common red fountain grass (*Pennisetum setaceum* 'Rubrum') in fall or winter, so they can renew themselves in spring. This will prevent unsightly plants with new leaves and blooms mixed in with the old. Keep a close watch on these grasses when rains begin in fall and winter. As soon as green growth commences at ground level, cut the whole plant down to a few inches above the ground. If frosts are frequent, wait until the weather warms up in spring and then cut back above the new growth (don't worry if you accidentally shear some off). Follow up with lawn fertilizer and water; the plant will soon bounce back. With evergreen warm-season types, remove faded and ratty flowers now after bloom or before new ones arise the following year; cut back or clean out the clumps of foliage when and if they become unsightly. Some evergreen grasses, such as pampas grass, rarely, if ever, need cutting back. For these types, cut off the flower stalks in winter or spring after last year's blooms get ragged-looking and before new blooms arise. (Leaves of pampas grass and some other grasses are razor sharp, so use long-handled loppers or a pole pruner; wear gloves, long sleeves, and pants.)

When to Cut Back Cool-Season Types. Cut back cool-season grasses that go dormant in summer to two-thirds of their height for fire protection when they die back in summer or cease to be attractive. Or leave them standing until fall and then cut them back above new growth. In nature, the tops of clumping cool-season grasses would be grazed or burned off, leaving a stumplike growth too thick and airtight to burn through. Do the same as a fire would. Don't cut stipa grasses, for example, all the way to the ground. Their meristem layer (the growth center where cells divide) is in that thick section at the bottom; cut it off and they'll die. Now in fall (or any time after midsummer), deadhead the flowers of spring-blooming grasses, such as perennial quaking grass (*Briza media*), that look tattered. If you have planted a small meadow of cool-season ornamental grasses, use a weed whacker to mow it two or three times a year.

The rage for grasses isn't just a California phenomenon; it's worldwide. Hence, while many of these plants do well here and are worth a try, finding those especially adapted to subtropical climate zones provides more of a challenge. No matter how pretty they are, avoid the invasive types. Greenlee's *Encyclopedia of Ornamental Grasses* offers a wealth of reliable information, including the virtues and vices of each grass. Here's a brief selection of ornamental grasses and tips for growing them:

- **Formosa Maiden Grass** (*Miscanthus transmorrisonensis*). Warm season. Big evergreen clump 3 feet tall and 5 feet wide. Red-brown flowers cascade to ground in summer. Likes full sun and moist, well-drained, fertile soil. Leaf tips go brown in dry soil.
- **Perennial Quaking Grass** (*Briza media*). Cool season. Clumping, with lovely nodding, spring-blooming flowers. Propagate by division; deadhead when blooms look ratty. Cut back if plant goes brown; fertilize and irrigate for quick rebound. Prefers moist, fertile soil and full sun; good with perennials.

- **Annual Quaking Grass** (*B. maxima*). Cool season. Charming seed heads on single stalks. Easy to grow from seed sown in fall in border or for cut flowers; seeds itself but controllable.
- **Blue Fescue, Sheep Fescue** (*Festuca cinerea* or *F. ovina* 'Glauca'). Cool season. Clumping evergreen grass that likes moist, well-drained soil but is drought tolerant. Grow in full sun on coast, partial shade inland. Cut back 3 or 4 inches above the crown once a year in fall or early spring. Replace clumps that die with fresh ones.
- **Foerster's Feather Reed Grass** (*Calamagrostis arundinacea* 'Karl Foerster'). Warm season. Attractive flowers on long, straight stems can be cut for floral arrangements. Well mannered with mound of green below. Prefers rich, moist soil, full sun.
- **Japanese Blood Grass** (*Imperata cylindrica* 'Red Baron' or 'Rubra'). Warm season. Upright foliage, up to 1 to 1½ feet tall. Forms colonies that spread slowly, with no flowers. Foliage starts out green with wine-colored tips that turn redder as year progresses, vivid red by fall, copper in winter. Needs full sun, partial shade inland; loves moist, sandy soil, good drainage. Pull it out if it reverts to invasive green leaves. Cut back in winter above new growth.
- **Red Fountain Grass** (*Pennisetum setaceum* 'Rubrum'). Warm season. Most popular ornamental grass because of ease of cultivation, but prefers moist, fertile, well-drained soil in full sun. Flowers April or May until fall. Keep well watered in hot interior valleys. Pick flowers for arrangements. Cut back in fall as described on page 239.

Lawn Care

Maintain regular feeding of warm-season lawns, such as Bermuda and zoysia, but hold off on fertilizing cool-season grasses, such as ryegrass, bluegrass, and fescue, for another month. (If you must fertilize, make it a very light feeding, and don't feed during or just before September's usual heat wave.) Continue mowing at summer heights. Also, mow off the fall flowers from lippia lawns to protect children and dogs from bee stings. Continue to water as you did during summer—deeply and as infrequently as possible for warm-season grasses, more frequently and less deeply for cool-season grasses except tall fescues (which are more drought resistant).

Plant Warm-Season Lawns. There's still enough warm weather to plant warm-season lawns now from stolons, with the exception of zoysia. It makes a much better start when planted in early summer. You can also plant warm-season lawns from seed, but it's better to wait until next spring, especially in inland areas. (Warm-season lawns can be planted from sod any month from spring through fall but not during winter dormancy.) Wait until October to plant cool-season lawns, unless you live close to the coast.

Dethatch Bermuda. If you didn't dethatch your Bermuda lawn in spring, or if the thatch was so thick it needs more than one treatment, now's the second-best time of the year to do the job. If you wait too late, the Bermuda won't have time to grow back and you'll have to put up with a bare muddy area all winter long. Do the job now while there's still enough warm weather to stimulate a fast recovery. (See page 82 for full instructions.)

Vegetable Gardening

Prepare Beds for Cool-Season Vegetables. Vegetable gardening is much like flower gardening this month: it's a matter of choice. Summer

How to Grow Peas

Peas are a good crop to plant early this month. Get them in before the usual heat spell; warm soil sprouts seeds fast to give you an early harvest.

- **Choose a Good Variety.** There are three basic kinds to grow: Chinese pea pods (also called snow peas), snap peas, and English peas. The first two are the easiest, and you eat them pod and all. English peas are delicious, but you have to shell them, and they take up more space.

- **Prepare the Soil.** Thoroughly dig up the ground with a spade to the depth of 1 foot or at least 10 inches, adding organic amendment (no manure). Work in a low-nitrogen fertilizer, such as 5-10-10 or 4-12-12.

- **Arrange North-South Rows.** Space rows so they run from north to south and are 18 to 24 inches apart. (Each row of earth will be planted with a double row of peas.)

- **Provide Strong Support.** Even dwarf varieties need some kind of trellis to climb on. Shove metal posts or several 8-foot-tall plastic-covered metal plant stakes into the ground down the center of the row. Tie hardware cloth, chicken wire, or reinforcing wire to the stakes. Or create an artistic support using pea stakes cut from shrubs and trees. A teepee shape works well for shorter varieties.

- **Make Twin Furrows.** Space twin furrows (narrow grooves in the ground) 3 to 6 inches apart, one furrow on each side of the trellis. Make the furrows 1 inch deep in coastal zones, 2 to 3 inches deep in interior zones.

- **Inoculate the Seed.** Unless you've grown peas in the same place within three years or plan to

fertilize with nitrogen, inoculate the seed with rhizobia for the largest possible harvest (as described on page 109).

- **Plant Close.** Plant the peas at intervals of 2 inches. (Or you can plant them 1 inch apart and thin them to 2 inches when the plants are 2 or 3 inches high.) Cover them with 1 inch of potting soil in coastal zones, 2 to 3 inches in interior zones. Pat it down gently.

- **Help Them Germinate.** Pea seeds germinate at soil temperatures from 40° to 75°F, but the warmer the temperature the faster they sprout. If you plant an old variety such as 'Mammoth Melting Sugar' in early September, they'll sprout fast, in three to six days. Some of the newer varieties of snap pea, such as 'Snappy' (my favorite) and the stringless 'Sugar Pop', don't germinate so easily. If they fail to come up, presprout more seed in the house, and put it in the ground as soon as it has sprouted. (Don't give up: presprouting is easy; see page 139.)

- **Foil Birds.** Cover the row with netting until the sprouts are 5 inches.

- **Water Regularly and Deeply.** Sprinkle the row daily to keep it damp until the seed germinates. Then water deeply and regularly, or use a drip system.

- **Tie Up the Vines.** Vines will hang on to supports with tendrils, but winter rains and wind can knock them down. Once they're 12 to 18 inches and before the rains, wind twine around the rows periodically to hold up new growth. (See accompanying box for another method.)

vegetables often keep on producing if given food and water, especially along the coast. If that's your case, wait until October to put in the winter garden. Or if everything is dead and dying, which usually is the case inland, you can now

🐌 Quick Tip

For the most even lawn appearance *and to avoid the washboard look of mowing, mow the lawn in at least two directions.*

Protect Peas from Birds and Support the Vines

Make a narrow, A-frame tent of netting by stretching a 2- or 3-foot-wide strip of Ross Garden Netting down each side of a planted double row. Secure the strips by covering the bottom of each with earth and tying the tops to several small bamboo stakes. (Twist-and-Tie garden twine works well.) The peas grow up inside this tent; when they reach the top, untie it and let them grow beyond. Besides foiling birds, this system helps the plants cling to their trellis; there's no need to wrap the row with twine to hold up sagging vines.

pull up, clean up, chop up, and compost the remains and begin again, by planting the fall and winter garden on Labor Day weekend. Put in plenty of manure and soil amendment. Add fertilizer according to package directions. Use organic fertilizers if you're an organic gardener, but be sure to provide crops with adequate nourishment in winter; when the weather's cool, nitrogen is less active in the soil.

Control Migrating Pests. A number of gardeners like to start planting in some areas while continuing to harvest in others. This works well if you grow vegetables on several levels or in raised beds. The only problem is you have less of a chance to get rid of all insect pests at once. Whiteflies in particular will tend to migrate off tomatoes onto something else. It's usually best to clean out the entire vegetable garden at one time and then wait a week or two before replanting.

   If you've planted flowerbeds with seeds of wildflowers nearby, be careful when chopping up tomato vines. Tiny green worms can crawl right off them and journey across the ground to

Quick Tip

How to Make a Straight, Shallow Furrow for Seeds. *Lay the handle of a hoe flat on its back on the seedbed. Press it down evenly. Measure the furrow with a ruler for correct depth.*

decimate your flower seedlings. If there's a very serious pest infestation—of caterpillars, say, or whiteflies—harvest all the vegetables you're going to eat and then spray the empty plants to kill the pests. Wait several days for the spray to take effect before pulling up the plants and disposing of them in the compost pile. (If you used a toxic spray, be sure to wear protective clothing when you remove the plants in order not to be exposed to pesticide.)

Start a First Garden. If this is your first vegetable garden, start with careful planning. Choose an area in full sun. (This is imperative for winter crops.) Prepare the soil by cultivating deeply with a spade; don't just scratch the surface with a fork or hoe. In order to have success, you must dig up the ground with a spade to a depth of 1 foot or, at the very least, to 10 inches. With the handle of the spade upright, put your foot on the upper edge of the spade and shove it all the way into the ground; then pull the handle toward you and lift the spadeful; turn it over, and hit the resulting clod of earth with the back of the spade to break it apart. If your soil is too hard for you to accomplish this, build raised boxes on it and fill them with good soil. Add all the soil amendments you can afford, fork them into the ground, and then level the area with a garden rake. Sprinkle a complete vegetable fertilizer onto the surface of the ground according to package directions and rake it into the top 6 inches.

Interplant Peas with Lettuce

If your rows of vegetables are 18 inches apart, skip a row between every two rows of peas. Plant lettuce in the skipped row. After the lettuce is harvested out, tie bamboo or twine across the tops of two rows of tall pea varieties, allowing them to grow across the gap. Children love going through the tunnel and picking peas.

Plant in late September or early October, and be sure to plant cool-season vegetables, not warm-season vegetables. These are the vegetables that are planted in earliest spring in cold-season climates, such as celery and all the cole crops (members of the cabbage family), plus the vegetables that can go into the ground year-round, such as carrots, beets, turnips, and radishes. When you go to the nursery, be careful to buy the right things, because this is one of those months when you can still find transplants of summer vegetables for sale side by side with winter ones. (Check the list in the following section to be sure.)

Fall is just as good a time to start a vegetable garden as spring. In fact, there are some advantages now. Winter vegetables take less care, pest problems are fewer in winter, and irrigation water sometimes falls from heaven. Winter vegetables are fun, surprisingly easy to grow, and far more delicious than the counterparts you can buy in the market.

Begin Planting Cool-Season Vegetables. Vegetables that can be planted now include beets, broccoli, Brussels sprouts, carrots, cauliflower, celery, fava beans, kale, kohlrabi, leeks, both head and leaf lettuce, mesclun, mustard greens, onions, parsley, peas, potatoes, radishes, rutabagas, spinach, Swiss chard, and turnips. (See the accompanying box for how to plant peas.) Technically, you could, if you wish, plant all these vegetables straight in the ground from seeds. In actual practice, however, it's easiest to plant broccoli, Brussels sprouts, cauliflower, and celery from transplants; plant potatoes from seed potatoes and onions from sets. (Wait until November to plant seeds of onions for slicing—the sets you plant now will give you scallions, not large onion bulbs.)

Parsley and lettuce are also often grown from plants you buy at the nursery—parsley because the seeds are slow to sprout, lettuce so you can have a quick harvest while you're waiting for the seeded rows to grow. (Lettuce seeds sprout easily.) Wait until midmonth to put in transplants of cauliflower, and wait until October to put in transplants of cabbages and artichokes.

When planting transplants of winter vegetables, I like to use a product containing humic acid (such as Roots or Grow More Humic Acid) as a transplanting fluid diluted according to package directions. Mix one of these products in a watering can and soak the ground around the roots of each plant. When I do this, I find that the roots grow to immense size and hence also the plant.

Adventuresome gardeners might like to try growing broccoli, Brussels sprouts, cabbage, cauliflower, and celery from seeds. It requires a fuss—the seedlings need nursing along with frequent applications of weak liquid fertilizer, such as fish emulsion—but it does allow a wider choice of varieties. If you're planting the seeds straight in the ground, a drip system will greatly increase your chances of success. Many gardeners grow their own transplants in flats or peat pots, but cole crops and celery actually don't like being transplanted; they form better roots when grown from seeds right where you want them. (When planting broccoli, Brussels sprouts, cauliflower, and celery from seeds, plant them early in September for best results, but plant cabbage seeds about midmonth.)

Though it's too late to plant summer vegetables, some gardeners in frost-free zones have been experimenting lately with planting a last crop of tomatoes or beans early in September. Choose an early variety, such as 'Early Girl Improved' tomatoes ('Celebrity' works, too) or 'Venture' beans. Many gardeners keep a few tomato plants going until December.

Purchase/Plant

❏ Transplant the biennials started from seed in July into the garden, 190

❏ Plant alstroemerias, 214

❏ Begin purchasing spring-flowering bulbs, 226

❏ Start planting bulbs, especially drought-resistant ones, 227

❏ Begin to plant lilies, 227

❏ Purchase plants or corms of cyclamen, 228

❏ Plant bulb covers over spring-flowering bulbs, 229

❏ Finish planting tropicals in coastal zones, 229

❏ Start planting cool-season flowers to bloom during winter and spring, 236

❏ Plant sweet peas from seeds for Christmas bloom, 236

❏ Plant warm-season lawns, except zoysia (though it's better to wait until spring), 240

❏ Start planting winter vegetables, 242

❏ Plant peas, 241

❏ Plant cool-season lawns in coastal zones, 225

Trim, Prune, Mow, Divide

❏ Continue to mow lawns at summer heights, 240

❏ Divide irises that need division in interior zones, 168, 228

❏ Stop pruning hibiscus, 230

❏ Prune oleanders by taking out whole stalks, 230

❏ Don't prune New Zealand tea trees in fall, 230

❏ Start disbudding camellias, 233

❏ Resume picking and deadheading roses, but don't disbud them, 234

❏ Wake up primroses and, if necessary, separate, divide, and replant them, 236

❏ Dethatch Bermuda if it needs it and if you failed to do the job in spring or if you are correcting a serious problem with several treatments, 240

❏ Mow off the flowers from lippia lawns, 199

❏ Start fall cleanup for perennials, 238

❏ Remove faded and ratty flowers from evergreen, warm-season ornamental grasses, 239

Fertilize

❏ Feed fuchsias, 168

❏ Continue to feed tuberous begonias, 185

❏ Feed ferns for the last time this year, 147

❏ Feed all container-grown succulents with a well-diluted complete liquid fertilizer, 195

❏ Feed and water cyclamen, 229

❏ Fertilize tropicals for the last time this year, only if they need it, 229

❏ Switch fertilizers on cymbidiums to a higher bloom formula to encourage flowering, 231

❏ To maintain the color of blue hydrangeas, start treating the soil with aluminum sulfate, 232

❏ Fertilize azaleas at month's end for the second and last time of the year; correct chlorosis if necessary, 233

❏ Fertilize Thanksgiving and Christmas cacti with 0-10-10, 234

❏ Continue to feed warm-season lawns; don't feed cool-season lawns until after midmonth, 240

❏ Fertilize roses (Rose-Pro gardeners resume use of urea), 234

Continued>>

Water

❏ Continue to water all garden plants according to their individual needs (with the exception of certain natives), 208, 225

❏ Check drought-resistant plants for signs of stress; give them a deep irrigation, if necessary, to tide them over to the winter rains, 208, 226

❏ Don't let fall-planted tropicals dry out, 230

❏ Keep citrus evenly watered to help prevent fruit from splitting, 230

❏ Don't let camellias dry out now or buds will fall off later, 233

❏ Water roses with up to 1½ inches of water twice a week, 183

Control Pests, Diseases, and Weeds

❏ Treat lemon trees for brown rot, 231

❏ Control rose pests and diseases, 72, 234

❏ Treat primroses and cyclamen for mites if necessary, 237

❏ Control migrating pests, 242

Also This Month

❏ Untie the fronds of palms transplanted in July, 220

❏ Start cleaning out flowerbeds and prepare the ground for fall planting, 236, 255

❏ Wake up cyclamen and primroses you summered-over, 236

❏ Make sure cymbidiums are in adequate light to produce bloom; also see that they get the range of temperatures necessary for bloom, 232

❏ Put Thanksgiving and Christmas cacti into natural light for two months so they will bloom, 234

❏ Prepare beds for cool-season vegetables, 243

❏ Start new vegetable gardens, 242

❏ Continue to harvest 'Valencia' oranges, 230

❏ Balance soil for acid-loving plants, 237

OCTOBER

The Year's Best Planting Month

October is almost always one of the pleasantest months of the year. Though we sometimes get our first rains this month and occasionally they're torrential, the rainy season doesn't officially start until next month. For the most part the weather is clear and sunny, though cooler—cool enough for working outdoors in the middle of the day even in interior valleys. That's good news for gardeners, because October is probably the busiest time of the year. It's the best time to plant almost all permanent additions to the landscape; the exceptions are tropicals (a bit late for them), bare-root plants (they get planted in January), native plants, and ground covers (wait until next month and they'll do slightly better). The idea behind fall planting is to get things into the ground ahead of the major rains. Roots get established during winter and reward you the following summer with a great surge of growth. It's the time-honored, easy, water-saving way to go.

October, like March, is a pivotal month when we make the switch from one Southern California season to another. In March we switch to the summer scheme. In October we switch to winter. Gardeners who put aside extra time for gardening this month will be rewarded with better results and less work to do later. This is the time to pull up the last remnants of summer vegetables and flowers and finish planting cool-season flowers and vegetables for winter and spring. Continue to cut back, clean out, plant, transplant, and revamp perennials. It's also the best time to plant most winter vegetables. Get them into the ground as soon as possible. Cool-season lawns can be seeded now, and it's time to prune, transplant, divide, and separate a great many garden staples. Continue to clean out the dead interiors of native plants. Cut out dead branches and shape the plants in readiness for winter growth.

Fall Planting for Desert Dwellers

Those who live in the desert can plant a wide range of vegetables and flowers this month. Both summer and winter vegetables can be planted now, with the exception of corn and melons, which should be planted in late January or early February. (Wait until November to plant onions, but buy the seeds of short-day varieties now.) Many flowers, including ivy geraniums and petunias, which thrive in the spring and summer along the coast, can be counted on for winter color in desert areas. For more planting ideas, see the selection of bedding plants at local nurseries.

Among permanent plants to put in now are flame vine (*Pyrostegia venusta*) and Easter lily vine (*Beaumontia grandiflora*). Flame vine blooms in fall and early winter, so now's the time to find it in nurseries. Planted in the low desert it can curtain walls and roofs with a solid sheet of vivid, orange color for several months, climaxing at Christmas, but it will also thrive in coastal zones if given a hot spot, such as a south-facing tile roof, to tumble over. Easter lily vine needs warmth, rich soil, plenty of fertilizer, protection from wind, and lots of water. (Some desert areas have ample water supplies, but don't grow it where water is scarce.) Its white flowers bloom fragrantly from spring to fall.

Trees, Shrubs, and Vines

Plant all trees, shrubs, and vines now to give them the best start possible. This is the finest time of the year to put in garden staples that last for years and become the backbone of the landscape. Tropicals are an exception; it's better to plant them in late spring or early summer, especially in interior zones. (Very tender plants like tropical hibiscus often die with the first frost when planted in fall.) But nurseries, understandably, may carry some plants only while they're in bloom, so fall may be the only time that you can find certain flowering trees and vines.

If you do plant tropicals now, don't fertilize them, do protect them from frost during winter, and ask your nursery if the plant you purchase is guaranteed to survive the winter. The reason fall planting benefits almost all other plants is that the soil is still warm enough to stimulate growth of roots, and winter rains will help them get established. You won't see much, if any, growth during the winter, but what you plant now will be ready to wake up and grow when the weather warms up in spring. Choose plants recommended for your climate zone, and take their eventual size and ability to withstand drought into consideration. Plant sun lovers in the sun and shade lovers in the shade, and always plant in zones, grouping plants with similar water requirements.

Among trees you might choose to put in now are all types of conifers as well as Chinese elm (*Ulmus parvifolia*), mayten tree (*Maytenus boaria*), many melaleucas, cork oak (*Quercus suber*—the thick-barked tree that Ferdinand the bull sat under), fern pine (*Podocarpus gracilior*), Australian and New Zealand tea trees (*Leptospermum laevigatum* and *L. scoparium*), and tipu tree (*Tipuana tipu*). Most shrubs used for hedges can be planted now, along with many shrubs used for accents and screens, including India hawthorn (*Rhaphiolepis indica*), photinia, pittosporum, lavender starflower (*Grewia occidentalis*), and yew pine (*Podocarpus macrophyllus*). Among vines and vinelike plants to put in now are Cape honeysuckle *(Tecomaria capensis),* Carolina jessamine *(Gelsemium sempervirens),* lilac vine *(Hardenbergia comptoniana),* and ivy. (Wait until next month to put in ground covers and California native plants.)

When purchasing *Rhaphiolepis indica,* be sure to choose a good variety. Flower color is poor on unnamed varieties. Among tall varieties, 'Dancer', 'Jack Evans', and 'Springtime' are good choices; 'Ballerina' is a stunning dwarf. Don't choose white varieties with single blossoms; their flowers go brown in rain and drop off in one week. If you don't specify to landscape companies which variety you want, you're likely to end up with inferior white or dull pink seedlings. (For more good varieties, refer to the list in the *Sunset Western Garden Book.*)

Fall Color

October is a good time to notice those plants that provide fall color year after year and perhaps add one to your garden. By purchasing now you can find the color that pleases you most. All the plants listed below can be put in now along the coast, and several can also be planted inland. (If you live in the interior don't plant tropicals this late in the season.)

For autumn leaves choose liquidambar for its colorful pink, red, yellow, or orange foliage or maidenhair tree *(Ginkgo biloba),* which has golden leaves in fall. (In order to avoid the sticky, malodorous fruit of mature female trees, plant only named male varieties, such as 'Autumn Gold' or 'Fairmount'.) The Hong Kong orchid tree *(Bauhinia blakeana)* has striking flowers ranging from cranberry to pink. Floss silk tree *(Chorisia speciosa)* blooms in burgundy or bright orchid to bright pink all over the top of the tree. (There's also a white species, *C. insignis.* Markhamia tree *(Markhamia hilde-*

brandtii) bears golden trumpet flowers from August through October. (It's best near the coast.) Chinese flame tree *(Koelreuteria henryi* or *K. bipinnata)* is named for its salmon-colored seedpods, which follow less significant yellow flowers.

Vines include cup-of-gold vine *(Solandra maxima),* which grows well even on the ocean-front, and flame vine *(Pyrostegia venusta),* discussed above in the desert section. Mexican flame vine *(Senecio confusus* or *S. angulatus)* is a yellow-to-orange vine for coastal locations. (It dies down in frost.) It may be hard to find but can be grown from seed or cuttings. Cut it back hard after bloom.

Deciduous Fruit Trees

In mild zones it's sometimes a problem to get deciduous fruit trees into winter dormancy. Don't follow the erroneous advice to feed them now in fall, though you may read it in books, magazines, and even some local newspapers. Fall fertilizing is an accepted practice in cold-winter climates, but in our region it forces growth at the wrong time of year. After midmonth hold back on water, but don't let the soil dry out completely. Dry conditions may encourage trees to drop their leaves and go dormant for the winter, as is desirable.

Plants to Divide, Trim, and Mulch

October is the main month for dividing plants that tend to grow in a clump. Some of these plants—clivia, iris, daylilies, and ginger, for example—are bulblike in that they grow from thickened roots, or rhizomes. Others are true perennials. The reasons for dividing are to propagate more plants, to make plants look better, to

How to Divide Daylilies

Divide daylilies every three to five years to keep them blooming. Old varieties bloom longer without division than new varieties.

- Dig up the clumps. Knock off excess earth. Separate large clumps by putting two garden forks back to back and prying them apart.

- To make individual sections, find the natural dividing point between two fans of leaves. Push downward between them with a large old screwdriver kept for the purpose, so that the fans break cleanly in two.

- Throw away broken parts. Trim the leaves of good divisions to 4 inches. Trim off any broken or damaged roots. Shorten overly long ones.

- Dig up the bed and loosen the soil to a depth of 1 foot; mix in bone meal, fertilizer, and organic amendments.

- For each plant make a shallow cone of earth. Replant the daylilies 12 to 18 inches apart, with their roots spread over the cone and covered with 1½ to 3 inches of soil. Mulch and water the ground. Give excess plants to friends.

keep them to a desired size, or to encourage bloom. (When crowded, some plants bloom better but others stop flowering.) Always water thoroughly the day before dividing.

Kahili Ginger. Once the rhizomatous rootstocks of Kahili ginger *(Hedychium gardneranum)* crowd the top of the pot, the plant will bloom less; this is a sign it needs to be either potted on or divided. Repot it, transplant it, or divide it now, to avoid destroying next year's bloom. To divide, slice down through the rhizomes with a knife or sharp spade to make large sections, 8 inches or more in diameter; trim off damaged roots only, and replant in pots or the ground, with the rhizomes just beneath the surface and the roots completely buried in humus-rich soil. Cut off faded blooms, but don't cut off the stalks or foliage; Kahili ginger needs its green leaves during the winter.

Clivia. October is the best time to divide clivia. They like to be rootbound, so don't divide them unless absolutely necessary (see the box on page 252).

Iris. Clean up and mulch existing beds. Continue dividing and transplanting overcrowded irises (as described on page 168). They won't bloom when crowded.

Daylily. Renew all evergreen daylilies *(Hemerocallis)* by cutting the leaves back to 4 inches. Mulch the beds and clean up dead leaves. Bait for snails and slugs. (If everblooming daylilies are still flowering, wait until month's end or even November in coastal zones.) Follow up with fertilizer to bring out fresh growth. In interior valleys divide overcrowded daylilies now; along the coast do it now or wait until March (see the accompanying box for directions).

Fortnight Lily. Fortnight lilies *(Dietes, Moraea)* eventually make huge ugly clumps with brown tips. Don't shear off the tops like rounded shaving brushes, as one often sees done; the tips will only go brown again, and new growth will stick up beyond the old in an ungainly fashion.

If you must shear fortnight lily, cut them straight across with electric hedge trimmers 6 or 8 inches above ground. Follow up with fertilizer and water.

How to Renew Gazanias

Gazanias are one of our finest drought- and disease-resistant ground covers. Divide the clumping kinds every three or four years to keep them like new.

- Dig up the clumps. Knock off excess soil.
- Divide the clumps by pulling and clipping them apart. Trim off any damaged roots and any dead leaves or flowers.
- Refurbish the bed by spading it deeply and adding soil amendment and fertilizer.
- Replant the divisions 8 inches apart. Keep them well watered until reestablished.
- You'll have plenty of plants left over; share them with friends or discard.

A much better way to treat them is to dig up the old clumps now with a garden fork and divide them. (The roots aren't deep.) Cut back their tops to 4 or 5 inches and replant them. Throw away the excess. (These are too common to give away.)

Bird of Paradise. Cut off the dead leaves of bird of paradise *(Strelitzia reginae)*. Pull out bloom stems after the flowers fade. Small plants can be divided with a sharp spade. They eventually make immense clumps that are almost impossible to divide. You may have to attack them with a chain saw. Replant salvageable sections.

Other Plants. Also divisible now, if necessary, are gazanias, ivy geraniums, lily turf, and all garden perennials that grow in clumps, including Shasta daisies. (Wait until November to divide and transplant agapanthus and Matilija poppies.)

Geraniums (Pelargoniums)

Prune Zonal (Garden or Common) Geraniums. Continue progressive pruning on zonal geraniums *(Pelargonium* x *hortorum)*. Remove dead and diseased leaves and branches. Cut back one or two of the longest branches, or, if you have been neglecting this job, take several. Make each cut straight across a branch and ¼ to ½ inch higher than a joint. Leave one or two healthy leaves on the branches you've cut back. (Bare stubs won't recover.)

With potted specimens dig out some of the old soil and refresh it with fresh soil. Feed geraniums occasionally during the winter with 20-20-20 or 18-20-16 or with an organic fertilizer. Continue to prune out one or two old leggy stems each month year-round. Save the most succulent cuttings to make new plants. Dip them in RooTone or Dip'N Grow and plant in fast-draining potting soil.

Cut Back Ivy Geraniums. Continue progressive pruning on ivy geraniums *(P. peltatum)*, cutting back one or two of the longest branches once a month. If, however, you have not been faithful to this task, now is your chance to cut back all the long and ungainly growth to about 6 to 8 inches from pot level. Remove dead branches, leaves, and debris. Remove a little soil and replace it with fresh mix. Feed them for growth and water them. If your ivy geraniums are growing in the ground, cut them back lightly and clean up the ground around them. Then mulch, feed, and water them.

Prune Martha Washingtons. Martha Washingtons *(P.* x *domesticum)* can become floppy if not pruned, but don't cut them back all at once. It's best to begin right after spring bloom and do the job progressively. Prune one or two leggy stems back to the lowest pair of leaves. Then cut more

How to Divide a Potted Clivia

Clivia like to be rootbound. Plants in the ground can go almost indefinitely without division. But you must divide clivia grown in pots when no soil is left and the roots push up out of the top, because then drainage becomes a problem. To divide them, take these steps:

- Use a large knife to cut around the inside of the pot or tub. Place the pot on its side. Direct strong water pressure up the drainage hole to loosen roots.

- To remove a plant that stays stuck, sit on the ground with your feet on the edge of the tub, grab the stalks close to the roots, and yank the monster out.

- Cut apart the individual stalks with a knife. Trim away some of the excess roots. Repot them in potting soil, three plants to an 18-inch container.

when regrowth begins. In coastal zones, progressive pruning can be continued through October.

Prune Species and Scented Geraniums. Cut back species geraniums lightly to keep them growing and in bounds. Some ground-cover types of scented geranium, including *P. tomentosum,* can be sheared with hedge shears. Remove dead and dying portions; clean up the ground. Follow up with a light application of a complete organic fertilizer like Gro Power; water it in.

Water Lilies

Lift Tropical Water Lilies in Interior Zones.
Tropical water lilies are the ones that hold their flowers high above the water and come in many exciting colors and a wide range of sizes. They usually can survive year-round outdoors in coastal climates, but if frost hits your garden every year they probably won't live through winter. If you know it's going to freeze, lift the tubers now, remove the soil, and store the tubers in damp sand in a garage or cellar for the winter. Plant them again in spring. If this sounds like a bother, buy fresh ones yearly. It's more expensive, but trying out new colors and sizes can add to the fun of growing these exotic plants.

Divide Hardy Water Lilies. Hardy water lilies are frequently smaller and less striking than tropical ones, but they're easier to grow, and many people prefer the way they float on the surface of the water rather than standing high above it, as tropical water lilies do. For the best bloom, divide hardy water lilies or pot them on every three years in October. (You can also plant more now.)

To repot hardy water lilies, lift the containers out of the pool. (Wear protective clothing and rubber gloves to avoid contact with algae, which can cause allergic reactions.) Inspect the roots; if they fill the container and the plants look crowded, it's time to repot. To do so, first clean up the plants by removing dead leaves and debris, and also take off any baby plants. (Plant these in separate containers as described on page 124.) Then remove some of the old soil from the roots of the parent plant and pot it on, filling in around the roots in the new larger container with Profile Aquatic Plant Soil or rich garden loam that contains no manure, peat moss, bone meal, perlite, or wood shavings. To keep the water from getting muddy and prevent fish from nibbling at roots, either cover the surface of the soil with a 1- or 2-inch layer of washed sand (or pebbles) or galvanized chicken wire.

Hardy water lilies that don't look crowded but do have yellow leaves and fewer flowers may simply need fertilizing. (The best feeding regimen is once a month beginning in April, as described on page 125.) Feed now by pushing slow-release tablets recommended for aquatic plants beneath the soil surface, or mix 1 pound of 5-10-10 slow-acting, granular fertilizer into the soil mix of every 5-gallon container. Replace the protective sand, pebbles, or wire netting on top.

Bulbs

Shop for Spring-Blooming Bulbs. If you didn't purchase bulbs and corms last month, don't wait any longer. The early shopper gets the best bulbs. Always purchase bulbs at a first-rate nursery. You'll pay a little more, but it's worth it. Bargain bulbs sometimes won't even bloom. Some mail-order catalogs are excellent sources of rare bulbs; a few offer the convenience of premium-size prechilled tulips, but many mail-order bulbs of common varieties are just as expensive and much smaller than those you can find at the best nurseries.

You can still plant the South African bulbs, such as babiana, croscosmia, freesia, ipheion (spring star flower; *Ipheion uniflorum*), ixia, sparaxis, tritonia, and watsonia. You can also plant oxalis and all the Tazetta types of narcissus, such as 'China lily' (Chinese sacred lilies), 'Geranium', and paper whites. Lilies (*Lillium*) should be planted as soon as you get them home. (See page 227 for more information on these bulbs.)

Another South African bulb that's worth a hunt is wand flower (*Dierama pulcherrimum*). It's not drought resistant, but if you can give it the moist, humusy soil it requires, you'll be rewarded eventually with a large clump of swordlike leaves and delightful arching flowers in May and June, followed by purplish blue berries that last two months or more and are stunning in flower arrangements. (Dropped berries can stain carpets.) Don't be discouraged if plants don't flower the first year after planting. You'll find this plant in old Southern California gardens and select nurseries, so treasure it once you find it. If you have a garden pond, plant wand flower next to it.

Buy anemones, daffodils, grape hyacinths, Dutch irises, and ranunculus now, but wait until next month to plant them. Keep them in a cool, dry place such as the garage. (Don't refrigerate them.) The temperature of the ground and of soil in containers is still too warm this month in most zones for safe planting of these bulbs. (In interior valleys daffodils and Dutch irises can be planted by midmonth, but it won't hurt to wait until November.)

Prechill Hyacinth, Tulip, and Crocus Bulbs. Hyacinths, tulips, and Dutch crocus (*Crocus vernus*) bulbs can also be bought now. The **Rule of Thumb** is: *To fool hyacinths, tulips, and crocuses into thinking they've had a cold winter, put the bulbs in the lettuce drawer of your refrigerator for six to eight weeks prior to planting.* Gardeners who live in interior valleys should start chilling these bulbs now for early December planting. Gardeners in coastal zones and air-drained, frost-free zones should wait until November to start the chilling process. Store them in a cool, dry place until then.

Before you refrigerate bulbs, put them in a brown paper bag, not plastic—it rots them. Write on the bag "Not onions, don't eat!" If your lettuce drawer takes delight, as some do, in regularly freezing lettuce, it's too cold for bulbs; store them on a low back shelf. They must not freeze. Also, beware of fresh fruits that give off ethylene gas, including apples, bananas, and pineapples. When these are stored in the same refrigerator with bulbs, make sure they're in airtight bags or containers; if the gas escapes it can cause flower bulbs to rot or grow roots and sprout.

🌿 Quick Tip

Off-Season Bulb Storage. *For tuberous begonias, caladiums, dahlias, gladioli, and other bulb and bulb-type plants, first line a wire hanging basket with fly screen and a handful or two of perlite or sponge rock. Roll the bulbs in bulb dust, place them in the basket, and cover them with more sponge rock. Hang them in a cool, dry spot high enough to be out of the reach of field mice. (They relish most bulbs and corms.)*

Divide Gladioli. When gladiolus stems have died, cut them off and dig up the corms. You'll probably be delighted, as I always am, to see how a new corm has grown on top of each old one. Sometimes you'll also find that several tiny new corms, called "cormels," have sprouted around the edges of it. Knock off the soil and lay the entire thing, stem and all, on newspaper to dry for a few days in sun along the coast, a week or two in shade inland.

After they're thoroughly dry, the corms will separate easily. Keep the new smaller, fatter corms that have grown on top to plant next year. Throw away the stem, the roots, and the old wider, flatter corm on the bottom. It's now worn out. You can leave the cormels attached if you wish, or separate them from the parent and either discard or plant them, but cormels are often difficult to sprout. To avoid this problem, prechill them in the refrigerator for two months, as described above for hyacinths, tulips, and crocuses. Then plant them 1 inch apart in flats or the ground in late winter, and let them grow until they're big enough to bloom; the process takes a year or two. Lift them in fall and plant them 6 inches apart the following year. (Occasionally the genetic structure of cormels will be different from the parent plant, and you'll get a mutation, a flower unlike its parent.)

Roll the new corms and cormels in bulb dust containing a fungicide, like captan, and a pesticide, like diazinon or carbaryl, and store them in a cool, dry place until next February, when once again it's time to plant glads. You can also treat the corms and cormels to control thrips before storage. To do so, soak the corms and cormels for six hours in a solution of 4 teaspoons of Lysol in 1 gallon of water. Dry the bulbs thoroughly before dusting with bulb dust and storing.

Divide Naked Ladies. Naked lady (*Amaryllis belladonna*) is among our most valuable but least appreciated drought-resistant South African bulbs. Look for good hybrids now in nurseries. The cheerful pink flowers of the old wild (unhybridized) type are often seen in backcountry gardens arising in straight, awkward rows on bare stems from dusty ground. They look best massed or mixed with aeonium, aloes, and statice (*Limonium perezii*) to cover a windswept bank near the sea, but they make a fine, informal bank cover in any frost-free zone. Once established inland they need only occasional water. Along the coast (Zone 24) they need little or no irrigation.

Eventually naked ladies form big clumps that push up out of the ground and need dividing. The **Rule of Thumb** is: *Divide naked ladies in early October, after bloom but while they're still dormant and before new roots or leaves have begun to grow.* If early rains stimulate growth, wait another year and dig them up a little earlier. They won't bloom for several years if divided during active growth.

Store Tuberous Begonias. Allow tuberous begonias to dry out after bloom. Slip the root ball out of the pot and let the whole thing dry in the sun. Leaves and stems will fall off by them-

How to Force Poinsettias to Bloom for the Holidays

Potted poinsettias saved from last Christmas can be forced into bloom again this year, if you start now. In most cases the time involved hardly pays, but the large tub and tree-size plants produced by growers in recent years can make the trouble worthwhile, considering the plant's beauty and original cost.

- Place a healthy poinsettia plant in a warm, protected place where it will get four to six hours of direct sunlight daily. Turn it for even growth.
- Begin on October 1 to keep the plant in a totally dark, cool place (65°F) for fourteen hours every night for ten weeks. For example, you could place it in a closet or in the garage under an upside-down trash can or cardboard box from 5 P.M. to 7 A.M. Don't allow even the tiniest glint of light to hit the plant during the nightly dark period, or flowering will be delayed. (Temperatures below 60°F will also delay bloom.)
- Every morning return the plant to a place where it will get four to six hours of direct sunlight during the day.
- Meanwhile, water and feed the poinsettia often with a complete liquid fertilizer high in bloom ingredients.
- When bracts on your plant begin to show good color, about the first week in December, discontinue the darkness regimen and enjoy the bloom.

selves. After the root ball is thoroughly dry, tear off the roots, roll the tuber in fungicide, and store it for the winter in sponge rock or perlite.

If you prefer, you can try keeping the tuber right in the pot or in the ground. Lay the pot on its side in a cool, dry, shady spot. Simply ignore the ones in the ground. Some may rot, but a few may come back next year.

Chrysanthemums

Stop feeding garden varieties of chrysanthemum (*Dendranthema grandiflorum*) as soon as buds begin to open. Sit back and enjoy the flowers of your labor. Bait for slugs and snails. Visit nurseries that specialize in chrysanthemums. For example, at Sunnyslope Chrysanthemum Gardens (8638 Huntington Drive, San Gabriel 91755; 626/287-4071), see how to grow chrysanthemums as spectacular cascades, hanging baskets, and bonsai. There are also annual displays at Descanso Gardens (1418 Descanso Drive, La Cañada 91011; 818/952-4400) and the San Diego Wild Animal Park (15500 San Pasqual Valley Road, Escondido 92027; 760/480-0100).

Roses

Give roses up to 1½ inches of water twice weekly. If you spray your roses, continue the use of Funginex to control diseases, but cease spraying with Orthene this month. Fertilize roses for the last time this year if you use commercial rose food; apply it early in the month. If you're following the Rose-Pro Method, do not fertilize this month. Continue to pick and deadhead roses to set the stage for next month's flowers, often the best of the year.

Annual and Perennial Flowers

Cool-Season Flowers. Depending on your climate zone and the condition of your garden last month, you may or may not have started to switch flowerbeds and containers from summer

Make a Ball of Primroses to Bloom All Winter into Spring

- Hang up a 14-inch wire basket. Wearing rubber gloves, create a neat edge by shoving premoistened sphagnum moss tightly through the two top lines of wire and clipping it into the shape of a smooth tube. Line the rest of the basket with more moist moss.

- Fill the basket with a good grade of soil mix, such as Bandini #105.

- Wrap the roots of twelve or fourteen malacoides (fairy) primrose transplants in a little moist sphagnum moss (like tiny blankets). Separate two wires on the side of the basket, push in the wrapped roots of one plant, and reclose the wires. By this means plant the sides of the basket solidly with primroses, in a zigzag pattern. Reserve four to six plants for the top. (The roots of these don't have to be wrapped.)

- Keep the ball in full sun along the coast or partial shade inland. Water by drip tube or hose. Feed with 20-20-20 liquid or 14-14-14 slow-release fertilizer.

to winter annuals, perennials, and biennials. (I am referring here to the plants that we grow as annual color and switch each season. See pages 92 and 236 for a rundown on this subject and how we grow these plants here.) October is the best month to complete this job, so if you still have flowerbeds and pots filled with warm-season annual flowers, get them pulled out before month's end. Dig up, amend, and fertilize the soil, and transplant or sow flowers for winter and spring bloom.

Flowers to put in from transplants now for cool-season color include calendula, cineraria, cyclamen, delphinium, dianthus, evergreen candytuft (*Iberis sempervirens*), flowering cabbage and flowering kale, foxglove, Iceland poppy,

🐞 Quick Tip

Keep Rabbits from Eating Pansies. *Nibbled tips on such plants as pansies, petunias, and lettuce may be rabbit damage. Sprinkle mothballs on the ground. (If you have a baby, substitute moth crystals, since mothballs are toxic and might be mistaken for candy.) Cats, dogs, opossums, and skunks are also repelled by the odor of mothballs.*

nemesia, paludosum daisy (*Chrysanthemum paludosum*), pansy, malacoides (fairy) primrose, obconica primrose, polyanthus primrose, snapdragon, stock, sweet alyssum, sweet William, and sweet violet (*Viola odorata*), johnny-jump-up, and other violas. Get them into the ground as soon as possible, provide them with adequate light, and feed them well for fast growth and bloom. The **Rule of Thumb** is: *If you get winter annuals to bloom before the holidays, you'll enjoy their flowers throughout winter. If you don't, they'll just sit there doing nothing until the weather warms up in spring.*

Even this late in the year you can plant from seeds, bring some of the flowers into bloom before Christmas, and have abundant flowers in spring; some varieties will continue to bloom through summer. Flowers to plant from seeds now include African daisy (*Dimorphotheca*), calendula, California desert bluebells (*Phacelia campanularia*), California poppy, clarkia, forget-me-not, globe candytuft (*Iberis umbellata*), godetia, hollyhock, johnny-jump-up, lavatera, linaria, nasturtium, Shirley poppy, snapdragon, sweet alyssum, and many wildflowers. Sweet alyssum, johnny-jump-ups, and linaria are usually the first to bloom, closely followed by calendulas. (For the most rewarding show grow tall calendulas such as 'Pacific Beauty', not the dwarf kinds.)

How to Grow Cineraria

Cineraria *(Senecio hybridus)* are the aristocrats of the shade garden. Put in transplants now, and care for them through winter. They thrive on cold weather, as long as it doesn't freeze, and then bloom fabulously in February, March, or April.

- For the finest display purchase transplants of medium or tall—not dwarf—varieties, or grow your own next year by planting seeds in August.

- Choose a spot in open shade under trees or overhangs. (Under the open sky to the north of a tall tree or house is ideal, if you protect the plants from frost.)

- Provide deep, well-drained acid soil. If that's not available, plant in 8- to 12-inch plastic pots, and sink them into the ground.

- Plant in a solid pattern all over the bed at intervals of 8 to 12 inches, depending on variety. Water regularly. Don't let the roots dry out.

- Feed every two weeks with a high-nitrogen fertilizer, such as Terr-O-Vite.

- Bait for slugs and snails, and use a systemic spray against leaf miners and aphids.

- When plants are robust and flower buds begin to show, switch the fertilizer to 0-10-10 or 2-10-10. Feed once a week until flowers open.

Permanent Perennials to Dig up, Divide, and Replant, or to Mulch. Most perennials, of course, are treated as permanent plants, not as annual color. They continue to grow and to flower in season for many years. Many gardeners combine these plants in the same bed with those treated mainly as annuals. Some permanent perennials, like the Shasta daisies already mentioned, should be lifted, divided, and replanted now (or you can throw them out and plant them again from seed). Others, like alstroemerias (Peruvian lilies) and clivia, prefer to

Quick Tip

How to Make a Hanging Basket Hang Straight. *Your hanging baskets will always hang straight instead of crooked if, before you attach their plant hangers, you bend all of their wires simultaneously. Grasp a three- or four-wire plant hanger so all the wires are held tightly together, and bend the ends of the wires all at once into a hook, about 4 inches from the tips. Then spread the wires apart. Hook each plant-hanger wire under the top basket wire or through a hole in a wooden or plastic basket, and then twist the hook closed.*

be left in the ground undisturbed. Still others, like daylilies and irises (as already discussed), need occasional division. And chrysanthemums, which are discussed as a separate category throughout this book, are best grown on new roots from fresh cuttings taken annually in spring.

I know of at least one Southern California gardener who treats his perennials in the same way that English gardeners care for their renowned herbaceous borders (flowerbeds planted with nonwoody plants). Every year in fall he lifts all perennial plants, digs up the bed, fertilizes and amends the soil, and then promptly replaces the plants, after first dividing those that require it. The only exceptions are those plants that detest being disturbed, and to these he gives a liberal topping of mulch.

Continue Fall Jobs. There's no better month than October for continuing the fall jobs begun in September—all the cutting back, pruning, mulching, moving, planting, and general cleanup that we do at this time of year. Here are some more specifics: Cut back Santa Barbara daisy *(Erigeron karvinskianus)* and pull it out when it's growing where you don't want it. Water and

A Foolproof Way to Grow Wildflowers

- Choose a spot in full sun. Spade or rototill the ground deeply, adding organic soil amendment but no fertilizer. (If you plant wildflowers for three years in the same bed, sprinkle the ground with a light application of complete fertilizer before planting for the third time.) Smooth and level the surface with the garden rake.

- Decide on a watering system. Drip tubes are best because they won't get the tops of flowers wet.

- If the area you're planting is too wide for you to reach all parts of it from the edges, either make wandering paths through it or place stepping-stones here and there between the drip tubes so you can walk on the bed without compacting the soil.

- Sprinkle seeds of western wildflowers all over the bed. Sprinkle individual types in drifts, putting tall varieties at the back or in the middle and shorter varieties at the front or around the edges.

- Rake the seed lightly into the soil.

- Intersperse pea stakes throughout the bed (see the accompanying box).

- Protect the seeds and sprouts from birds: stretch Ross Garden Netting over the stakes. Fasten the edges down with rocks or wire staples. (After the plants are up 4 to 5 inches, take off the netting but leave the pea stakes in place to support the plants through wind and rain.)

- Sprinkle the bed by hand twice a day until seeds germinate. Then start watering with a drip system or by soaking the bed when rains aren't adequate.

- After the plants are up and growing, stand or lean your hands on your paths or stepping-stones to weed and thin the bed. Bait for slugs, snails, and cutworms. Later, use the stepping-stones when picking and deadheading the flowers.

- Use canes pruned from climbing roses to protect the bed from being smashed by skunks or other animals in spring (see page 47 for directions).

---

fertilize it for regrowth. Cut back *Gaillardia* 'Yellow Queen', *Rudbeckia fulgida* 'Goldsturm', and goldenrod *(Solidago)*. After Russian sage *(Perovskia* 'Blue Spire') and other late-summer and fall bloomers stop flowering, deadhead and trim them. Cut back pincushion flower *(Scabiosa)* now; if you don't, it gets to be a mess. *S. africana* is the best one to grow here and spreads well. *S. columbaria* is good in coastal zones (unfortunately, the one you usually find is *S. caucasica*).

Verbena bonariensis blooms through September. Cut it back now; it has wonderful basal growth underneath. Society garlic *(Tulbaghia violacea)* needs no cutting back; deadhead it if you haven't done it already, divide clumps that are dying in the middle, and throw away the

brown parts. Crown-pink *(Lychnis coronaria)*, which comes in white or cerise, comes up all over the place; move it around now. It looks good next to blue or purple plants like the sea lavender *Limonium perezii*.

Divide and replant perennials that bloomed in spring and summer, including Shasta daisies, as described above. (Plants with fleshy roots that go dormant in winter—saponaria is an example—are better divided in late February.) Pull up and move, toss out, or give away plants that are coming up from seed in the wrong places. Gaura, *Verbena* 'Bonny Blue', and some ornamental grasses are especially notorious.

If rains come early, keep a close watch on your ornamental grasses. Those that go dormant in summer need cutting back when they begin to grow again, which often happens with the first fall rain. Even warm-season ornamental grasses, including red fountain grass (*Pennisetum setaceum* 'Rubrum'), have such a short dormancy here that they often sprout fresh green leaves at ground level as soon as rains start. When you see growth begin, cut off all the old, brown leaves and flowers just above the new growth. Follow up with a lawn fertilizer and water. (See page 239 for more about pruning ornamental grasses.)

Japanese anemones (*Anemone hybrida*) are in full bloom now, brightening up the shade. If you don't already have this elegant plant that seeds itself in places where it's happy, look for it now in nurseries.

Wildflowers

One of the greatest joys in gardening is growing wildflowers. Plant them early this month for a flower display that begins before Christmas and lasts through June—sometimes throughout summer.

One of the best ways to go is to buy several packaged mixes of California or western wildflowers and add some choices of your own, such as extra linaria, California poppies, and larkspur. Put in some splashes of scarlet flax (*Linum grandiflorum* 'Rubrum') and an edging of nemophila. Notice that the labels of some mixes indicate whether the seeds are those of annuals or perennials and whether they're easy to grow. Labels often also tell the season when you can expect the flowers to bloom, whether they need dry or moist soil, whether they prefer sun or shade, and the average height of the plants.

Purchase seed from seed racks or catalogs. One source is Larner Seeds, P.O. Box 407, Bolinas, CA 94924 (415/868-9407). The Theodore Payne Foundation in Sun Valley (818/768-1802)

Use Pea Stakes to Protect Flowers from Heavy Rains and Wind

Use English pea stakes (originally devised to support peas) to prevent flowers from being damaged by wind or rain. Cut 2- to 4-foot-tall branches with many twigs from shrubs, such as Victorian box (*Pittosporum undulatum*). Ideally the branches are straight and strong and the twigs splay like the ribs of an upside-down umbrella. Remove the leaves.

Shove the bottoms of the sticks into the ground all over flowerbeds after planting. Annual and perennial flowers will grow up through the branches, lean on the twigs, and won't get knocked down by winter weather. By the time the beds are full grown, the twigs should be largely hidden by foliage and flowers.

sells seed of California wildflowers and also a book on the subject by Connelly, *The Gardener's Guide to California Wildflowers*.

If you want spring flowers, look for seed mixes that concentrate on spring-flowering annuals. If you'd like longer-lasting color, choose seed mixes that combine annuals with perennials. If you want long-lasting bloom in a sunny bed, your best bet is to choose a mixture of western wildflowers that contains both annuals and perennials and that needs dry soil in full sun. In good years when we have adequate rains, the wildflowers in these drought-resistant mixes can survive through winter and spring on little more than natural rainfall, but they perform better and last months longer when irrigated regularly once the rains cease. If you irrigate them once a week in hot weather, they'll provide an ever-changing and delightful flower display from Christmas until fall, at which time you can replant. Mexican hat (*Ratibida columnifera*) will come back year after year in a hot spot that it likes and give you masses of informal color all summer long with little care. (A word of warning: If you live in a suburban area, steer clear of wildflower mixtures that contain grasses along with the flowers. These are fine for country meadows, but they look weedy in suburban gardens, and the grasses may reseed themselves in lawns, ground covers, and shrubbery.)

Another way to plant wildflowers is to make your own mix with such easily grown selections as California poppies, Chinese houses (*Collinsia heterophylla*), godetia (*C. amoena*), larkspur, linaria, nemophila, phacelia, Rocky Mountain clarkia, improved (*Clarkia unguiculata*), and scarlet flax (*Linum grandiflorum* 'Rubrum'). This mix of flowers will bloom through June. If desired, dot the bed with seeds of tall orange calendulas. They'll bloom ahead of the California poppies to provide a happy contrast with the soft lavender tones of the linaria.

Lawn Care

Cool-season lawns such as ryegrass, bluegrass, and fescue are beginning to speed up now, and warm-season lawns such as Bermuda, zoysia, and St. Augustine are beginning to slow down. That means it's time to reset the blades on your lawnmower (as described below). Many lawn owners like to mulch their lawns with manure or a fine-grained soil amendment now, before the winter rains. This is also a good time to aerate lawns with a machine made for the purpose (see the accompanying box). Aeration aids growth by getting air to the roots.

Cool-Season Lawns. Reset mower blades to cut cool-season grasses shorter now, to 1½ inches. Improved varieties of tall fescue can also be cut at this shorter height now. Make sure the mower is sharp so it doesn't mangle the tips of fescue's tough grass blades.

Help cool-season lawns wake up and grow by feeding them with a complete lawn fertilizer for both root and top growth. If your lawn's been plagued with fungus and you haven't done anything about it, tackle the problem now, ahead of the rains. Many products are available. Some contain fertilizer, which makes them easier to spread evenly.

Dethatch cool-season lawns and uproot any crabgrass in it in early fall. This is an annual task that can transform a lawn (see the box on page 261). Crabgrass can't get started in a thick, healthy lawn. It's nice to know that once you've dethatched and started a good program of water and fertilizer your problems will mostly be confined to the edges. October is also the best time of the year to plant a cool-season lawn from seed (see box on page 262).

Warm-Season Lawns. Continue to cut warm-season lawns at the same height that you cut them throughout summer. Cutting them longer in winter, once a common practice, will simply increase thatch. Keep warm-season lawns green longer by continuing your feeding program through October.

In desert zones, feed St. Augustine now and continue throughout the winter. During the summer St. Augustine grass needs a great deal of water when grown in the desert, but the advantage is that you can keep it green throughout the winter by feeding it every six weeks with a pound of nitrogen for each 1,000 square feet.

Overseed Bermuda grass with annual winter ryegrass, if desired, for a green lawn in winter. Cut Bermuda short before overseeding, and mulch with manure or a fine-grained, dark-colored soil amendment in a ¼-inch layer over the seeds, to speed germination. Keep the

How to Aerate a Compacted Lawn

When the soil under a lawn becomes compacted from foot traffic or heavy equipment, it loses its springy texture and becomes hard as a rock. Water puddles or runs off, and lack of air to the roots causes the turf to deteriorate in appearance and vigor; it often develops thin or bare patches. To correct this condition take these steps:

- Mow the lawn; then make holes in the sod by running a rented aeration machine over it. Or do the job by hand with a tool made for the purpose.

- Rake up the plugs.

- Spread 40 pounds of gypsum and 15 cubic feet of organic soil amendment (such as fine-grained nitrolized redwood or finely ground bark) over each 1,000 square feet of lawn.

- Optional step: Substitute Profile Professional Soil Conditioner for the organic soil amendment. Spread Profile with a drop spreader set to the largest opening. Rake it into the holes. (Profile, unlike organic amendments, makes a permanent improvement in soil. It is made up of tiny particles of porous ceramic, kiln-fired minerals that hold water and oxygen and last year after year. There is a type for clay soil and another for all other soils.)

- Apply a complete lawn fertilizer according to package directions. When the soil or thatch is hydrophobic (so dry it sheds water), also spread on a pelletized penetrant, such as Water In or Soil Air, according to package directions.

- Rake these materials into the holes. Follow up by watering deeply.

---

ground damp until the seeds are sprouted. Be aware that in some areas, particularly warm coastal regions, there isn't enough summer heat to get the rye to completely die out in summer. The result can be a shaggy-looking summer lawn. So before overseeding with winter rye, observe local lawns to see the final effects on your kind of Bermuda.

Dethatch kikuyu grass now to keep it in bounds (see the box on page 82). Collect and bag the stolons. Don't put them in compost.

Vegetable Gardening

It's time to put in the winter vegetable garden or, if you started planting last month, to continue the job. First, pull up and throw out or compost the remains of your summer garden. A thorough cleanup now really pays off in fewer bugs and diseases later. Dig up the soil deeply with a spade, turning it over, aerating it, and breaking

 Quick Tip

How to Plant a Gopher-Proof Lawn. *Prepare and level the ground for planting. Reserve some amended soil. Cover the ground with chicken wire (½-inch mesh) laid flat, and wire the sections together. Cover the chicken wire with 2 or 3 inches of soil. Then plant the lawn from seed. When planting from sod simply cover the prepared ground with chicken wire, and overlap the edges of the wire strips by 1 or 2 inches. Lay the sod directly on top of the wire.*

up the clods as you go. Then use a garden fork to mix in such organic amendments as steer manure, chicken manure, seaweed, homemade or commercial compost, and whatever source of humus you've got. Also, at this time of year, you have the opportunity to permanently improve sandy soil so that it will retain more water and to improve clay soil so that it will drain better by adding the correct Profile Professional Soil

How to Plant a Cool-Season Lawn

If you want an instant lawn, order sod. (Be sure to prepare the ground thoroughly. Grade the soil ½ inch lower than walks to allow for the thickness of the sod, and before installing it level the ground carefully.) If you're going to plant from seed, take these steps:

- Choose turf grass adapted to your area. See page 106 for a discussion of varieties and cultivars.

- Amend the soil. Rototill the ground to a depth of 8 inches. Spread 3 to 4 inches of organic amendment on top and mix it in. Additionally, if possible, mix in a 1-inch layer of Profile Professional Soil Conditioner or one 40-pound bag to every 20 square feet worked into the top 6 inches of soil. Purchase the Profile product that is correct for your soil (sand or clay). Also, for clay soils apply gypsum at the rate of 10 pounds to every 100 square feet and mix it in.

- Level the ground, using a rented leveler or a handmade drag bar or leveler (as described on page 83).

- Install a sprinkler system.

- Rent a seed sower or use a handheld sower. Spread the seeds precisely according to the directions for the variety you're planting. Sow half the seeds while walking back and forth in one direction, the other half while walking at right angles to the original direction.

- Rake the soil lightly with a garden rake so the seed will be covered with no more than ¼ inch of soil. (Rake in one direction only so the seeds won't be buried too deeply.)

- Optional step: Instead of raking the seed into the ground use a squirrel cage (a rentable mulch spreader) to cover the seeds. Cover them with not more than ¼ inch of ground bark or screened manure or the amount directed for the seeds you're using.

- Spread a lawn fertilizer according to package directions.

- Roll the lawn with a lawn roller one-third full of water. Erect a barrier, such as Weathashade Fence-It, to keep children and dogs out of the area.

- Use a fine spray of water to wet the soil at least 4 inches deep. (Be careful not to create puddles, because that will float the seed to the surface.) Then sprinkle lightly three or more times a day as needed to keep the surface soil moist until the grass sprouts. (Tall fescue and ryegrass germinate in about ten days. Bluegrass takes about one month.)

- When grass is about 2 inches high, mow it to 1½ inches. Use a sharp mower and mow when the soil is somewhat dry, so you don't tear out young grass plants.

Conditioner for your soil type. Add Profile year after year until, eventually, your soil contains the optimum amount of 15 to 20 percent. Profile can improve the structure of soil, but you will still need to add organic amendments once or twice a year in order to have healthy, fertile soil and thriving plants. Add commercial fertilizer for vegetables according to package directions; work this into the top 6 inches of soil. If you're an organic gardener, instead use blood meal, cottonseed meal, and bone meal, or a bagged or-

ganic vegetable food. Then use a garden rake to level the ground. Use a hoe to make furrows between rows in heavy soils.

Plant tall crops to the north and short crops to the south. Full sun is needed for all winter vegetables.

Plant Vegetables from Seeds and Transplants. Plants that can be put in from seeds now include beets, broccoli, cabbage, carrots (see boxes), cauliflower, celery, fava beans, kale, kohlrabi,

How to Dethatch Cool-Season Lawns and Control Crabgrass

Some cool-season lawns, such as bluegrass and the new, finer-textured tall fescues, make lots of thatch. Others, such as ryegrass, make little or none. (See page 81 for a description of thatch and how to gauge its thickness.)

- Annually dethatch cool-season lawns that need it in early fall.

- Mow the lawn short. Mow several times in different directions, adjusting the blades lower with each mowing. (This part of the process is much the same as that used on warm-season lawns in spring, as described on page 82, but don't scalp cool-season lawns right down to the ground.)

- If the thatch isn't very thick, you can dethatch a cool-season lawn by hand; rake vigorously with an ordinary metal grass rake or a special de-thatching rake. Or do the job with a rented vertical mower, as described for warm-season lawns.

- Gather the piles of thatch into bags, and send

them to the dump. Don't compost them, because they contain weed seeds.

- As you use a rake, you may notice certain grasses standing up much higher than your lawn grass. This is usually crabgrass. It grows low and crablike, spreading out into a thick clump, but when you rake it the stolons stand up taller than the lawn grasses. Pull it up by the roots now and throw it away along with the thatch. (Use pre-emergent herbicides in late winter.)

- Roughen up and reseed any bare spots left by crabgrass. Cover the whole lawn with dark-colored mulch, such as manure or ground bark. (If desired, also cover reseeded areas with Reemay Grass Seed Starter, a spunbound polyester material you can reuse year after year.)

- Spread a slow-acting fertilizer such as Milorganite all over the lawn except on the parts you reseeded. (Fertilizers inhibit germination.)

- Water deeply and keep newly seeded areas moist.

---

lettuce, mustard greens, parsnips, green peas, snap and other edible-pod peas, radishes, rutabagas, spinach, Swiss chard, and turnips. Though all of the above technically can be planted from seed, it's better to put in celery and most cole crops, including broccoli, Brussels sprouts, cabbage, cauliflower, and collards, from transplants instead of seed. It's a little late to plant these vegetables from seed. Also plant lettuce from transplants for an early harvest; plant it from seed for later crops. (Send away for gourmet varieties—for example, a mesclun.)

Parsley grows well from seed, but it's slow to germinate. (Keep it damp for twenty days.) Most gardeners find it easier to grow from transplants. Put it in a row now, feed it well, and you'll have masses of parsley all winter—so con-

venient for stuffing turkey and garnishing your holiday dishes.

Plant curly cress, cilantro (coriander), and arugula (rocket) from seeds. All three grow rapidly, love cool weather, and are expensive to buy in markets. Garden cress tastes like watercress. Cilantro and arugula are unique, acquired tastes but delightfully addictive. Use cilantro in Chinese and Mexican cooking, salads, soups, and lamb stew. (Add it at the last minute.) Use arugula in salads, as a sophisticated garnish, with Italian food, in sandwiches, and as a flavorful raw accompaniment to oxtail soup made from the dry mix. Both seed themselves if you let them.

You can now also plant potatoes from seed potatoes, raspberries (choose mild-winter

OCTOBER

How to Presprout Carrot Seeds

Some gardeners have trouble getting carrots to germinate, especially in dry or windy weather. This usually comes from not keeping them damp long enough. (It can take two to three weeks.) If you've had this problem or have difficulty at certain times of year, try presprouting carrots (or see the tip on this page for another method).

- Mix the seeds into a handful of damp peat moss. Spread the mixture on a paper plate.

- Put the whole thing into a zip-locked bag, seal it, and freeze it for twenty-four hours.

- Remove the plate from the freezer, and, leaving it inside the zip-locked bag, give it bottom heat—for example, on the TV or VCR (75° to 80°F)—for up to three days. Inspect it daily for sprouting.

- As soon as the seeds sprout, take them out of the bag and sprinkle them, moss and all, into a prepared row. Lightly cover the row with potting soil, and keep it well watered until the sprouts come through. You'll get carrots two weeks earlier than otherwise, and they'll be uniform in height.

varieties) from plants or bare roots, globe artichokes from seedlings or bare roots, and horseradish and rhubarb from bare roots (though rhubarb doesn't grow well here, so I don't recommend growing it). Onions can be put in from sets but, as explained on page 285, you won't get globe onions from them; you'll get scallions.

Confine horseradish in its own bed; it's an invasive though culinarily useful weed. If you've been growing it, now's the time to dig up the large roots. Peel the root, grind it (easily done in a food processor), and then purée it with a little water and a splash of vinegar. (Wear gloves, and don't get fumes up your nose.) Hand-mix a portion of the purée with sour cream and sugar to

🌿 Quick Tip

How to Speed Germination of Seeds of the Parsley Family. *Carrots, like parsley, parsnip, and the ornamental wild carrot, Queen Anne's lace (Daucus carota), are all members of the parsley family (Umbelliferae), and as a group their seeds are slow to germinate. To hasten the process, sprinkle the seeds on prepared soil and pour boiling water over them, straight from the kettle. Cover the seeds with potting soil. Keep them damp until they've sprouted.*

use right away, and freeze the rest in ice cube trays to use as needed.

Wait until early November to plant strawberries and globe onions. Look for seeds of short-day onion varieties, including 'Grano', 'Granex', or 'Crystal Wax', now if you didn't do it in September, so you'll have them on hand.

Cut Down Brown Stems of Asparagus and Plant New Beds. Leave the stems of asparagus on the plants as long as they remain green. When they've turned brown, which should occur sometime between now and January, cut them off at ground level and top-dress the bed with manure. Asparagus doesn't mind salty soil, but it needs rich and preferably sandy soil, full sun, good drainage, lots of water, and plenty of room.

Asparagus also càn be planted now (as described on page 84). It's best to plant a variety developed for this area by the University of California, such as 'UC-157'. Asparagus is a reliable perennial vegetable, and once planted a bed of it can bear crops for as long as fifteen years if you give it good care.

Prechill Strawberry Plants for November Planting. In mid-October cut off the runners

How to Grow Carrots

Carrots sprout at ground temperatures of 45° to 85°F—80° is best—and thus can be planted any month year-round. (The seeds sprout slowly.)

- Choose a gourmet variety, or choose several varieties for comparison.

- Dig and prepare a bed of deep, loose, well-amended soil—sandy soil is best. A raised bed works well. Or grow carrots in a half barrel filled with planter mix. Add bone meal and low-nitrogen vegetable fertilizer but no fresh manure—it makes carrots fork or grow many hairy roots. Water the bed deeply and allow it to settle overnight.

- Plant the seeds all over a raised bed or in a straight row next to a buried drip tube. For the latter, press the back of a hoe handle into the soil to make a shallow trench.

- Carrots have tiny seeds, so mix them with a little sand in the palm of your hand to make them easier to sprinkle evenly. Pelletized seeds are available in some catalogs. You can grab these one by one and space them so they won't require thinning.

- Sprinkle the seeds thinly and evenly on the bed or down the row. Cover them lightly with ¼-inch potting soil. Pat it down gently to create good contact.

- Cover the bed with burlap strips or floating row cover if the weather's hot and dry.

- Sprinkle the bed once or twice daily with a fine spray for one to two weeks to keep the ground thoroughly moist until the seeds sprout. (Don't let it dry out.)

- If you're using burlap, peep under it daily. As soon as sprouts show, remove it.

- If you're not using a drip system, wait until the ground is dry 4 inches down or until the sprouts just begin to wilt before watering again. Then commence regular deep watering. (This encourages a taproot to go straight down and can produce a straight carrot even in clay soil.)

- Thin the carrots according to package directions. Eat the thinnings. Carrots cannot be transplanted; it makes them grow in inedible, forked, and twisted shapes.

you've been encouraging your strawberries to grow (see page 203), thus severing them from the parent plants. Gently dig up these runners, and bare their roots by brushing or shaking off the dirt. Clip off all but two or three leaves from each new little plant. Gather them into bunches and tie them loosely together. Place the bunches in a plastic bag, and put it on a low back shelf of your refrigerator or, if your refrigerator doesn't freeze lettuce or other vegetables, into the lettuce drawer. Leave them there for twenty days before planting them next month, on or before November 10. Prechilling strawberries fools them into thinking they've had a cold winter. Once the plants have become reestablished in the ground, and as soon as the days lengthen

Quick Tip

How to Prevent Green Shoulders. *Some carrot varieties tend to push up out of the soil as they grow. The exposed portions turn green or red and develop a bitter flavor. Prevent this problem by mulching the row or by mounding some soil around the base of the plants when the tops are 4 inches tall.*

and the weather begins to warm up in late winter, they'll be stimulated to produce fruit instead of more vegetative growth. Meanwhile, dig up the bed, throw away or compost all the old plants that bore this year, choose another spot for planting your new strawberry plants, and plant something else in the old bed.

Purchase/Plant

❏ If you grew your own transplants of cool-season flowers and vegetables, plant them out in the garden now, 247

❏ Plant all types of permanent landscape plants other than bareroot plants, tropicals, and native plants, 247

❏ Desert dwellers can plant most summer and winter vegetables now, and many flowers, 248

❏ Plant flame vine in all mild zones; in the desert include Easter lily vine, 248

❏ Plant trees, shrubs, and vines, 248

❏ Choose and plant for permanent fall and winter color, 249

❏ Continue to shop for spring-blooming bulbs and plant the ones that can be put in now, including South African bulbs, oxalis, and Tazetta types of narcissus, 253

❏ Plant lilies as soon as you get them home, 253

❏ Buy anemones, daffodils, Dutch irises, grape hyacinths, and ranunculus; keep them in a cool, dry place until planting time, 253

❏ Purchase hyacinth, tulip, and crocus bulbs and prechill them in the refrigerator, 253

❏ Plant cool-season flowers for winter and spring bloom, 253

❏ Plant cineraria for late-winter and early-spring bloom, 257

❏ Plant wildflowers, 258

❏ Plant cool-season lawns; this is the best time of year for this job, 262

❏ Overseed Bermuda grass with annual winter ryegrass, if desired, 260

❏ Plant cool-season vegetables and year-round vegetables, including carrots and some perennial vegetables, 261

❏ In cold, low-lying gardens plant hardy flowers for winter color; avoid tender bedding plants, 256

❏ Plant celery, 302

Trim, Prune, Mow, Divide

❏ Thin out sweet peas and pinch them back to force branching, 235

❏ Divide, trim, and mulch plants that tend to grow in a clump and that need to be divided, including bird of paradise, clivia, daylily, gazanias, fortnight lily, iris, Kahili ginger, lily turf, and perennials like Shasta daisies, 249

❏ Continue progressive pruning of zonal, species, and ivy geraniums, 251

❏ Finish pruning Martha Washington pelargoniums, 251

❏ Continue to shape and clean out the dead interiors of native plants, 299

❏ Divide hardy water lilies, 252

❏ Lift, dry, separate, and store gladioli, 252

❏ Divide naked ladies, 254

❏ Dig up, divide, and replant perennials, or mulch them, 256

❏ Cut branches out of shrubbery to make pea stakes, 259

❏ Reset mower blades to cut cool-season lawns shorter for the winter growing season, 260

❏ Continue to mow warm-season lawns short, 260

❏ Dethatch kikuyu grass to keep it in bounds, 261

❏ Cut down asparagus stems after they go brown, 264

❏ Cut off runners from strawberries, gather them in bunches, and prechill them for November planting, 264

❏ Watch red fountain grass (*Pennisetum setaceum* 'Rubrum') for new growth, the sign to cut it back, 259

❏ Cut back clumps of sheep fescue (*Festuca ovina* 'Glauca') now or in early spring, 240

Fertilize

❏ Feed fuchsias, 168

❏ Continue to treat blue hydrangeas with aluminum sulfate, 232

❏ Fertilize hardy water lilies that appear to need it, but don't fertilize tropical ones, 252

❏ Stop fertilizing chrysanthemums, and enjoy the blooms, 255

❏ Fertilize poinsettias with a complete fertilizer high in bloom ingredients, 255

❏ Feed roses early this month (Rose-Pro gardeners stop fertilizing now), 255

❏ Feed cool-season lawns with a complete fertilizer, 260

❏ Continue to feed warm-season lawns to keep them green longer, 260

❏ Feed St. Augustine grass in desert zones, 260

Water

❏ Water all garden plants according to their individual needs, your soil, your climate zone, and the weather (reducing water if rains start early), 247

❏ Water deciduous fruit trees more sparingly in fall, 249

❏ Water roses with up to 1½ inches of water twice a week, unless rains do the job for you, 255

❏ Continue to water lawns when rains aren't adequate, 260

Control Pests, Diseases, and Weeds

❏ Treat gladiolus corms for fungus and thrips (but avoid putting fungicide on those you plan to prechill), 254

❏ Protect pansies, petunias, and lettuce from rabbits, 256

❏ Treat cool-season lawns with fungicide if required, 260

❏ Create a gopher-proof lawn by burying chicken wire under it prior to planting, 261

❏ Get rid of existing crabgrass by hand-pulling, 221

❏ Continue to control diseases on roses, 72

Also This Month

❏ Harvest macadamia nuts when they fall to the ground, and cure them properly, 98

❏ Lift tuberoses and store in perlite until next May, 151

❏ Untie the fronds of palms transplanted in August, 220

❏ Tie up sweet peas and edible peas to prevent them from being knocked down by wind or rain, 235

❏ In interior zones where frost can be expected, lift and store tropical water lilies for the winter, 252

❏ If you want to try growing the cormels (tiny sidebulbs) of gladioli, prechill them in the refrigerator, 254

❏ Store tuberous begonias for the winter, 254

❏ Begin forcing potted poinsettias for Christmas bloom, 255

❏ Finish pulling out faded annual flowers and cleaning pots and beds for fall planting, 256

❏ Make a ball-shaped basket of malacoides (fairy) primroses, 256

❏ Straighten hanging baskets by attaching new wires if necessary, 257

❏ Aerate lawns that are compacted from foot traffic or heavy machinery, 261

❏ Thoroughly clean up the vegetable garden; pull up the last of the summer crops and compost the remains, 261

❏ Dethatch cool-season lawns by hand or machine, 263

❏ Harvest horseradish, 264

❏ Continue fall maintenance of perennials, 257

NOVEMBER

The First Month of the Rainy Season

Throughout most of the United States November signals the onset of cold and icy weather. After a short respite of late warm weather, the Indian summer, the sun dips low on the horizon and winter sets in for good. Gardeners throw mulch over tender roots and wrap up roses ahead of the snow. But in Southern California November heralds the return of the rainy season.

This is an active time for us and for many of our plants. Out in the backcountry, in canyons and on hillsides, the native landscape wakes up from summer dormancy and starts to green up and grow. In our gardens we look forward to color from many flowering plants programmed by nature to bloom in winter. Roses give us some of their best blooms in November. If you did most of your fall planting in October, November is an easy month in the garden. But if you didn't plant last month, don't wait any

longer—do it now. Regardless, there are a number of plants—onions, strawberries, native plants, ground covers, and many bulbs—that are best when planted in November.

Our Cyclical Rains

Ever since certain events in the 1860s, it's been apparent that California's rains are not only seasonal (wet winters, dry summers), but they're also cyclical (several years of ample rains followed by several years of drought). In 1861–62 California had the heaviest rains ever recorded. In Los Angeles it rained for twenty-eight days without stopping, San Francisco had 49 inches, and the Central Valley turned into a lake. This disaster was followed two years later by the worst drought in California history. Tree rings tell the story, and they have longer memories than people—who tend to forget about bad

Pitcher Irrigation

You can provide controlled irrigation by burying porous clay pots in strategic locations and periodically filling them with water by hand or a pipe network. Use several of these in a ring around the drip line of a tree; use two or three to water a shrub, or bury a central pot to provide water for a circle of vegetables, like beans or peas. Pitcher irrigation has been used in China for more than two thousand years. Brazilian research finds pitcher irrigation more efficient than drip.

years when the rains are good. Heavy rainfall makes them wonder, "What's all this fuss about drought?" But wise gardeners always remember, first, that it could happen again, and second, that they can never be sure how much rain there will be.

Some years the rains are torrential, smashing garden flowers and causing such bad botrytis (gray mold) that all gardeners wish they would stop. In the winter of 1997 and 1998 rainfall totals averaged 231 percent of normal, more than any years since 1883. Other years there's not nearly enough rain, and gardeners have to pour on water from the hose. Every year or two the media interprets a new scientific study to mean that our local weather pattern is changing. Of course, no one really knows the effects of global warming, but our wet-dry cycles, lasting about seven years for each phase, have existed for centuries and so have the warming and cooling ocean patterns, lasting roughly sixty years. Ten years ago few people had ever heard of the weather phenomenon called El Niño that is now blamed for torrential rains. But El Niño is an ancient cyclical pattern; only our knowledge of it is new (see the accompanying box).

Another factor, and one that's not so easy to forget, is that here in Southern California we're largely dependent on water brought from somewhere else. In the 1920s and 1930s there was an overabundance of imported water. Homeowners, gardeners, and industrialists became accustomed to using water in wasteful ways. Gardens took on the grassy New England or tropical jungle look. Now we're overcrowded and there's not enough water to go around. When you combine our cyclical rainfall with the fact that irrigation water is in ever shorter supply, you have a very serious problem for thirsty plants. In periods of rationing many could die. That's why we need to concentrate on establishing a basic landscape of plants that can survive drought. Now's a good time to begin.

California Native Plants

Many California native plants are well worth considering for home gardens, and November is the best time to plant them. Our state is blessed with a wealth of lovely wild plants, many of which have been improved by selection and hybridizing; yet they're often more widely planted in English gardens than here. Part of the reason may be that they require excellent drainage, they're difficult to raise in nursery containers, and summer watering combined with our hot temperatures sometimes leads to root rot. One way to avoid these problems is to purchase your native plants from nurseries that specialize in them, like Tree of Life in San Juan Capistrano (714/728-0685), or find them at such botanical gardens as The Santa Barbara Botanic Garden (805/682-4726), Theodore Payne Foundation in Sun Valley (818/768-1802), and Rancho Santa Ana Botanic Garden in Claremont (909/625-8767). Also, prepare the ground properly, grow native plants on banks and in raised beds, concentrate on the best and easiest to cultivate, and learn their watering requirements.

El Niño and What It Means to Gardeners

El Niño is a global weather phenomenon caused by shifting patterns of sea surface temperatures in the Pacific Ocean. During an El Niño year, an enormous pool of warm water that normally resides in the western waters of the Pacific drifts toward South America. This movement weakens the prevailing east-west tradewinds, heating the ocean surface and upsetting the world's normal weather patterns. Some geographical areas that are normally dry experience floods, while others accustomed to rains suffer from drought. In Southern California El Niño means strong winds, heavy rains, and storms resulting from what is called the "Pineapple Express" crossing the Pacific from Hawaii, instead of, as is normal, storms wheeling down from the Gulf of Alaska.

For gardeners El Niño means that their plants can be damaged by soil erosion on slopes and by flooding in low-lying areas. Plant roots can drown in waterlogged soils when their roots are deprived of oxygen. Wet soils also increase the incidence of water molds that kill plant roots. When an El Niño is predicted, take steps to protect plants from excess moisture. Make sure your garden has good surface drainage. Design the landscape so surface water flows from the highest parts of the property to an outlet such as the street or a drainage ditch. Check runoff from slopes, roofs, and patios to make sure these do not flood plants. If water stands in a particular area after rain, take action to improve the drainage. Remove obstructions stopping the flow of surface water or install a catch basin feeding into a drainpipe with an outlet at a lower elevation. If water stands in irrigation basins for several hours, remove some earth so the water can flow out.

Not all native plants are drought resistant. Some are native to streambeds and need lots of water. Other native plants are so well adapted to our wet winters and dry summers that they can accept no summer water at all. Still others are more adaptable to garden conditions. They can take water in summer if it's given to them but will survive without it if necessary. Many drought-resistant plants from other parts of the world mix well with California natives. Perry's *Trees and Shrubs for Dry California Landscapes* and *Landscape Shrubs for Western Regions* are excellent books on the subject.

Among the hundreds of fine native plants that are well adapted to landscape use are California tree mallow *(Lavatera assurgentiflora)*, Catalina cherry *(Prunus lyonii)*, Cleveland sage *(Salvia clevelandii)*, lemonade berry *(Rhus integrifolia)*, monkeyflower *(Mimulus hybridus)*, with many lovely new hybrids available, St. Catherine's lace *(Eriogonum giganteum)*, sugar

Quick Tip

Pine Needles Are Precious. *When you rake fine-textured pine needles from a driveway, don't throw them away. Save them to mulch acid-loving plants, such as camellias, azaleas, and blueberries, or to cover informal, woodland, or vegetable-garden paths.*

bush *(R. ovata)*, Torrey pine *(Pinus torreyana)*, toyon (California holly; *Heteromeles arbutifolia)*, and western redbud *(Cercis occidentalis)*. Two outstanding native ground covers are trailing manzanita *(Arctostaphylos* 'Emerald Carpet')*, which prefers shade inland, and evergreen currant *(Ribes viburnifolium)*, a plant from Catalina Island that thrives in shade in all zones. Also don't overlook California lilac *(Ceanothus)*, which has many fine species and named varieties to choose from. Select plants for color, growth habit, and adaptability to your soil and climate.

How to Divide and Plant Matilija Poppy

Matilija poppy *(Romneya coulteri)*, one of the loveliest of California natives, has fragrant white flowers like crepe paper with large yellow centers that cover the plant all summer, complementing its handsome gray foliage. At any time of year you can, if you wish, purchase selected varieties already growing in containers from native-plant nurseries (such as those mentioned on page 270). But if you want to propagate a plant already growing in your own garden or a friend's, do the job sometime between now and January, while the plant is in its brief dormancy and just before it begins to grow again. There are two ways to propagate this plant. The first and easiest way is to dig up a whole clump; lift it into a bucket or basket to transport it. Prepare the soil as described below for root cuttings, and plant the clump at the same depth you originally found it. The second method is to take root cuttings. (This method is best if you want to start many of these plants.)

- For root cuttings dig around the parent plant with a trowel; look for roots about pencil-thick in size with small but visible buds on them. (Small pieces work fine; take several cuttings to ensure success.)

- Unless you plan to plant the cuttings immedi-

ately, place them in a plastic bag filled with moist potting soil so they won't dry out. (Take them home this way if you're getting them from a friend.)

- If possible plant in well-drained soil. Loosen it first with a spade, and then plant the roots by placing them horizontally and covering them with an inch of soil.

- If you must plant in hard clay soil, first spade it deeply, adding soil amendment. Then water the ground and let the area settle overnight. The next day spread a 3- or 4-inch-high layer of sand on top of the prepared area. (Use as much sand as you want; two or three bucketfuls are ample for a good start.) Plant the roots 2 inches down in the sand. The roots will grow right between the sand and the clay. (Never mix sand with clay—this makes clay even denser. In this case, you're stacking them to make a raised bed.)

- Keep the soil damp but not soggy until the cuttings sprout and you see growth begin; then water regularly until they're established. Summer water produces longer bloom.

- When the foliage dies back in late fall, cut down the plants to 4 to 6 inches. New growth soon springs again from the roots.

Within your landscape of native plants, why not use native grasses to create a natural California meadow? Include nodding feather grass *(Stipa cernua)*, a historic cool-season grass that grows in clumps 1 to 2 feet tall and wide. For centuries this perennial bunchgrass covered much of California until it was grazed almost to extinction by cattle during the nineteenth century and replaced by the imported annual European grasses that cover our hillsides today. Plant feather grass from seeds or plugs in fall or winter; it needs no summer water once established. Native grasses can also be used to make rustic

lawns in hot inland valleys and for erosion control.

Seeds of California native plants, including wildflowers, can also be planted this month. The seeds of many native plants are difficult to germinate without special treatment prior to planting. In some cases this means subjecting them to fire in an aluminum pie pan beneath a handful of burning pine needles. Methods for germinating seeds of native plants are given in such books as Lenz's *Native Plants for California Gardens.* (Directions for planting wildflowers are given on page 258.)

Special Tips for Planting California Native Plants

- When purchasing a native plant, gently slide it out of its container and check the roots. Don't choose a plant with a lot of top growth and too many roots in the can. (If it has been in a container too long, its roots will have become hard and taken on the shape of the can, and it won't readapt as well to the ground. Choose another one.)

- In clay soil plant on raised terraces or on a slope with a sleeve drain (see page 34).

- Dig a planting hole, fill it with water, and let the water drain out.

- Water the plant in the container prior to planting.

- Carefully remove the plant from the can and gently lower it into the hole. Native plants are fragile; take care not to break the crown or roots.

- Before filling the soil in around the plant, lay a stick across the hole and check how high you have placed the plant. Make sure the top of the root ball will end up 2 inches above the surrounding soil; this is especially important for native plants. Don't bury the crown in soil, or it will rot.

- Backfill the hole with native soil, gently pressing it down around the roots with your hands.

- Build a watering basin. Put a layer of loose mulch over the roots to keep them cool and moist.

- Water deeply. Thereafter water regularly to keep the soil damp but not soggy. During rains open the berm of the watering basin to let water out.

- Once the plant is established, decrease irrigation. Eventually water it only as needed in summer.

Pruning

Prevent Storm Damage. November, with its wind and rain, brings a natural cleanup, but unless you prepare for it, it can often cause damage. Open up spaces in dense trees. Allow the wind to pass through. A full tree with no gaps in it acts like a sail on a mast. A strong wind may capsize it, especially if the ground is wet. Remove dead and weak branches.

Make sure young trees are well staked. Tie them loosely, so they can move back and forth in the wind without being toppled. Trees need to flex in wind in order to develop strong trunks. When using wire for tying, run it through a section of old hose so it doesn't damage bark. Check all staked trees now to make sure no wires are restrictive. Once trees have become well rooted remove the stakes and wires, so bark doesn't grow over them.

Prune Acacias. Cut back top-heavy shrubs, such as acacia. Where necessary remove whole branches to allow wind to pass through. Head back young acacias to force branching and strengthen their trunks. With proper pruning these fast-growing, brittle but beautiful shrubs and small trees, often listed as short lived, can be kept going almost indefinitely.

Prune Cane Berry Plants. Prune selected cane berry plants, including blackberry, boysenberry, loganberry, and spring-bearing raspberry. Cut the old canes down to the ground, leaving the new ones that grew this year. On fall-bearing raspberry plants (which grow well only in the mountains) cut off the top of the cane that has borne fruit. Leave the bottom of the cane to fruit in spring.

Don't prune the canes of subtropical (low-chill) raspberries, like 'Bababerry', 'Fallgold',

How to Force Narcissus Bulbs in a Basket for Holiday Bloom

- Purchase plump premium bulbs of Chinese sacred lilies, 'Cragford', 'Geranium', 'Grand Soleil d'Or', or paper whites.

- Choose a suitable flat basket—one approximately 6 to 9 inches in diameter and 3 to 4 inches high. Leave it plain or spray it with quick-drying paint.

- Line the basket with a circle of heavy-gauge (4-millimeter) plastic sheeting cut to fit.

- Fill the basket halfway to the top with clean pebbles or gravel. Add six or eight bulbs, fitting them closely together. Fill in with more pebbles to hold them upright.

- Cover the pebbles with sphagnum moss. (This is optional for a pleasing appearance.)

- Add water to the rim of the plastic. Add more every two or three days.

- Cover the basket with an upside-down cardboard box. Place it in a cool spot, such as the garage, for one and a half weeks or until sprouts are up 3 or 4 inches.

- Uncover the basket and place it in a sunny window or in the sun on your patio or porch until the flowers open. Direct sun keeps the stems from growing too long and floppy, but if you put the basket outside bring it in at night for warmth. Turn it daily for even growth.

- Enjoy the fragrant flowers in the house during Christmas or Hanukkah, or make these baskets for gifts. If you plant six weeks before Christmas, a few flowers will open that day. Allow six and a half weeks for fully open flowers.

- Discard the bulbs after flowers fade. Bulbs forced in water can't be reused.

'Oregon 1030' (also called 'California'), and 'Rosanna'. These are the only kind of raspberries to grow in most Southern California climate zones, and all of them produce their best berries on new wood. Wait until December or January; then prune these by cutting them nearly to the ground. Dig up the suckers (sprouts coming up near the old plants) to make new rows (see page 298).

Shrubs and Young Trees

Now through January is the best time to move shrubs and young trees that are growing in the wrong places. For evergreen shrubs and trees dig a deep trench around each one. Then cut through the earth under the root ball, saving as many of the roots as possible. (You may unavoidably have to slice through some.) Ball the roots in burlap or chicken wire before lifting

 Quick Tip

Plant Double for Twice the Show. *Plant a layer of daffodils 8 inches deep. Half-cover them with potting soil. Fit a second layer of bulbs into the spaces between the tips of the lower layer. Cover these with soil mix. The upper layer will bloom first, then the lower.*

them from the hole. Once the plant is in its new hole, remove the chicken wire; but if you have gophers it may help to leave it in place and let the roots grow through it. Burlap may be either removed or opened up and left in the hole to rot, as desired. After transplanting, stimulate root growth by soaking the ground with a product containing humic acid, such as Roots or Grow More Humic Acid, diluted according to package directions.

Transplant deciduous plants after the leaves fall and the plant has gone completely dormant.

Then dig up as large a root system as possible, knock off all soil, and replant as for bare-roots, by holding the plant so its soil line is even with the surrounding ground and sifting the soil in with a trowel. Prune the top, to balance it with the loss of roots.

Ground Covers

November is the traditional month for planting carpetlike ground covers. Many gardeners find the term "ground cover" confusing. All plants that cover and hide bare ground are customarily lumped together under this general term. Many vines, shrubs, perennials, wildflowers, bulbs, and herbs are used for this purpose; often they're among the best choices for a particular task, but in most cases this is not the right time to plant them. Here we're discussing only those low-lying creepy-crawly things generally sold in flats and used to replace lawns. Some can be walked on; others cannot. These true ground covers are among the most important plants in the landscape and the most difficult to choose.

Some nurseries carry a wide assortment of ground covers. Before making a final choice, consider the site, the conditions, and your requirements. See displays in botanical gardens, such as the Los Angeles Arboretum. Also study lists in the *Sunset Western Garden Book* and pictures in Mathias's *Flowering Plants in the Landscape* and Sunset's *Lawns: How to Plant and Care for a Healthy Carpet of Green.*

Colorful iceplants, gazanias, pelargoniums, trailing African daisy *(Osteospermum fruticosum),* cape weed *(Arctotheca calendula),* pork and beans *(Sedum rubrotinctum),* and lippia are among many fine choices, of varying drought resistance, for full sun. Beware of red apple iceplant *(Aptenia cordifolia* 'Red Apple'); it needs a lot of water and frequent fertilizing with a high-nitrogen fertilizer, like calcium nitrate, to look good. It's fine for quickly covering and holding a bank but builds up thickly and needs replacement in about six years.

For shady spots fine-textured needlepoint ivy *(Hedera helix* 'Needlepoint'), Indian mock strawberry *(Duchesnea indica),* carpet bugle *(Ajuga reptans),* and star jasmine *(Trachelospermum jasminoides)* are among possible choices. (Some of these can also grow in sun if well watered.) For small spaces and between stepping stones blue star creeper *(Laurentia fluviatilis),* common thrift *(Armeria maritima),* creeping thyme, Irish and Scotch moss (in coastal zones only), and—in moist shade—baby's tears *(Soleirolia soleirolii)* are possible choices. Sprenger asparagus *(Asparagus densiflorus* 'Sprengeri') is drought resistant. It's sold in cans—not flats—and it's highly invasive, but it's useful nonetheless for holding steep shady slopes.

On large slopes in full sun it's always better to combine shallow-rooted ground covers with taller, deeper-rooting plants, such as prostrate acacia *(Acacia redolens* 'Prostrata'), bougainvillea, Cape plumbago *(Plumbago auriculata),* and lantana. A combination of these four plants can provide a permanent bank cover with stunning color year-round. (Wait until next spring to plant all except acacia. It's too late to put in tropicals and subtropicals now except in the mildest zones, and then only during warm years.)

Bulbs

You don't have to wait any longer to put in anemones, daffodils *(Narcissus),* Dutch irises, grape hyacinths, and ranunculus. It's a fine time for planting these and all other spring-flowering bulbs you haven't yet planted, except tulips, hyacinths, and crocuses. Put the last three in brown paper bags and chill them in the refrigerator for six

How to Plant a Pot of Daffodils

This is simply a method for growing daffodils in containers so you can enjoy them on your patio or porch at their natural time for blooming. You're not forcing the bulbs, so you can keep them if you wish; they may flower again next year. (Each cultivar will bloom according to its built-in time schedule and your climate zone. The popular trumpet daffodil 'King Alfred' usually blooms here in February or March.)

- Buy the largest bulbs you can find. Leave double- and triple-nosed bulbs whole. They'll produce a flower from each point.

- Choose a container of appropriate size. (Five to six bulbs will fit in a 12-inch pot, more if you crowd them.)

- Cover the drainage hole in the bottom of your pot with a piece of broken crockery or plastic fly screen.

- Place a layer of fast-draining potting soil in the bottom of the container. Add a handful or two of bone meal. Cover this with more soil.

- Add the bulbs. Jamming them in as close as possible won't impair their growth, but it's wiser to leave a little space around each one so they don't touch each other or the sides of the container. That way if one rots you won't lose them all.

- Cover the bulbs with potting soil. When you've finished, the top of the soil should be 2 inches lower than the edge of the pot and the tips of the bulbs should be just below or even with the surface of the soil.

- Water the pot, and add more potting soil, if necessary.

- Place the pot in a cool, shady place, near a hose bib for convenience. Cover it with an upside-down cardboard box to keep it dark.

- Water the pot daily. When rain falls, uncover the pot and let nature do your watering; then re-cover it when rain ceases.

- Once the leaves are up 3 or 4 inches, remove the cover for good. Move the pot into bright light; put it in "skyshine" (under the open sky but not in full sun). Keep it there, or in cool semishade, until you see the first flower buds.

- Once buds appear, move the pot into full or half-day sun. The flowers will face the sun, so put them where you can see their smiling faces. Once they open, they'll last longer in partial shade.

- After the flowers fade, clip them off. You can then either dump the bulbs out of the pot and discard them or plant them in the ground; leave the roots and bulbs all together as a clump and keep them damp. Sometimes the leaves will stay green for several months; don't cut them off until after they go brown.

to eight weeks prior to planting time in late December or early January. Make sure they don't freeze, and mark the bags so you know what's in them. Species tulips (wild tulips) *Tulipa bakeri* 'Lilac Wonder', *T. clusiana* (lady tulip), *T. saxatilis,* and *T. sylvestris* do not need chilling. Plant them right away in pots or the ground. Choose spots up front in the border or by paths; they aren't tall, but they are charming and will come back year after year.

Bulbs look best planted in natural drifts rather than rows. Prepare the soil, toss the bulbs on the ground, and plant them where they fall. Consult a bulb chart for proper planting depths. Put a little bone meal under every bulb you plant in the ground, and cover it with an inch or two of soil before adding the bulb. You can also plant bulbs in containers. Daffodils of all types are especially good candidates for container planting. (For instructions, see the accompanying boxes.)

What Is a Daffodil? If you're confused by the names "narcissus," "daffodil," and "jonquil," you're not alone. Even longtime gardeners muddle these terms, but the solution is quite easy. The words "narcissus" and "daffodil" have exactly the same meaning, but *Narcissus* is the botanical name for a whole genus of bulbs encompassing more than twenty-six species and innumerable cultivars. Daffodil is the common name for all of them. (Tazetta and Tazetta hybrids, however, are seldom called "daffodils" in actual practice. Gardeners and bulb catalogs alike usually refer to these only by the botanical name *Narcissus,* though without italics.) Jonquil is the name of one small group of narcissus that bear a cluster of little blooms on a single stem, bloom late, and are usually yellow and fragrant. Jonquils are very hardy, and they're more common in the East and Middle West than here.

Begin Forcing Tazetta Narcissus. Tazetta and Tazetta hybrid narcissus, including 'Cheerfulness', Chinese sacred lilies, 'Geranium', 'Grand Soleil d'Or', paper whites, and others, have bunches of tiny fragrant flowers on each stem. They can be planted outdoors here as early as September, and they bloom in fall and winter; some of these may be already in bloom now. You can also begin now to force, in pebbles and water, the Tazetta and Tazetta hybrid bulbs you've set aside for this purpose. By the method described in the box on narcissus on page 274 you can make them bloom in six weeks and schedule them to bloom just when you want them to do so. This method of forcing bulbs is also used for indoor bloom in cold-winter climates.

Gardeners in cold-winter climates also force many bulbs by another method; they subject the bulbs to a certain period of winter chill outdoors in buried pots. They then bring the bulbs indoors and place them in a sunny window to force bloom in the dead of winter, months ahead of the bulbs' natural schedule. Here, there's no point in forcing bulbs in this manner and it's not even possible, so ignore the sections pertaining to this process that you find in most bulb books; they don't apply here. (All bulbs that have been forced, regardless of the method used, must be thrown out after the blooms fade. They'll never bloom again.)

Quick Tip

How to Make Small Holes for Small Bulbs. *When planting just a few small-size bulbs, such as ranunculus, anemones, sparaxis, and oxalis, dig individual holes with a melon scoop.*

Annual and Perennial Flowers

There's still time to plant spring flowers. November planting is not quite as good as October, but it's a thousand times better than waiting until spring, seeing everything in bloom and regretting that you didn't plant in fall. First-time gardeners often fall in love with annual spring flowers when they see them blooming in April, then buy them and plant them at great expense. But instead of six months of bloom from December through May they get a month or two, at the most, and decide they have purple thumbs. Not so; it's just their timing that's wrong. Remember this all-important **Rule of Thumb:** *For colorful spring flowerbeds, the time to plant is fall.*

Plant Cool-Season Annual Flowers. Annuals and perennials used as annuals that can now be put in from pony packs and color packs include calendula, cineraria, columbine, coral bells,

How to Plant Ranunculus

Ranunculus provides longer-lasting color than any other spring-flowering bulb. Each large-size tuberous root will give as many as fifty to seventy-five blooms.

- Choose a good strain, such as Tecolote Giants. Plant in mid-November.

- Choose a spot in full sun where ranunculus hasn't grown for three or four years. (If sprinklers keep the bed soggy, presprout the tubers in flats of damp sand; as soon as they've grown some roots, plant them in the bed.)

- Cultivate the soil deeply, adding organic soil amendment, bone meal, and flower fertilizer according to package directions. Water the bed and let it settle overnight.

- Toss the tubers in drifts onto the bed. Rearrange them slightly so they're approximately 6 inches apart.

- Plant each tuber where it fell, making sure the points face down. Cover them with 1½ inches of soil in heavy ground or 2 inches in light, sandy soil.

- Soak the bed deeply. Except in dry, sandy soil or very dry weather, don't water again until green growth shows. Then, if rains are mere sprinkles, water often enough to keep the soil moist but not soggy. The tubers can rot if they're soaked prior to planting or if they're planted in soil that stays soggy wet. (See note above about presprouting.)

- Protect the sprouts from birds with wire or plastic garden netting until they're up 4 inches.

cyclamen, delphinium, dianthus, English daisy, evergreen candytuft, foxglove, flowering cabbage and flowering kale, hollyhock (for summer bloom), Iceland poppy, johnny-jump-up, nemesia, pansy, paludosum daisy (*Chrysanthemum paludosum*), phlox, primroses (polyanthus, malacoides [fairy], obconica, and others), schizanthus, snapdragon, stock, sweet alyssum, sweet William, and viola. Get them into well-prepared ground, feed them often with a product high in nitrogen as well as phosphorus and potassium, and, when rains aren't adequate, water them deeply. Even planting now you'll have a gorgeous display beginning for sure in February—maybe sooner—that will peak in April and last until June.

Plant Nasturtiums and Wildflowers from Seeds. If you regret you didn't plant from seeds earlier, you can still plant some types now. In fact, this is the best month to plant nasturtiums.

Nasturtiums will grow and come back year after year if thrown, yes, simply tossed, onto a north-facing hillside—that is, they will if the hillside is just right, damp enough and earthy enough for them to take hold. But this fact shouldn't be taken to imply that this is the correct way to plant nasturtiums. Both wildflowers and nasturtiums do much better if you prepare the ground, dig deeply, add soil amendment (no fertilizer), cover the seeds according to package directions (rake wildflowers in lightly), and protect them from birds.

Wildflowers to plant from seeds now include baby blue eyes (*Nemophila menziesii*), California poppy, Chinese houses (*Collinsia heterophylla*), clarkia, larkspur (it blooms in June), linaria, southwestern species of lupine (see the accompanying tips for success), scarlet flax (*Linum grandiflorum* 'Rubrum'), sweet alyssum, and mixed packages of western and southwestern wildflowers.

Plant wildflowers in full sun. Keep the seedbed damp by sprinkling it by hand every day, or twice a day if it's dry and windy. Be patient. At November's cooler temperatures it's going to take a little longer for the seed to germinate; don't let the bed dry out or all is lost. (See page 258 for more on growing wildflowers.)

Feed Flowers Planted Earlier. If you've already planted flowerbeds with wildflowers and other cool-season annuals and perennials, they should be spreading out and growing now. A few may start to bloom. Protect them from snails, bait for cutworms, and water when rains aren't adequate. Plants put into the ground when small build better roots in the ground. Iceland poppies, for example, bloom better and longer when planted early from tiny plants instead of later from more expensive 4-inch containers.

Don't forget that it's a race between you and the weather to get such winter-blooming plants as Iceland poppies, cyclamen, primroses, and pansies to bloom before Christmas; feed them for both growth and bloom. The trick with winter-blooming annuals is to fertilize them often, because nitrogen is less active in cool soil. You can use granulated or pellet-type flower fertilizer if you wish. Just toss it on the bed once every month or six weeks and water it in. But cool-season flowers respond best when fertilized every two weeks with a liquid product high in growth as well as bloom ingredients. (Liquid or slow release is always best for plants in pots.)

Continue to feed cineraria with a high-nitrogen product for growth, such as Terr-O-Vite. Don't fertilize wildflowers at all—they don't need it unless you've grown them for several years in a patch of poor soil and you notice yellow leaves and an obvious decline in vigor. In that case, only fertilize after they're up and growing with

---

Tips for Success with Lupines

- Choose a western variety, such as arroyo lupine *(Lupinus succulentus).*

- Scarify the seed (see page 155). For a quick start also presprout the seed indoors, as for corn and beans (page 139).

- Prepare ground that's in full sun for planting wildflowers (see page 258).

- Plant the seeds 4 to 6 inches apart. Cover them with ¼- to ⅛-inch potting soil.

- Thin the plants to 6 inches apart when they're 2 or 3 inches tall. Bait for cutworms, and use BT against caterpillars.

---

a light application of granulated 6-10-5 flower food. Spraying the ground with Roots can also help a sluggish stand of wildflowers take off and grow. In ordinary circumstances, fertilizer makes wildflowers grow too much at the expense of bloom. Most western wildflowers are more drought resistant than other garden flowers. They can often survive on natural rainfall, but keep an eye on them and water when rains aren't adequate to keep them growing.

Plant Flowering Cabbage and Flowering Kale for Winter Color. Flowering cabbage and flowering kale are two similar plants that are not only decorative but also edible. They can be cooked, though the result won't win a prize for taste. A better culinary use is as a colorful raw garnish under salad greens and with such edible flowers as violas and daylilies. Grow the plants in full sun as winter bedding plants, flowerbed edgings, unusual additions to hanging baskets, or ornamental touches in your vegetable garden. They do well in large containers and mix well with other flowers. Flowering kale and flowering cabbage are among the best plants for winter color in the cold low-lying valleys that regularly get winter frost. Frost, far from fazing them, improves them by making their colors more brilliant.

Don't feed flowering kale or flowering cabbage for bloom; this stimulates bolting. Frequent applications of a light-nitrogen fertilizer, such as fish emulsion, produce the best results. Protect the plants from cabbage worms with BT.

Continue to Plant, Divide, and Deadhead Perennials. Several perennials continue to bloom throughout October. *Hypoestes aristata* 'Lavender Cloud' is at its best now. This plant makes a very pleasant looking green shrub for most of the year and then bursts into its full glory in November, just when we're happy to have a splash of color in the garden and to use the long salvia-like sprays in flower arrangements. Look for plants now at specialty nurseries or ask friends for seedlings. This plant is amazingly drought resistant and trouble-free, and it seeds itself around the garden. Cut back *Tagetes lemmonii* and other late bloomers, like tall rudbeckias, to good basal growth after flowers fade. You can deadhead and clean up Mexican sage (*Salvia leucantha*), but don't cut this one back too far—it may die during the winter rains; wait until spring. Lift and divide summer phlox (*Phlox paniculata*). This phlox does well inland and even thrives in full sun as long as the roots are mulched. The stalks may reach 5 or even 6 feet tall. Cut down any of these that may remain and divide the plants every few years, throwing away the centers and replanting the young shoots growing from the outside of the clump. Continue to deadhead bulbine; it blooms almost year-round along the coast. Cut off faded flowers from coreopsis and any wooden stalks sticking above the clump. Remove faded flowers from *Sedum spectabile*. Continue to watch orna-

mental grasses for new growth springing from the ground when rains begin. When you see it, cut off the faded foliage and blooms down to the new growth. (With evergreen types deadhead only. See page 239 for more information and cautions on cutting back ornamental grasses.)

Cut off dead bloom stalks down into the basal leaves of asters, Jerusalem sage (*Phlomis*), kangaroo paws (*Anigozanthus*), lavender, lion's tail (*Leonotis leonurus*), pincushion plants (*Scabiosa*), sea lavender (*Limonium perezii*), and Shasta daisies. Clean up ornamental grasses by removing fistfuls of dead leaves and unsightly flower stalks. Clean up parts that have died out of lamb's ears (*Stachys byzantina*) and Jerusalem sage (*Phlomis*). Mulch the bare ground. Cut back *Helichrysum* 'Limelight' and others to control their spreading growth. Make the cuts to an adjoining branch so that the plant does not look as though it has been pruned.

Chrysanthemums

Cut back chrysanthemums (*Dendranthema grandiflorum*) growing in the ground after bloom, leaving 6- to 8-inch stalks. New growth will spring from these stalks. In March take fresh cuttings from them, dig up and discard the old roots, and start over with the new plants.

After cutting the plants back, clean up the ground and discard dead leaves. Chrysanthemums are notorious disease carriers, so don't add their remains to the compost pile. When cutting back potted chrysanthemums after their blooms fade, never cut them back to short, bare stubs. Just take off the flowers and cut back the stalks lightly. They need their leaves to survive. When fresh growth begins, cut off the old leaves and stalks above the new growth.

Roses

In most climate zones roses will continue to grow and to flower throughout November and December. In fact, if you've taken good care of your plants, November's blooms are often the best of the entire year. The flowers are rendered all the more pleasing by the lack of care roses need at this time of year. You can, if you wish, continue to pick and deadhead roses this month, but there's no need to spray them. Don't fertilize them now, and water them only until mid-month and then only if rains aren't adequate. Calculated neglect now encourages roses to slow down and get ready to drop their leaves and go dormant in December or January.

Citrus, Avocado, and Macadamia Trees

Wrap the trunks of young citrus, avocado, and macadamia trees with an insulating material of some kind, such as fiberglass, wood pulp, corrugated paper, or Gardener Protective Tree Wrap, by mid-November, to protect them from frost damage. Thoroughly cover the trunk, from the soil line to the main scaffold branches. Tie or tape the material in place. Once the trees are two or three years old and have grown a good head of branches with a rooflike covering of leaves they usually don't need this protection.

Don't let the roots of young citrus, avocados, and macadamias—or mature trees either, for that matter—go dry in cold or frosty weather. Wilted leaves are more susceptible to frost damage.

Control of Peach Leaf Curl

Spray peach and nectarine trees against peach leaf curl, an airborne fungal disease that impairs fruiting and can eventually kill a tree. This disease thickens and stunts new shoots, and it puckers, thickens, and curls fresh leaves from the time they first emerge in spring. Affected leaves are red or orange when they first emerge, and later they turn pale green or yellow. Later still, a grayish white powder appears on them, and finally the leaves drop prematurely from the tree. Affected trees bear poorly, and the fruit that survives is usually deformed by wrinkles, raised areas, and irregular lesions. Be sure to spray all your peach and nectarine trees—even dwarf ones growing in containers—against this dread disease, even if they've never shown symptoms. Because peach leaf curl is caused by an airborne fungus it's carried everywhere, though it's at its worst in wet years. Virtually all unsprayed peaches and nectarines fall prey to it eventually, and once the leaves have emerged there's no cure for the problem.

Before spraying your peach and nectarine trees, clean them up by removing any loose leaves or mummified fruits and by raking up and destroying all debris in, under, and around each tree. Spray the entire tree, carefully going over the trunk, the branches, and the twigs; also lightly spray the ground under the tree. Spray twice during winter while the trees are dormant, once as soon as the leaves have fallen and again before the buds swell in spring. (The exact timing will differ according to your climate zone, but usually you'll need to apply the first treatment sometime between mid-November and mid-December and the second in late January or early February.)

For your first spray treatment (now in November or in early December), use lime sulfur or, better yet, Ortho Multi-Purpose Fungicide, which contains the fungicide Daconil. Daconil controls peach leaf curl and also shot hole fungus (*coryneum blight*). Lime sulfur (calcium polysulfide) controls peach leaf curl but not shot hole fungus. You can, however, mix lime-sulfur

How to Grow Strawberries

You can, if you wish, grow strawberries on flat ground, in a raised bed edged with wood, or on raised vegetable rows between furrows; you can water them individually by hand, with overhead sprinklers, or by flooding the furrows. If you want to plant and water in any of these ways, follow the instructions below only insofar as they pertain to your particulars. But the mound method watered by a drip system, as described here, produces berries most successfully and with the least work in the long run.

- Plant a prechilled, locally adapted variety between November 1 and 10. (If you chilled your own plants, get them in the ground no later than November 5; you'll have fruit in one and a half months.)

- Provide deeply spaded, rich, slightly acid, preferably sandy soil with a high proportion of organic matter.

- Construct mounds 6 to 8 inches high and 2½ to 3 feet wide, flat on top and with slightly sloping sides. Leave 18 inches between the mounds.

- Fertilize by mixing into the top 6 inches of soil a complete time-release fertilizer, such as Osmocote 15-15-15, according to package directions. Fertilize again in spring and then once more in summer.

- Set the plants in alternate positions 12 inches apart, in two rows that are 13 to 14 inches apart on top of the mound.

- For each plant make a crevice with a trowel, fan out the roots, and close up the hole so that the middle of the crown is even with the soil line. (If you plant it too deeply the crown will rot, but if you plant it too shallowly the top roots will dry out.)

- Install two drip lines of a type like Drip-In that is designed for watering row crops, one drip line for each row of plants. Arrange the drip lines on top of the ground so that the crowns of the plants will be dry and the roots moist.

- Water lightly every day for a week, or until the plants are established. After that water once a week when it doesn't rain.

- In mid-January cover the entire bed with clear plastic mulch. Carefully cut an X or a round hole 4 inches in diameter directly over each plant. Gently slip the plants up through the holes. Cut the plastic to fit the bed, and bury the bottom edges in soil to prevent it from blowing away.

- Harvest berries daily as they ripen. Cut runners off as they occur.

- Bait for sowbugs, slugs, and snails. Protect the plants from birds with netting.

- After fruiting stops, let runners grow and remove the plastic to allow them to root in the ground. Then dig up the runners, bare their roots, and prechill them (as described on page 264). Replant them in the same bed for three years; then choose another spot.

sprays with Volck Oil to simultaneously control overwintering pests. You must not mix Daconil with Volck Oil. So, if you use Ortho Multi-Purpose Fungicide (Daconil 2787) now, you should spray again in January with a lime-sulfur spray, such as Ortho Dormant Disease Control, and mix it with Volck Oil to control peach leaf curl and also smother overwintering pests.

(Some gardeners spray their trees three times—in November, December, and January—and that's even better.)

When you purchase fungicides, read the labels. Lime sulfur and Daconil can be used against other diseases and on plants in addition to those discussed here. Some lime-sulfur products contain only 10 percent lime sulfur; Ortho Dormant Disease Control Lime-Sulfur Spray contains 27 percent and works better. While you're about it, don't forget to use dormant spray on all your other deciduous fruit and nut trees and your roses, too, after you've pruned them. Follow package directions exactly. (For more information on dormant spraying, see pages 47, 69, and 297.)

Lawn Care

Cool-Season Lawns. There's still time, if you didn't do the jobs last month, to plant cool-season lawns (page 262); to overseed Bermuda with annual ryegrass (don't wait any longer; it has a short growing season, described on page 260); to dethatch cool-season lawns that need it; and to get rid of crabgrass (page 221). Continue to feed all cool-season grasses regularly—once a month, every six weeks, or less frequently according to the product you buy. This is their best growing season. Water them when rains aren't adequate. Mow these grasses short—to 1½ inches.

Warm-Season Lawns. Warm-season lawns are beginning winter dormancy. Stop fertilizing and mowing them when their growth slows. Renovate kikuyu—cut it right down to the ground—if you didn't do this job last month.

Gopher Traps. Mankind's war with gophers is probably as ancient in these parts as the history of agriculture. Almost anywhere in Southern California where you grow a garden—unless it's protected by a natural barrier of underground rock—gophers will move in, push up disfiguring mounds of earth, and help themselves to the roots of your plants. For example, one local gardener who planted a new lawn woke up one morning to discover an army of gophers had invaded overnight and ruined the lawn. He tried

various methods of attack, including flooding, poison bait, toxic gas, and metal traps; he even bought a cat. (His dog killed several gophers, too, but did more damage digging up the lawn than the gophers had done.) This gardener finally conquered the gophers when he discovered the Blackhole, a trap made by FBN Plastics in Tulare, California.

The Blackhole trap is smaller than box-type traps, and though it's slightly more expensive than they are it's easier to use. It's shaped like a tube and contains a lethal wire snare that kills the gopher instantly. You dig down and fit it into the gopher's run. Your victim comes charging along its tunnel, sees light ahead, and runs right into the trap; that's when his light goes out. The Blackhole trap is available at many local nurseries.

Vegetable Gardening

Continue to plant beets, carrots, kale, kohlrabi, lettuce, mesclun, mustard greens, radishes, spinach, and turnips from seeds to keep fresh crops coming along. If you're late in planting vegetables, there's still time to put in transplants of broccoli, Brussels sprouts, cabbage, cauliflower, celery, parsley, and Swiss chard, as well as seeds of fava beans, peas, globe onions, and parsley (see page 264 for tips on speeding parsley's germination). It's best to plant earlier, but in most climate zones it's still warm enough in November to germinate seeds as long as the weather doesn't turn cold and wet. You'll just have a shorter harvest. Do plant as soon as possible, though. Among plants that are well adapted to November planting, artichoke, strawberries, and rhubarb can be put in bareroot, though I personally don't recommend rhubarb. (Hot summers inland rot the roots, and along the coast there's not enough winter chill to

How to Grow Globe Onions

- Choose a short-day variety, such as 'Granex', 'Grano', or 'Crystal Wax'; plant from seed, and put the seed in the ground between November 1 and November 10.

- Prepare a row of loose, well-drained (preferably sandy) soil with a high content of humus, in full sun.

- Add vegetable fertilizer according to package directions. Water the bed and let it settle overnight.

- Sprinkle the seeds thinly in a wide, shallow row.

- Cover the seeds with ¼-inch potting soil. Pat it down with the palm of your hand.

- Install a drip line down the row, such as Drip-In, that can be used for watering row crops. (This is the easiest way to water onions, but if you wish you can use any other method commonly used for watering vegetables.)

- Sprinkle the bed by hand, to make sure it stays damp, when rains aren't adequate. (Or, if possible, adjust the drip system to water daily until the seeds have germinated.)

- Once the seedlings are up, let the drip system kick in to keep the rows evenly moist throughout the growing season.

- Remove weeds when they're small, and continue to weed regularly. (Because onions have shallow roots, they don't compete well; weeds will stunt their growth.)

- Thin the seedlings in late December or early January. No need to throw out all the thinnings—transplant some to another row.

- Leave the biggest ones in the existing row, spaced 4 to 5 inches apart.

- Give onions frequent light applications of balanced fertilizer throughout their leafy green stage to maintain a steady rate of growth. Stop feeding them in early- to mid-March. (Fertilizing onions with nitrogen after they begin to form a bulb makes them split.) The previously straight plants will suddenly grow fat. Start to pull and eat them in early May. When necks weaken and tops begin to fall over (usually before the end of May), turn off the drip system to let them cure. Dig up the remainder of the bulbs when the tops die.

- Place the onions in a shady, well-ventilated area until they're thoroughly dry. Then store them in a cool place. Mild onions don't keep as well as pungent types, but they will last several months if properly cured and stored.

stimulate the growth of tender, pink stalks. The leaves of all rhubarb plants are highly poisonous, and I have a hunch that the stalks, when they're overly sour and green or brownish in color, contain too much oxalic acid for good health.) Potatoes can still be planted from seed potatoes and scallions from onion sets.

Also plant garlic now. Purchase large globes with good-sized sections in any market or elephant garlic at the nursery or produce market. (It's a different species, and milder, but grown much the same way.) Break up the garlic cloves and plant them individually, with the points fac-

ing up, in fertile soil rich in humus. Plant them in full sun, 4 inches apart and 2 inches beneath the soil surface. Some gardeners have told me that interplanting garlic with cabbage crops reduces problems with cabbage worms and aphids. However, test data, plus my own experience, make me doubt the efficacy of this method. Heavy rains and cold weather usually have more to do with reducing the numbers of aphids and cabbage butterflies, whose larvae do the damage. I recommend BT against cabbage worms and Safer insecticidal soap against aphids. (Both are harmless to humans.)

The Secret Lives of Strawberries and Onions. Strawberries and onions seem at first glance to be an unlikely pair to lump together for discussion, but they share certain characteristics. In order to grow abundant harvests of large, luscious strawberries and premium globe onions, you have to understand some of their innate secrets.

Both are regional crops—that is, varieties of each are designed to be grown in certain geographical areas and not in others. Both have specific temperature requirements that, for best results, require their being planted during an identical and extremely short slice of time— sometime between November 1 and 10—though they require this schedule for somewhat different reasons.

Exhaustive tests by the University of California Agricultural Extension, paid for by strawberry growers, have proved that strawberries planted between November 1 and 10 get winter chill at the precise moment in their growing schedule to trigger fruit production rather than foliage. When planted at the wrong time they'll put out runners but won't produce much, if any, fruit. (Watch any professional strawberry growers near you as a good indication of when to plant.)

Either plant runners from your own garden that you've already prepared as prechilled, bare-root plants (as discussed on page 264) or plant from bare-roots purchased from nurseries now. (See the accompanying box for planting instructions.) As a general rule, don't order strawberries, other than alpine varieties, from catalogs, because they usually don't carry varieties that are adapted to our climate. Strawberries are a highly regional crop—even more so than onions. Just a few hundred miles up the California coast entirely different strawberry varieties are grown, so be sure that you plant a locally adapted variety, such as 'Chandler', 'Douglas', 'Sequoia', 'Tioga', or 'Tufts'.

Onions are photothermoperiodic—that is, they're sensitive to temperature and also to day length. An onion plant is stimulated to stop making leafy growth and to start making a bulb not so much by temperature as by the lengthening of days, as the sun moves north in spring and summer. Each variety will form a bulb only after it has received a certain number of hours of daylight each day for a certain number of days. However, varieties vary greatly in the number of hours of daylight they need. Accordingly, all onions are categorized into long-day (northern), intermediate-day (central), and short-day (southern) varieties.

Long-day varieties, grown in northern states and in Canada, need fourteen to fifteen hours of daylight to make a bulb. Northern European and Alaskan varieties need sixteen hours or more. No long-day varieties can possibly receive enough hours of daylight in Southern California to make a bulb. If you plant them your crop will always fail, and yet you can often find seeds of long-day onions on local seed racks, and almost all onion sets are of long-day types. These sets can be used only for growing scallions (green onions). Here, in order to get the best globe onions, we must plant seeds of short-day (southern) varieties in fall or, alternatively, plant intermediate varieties in late winter.

Also, once an onion has reached a certain critical size, which differs by variety, temperatures of between 40° and 50°F will make it go to seed prematurely, or bolt. The way to grow good bulb onions here and avoid bolting is to follow this **Rule of Thumb:** *Plant globe onions only from seeds, never from sets (small bulbs). Plant only such "short-day" (southern) varieties as 'Grano', 'Granex', and 'Crystal Wax'; and put the seeds in the ground between the first and*

285

tenth of November or plant these varieties bare root in January).

'Grano', 'Granex', and 'Crystal Wax' are sweet, mild flavored, and juicy like 'Vidalia' and 'Maui' onions. Eat them raw in sandwiches and salads. Nothing better. 'Crystal Wax' also makes good pickling onions when closely planted. Neither 'Crystal Wax' nor 'Grano' keeps well; on this score 'Granex' is a little better. Seeds of intermediate day-length onions, including 'San Felipe' and 'Pronto S', will also produce a bulb if you plant them in February; they'll ripen in summer. Onion seeds sprout extremely easily; there's no problem involved. I've often planted onions on the same day I took off for a two- or three-week vacation, and left them with an auto-matic drip system as a baby-sitter; when I came home my onions were always up and growing. (See the accompanying box for instructions.)

By all means plant a row of onion sets now, if you want them only for scallions. For best flavor pick scallions when they're young, and plant successive crops. If you leave them in the ground too long you may eventually get a large onion, but it will be green through the middle, and it will have a thick stalk on top that won't dry out properly, so your onions will rot. Some gardeners think the way to cure thick stalks is to knock the tops over in spring when the globes are full grown, but tests have shown this practice to have no influence whatsoever on the proper ripening of onions.

Purchase/Plant

❏ Continue to plant wildflowers, 278

❏ Plant California native plants, 270

❏ Now through January transplant shrubs and young trees that are growing in the wrong places, 274

❏ Plant ground covers, 275

❏ Plant anemones, all kinds of daffodils, Dutch irises, grape hyacinths, ranunculus, and all other spring-flowering bulbs except tulips, hyacinths, and crocuses, 275

❏ Plant daffodils in pots, 276

❏ Plant a basket of narcissus for holiday bloom, 274

❏ Finish filling flowerbeds with cool-season flowers for winter and spring bloom, 277

❏ Plant nasturtiums and continue to plant wildflowers from seeds, including lupines, 278

❏ Plant flowering kale and flowering cabbage, especially in interior zones, 278

❏ Plant cool-season lawns from seeds early this month, 283

❏ Overseed Bermuda with annual ryegrass if desired, 283

❏ Continue to plant winter vegetables, including garlic, 283

❏ Plant bare-root artichokes, 283

❏ Plant bare-root strawberries between November 1 and 10; use the runners you prechilled or purchase plants at a nursery, 285

❏ Also between November 1 and 10 plant globe onions from seeds of short-day varieties, 285

❏ Continue planting perennials, 280

Trim, Prune, Mow, Divide

❏ Prune pine trees and other conifers now through February, 191

❏ Divide and transplant agapanthus, 251

❏ Divide Matilija poppy, 251

❏ Open up spaces in dense trees to allow wind to pass through, 273

❏ Prune acacias, 273

❏ Prune cane berries other than low-chill raspberries, 273

❏ Cut back chrysanthemums after bloom; clean up the ground, 280

❏ Watch red fountain grass (*Pennisetum setaceum* 'Rubrum') for new growth, the sign to cut it back, 259

❏ Continue to divide and deadhead perennials, 280

Fertilize

❏ Fertilize cool-season bedding flowers; don't feed wildflowers, 279

❏ Continue to fertilize cineraria for growth, 279

❏ Don't feed roses this month, 281

❏ Continue to fertilize cool-season lawns; stop fertilizing warm-season lawns when their growth slows, 283

Continued>>

Water

❑ Once rains arrive, stop watering succulents growing in the ground, 195

❑ Water all garden plants less frequently now as weather cools and rains begin, but if rains don't arrive be alert to signs of stress and water as necessary, 269

❑ Install pitcher irrigation, 270

❑ Water bulbs, especially potted ones, 73, 276, 292

❑ Water roses until midmonth, only when rains aren't adequate, 281

❑ Don't let citrus go dry in cold or frosty weather, 281

❑ Water cool-season lawns when rains aren't adequate; stop watering warm-season lawns when they go brown, 283

Control Pests, Diseases, and Weeds

❑ Bait flowerbeds, especially wildflowers, for cutworms and slugs and snails, 91

❑ Spray peach and nectarine trees against peach leaf curl after leaves fall, 281

❑ Trap gophers on lawns and elsewhere in the garden, 283

Also This Month

❑ Use pine needles as mulch, 271

❑ Stake young trees loosely so they can develop strong trunks, 273

❑ Prechill tulips, hyacinths, and crocuses, 275

❑ Begin forcing paper whites, Chinese sacred lilies, and other Tazetta and Tazetta hybrid narcissus in water and pebbles, 277

❑ Wrap the trunks of young citrus and avocado trees with an insulating material to protect them from frost damage, 281

DECEMBER

The Holiday Month

If there's one thing we can say for sure about December weather in Southern California, it's that we can never be sure just what it's going to be. December is supposed to be a winter month, and sometimes it acts like one. Snow blankets the mountains and frost hits all zones. At other times there's a heat wave between Christmas and New Year's that reminds us of August—unless we go to the beach and stick a furtive toe in the icy sea. The weather forecaster is forever informing us that this is the coldest (or hottest) temperature ever recorded for the particular date. And we're inclined to chorus, "What unusual weather we're having!" as if that weren't the most usual thing in the world. So be alert this month: on the one hand protect tender plants from possible frost, but on the other hand continue watering if the weather's hot, dry, and

windy. If you garden in an interior zone, don't be fooled by this month's sunny days. An ice-cold javelin may be hidden behind December's back, ready to strike at night.

If you're too busy to give the garden much attention this month, you're in luck. Most plants will roll along quite happily with only an occasional boost from you. Gardeners who prepared for winter in the fall, when time was easier to come by, can rejoice now because their gardens will cooperate in December by making fewer demands. Plant lovers overwhelmed by the holiday rush can let many jobs slide. But if you're an eager beaver or were an early shopper, you can get the jump on the New Year by tackling a few of January's chores, such as pruning deciduous fruit trees or planting bare-roots. Nurseries stock them beginning this month.

How to Make Poinsettias Last Indoors until March

- Purchase one to three premium plants—healthy specimens of such varieties as 'Eckespoint', 'Pixie', or 'Everlasting Star' (which holds onto its foliage longest).

- Line a large ornamental basket with several layers of plastic cut to fit.

- Pour in a layer of styrofoam packing pellets, to hold the roots above water.

- Arrange the poinsettias in the basket on top of the styrofoam pellets.

- Surround the poinsettias with four to six low-profile green houseplants, such as Chinese evergreens (*Aglaonema modestum*) or 'Dallas' or 'Kimberley Queen' ferns, to add beauty and provide the moist atmosphere that's highly beneficial to poinsettias.

- Place the entire arrangement out of drafts in bright light, such as 18 inches to 2 feet below an electric light source, but away from direct sunlight. This should provide the required temperatures; 70°F in the daytime and 60° to 65°F at night are ideal. Don't subject blooming poinsettias to extremes of temperature—80°F days and 50°F nights will make the leaves and bracts fall off. (So will drafts and over- or underwatering.)

- Water the plants when the surface of the soil feels dry to the touch; then water them enough to make excess water flow out the bottom of the container. Beginning in late December start feeding them occasionally with a weak, balanced fertilizer.

Preparing for Frost

In areas where frost is expected, move tropical and other frost-tender container-grown plants under eaves, under spreading trees, or into shade houses. Don't forget to water them. Plants withstand cold weather much better when provided with adequate moisture. Some tropicals, including species often grown as houseplants and tubbed specimens of plumeria, can be brought indoors for the winter. Keep these in bright light or filtered sun, and let them go somewhat but not totally dry. Plumerias will probably go semidormant and drop their leaves but will come back when you put them outdoors again in spring. (See page 295 for more about frost protection.)

Poinsettias

If you've been subjecting a potted poinsettia to fourteen hours of darkness nightly since October, it should be in full bloom now. Stop fertilizing it for now, and bring it into the house to enjoy. For bloom that lasts several months, give it the light, food, and water described in the accompanying box.

Buy more potted poinsettias early this month if you want them to give as gifts or to decorate your home or entryway. The best plants are usually sold early. Wherever you purchase your plant, be selective. Choose a plant that hasn't already been abused. Exposure to extremes of temperature and over- or underwatering can occur before you get your plant, and these factors can make the green leaves fall off prematurely, a common fault of poinsettias. The colorful bracts should look healthy, not wilted, and the leaves should be green and firmly attached to the stalk. If several have fallen off, that's a bad sign. Also inspect the flowers, the tiny little buttons in the center of the colorful bracts. Make sure they're fresh looking, not brown or mildewed.

When you get your plant home, give it the location, light, and other conditions that will help it last, as described in the box. (One of the worst places to keep a poinsettia is on top of the TV.) If you leave the foil on the pot, don't allow the plant to suffer wet feet—tear holes in the foil so water doesn't collect in it. The best way to water is to put your plant in the kitchen sink, water it thoroughly, and let it drain before putting it back on display.

Cymbidiums

Many cymbidiums start to flower in December, some as early as November. Most bloom between February and May, a few in May and June, and one or two year-round. Choose wisely and you can have these exotic orchids decorating your home, patio, and garden for six months or more.

Protect cymbidiums' bloom spikes from snails. Stake the spikes to avoid breakage, but allow each spray to maintain its natural, arching form. Allow miniatures in hanging baskets to cascade naturally. Continue to feed the plants for bloom (as described on page 231) until buds open. Once they bloom stop feeding the plants, but keep them damp, though not soggy. For longer-lasting flowers move blooming plants into more shade and away from bees. (The flowers "blush" and fade after pollination.)

Once cymbidium spikes have set buds, you can force some into bloom for holiday decoration ahead of their natural schedule. Wait until the buds on the bloom spikes are full size and look fat and ready to open. Then take the plant into the house and place it in bright light. The warmth plus the longer day will open the buds quickly. Continue to enjoy the plant indoors or, for a longer-lasting display, place it outside again.

There's one drawback, however; plants you force into bloom early won't perform as well next year. You'll get a few spikes but not as many. This is also a factor to consider when buying new varieties. Some may have been forced into bloom, and you won't get as many spikes the following year. Wait for the third year, and they'll be loaded.

Sasanqua Camellias and Early-Flowering Azaleas

Choose sasanqua camellias for winter color that will return year after year. They're in bloom now. *Camellia sasanqua* 'Yuletide' is one of the best. Bright red blossoms with yellow centers dot the handsome, small-leafed foliage from November into January. Although sasanqua flowers are usually smaller and not as long lasting as those of *C. japonica,* the plants bloom abundantly and can take more sun, and the flowers are usually immune to blossom blight.

Also look for early- and long-blooming varieties of azalea. A collection of them can provide color fall through spring in frost-free zones. Combine them with camellias on north-facing slopes and the north side of your home. Some varieties to look for include 'Alaska', 'Albert and Elizabeth' (note that it rarely survives in Zone 24), 'Avenir', 'California Peach', 'California Sunset' (inland only—it dies or does poorly in Zone 24), 'Carnival Time' (and other members of the Carnival series), 'Chimes', 'Eric Shame', 'Lucille K.', 'Nuccio's Happy Days', 'Red Wing' (sometimes called 'Red Bird'), 'Rosa Belton', and 'Vervaeneana Alba'.

Roses

Don't fertilize or prune roses this month. Let the flowers stay on the bush, and don't water them. These steps help roses harden off for winter.

Perhaps your garden isn't properly zoned and you have heavy water users like roses growing next to drought-resistant plants such as bougain-villeas. Winter is a good time for moving roses to a better spot. Prepare the new beds now; dig up the roses and move them there next month. Despite the demands of holiday activities, some gardeners also find time this month to prepare the beds for January bare-root planting. To do so, spade the ground deeply and put in plenty of soil amendment. Don't be dismayed if you have clay soil. Roses thrive in it, but be sure to test the drainage, and if it's severely impaired dig in gypsum, install drains, or build raised beds for your roses. For permanent soil improvement, work in the recommended quantity of Profile Professional Soil Conditioner (there's a special type for clay soils).

Study your rose collection with the idea of weeding out poor performers. Why struggle along with a plant that's worn out or simply not right for your climate zone? In the interest of water conservation, it's far better to grow a handful of choice roses than a great many mediocre ones.

If you are going to plant a few roses next month, plan your color scheme now so decisions will be easier later. All too often roses are planted with a shotgun approach; no thought is given to color compatibility. Don't, for instance, put one of the new brilliant oranges next to a bluish red. The best-looking rose gardens are designed like a rainbow, with a progression of harmonious colors flowing from one side to the other. Clashing colors are well separated. For a bigger display, plant at least three roses of one variety together. It's easier to take care of roses when they are growing in a separate rose garden, but roses have far greater charm when grown as companions in mixed flowerbeds. Use climbing roses wherever possible to add vertical accents.

Bulbs

Finish Planting Spring-Blooming Bulbs. If you bought bulbs this fall but didn't plant them when you should have, don't despair; you still have a little time to get them into pots or the ground. The **Rule of Thumb** is: *Finish planting spring-flowering bulbs such as daffodils on or before Christmas Day.* When planted later the flowers will be smaller and fewer. The exceptions are tulips and hyacinths (crocuses too, if you live in an interior zone). They need cold earth, so start planting them between Christmas and New Year's Day, unless there's a heat wave. If that occurs wait until early January; plant before the tenth.

Leave the bulbs in the refrigerator until you're ready to plant. If you choose to plant tulips in pots, keep the planted pots in a cool place and cover them with an upside-down cardboard box to cut out light and encourage the growth of good root systems. Water them often. When the foliage is 2 or 3 inches tall, remove the covering and bring the pots out into the sun. Try to keep the roots from heating up by shading the containers in cool foliage, or by double-potting. Water daily unless rains are adequate.

Tulips do well in half barrels and in the ground to the north of trees or houses. Study the shadow pattern annually, and plant them where the ground is cool and shady in winter and then sunny beginning in February or March. Or plant them in full or morning sun and shade the ground over them with a bulb cover, such as johnny-jump-ups, paludosum daisies (*Chrysanthemum paludosum*), or violas. They respond well to a treatment of light liquid fertilizer, such as bulb food, once at planting time and again when the leaves show.

Hyacinths grow well in the ground, planted 5 inches deep and 6 inches apart, or in shallow pots of fast-draining soil mix, planted just below or at the soil surface. Bury some bone meal under each bulb. (Keep the pots watered, cool, and darkened, as described above for tulips.) Or force them in pebbles and water or a special reusable "hyacinth glass," which keeps the roots immersed in water. Keep these forced ones cool and dark, under an upside-down cardboard box, until the tops are up 3 or 4 inches; then place them in a sunny window or outdoors in sun every day when the weather's warm (bring them in at night.) Turn the ones on window ledges to make their stems grow straight.

Plant crocuses in either low pots or the ground. Because the flowers are low they often show up better in low-level pots. Nestle them among well-placed rocks and a few pebbles to add charm and keep the soil cool.

Lift Dahlias. When dahlias have gone totally dormant, in early December, dig up the tubers. First cut back the tops to 6 or 8 inches; then use a spade to slice down through the soil and loosen it in a circle 12 to 14 inches out from each plant. Finally, use a garden fork to carefully pry up the tuber, which you will find has now grown into a round clump of tubers, all attached to a central stem in the same way the spokes of a wheel are attached to the hub. Shake off the soil, cut the tops back to 2 inches, and lay the whole unseparated clump on newspaper in the sun to dry until evening. Continue the drying process for a day or two in a dry shady place, such as the floor of the garage. Then dust the clumps with bulb dust or sulfur and pack them, not touching each other, in perlite. Store them for the winter in a cool dry area, in hanging baskets lined with newspaper or in boxes.

Divide the clumps in spring when growth begins and you can see the eyes (growth buds) beginning to form; cut each clump into individual sections. Each must have an eye. (Throw out the old center stalk.) Dust the cut portions in sulfur and allow them to callus off overnight. Plant each tuber separately. You may have extras to share with friends.

Prepare Amaryllis to Bloom. Amaryllis *(Hippeastrum)* bulbs are on sale at nurseries now; you can also purchase them from mail-order companies. Many are preplanted and already starting to grow. These are entertaining bulbs to grow for holiday color (they'll bloom for Christmas) and make excellent hostess gifts.

Place a preplanted amaryllis whose growth has begun in a sunny window and turn it daily so the stalk won't bend toward the light. Keep it well watered but not overly wet. If growth has not yet begun, water the plant and keep it cool and dark until growth begins; then move it into a warm, sunny location. A thick scape (stalk) will emerge from the bulb and shoot rapidly upward, often to 15 inches. Sometimes two will appear, each one bearing three or four spectacular blossoms. When the bloom begins to show color, move the plant to a cooler spot, where it will last longer.

After the flowers fade cut them off, but leave the tall scape in place until you can see that the juices have gone back down into the bulb. Then cut it off. This nourishes the bulb. Put the plant outside in semishade for the summer. Feed it occasionally and protect it from snails and slugs. In September lift it from the container and let the root ball dry out. Cut off the leaves when they die. Brush the dry root ball with bulb dust or sulfur, slip it back into the pot, allow it three months of complete dormancy, and then start the process over; this time it will bloom in spring. (Once an amaryllis has been forced to bloom at Christmas you can't repeat the process.)

Quick Tip

A Long-Handled Scoop Keeps Fertilizer Dry.
Most powdered fertilizers contain a plastic measuring scoop. Use household wire to bind it firmly to the end of a thin, 18-inch bamboo plant stake. Use a second stake to scrape off the excess powder when measuring. Wet hands won't touch the scoop, and the fertilizer will stay dry.

If you purchase a bare, unplanted amaryllis bulb now, choose one that has just begun to sprout but has not yet pushed up a flower scape. Plant it in rich, fast-draining soil mix in a small pot—just 4 inches wider than the bulb. Before putting the bulb in the pot, though, place a few tablespoons of bone meal in the soil in the bottom. Cover this with a little plain potting soil. Plant the bulb with its upper half above soil level. Water it and treat it as described above. Repot amaryllis bulbs annually into the next size of container.

Winter Color

Permanent landscape plants that are colorful in winter enliven gardens and make good gifts. Choices include purple princess flower (*Tibouchina urvilleana*), Mexican flame vine (*Senecio confusus*), marmalade bush (*Streptosolen jamesonii*), Carolina jessamine (*Gelsemium sempervirens*, an attractive, evergreen, yellow-flowered vine though unfortunately poisonous), variously hued New Zealand tea trees (*Leptospermum scoparium*), and strawberry tree (*Arbutus unedo*). The last two are among our finest slow-growing, drought-resistant plants that can be grown as shrubs and eventually become small trees. Both develop interestingly shaped trunks. Strawberry tree bears its flowers and colorful fruit now. (The fruit is edible but not flavorful.) There are striking dwarf forms that grow naturally into eye-catching shapes.

Annual and Perennial Flowers

Care for Cool-Season Flowers. If you planted annual flowerbeds in September or October, by now the garden should be full of color. If not, remember that the trick is to get things into bloom before Christmas and they'll bloom all winter. Once cold nights begin, cold-season annual plants slow down and won't bloom until the weather warms up, in February or March. Of course, some plants are naturally programmed to bloom in late winter, spring, or early summer. We don't expect them to bloom ahead of time. But among the flowers you can expect to be colorful prior to Christmas in most zones are calendula, dianthus, flowering cabbage and flowering kale (ornamental members of the cole or cabbage family that are grown for their colorful foliage rather than flowers), Iceland poppy, linaria, nemesia, paludosum daisy, primroses of all kinds, pansy, schizanthus, dwarf stock, sweet alyssum, sweet pea, sweet William, viola, and wallflower (*Erysimum cheiri*). With the exception of linaria and sweet pea, feed these plants regularly to speed them into bloom, with a liquid fertilizer high in nitrogen and bloom ingredients such as 20-20-20.

Linaria and sweet peas can be speeded into bloom with 0-10-10 if desired, but it usually isn't necessary. (Don't give them nitrogen; wildflowers seldom need it, and sweet peas grow at the expense of bloom if given too much of it.)

Dwarf delphiniums ('Dwarf Blue Mirror') and dwarf foxgloves ('Foxy') bloom in fall or early winter shortly after planting. Cut off spikes that have bloomed now, and follow up with fertilizer. Delphiniums will bloom again in spring; dwarf foxglove 'Foxy' will also if it has sprouts that haven't yet flowered. (Tall varieties of delphiniums, foxgloves, and stock also bloom in spring.)

Dwarf snapdragons bloom in fall through winter but are easily decimated by caterpillars and are highly susceptible to rust. (Spray them with a product containing mancozeb or tri-adimefon every five to eighteen days against rust and with BT to control caterpillars. Next year grow taller, rust-resistant varieties, from seeds planted in September or from transplants in October.)

Deal with Frost. What if you planted early but nothing's in bloom? One possible reason is that you live in an interior zone and cold nights have held things back. If this is the case, don't worry: you'll just get flowers a little later. Some gardeners feel that frost is a natural kind of pinching, making their plants stronger and bushier in the long run and keeping things from growing too rank. Trial and error is the best way to find out which plants perform best in your climate zone, under local conditions, and with the care you give your plants.

In very cold low-lying gardens, like those in Zone 20, frosts kill some of the more tender bedding plants such as primroses, pansies, and cineraria. The best bets for winter color under such conditions are hardier plants like flowering cabbage and kale, tall calendulas, snapdragons, and bulbs, particularly paper whites and oxalis. Stock and many wildflowers will survive the cold winter and bloom in spring.

It's important even in coastal zones to protect tender annuals, especially cineraria *(Senecio hybridis)*, from frost. This plant can fool gardeners because it so obviously loves cold weather and grows best and fastest in it, but frost "melts" its

🐚 Quick Tip

How to Attach a Vine to a Smooth Wall or Fence. *To make inexpensive invisible wall hangers for vines, glob dots of clear silicone sealant where needed. Stick the center of a short piece of twist tie into each glob. Allow it to dry overnight. Come back the next day and tie up the vine.*

leaves and turns them black or brown. It actually prefers night temperatures of 45° to 50°F with a daytime increase of no more than five or ten degrees. What place on Earth would provide such a narrow range of temperatures for a wild plant? The explanation is that cineraria is not a wild plant; it's a nonhardy manmade "species" of uncertain ancestry that was developed in the nineteenth century to be grown in cool greenhouses. So when growing cineraria in your garden, cover the beds with a tent of sheets or beach towels, supported on bamboo poles, on nights when frost is expected. Take off the covers first thing in the morning, before the sun hits the bed. (Cineraria is well worth this trouble.) Plants under a tree or overhang usually survive unharmed. Here again, trial-and-error is the best teacher. Continue to feed cineraria with Terr-O-Vite for growth.

Grow Plants in Adequate Light. Another factor inhibiting winter bloom is too much shade. New gardeners are sometimes unaware of how the movement of the sun in winter creates shade to the north of trees and buildings where it didn't exist in summer or fall. (See page 184 for an explanation of the movements of shade.) If you have this problem, wait until the sun comes back in spring; your flowers will then bloom. If you have plants such as malacoides (fairy) or polyanthus primroses that are full grown but just sitting there doing nothing, try feeding them with

0-10-10 or 2-10-10 liquid once a week during December. This can stimulate bloom in areas that are too shady. Once flowers open, switch back to a fertilizer high in both bloom and growth ingredients.

In the future, use these shady areas to plant cyclamen, cineraria, bulbs, azaleas, and obconica primroses, which will bloom in darker shade than other primroses. Under north-facing overhangs clivia and camellias are good choices for winter bloom. If plants in containers aren't blooming, move them into more sun and continue to fertilize them with a product high in both nitrogen and bloom ingredients.

In Coastal Zones Plant Annual Flowers Even Now. It's too late this year to plant annual flowers in most interior zones. But let's say you've just moved into a house in a mild or coastal zone and it has some bare beds that need filling, or you were too busy in fall to tackle the job. You don't have to wait until spring to plant winter and spring flowers. That's the joy of living here. Seeds that can be planted now include African daisy *(Dimorphotheca)*, ageratum, calendula, California poppy, clarkia, coreopsis, forget-me-not, gaillardia, godetia, hollyhock, larkspur, lavatera, nemophila, annual phlox *(Phlox drummondii)*, schizanthus, Shasta daisy, sweet alyssum, and mixed wildflowers. You'll just get later bloom, and some plants, such as larkspur, may not grow quite as large. Follow the planting directions beginning on pages 236 and 255. Plant early in the month, and be sure to plant in full sun. These seeds won't germinate in partial shade, especially now.

Sprinkle the bed faithfully every morning until the seeds come up and then water as necessary. For a faster effect, in full sun put in bedding plants of calendula, candytuft *(Iberis)*, columbine, coral bells, English daisy *(Bellis perennis)*, Iceland poppy, nemesia, pansy, polyanthus primrose, sweet alyssum, sweet William, viola, and wallflower. For semishade use cyclamen as well as malacoides or obconica primrose. Put these in a flowerbed now, and much of the bed should be in bloom before April.

Care for Perennials. Many perennial plants are in total dormancy at this time of year, particularly in interior zones. If your garden is subject to heavy frost, cover the ground over tender plants with mulch. But gardeners who live in valleys or on mesa tops where frost hits also have the advantage of growing a wider range of those plants we so often think of as "eastern" here in California. Now is the time they can get the winter chill they need for best performance.

By month's end when blooms have faded on *Hypoestes aristata* 'Lavender Cloud', cut flower spikes down to 16 inches in height and shape the plant. Look around the garden for those that may have seeded themselves last fall and move them now or next spring into sun or partial shade.

The ubiquitous heliotrope, an old-fashioned plant beloved for its fragrance and purple or white flowers, needs protection from frost—grow it in pots if necessary. It blooms throughout winter in mild climates given adequate water and good drainage; soggy roots mean quick death.

Brunfelsia pauciflora 'Macrantha', usually sold as 'Royal Purple', is an exception to all other plants that I can think of. It likes a double shot of nitrogen twice in winter during the coldest time of the year, treatment that would kill any other plant. Grow this spectacular subshrub in well-amended acid soil, in the ground if there are no competing tree roots, or in pots or hanging baskets. When treated right it literally drips with blossoms in June and it will bloom in more shade than almost any other plant, including clivia. The trick is to now drench the soil around the roots with a nitrogen fertilizer—Terr-O-Vite is ideal—mixed, believe it or not, double-strength. Do the job again in January.

When other late bloomers like Japanese anemones, lion's tail (*Leonotis leonurus*), common sneezeweed (*Helenium autumnale),* and *Verbena rigida* stop blooming, cut back the bloom spikes down to basal foliage and remove dead and dying portions. Remove the old bloom spikes and dead growth from lamb's ears. It's best to cut baby's breath (*Gypsophila paniculata)* almost to the ground at the end of December to produce a compact plant with strong flowering stems next season. Deadhead and cut back *Knautia macedonica,* a scabiosa look-alike (often incorrectly labeled) that blooms later than scabiosa, has wine-colored flowers on taller stems, and has more character though it is rangier. Look for *Loropetalum chinense rubrum* 'Monraz' with fringelike, ruby pink blossoms and burgundy or variegated foliage. Vibrantly colorful now in winter, it blooms heavily again in spring and lightly throughout the year, needs acid soil and good drainage—like an azalea—but with full sun along the coast, part shade inland. Some varieties can grow tall; all are brittle—don't put it where it can get hit by an edging machine. Also for winter color is *Cestrum fasciculatum* 'Newellii', though it blooms all year with red flowers followed by red berries. It's often still going strong now. Cut red and orange cestrums back after each wave of bloom to force fresh foliage and keep them shaped. (If burned by frost, they soon bounce back.) Though cestrums' fruit and sap are poisonous to humans, their tubular flowers attract hummingbirds.

Pruning

A number of plants can be pruned this month, but don't prune such tender or tropical plants as bougainvillea, eugenia, hibiscus, lantana, Natal plum, or philodendron. Pruning tropicals now will stimulate growth that could be nipped by frost.

Deciduous Fruit Trees. Once deciduous fruit trees have gone dormant and dropped their leaves, they can be pruned. You can do this job now or wait until next month. Every type of deciduous fruit tree needs different treatment. Personally, I study more than one reliable manual on pruning western trees before tackling this complicated and all-important job, because they all say things slightly differently and in various depths on the various trees; what is omitted in one book may be covered in another. (The pruning of deciduous fruit trees is discussed in more detail beginning on page 35.) Follow up your pruning with dormant spray. Dormant spray is best used more than once, so even if you don't prune this month it's wise to use dormant spray now (as described beginning on page 47) on all deciduous fruit trees and the many ornamental trees that drop their leaves in winter.

Grapes. Prune grapes this month. There are three major pruning methods, depending on the type grown. Young plants of each type must be pruned differently from those that are mature. (The *Sunset Pruning Handbook* contains diagrams and a good basic explanation of this subject.)

Save the trimmings to make ornamental wreaths and baskets. Start a wreath by wiring one bendy stem into a circle; then wind others around it. Add ribbons, dried flowers, and berries, and use the wreath in holiday decorations. Begin a basket the same way; then weave

How to Make the Classic Southern California Succulent Wreath

- Gather about a hundred cuttings and little rooted plants of various succulents. Good candidates are panda plant (*Kalanchoe tomentosa*) and the many different species and cultivars of crassula, echeveria, and sedum.

- Let the cuttings sit for a day or two to callus off so they'll root and not rot.

- Purchase two wire-form rings, green florists' wire, and fern pins from a crafts or florists' supply store. You'll also need clear vinyl fishing line.

- Line one ring with premoistened sphagnum moss. Fill this with potting soil mixed with a teaspoon of slow-release fertilizer. Wad more sphagnum moss on top.

- Cover this ring with the other, empty one and wire the two together. Clip off excess moss on the outside to make it smooth.

- Make a hole with a chopstick, through the sphagnum moss, to the same depth as the length of the stem of a cutting, insert the cutting, and secure it with a fern pin. Vary the types of suc-

culents, the textures, and the colors as you work, fitting them together closely.

- It takes three months for cuttings to anchor themselves, so tie fishing twine to the frame and wind it around as you go to make cuttings more secure.

- Leave room for a bow at the bottom. Place a hook on the back of the wreath, and hang it.

- The finished wreath should look like a piece of della Robbia pottery. (Rose-shaped echeverias, especially, provide this look.)

- After the holidays, hang the wreath in semishade where rains will provide adequate moisture during the winter and spring. During summer and fall squirt it with a hose occasionally, or soak it in water once a week. Recycle your wreath for several years, by snipping off leggy cuttings in November or December and replacing them closer to the form, and by filling in with fresh cuttings. Feed it occasionally with a well-diluted, complete, liquid fertilizer.

cross-pieces to form the base. Attach a handle if desired. Line the basket with sphagnum moss and a layer of plastic, make holes for drainage, fill it with potting soil, and plant it with winter annuals. (These baskets last several years.)

Low-Chill Raspberries. Before the arrival in 1978 of the low-chill red raspberry called 'Oregon 1030' (also called 'California'), Southern Californians couldn't grow real red raspberries like the ones that grow in cold-winter climates. Now several additional varieties have been discovered or developed that will bear good crops here, including 'Bababerry', 'Fallgold', 'Rosanna', and 'San Diego'. These "subtropical" raspberries are now grown here commercially as

well as in home gardens. They require different and much easier pruning than other types of cane berries.

All low-chill raspberry varieties bear their berries almost year-round on new wood that they put out almost continually. The simple pruning method for all low-chill types of raspberry is to cut all the canes down to 3 or 4 inches, now or in January. New growth will spring from the ground. Dig up the suckers to form new rows of plants; if you let your existing rows get too wide, they'll become unmanageable.

Fertilize raspberries in spring when they start to grow, with an evenly balanced fertilizer such as 16-16-16, and give them plenty of water.

How to Make a Miniature Western Ranch

- Buy two 1-gallon-size Tam junipers (*Juniperus sabina* 'Tamariscifolia'), one gallon-size lavender starflower (*Grewia occidentalis),* and a flat of Irish moss (*Sagina subulata).* Purchase tiny toy cowboys, a fence, a bridge, horses, and wildlife at a cake-decorating store. You'll also need red plastic plates, an old (preferably brown) plastic wastebasket, a few small rocks, and a small bag of blue gravel; it's available at aquarium supply stores.

- Make several holes in the bottom of a flat, 18-inch plastic dish designed to fit under a large planting tub. (The Quick Tip on page 301 tells how. Pottery dishes are too heavy and too shallow, and it's impossible to drill holes in them.) Cover each hole with a piece of broken crockery.

- Cut the walls of a barn from the centers of the red plastic plates. Cut the roof out of the plastic wastebasket. Fix these together inside the barn with tear-proof package-wrapping tape.

- Fill the bottom of the plastic dish with a 2- or 3-inch layer of potting soil. Shape the junipers into bonsai "cypress trees" and the lavender starflower into an "apple tree" by pruning the roots and clipping off excess foliage from the trunks and branches. Plant these in the dish, and surround them with rocks.

- Plant a "meadow" of Irish moss, cut to fit. Cut a winding streambed through it and fill this with the blue aquarium gravel. Add the barn, cowboys, fence, bridge, and animals.

- Water the plants and let the dish drain. Keep it in the house for one week if desired; thereafter keep it outdoors in sun or semishade. Water it regularly, feed it occasionally, and prune as necessary. In a year or two take out the bonsai, reprune their roots, and replace them.

Spray them regularly with BT against caterpillars; they relish raspberry leaves. (If you didn't prune other cane berries, like blackberries, boysenberries, and loganberries, last month, do it now, as directed on page 273.)

Native Plants. Native plants can be pruned any time during the winter growing season, with the exception of ceanothus, which is better pruned after bloom. Some gardeners prefer not to prune natives at all except to remove dead and diseased branches. Other gardeners prune to show the "good bones" of certain plants. A little judicious pruning can often uncover an artistic shape that's already there but hidden by foliage. Remove spent stems from Matilija poppy (*Romneya coulteri)* to encourage new growth and heavier spring flowering. Lemonade berry *(Rhus integrifolia)* and sugarbush *(R. ovata)* can be easily shaped into hedges, espaliers, or small trees.

Wisteria. If you didn't prune wisteria in summer, do it now. Study the buds first. Small, narrow buds are leaf buds; round, fatter buds, often found on short stubby growth called "spurs," are flower buds. Don't cut off the flower buds or flower-bearing spurs. Prune off long "streamers" or "twiners" (thin, young stems that grew rapidly this year). Carefully untangle them from older wood if necessary and cut them back to two or three buds to stimulate the growth of more flower spurs. Retain twiners going in desired directions and tie them loosely in place. If an established wisteria never blooms, cut into the ground around the plant with a sharp spade to prune the roots. This may stimulate bloom, perhaps not next spring but the year following.

A Freewheeling Way to "Bonsai" Nursery Plants

Cut off half the roots of a well-shaped 1-gallon-size Tam juniper removed from its container. Cut off unwanted branches, bare the trunk, and clip all foliage from under the branches, leaving the top foliage intact. Choose one strong root near the top of the root ball, and wind it tightly around the trunk just beneath the soil line. Plant the juniper in a Japanese bonsai pot. As the root you wound around the trunk grows, it will slow the growth of the plant.

Homegrown Holiday Decorations

Look around the garden to see what can be used to make the house look festive for the holidays. Some gardeners recycle tubbed pine trees, bringing them indoors year after year to do the annual stint as Christmas trees. Gardens can also provide sweet-smelling evergreen cuttings from pines, firs, cedars, and cypresses. Red berries from pyracantha and toyon and the leaves and berries of English holly are naturals, though not as long lasting as conifer foliage. (Sprays such as Keeps It are available at florists' supply stores and can keep berries and foliage fresh longer.) Cuttings of succulents such as jade plant and echeveria last all month and mix well with ornaments.

Other possibilities to dye, paint, glitter, or leave plain are pinecones, strawflowers, bunches of dried herbs, thistles, agapanthus stalks, and the decorative seedpods of plants including jacaranda, certain acacias, lotus, and eucalyptus (the heavy pods of flame eucalyptus *[Eucalyptus ficifolia]* are especially prized for their unique shape). For a last-minute touch, tape fresh red geraniums to packages; they'll last only a day. A tall dried stalk of century plant with the seed-pods still in place can be held upright by rocks hidden in an earthenware tub. Festoon it with decorations for a southwestern-style Christmas tree.

Gifts for and from the Garden

Nurseries and garden supply stores are great places to do Christmas shopping. Lines are usually short, parking easy, stocking stuffers abound, and children can find inexpensive gifts, such as a rain gauge or a hummingbird feeder. Some ideas: tools of all kinds; gadgets such as thermometers that record high and low temperatures (good even for nongardeners); soil augers; tensiometers; heat cables for sprouting seeds; ornamental objects, such as bronze faucets, bird baths, and garden sculpture; houseplants; bare-root roses; fruit trees; soil-test kits; and miniature greenhouses.

For a personal gift that doesn't need wrapping choose a sturdy basket for bringing in vegetables or flowers. Stuff it with a colorful apron, a pair of gloves, a trowel, a book or two, a few packs of seed, and a potted plant.

Make a Child's Fantasy Garden for Christmas or Hanukkah. A dish garden with a playful theme can spark the imagination of a child and create an interest in gardening at an early age. Make one yourself and give it to the child to play with. Better yet, give the ingredients with a promise to help make it. Older children can be given a construction kit with a set of instructions. (If you go this route stick to succulents, and give cuttings rather than plants. They're easier to deal with.)

Arrangements using houseplants and succulents can be kept indoors for as long as a year. For these, don't make a hole in the bottom of the container; put a layer of fine gravel on the bottom mixed with agricultural charcoal, to keep drainage water pure. Some possible themes: zoo, tropical jungle, Mickey Mouse garden, space stations among weirdly shaped succulents, forests of ferns and miniature cycads inhabited by dinosaurs, Indians stalking cowboys in a desert scene of rocks and succulents, or a western ranch (see the accompanying box) complete with trees and stream.

Make Homemade Gifts for Adults. Start early to pot such bedding plants as primroses, pansies, and miniature cyclamen in baskets and containers for holiday and hostess gifts. Line baskets with dry sphagnum moss and then line the sphagnum with plastic. For outdoor arrangements, make holes in the bottom of the plastic lining and fill it with potting soil and bedding plants in bud, fitting them closely together for the best effect. Keep the basket in sun and feed the plants to get them blooming before the holidays. When working with sphagnum moss, always wear waterproof garden gloves. Don't let damp sphagnum moss come into contact with cuts or abrasions.

For indoor arrangements make no holes in the plastic; place a layer of gravel for drainage and agricultural charcoal to absorb impurities in the lined basket before adding soil mix. Then fill it with small houseplants, varying the colors and shapes. If gray-leafed ivy is available, drape it over the side. For a finishing touch, pop a red African violet in one corner. Keep indoor baskets in bright light but out of direct sun, and feed them with high-bloom fertilizer.

Another idea is to make an outdoor entryway arrangement. Spray-paint a basket white, add chains for hanging, and fill it with poinsettias, kalanchoe, cyclamen, or an azalea. Or make dishes of succulents from your garden. In a

Quick Tip

How to Make Holes in the Bottom of a Plastic Container. *Hold a plastic container, upside-down, steadily over a lit candle until a spot visibly softens; it will bubble up slightly and may change color. Then lay the container right-side-up on a wooden board. Use a hammer and chisel to cut a square or triangular hole.*

terra-cotta pot combine driftwood with jade plant, gray-foliaged shore juniper (*Juniper conferta*) (draping it over the side), and pink cyclamen. You might also fill a footed Mexican pot with cacti and euphorbias plus a rock or two, and cover the surface of the soil with gravel. Or pot individual herbs, and present them in a wooden crate.

Herb Gardening

Herbs have been cultivated, used, and treasured by men and women for thousands of years. Many are ornamental as well as useful. Even a few of them can add charm, history, and mystique to any garden. You can grow enough culinary herbs, such as marjoram, parsley, rosemary, sage, and thyme, in your garden for your Christmas turkey, or plan to plant a whole garden of herbs next spring.

You can now, if you wish, plant culinary herbs in individual pots and grow them indoors on a sunny kitchen windowsill, and then, in spring, plant them outdoors. Pot the 2-inch nursery size into 4-inch containers when you purchase them; then repot them into 6-inch containers as soon as their roots fill the smaller size. When you grow herbs indoors they grow fast at first and then slow down. You can keep them to size by pruning off leaves now and then for cooking. Too much fertilizer makes herbs

301

Grow Sweet, Crisp, Juicy Celery

When you bite into a stalk of celery grown this way, juice will squirt into your mouth and run down your face.

- Dig a trench 14 inches wide in rich, well-drained soil in full sun.

- Add manure and homemade compost or commercial soil amendment.

- Cultivate fertilizer into the top 6 inches and then water the trench. (Finished planting area should be 3 inches lower than surrounding soil.)

- Plant celery transplants 6 inches apart down the center of the trench. Water them deeply.

- Water frequently throughout the growing season to keep the celery growing fast.

- Beginning six weeks after planting, feed the celery every two weeks with liquid fertilizer.

- Control slugs; they can ruin celery.

- A month before harvest, blanch the stalks by wrapping them with newspaper and tying firmly. Push earth around the bottoms of the stalks, and continue to water and feed them.

overgrow and lose their savor, but when they're grown in containers they do need occasional light fertilizer because potting soils are low in nutrients.

In spring plant culinary herbs outdoors in the ground in your vegetable garden, mixed in with any garden plants, in a special herb garden, or in a small space right outside your kitchen door. One organized and artful way to grow them in a small space is to lay an old ladder or wagon wheel on the ground and plant in the spaces. (When you clip leaves from an herb for cooking, choose which ones you take so that you're also controlling the plant's size and shape.) Another way to grow just a few herbs is to plant them in a strawberry pot or hanging basket. (For easy care, attach containers to a drip system.) Here are some basic facts about herbs:

- An herb is any plant used for medicine, fragrance, or flavoring. (In botany the word "herb" means any nonwoody plant. In cold-winter climates all these plants die down in winter, but many biennial and perennial herbs are evergreen when grown here.)

- *Not all herbs are edible. Some medicinal herbs, such as comfrey, rue, and tansy, contain toxic chemicals. They must not be taken internally by anyone and especially not by pregnant women.*

- Fresh culinary herbs from your garden are not only tastier than the dried herbs you can buy but safer. (Dried herbs purchased in markets are often imported and have frequently been sprayed with chemicals not allowed in the United States.)

- Herbs thrive in our mild climate and adapt to most soils, but they prefer good drainage, which you can provide by growing them in rock gardens or raised beds.

- Unless you grow your herbs in containers, as described above, don't fertilize them; it makes them less flavorful. (An exception is an herb like sage that's been in the ground for several years, has often given its leaves to you, and shows an obvious decline in vigor. You can pull it out, amend the soil, and replace it; or you can feed it lightly and mulch its roots to bring it back.)

- Some herbs, such as mint and watercress, need lots of water. Others, such as rosemary and society garlic, are useful drought-resistant plants; these two are grown as ornamentals more often than as culinary herbs.

Lawn Care

Cool-Season Lawns. Feed cool-season lawns every month to six weeks during the growing season. If the grass blades turn red-brown and brown dust gets on your shoes, it's rust. Don't spray the lawn with chemicals; just feed it. The rust will clear right up. Mow weekly and water when rains aren't adequate.

Warm-Season Lawns. Most warm-season lawns, such as Bermuda and zoysia, are dormant now and require little, if any, care. Once the grass has gone completely brown and stopped growing, you can turn off the irrigation water and stop mowing. The exception is Bermuda that's overseeded with winter ryegrass. Treat this like cool-season grasses, feeding it to keep it growing and mowing it to keep it looking nice. If we have warm weather, St. Augustine may continue to grow; mow it if needed. Once the weather gets cold it won't need mowing.

Vegetable Gardening

December is an exciting time in the vegetable garden because most winter crops are in full swing, and some are starting to produce. As crops are harvested, plant more. Among crops that can be planted this month are artichokes, asparagus 'UC-157', beets, broccoli, Brussels sprouts, cabbage, carrots, cauliflower, celery (see the accompanying box), kale, kohlrabi, head lettuce, leaf lettuce, mesclun, peas, potatoes, radishes, Swiss chard, and turnips.

Tie the leaves over the heads of cauliflower as soon as they begin to make a head in order to prevent the curds from turning green, and watch them carefully; once cauliflowers begin to expand, they grow rapidly to maturity. Purple cauliflower doesn't need this blanching (it tastes like broccoli). Some cauliflower is "self-blanching"—the leaves naturally cover the heads. Even so, tie the leaves together and you'll get a better product in the end. Occasionally gardeners have a problem with cauliflower "buttoning"; a tiny little curd forms prematurely, the leaves stay small, and you never get a big head. This can result from buying stressed plants at a nursery or from temperatures below 40°F, insufficient nitrogen, too much salt in the soil, or letting the plants go dry.

Take off the bottom sprouts and bottom leaves from Brussels sprouts. Control aphids with insecticidal soap and beneficial insects. Cut broccoli as soon as it makes a head, and leave the stalk in the ground to produce side sprouts. (See page 60 for more about harvesting cole crops.) Pull beets, carrots, kohlrabi, and turnips while they're still young and tender. Pick peas to keep them coming. Start harvesting the outside stalks of celery. Harvest outside lettuce leaves as needed or cut off the whole head. Harvest mesclun by cutting with scissors or by pulling up whole plants, as described on page 85. (Leave the stalk in the ground and feed and water it; it'll grow another head.) Control slugs on celery, lettuce, and mesclun.

Side-dress rows with fertilizer, according to the individual needs of vegetables, to keep them going. In general, if you're planting from seed, begin when the plants are 2 to 3 inches high to side-dress the rows with fertilizer every six weeks, or begin then to feed them once a week with liquid fertilizer. When you're growing vegetables from transplants, you should usually side-dress the rows with additional fertilizer six weeks after planting. Quick crops like radishes will need no additional fertilizer if you fertilized the soil, as you should have done, prior to planting. Give long-term crops, like broccoli and Brussels sprouts, additional fertilizer at intervals of six weeks throughout their growing season.

Onions grow best with slightly more frequent and lighter doses of fertilizer. (Thin your onions by month's end and transplant the thinnings into another row. Don't neglect to weed them regularly.)

Purchase/Plant

❏ Begin planting bare-root roses, trees, vines, berries, and vegetables, if you wish, 289

❏ Purchase poinsettias early in the month, 290

❏ Choose and plant sasanqua camellias and early- and long-blooming azaleas, 291

❏ Finish planting all spring-flowering bulbs, except tulips, hyacinths, and crocuses, on or before December 25, 292

❏ Plant tulips, hyacinths, and crocuses between Christmas and New Year's Day, 292

❏ Purchase permanent plants that are colorful in winter, to plant or use as gifts, 294

❏ Continue to plant cool-season flowers in coastal zones only, 296

❏ Purchase gifts from nurseries and garden supply stores, 300

❏ Plant a child's fantasy dish garden, or give the ingredients and a promise to help make it, 300

❏ Plant bedding plants in baskets and pots for holiday and hostess gifts. Also use indoor plants, succulents, herbs, and plants in bloom, 301

❏ Plant culinary herbs in pots for use in turkey stuffing, 301

❏ Continue to plant winter vegetables, 303

❏ Plant celery, 302

Trim, Prune, Mow, Divide

❏ Stop picking and deadheading roses; leave the hips on the bush, 291

❏ Cut off flower spikes that have bloomed from dwarf foxgloves and delphiniums, 294

❏ Start pruning deciduous fruit trees, if you have time, 297

❏ Don't prune tropicals, 230

❏ Prune grapes, 297

❏ Prune low-chill raspberries, 298

❏ Prune native plants, 299

❏ Prune wisteria by cutting off unwanted long twiners, and prune roots of vines that fail to bloom, 299

❏ Pick plant materials from the garden to use as holiday decorations, 300

❏ Mow cool-season lawns, including Bermuda that's overseeded with winter ryegrass, 303

❏ Don't mow warm-season lawns, except St. Augustine if it continues to grow, 303

Fertilize

❏ Stop fertilizing potted poinsettias; bring them into the house to enjoy, 290

❏ Continue fertilizing cymbidiums until flowers open, 291

❏ Don't fertilize roses, 291

❏ Feed cool-season flowers with a complete fertilizer for growth and bloom, 294

❏ Continue to feed cineraria for growth, 279

❏ Feed shade plants for bloom; give them adequate light, 295

❏ Feed cool-season lawns, but don't feed warm-season lawns except for Bermuda that's overseeded with winter ryegrass, 303

❏ Side-dress vegetable rows according to the individual needs of plants, 303

❏ Drench the ground under *Brunfelsia* 'Royal Purple' with Terr-O-Vite mixed double-strength, 296

Continued>>

Water

❏ Don't water succulents growing in the ground, 195

❏ Continue to water if the weather's hot, dry, and windy; include California native plants now because this is their growing season, 144, 271

❏ Keep cymbidiums damp but not soggy, 291

❏ Remember to keep all bulbs, but especially potted ones, well watered, 292

❏ Don't water roses, 291

❏ Water cool-season lawns when rains aren't adequate, 303

❏ Water St. Augustine grass if it continues to grow, 303

❏ Turn off the irrigation systems of all other types of warm-season lawns once they have gone brown, 303

Control Pests, Diseases, and Weeds

❏ Spray peach and apricot trees for peach leaf curl if you didn't do so in November, 281

❏ Protect cymbidiums' bloom spikes from snails, 291

❏ Control rust on dwarf snapdragons, 295

❏ Use dormant spray on deciduous fruit trees and other woody plants that drop their leaves in winter, 297

❏ Control rust on cool-season lawns by fertilizing and mowing them, 303

❏ Control aphids with insecticidal soap and beneficial insects, 303

❏ Control slugs on celery, lettuce, and mesclun, 91, 302

Also This Month

❏ Prepare for frost in areas where it is expected by sheltering tropical plants growing in containers, 290

❏ Force budded cymbidiums into bloom for the holidays, if desired, 291

❏ Keep an eye on the growth of potted bulbs; remove covers when they reach the right height, 292

❏ Prepare beds for planting bare-root roses next month, 292

❏ Lift dahlias and store them for the winter, 293

❏ Prepare amaryllis to bloom, 293

❏ Protect tender annuals, especially cineraria, from frost, 295

❏ Tie up permanent vines so they don't get knocked down by rain or wind, 295

❏ Use the bendy stems of grapevines to make wreaths and baskets, 297

❏ Make a holiday wreath from succulents, 298

❏ Harvest winter vegetables as soon as they mature, 303

SEED AND PLANT SOURCES

Buena Creek Gardens
418 Buena Creek Road
P.O. Box 2033
San Marcos, CA 92069
760/744-2810

W. Atlee Burpee & Company
300 Park Avenue
Warminster, PA 18974
800/888-1447
Web site:
www.burpee.garden.com

The Cook's Garden
P.O. Box 535
Londonderry, VT 05148
800/457-9703
Web site:
www.cooksgarden.com

The Gourmet Gardener
8650 College Boulevard
Overland Park, KS 66210
913/345-0490
Web site:
 www.gourmetgardener.com

Heritage Roses of Tanglewood Farms
16831 Mitchell Creek Drive
Ft. Bragg, CA 95437
707/964-3748

High Country Gardens
2902 Rufina Street
Santa Fe, NM 87505
800/925-9387
e-mail: plants@highcountrygardens.com

Jackson & Perkins Co.
2518 South Pacific Highway
Medford, OR 97501
800/292-4769
Web site:
www.jacksonandperkins.com

Le Jardin du Gourmet
P.O. Box 75
St. Johnsbury Center, VT 05863
802/748-1446
e-mail:
flowers.herbs@kingcon.com

Judy's Perennials
436 Buena Creek Road
San Marcos, CA 92069
760/471-8850
(Phone for days open.)

Pacific Tree Farms
4301 Lynwood Drive
Chula Vista, CA 91910
619/422-2400

Park Seed Company
1 Parkton Avenue
Greenwood, SC 29647
800/845-3369
Web site: www.parkseed.com

Renee's Garden
7389 West Zayante Road
Felton, CA 95018
888/880-7228
e-mail: renees@pacbell.net

Shepherd's Garden Seeds
30 Irene Street
Tarrington, CT 06790
860/482-3638
Web site:
www.shepherdseeds.com

Territorial Seed Company
P.O. Box 157
20 Palmer Avenue
Cottage Grove, OR 97424
541/942-9547
Web site:
www.territorial-seed.com

Thompson & Morgan
P.O. Box 1308
Jackson, NJ 08527
800/274-7333

Tree of Life Nursery
P.O. Box 635
33201 Ortega Highway
San Juan Capistrano, CA 92675
760/471-8850
(Phone for days open.)

Wayside Gardens
P.O. Box 1
Hodges, SC 29695
800/845-1124

ROSE-PRO CALENDAR

Month	Planting	Pruning	Spraying
January (p. 44)	Plant bare-root roses.	Prune rosebushes and ever-blooming climbers.	Dormant spray with a mixture of Ortho Dormant Disease Control Lime-Sulfur Spray and Volck Oil.
February (p. 71)	Finish planting bare-root roses purchased locally.	– – – – –	Spray once a week with Funginex beginning at midmonth.
March (p. 94)	Finish planting bare-root roses purchased from mail-order catalogs.	Begin disbudding hybrid teas and grandifloras.	Continue spraying once a week with Funginex, and add Orthene. Also mix Miracle-Gro or Super K Gro into the spray. Or, if mites are a problem, substitute Orthenex Insect and Disease Control Formula III.
April (p. 122)	– – – – –	Pick blooms or deadhead spent flowers. Also disbud hybrid teas and grandifloras.	Spray once a week with Funginex, Orthene, and Miracle-Gro or Super K Gro (or substitute Orthenex for Funginex and Orthene).
May (p. 146)	Plant roses from nursery containers.	Pick or deadhead flowers. Also disbud hybrid teas and grandifloras.	Spray once a week with Funginex, Orthene, and Miracle-Gro or Super K Gro (or substitute Orthenex for Funginex and Orthene).
June (p. 170)	Plant roses from nursery containers.	Pick or deadhead flowers. Also disbud hybrid teas and grandifloras.	Spray once a week with Funginex, Orthene, and Miracle-Gro or Super K Gro (or substitute Orthenex for Funginex and Orthene).
July (p. 183)	– – – – –	Stop disbudding. Continue picking or deadheading. Prune climbers that bloom only once a year.	Spray once a week with Funginex, Orthene, and Miracle-Gro or Super K Gro (or substitute Orthenex for Funginex and Orthene).
August (p. 213)	Plant roses from nursery containers.	Give all roses a light pruning to encourage fall flowers.	Spray once a week with Funginex, Orthene, and Miracle-Gro or Super K Gro (or substitute Orthenex for Funginex and Orthene).
September (p. 233)	Plant roses from nursery containers.	Pick blooms or deadhead spent flowers.	Spray once a week with Funginex and Orthene. Stop spraying with Miracle-Gro or Super K Gro (or substitute Orthenex for Funginex and Orthene).
October (p. 255)	Plant roses from nursery containers.	Pick blooms or deadhead spent flowers.	Continue spraying once a week with Funginex. Stop spraying with Orthene.
November (p. 281)	– – – – –	Pick blooms if desired but stop deadheading them.	– – – – –
December (p. 291)	– – – – –	– – – – –	– – – – –

Please note: Detailed explanations of tasks on this chart and alternative methods of fertilizing, pest control, and disease control are given in the month-by-month chapters. Refer to the page numbers listed above.

Month	Irrigating	Fertilizing	Other Activities
January	Water new plants every other day for the first three weeks after planting.	Give all plants 2 tablespoonfuls of Epsom salts. Also give all newly planted roses 1 cup of superphosphate and all established plants $1/4$ cup of superphosphate.	Apply mulch. Attend public demonstrations of rose pruning.
February	Begin watering all plants with 1 inch of water per week when rains aren't adequate.	Give each plant 1 cup of Milorganite at midmonth. (Give 2 cups of Milorganite to large established climbers.)	Early this month apply 1 cup of gypsum to the ground over the roots of each plant.
March	Apply up to 2 inches of water once a week when rains aren't adequate.	Give 1 tablespoon of sulfate of potash to each plant early in the month. Also give each plant 1 tablespoonful of sulfate of ammonia once a week.	— — — —
April	Apply up to $1^{1}/2$ inches of water twice a week.	Once a week give each plant 1 tablespoonful of sulfate of ammonia.	Attend rose shows.
May	Apply up to $1^{1}/2$ inches of water twice a week.	Every other week give each plant 1 tablespoonful of urea.	— — — —
June	Apply up to $1^{1}/2$ inches of water twice a week.	Every other week give each plant 1 tablespoonful of urea.	Attend rose shows.
July	Apply up to $1^{1}/2$ inches of water three times a week.	Every other week give each plant 1 tablespoonful of urea.	Renew mulch where necessary.
August	Apply up to $1^{1}/2$ inches of water three times a week.	Give each plant one application of 2 tablespoonfuls of Epsom salts and $1/2$ cup of Milorganite.	— — — —
September	Apply up to $1^{1}/2$ inches of water twice a week.	Once a week give each plant 1 tablespoonful of urea.	— — — —
October	Apply up to $1^{1}/2$ inches of water twice a week.	— — — —	Attend rose shows.
November	Water until midmonth if rains aren't adequate. After midmonth withhold water.	— — — —	— — — —
December	Withhold water.	— — — —	Prepare beds for bare-root planting. Remove weeds and fallen leaves.

This schedule of rose care is adapted from rosarian Richard Streeper's calendar of rose care.

Caution: Use Epsom salts with discretion. Too much can cause calcium magnesium imbalance and resultant soil compaction.

GLOSSARY

Actual nitrogen. The amount of pure nitrogen in a fertilizer. To determine the number of pounds of a specific fertilizer you must use in order to give a plant 1 pound of actual nitrogen, divide 100 by the first number on the package.

Air-layer. To propagate a plant by growing roots from an aboveground node of a branch or trunk. The node is wrapped with sphagnum moss and kept damp (usually by covering it with plastic). The entire portion of the plant that includes the new roots can then be severed to create a new plant. (Compare *layer.*)

Ammonic. Containing ammonia (NH_4), a primary source of nitrogen in such fertilizers as ammonium sulfate, which will acidify soils as well as fertilize them. Ammonium sulfate (21-0-0) is a cheap source of fast-acting nitrogen that dissolves quickly in water, but it can burn plants if not watered in well.

Annual. A plant that completes its life within twelve months. An annual germinates, grows, blooms, sets seed, and dies all in one season. Warm-season annuals begin life in spring and die when the weather gets cold in fall. Cool-season annuals begin life in fall and die when the weather gets hot in summer. Some perennial plants, such as delphiniums and petunias, are grown mainly as annuals. Some perennials that are grown as annuals in other parts of the country, such as impatiens and geraniums (pelargoniums), are grown here as true perennials.

Anther. The pollen-bearing flower part. It consists of pollen sacs and is located on the end of the stamen, the male reproductive organ of flowers.

Antitranspirants. Products sprayed on leaves that leave a film in order to slow transpiration and thus prevent wilting. They can help plants survive heat, cold, dryness, salt spray, and transplanting.

Areoles. Spine cushions. They're found on all cacti but not on any other succulents. (Many other succulents, including the cactuslike euphorbias, have spines, but they do not have spine cushions.)

Axillary bud. A bud that occurs in the leaf axil (the upper angle where the leaf joins the stem). Tomato suckers arise from axillary buds.

Balanced fertilizer. A widely used but somewhat vague term for a fertilizer that contains all three major elements (nitrogen, phosphorus, and potassium) that plants need. (See *complete fertilizer.*)

Bare-root. A plant that has had all soil removed from its roots. Many deciduous plants are sold bare-root during the winter months.

Beneficials. Insects, arachnids, nematodes, and other organisms that eat or parasitize pest insects and mites. Many, such as spiders, exist in our gardens; others can be purchased for release.

Biennial. A plant that requires two growing seasons to flower and then sets seed and dies. Bedding plants that are biennials are usually planted in fall; seeds of biennials are planted in summer to bloom the following year. Some biennials, such as the foxglove 'Foxy' and the sweet William 'Wee Willie', can be grown as annuals.

Biodegradable. Capable of decomposing by natural biological means.

Blossom-end rot. Black, sunken, leathery areas on the bottom of tomatoes (and also found on peppers, squash, and watermelons) caused by insufficient calcium. The insufficiency is caused by uneven moisture in the soil or by roots damaged from cultivation, salty soil, or extremely wet soil.

Bolt. To go to seed prematurely. Typically describes vegetables, such as onions.

Botrytis. A fungal disease characterized by fuzzy, wet filaments and the blackening and swelling of plant parts, especially flowers, leaves, and stems. Promoted by prolonged wet weather or frequent overhead irrigation.

Bract. A leaflike organ between the flower and the leaves or one that is part of an inflorescence or that has taken on color to look just like a petal, as on poinsettias.

Branch collar. The swollen area surrounding a tree branch where it meets a larger branch or the trunk.

Broad-spectrum pesticide. A pesticide that kills a large number of various pests rather than being designed to control one specific pest. In general, specific pesticides are better because they protect beneficials. (See *integrated pest management*.)

BT. *Bacillus thuringiensis,* a bacterial disease that kills caterpillars and is sold under several trade names (such as Attack, Dipel, and Thuricide) in liquid or powder form to be used as a spray or dust. Caterpillars that ingest treated leaves stop eating and die in about three days.

Bud union. The location on a grafted plant where the variety was grafted onto the rootstock. It may or may not be swollen. On older plants it often becomes difficult to distinguish where the bud union is, but in some cases it's easily seen. On citrus, for example, there may be a change in the size of the trunk from smaller to larger, or vice versa. On bare-root trees the bud union is often no more than a slight bend in the trunk. On roses the bud union is the knob, bump, or large swollen area from which the canes arise. (On old roses bud unions can grow to enormous size, sometimes a foot or more long.)

Bulb. A modified subterranean leaf bud; it has a basal plate above which are food-storing scales (rudimentary leaves) surrounding a bud from which comes a plant. Also used loosely to describe all plants that grow from thickened underground food-storage organs.

Caliche. A highly alkaline type of soil found largely in desert areas. Its high lime content may be visible as white flecks throughout or as a white crust on top of the soil, or it may occur in a hard buried layer.

Callus. The dry crust of plant cells that forms over the open cut on a cutting. (To develop the crust is to "callus over.")

Cane. The woody stem of a rose or cane berry, such as raspberries and blackberries, or a somewhat flexible, jointed, and often hollow or pith-filled stem arising from the ground, as on bamboo, sugarcane, and cane begonias.

Chaparral. A dense growth of various native shrubs that are stiff, drought resistant, evergreen, and sometimes thorny.

Chelate. Technically, an organic molecule that prevents iron, manganese, and zinc from being "locked up" (becoming insoluble) in alkaline soil by binding itself to them. In this combined form they stay soluble, and thus plants can use them. *Iron chelate, chelated iron,* or a *chelated* or *chelating* formula are included in products that contain the trace elements iron, manganese, and zinc in a form plants can use.

Chilling requirement. The number of hours between 45° and 32°F that a plant needs to overcome dormancy in order to grow, flower, and fruit properly. (When the temperature drops lower than freezing, little action occurs within the tissues of the plant.) A plant with a low chilling requirement is one that needs few, if any, hours between 45° and 32°F in order to bloom and bear fruit.

Chimney drain. A narrow drain, dug with a spade, crowbar, or post-hole digger, in the bottom of a planting hole on flat ground, when the cause of poor drainage is a layer of hardpan that is thin enough to break through with hand tools. The hole is then filled with sand or ground bark to allow water to escape through the layer of hardpan down into a layer of soil that drains.

Chlorosis. Condition denoting a lack of chlorophyll (a green pigment in plant cells) often brought about by a lack of sufficient soluble iron in the soil. A chlorotic plant has yellow leaves and dark veins. Sometimes especially in citrus, this is caused by waterlogged soil. Also, highly alkaline soil can cause chlorosis by preventing plants from absorbing enough iron, zinc, and manganese for plant health.

Clay. A fine-grained earth made up of tiny mineral particles less than 0.002 millimeter in size. When you grip a damp handful it holds together. Pure clay is good for little else than making bricks or pottery, but "clay soils" contain humus and may also contain some admixture of sand or silt.

Climate zone. A geographical area in which the yearly temperature range, length of seasons, average precipitation, humidity, amount of sunshine, and other factors combine to make certain plants grow better than others. The climate zones described and mapped in the *Sunset Western Garden Book* make up the zone system most widely used by western gardeners.

Cole crop. Any member of the cabbage family, including cauliflower, broccoli, and Brussels sprouts.

Complete fertilizer. The correct term for describing a fertilizer containing all three major elements (nitrogen, phosphorus, and potassium) that plants need. The formulas—the relative amounts of the three—may vary widely, however. A complete fertilizer high in growth ingredients has a high first number, and a complete fertilizer high in bloom ingredients has a high second number or second and third numbers.

Compost. A soil amendment made by farmers and gardeners by piling up organic materials and keeping them damp until they rot.

Cool-season flower. An annual, biennial, or perennial flower that's native to a cool climate and that grows and flowers best at cool temperatures.

Cool-season lawn. A lawn variety that's best adapted to a cool climate and thus grows best and fastest during late fall, winter, and early spring.

Cool-season vegetable. A vegetable that originated in a cool climate and grows best at cool temperatures.

Corm. A thickened subterranean stem that is a solid piece of food-storage tissue and that produces a plant from buds on top. Gladioli and freesias grow from corms.

Corolla. The collective name for the petals of a flower. The collective name for the sepals is the calyx. The corolla and calyx combined make up the perianth. (On a fuchsia the corolla is the usually downward-facing "skirt" of the flower, and it may be of any color available in fuchsias; the sepals of a fuchsia flare back toward the stem and are always red, white, or pink.)

Crabgrass. An annual weed forming a thick clump of coarse grass that spreads out like a crab, turns red at the first frost, and dies out in winter.

Crop rotation. A system used by farmers and gardeners since ancient times to preserve the fertility of soil and minimize pest and disease problems. It consists of planting those crops (including flowers) that are subject to specific soilborne pests and diseases on a particular piece of ground no more than once every three years.

Crown. The place at soil level where a plant's roots end and its trunk or stem (or group of stems) begins. Also used to denote the top of a tree's canopy of branches.

Crown rot. A general term describing any number of fungal diseases that can attack the crown of a plant. Usually it's the result of planting too low or allowing water or mud to collect around the plant's trunk or stem (or stems).

Cultivar. See *variety.*

Curd. The white head of a cauliflower or the individual sections of a head.

Cutting. A section of a plant that's cut off for grafting or rooting.

Cutworm. A large black, brown, or gray hairless and fleshy caterpillar that curls into a C shape when disturbed. Often found underground or under fallen leaves when you dig or cultivate. Surface cutworms chew off stems at ground level overnight. Subterranean cutworms eat roots. Climbing cutworms destroy fresh shoots and young foliage.

Deadhead. To clip off faded flower heads before they can set seed.

Deciduous. Describes plants that drop all their leaves once a year.

Decollate snail. A small African carnivorous snail introduced here to eat brown garden snails. (Their use is not legal in all counties. Check with the nearest University of California Cooperative Extension office.)

Decomposed granite. A grayish, creamy, or light brown, granular, and sometimes flaky soil composed of small particles of granite. It drains well and is high in potassium.

Diatomaceous earth. A powder made of a mined product that's filled with the sharp skeletons of tiny diatoms, one-celled algae. The silica in diatomaceous earth kills pests by piercing their bodies like broken glass.

Divide. To break apart the roots or to separate the bulbs of a plant that has formed a clump in order to make new plants, to limit the plant's size, or to renew the plant.

Dormant. Describes the "sleeping" state when a plant isn't growing though it remains alive.

Dormant spray. A pesticide and/or fungicide, such as oil or lime sulfur, used in winter on deciduous plants that have gone dormant and dropped their leaves. Dormant sprays are usually too concentrated for use on foliage; in most cases, they would burn the leaves.

Drain. See *chimney drain, French drain,* or *sleeve drain* and *sump.*

Drainage. The passage of water through soil and the soil characteristics that support it. When drainage is good, water passes rapidly downward through the soil. When drainage is poor, water puddles on the surface or is held for a long period within the soil, traveling downward very slowly if at all. If the passage of water is seriously impeded, plant roots can die from being deprived of necessary oxygen. Sandy and decomposed granite soils usually have fast drainage; in clay soils it is usually slow. Hardpan or buried rock can also seriously impede drainage.

Drift. A gracefully shaped area with rounded edges in a flowerbed, planted with one type of plant or one color. Drifts extend from the foreground to the middle ground or from the middle ground to the background as well as from side to side in the bed.

Drip line. An imaginary line

encircling a tree directly under the outermost tips of the branches. (Also, often used loosely to describe the various tubes and hoses or tube-type emitters, either buried or above ground, that are used in drip irrigation.)

Drip system. A method of watering plants by which water at controlled low pressure is fed through a hose that in turn feeds small tubes leading to individual plants, where emitters release water to the root zone or mist it on foliage. (In some cases emitters are attached directly to the primary hose. See *header.*)

Drought. Lack of adequate rainfall or less-than-normal rainfall lasting for a prolonged period—several months, a season, or several years. "Summer drought" describes our customarily dry summers.

Drought resistant. Describes plants from dry regions of the world that have developed various means of enduring drought without dying. Drought-resistant plants require less irrigation than do others once they are established.

Drought tolerant. A term often used to describe a plant that, once established, can survive on natural rainfall alone, with little, if any, irrigation.

Emitters. Various types of plastic gadgets that release measured quantities of water. They attach to microtubing and, in some cases, to headers by simple push-pull methods. Emitters are not all interchangeable; they have to be the right size for the tubing used.

Epiphyte. A plant that grows by attaching itself to another plant but doesn't sap nourishment from the host plant, as do parasites.

Espalier. To train a plant into a flat, formal shape on wires or

against a wall or fence. Also the trained plant and sometimes the framework it grows on.

Eye. The center of a flower when it has a different color from the outer petals; the bud on a tuber; a cutting that has only one bud; or an undeveloped bud, which looks like a line, bump, depression, or other demarcation on the stem of a plant.

Farm Advisor. The title that designates agricultural scientists who are representatives of the agricultural and natural resources advisory system that's supported by state, county, and federal governments through the University of California. Reach them at your local county's UC Cooperative Extension office.

Fertilizer. Any material, either organic or inorganic, that's applied to soil or foliage to feed plants and aid their growth.

Fireblight. A bacterial disease that causes blackening and dieback of leaves, twigs, branches, and fruit on apple trees, evergreen pear *(Pyrus kawakamii),* pyracantha, and other members of the rose family.

Force. To make a plant bloom months ahead of schedule by simulating natural conditions that make it bloom.

Frass. The dust or pelletized excrement of insects, such as residues of boring left by bark beetles.

French drain. A trench in which perforated pipe has been laid and then covered with a 3-foot layer of sand or gravel. It's used to drain excess water from flat or sloping ground. The top of the gravel in the completed French drain may be level with the surface of the ground or buried at any depth underground. If buried, the top of the gravel should be covered with plastic sheeting or

landscape cloth prior to burying so that clay soil above the French drain can't drift down into it and clog the spaces in the gravel.

Full slip. Characterizes a ripe cantaloupe; a crack forms around the stem end so the melon slips off the vine easily, without tearing.

Furrow. A groove or trench made in garden soil for the purpose of planting, carrying irrigation water between rows, or controlling erosion.

Genus. A group of plants of one or several species that are related structurally and belong to the same family but that differ from other genera within the family. Designated by the capitalized first word in a botanical name, which is followed by the uncapitalized species name.

Glochid. A short, barbed, almost invisible, and hairlike spine. Glochia grow from the areoles of some but not all cacti.

Glyphosate. A nonspecific weed killer made of a biodegradable salt that works by being absorbed through leaves and traveling down inside the plant to kill the roots.

Graft. To propagate a plant by inserting a section of one plant into another.

Green manure. A plant or plants, in most cases a legume, grown on a plot of land for one growing season (usually over winter) for the purpose of being plowed, tilled, spaded, or otherwise worked into the ground to improve soil fertility.

Gypsum. Calcium sulfate $(CaSO_4\text{-}2H_2O)$, a natural rock product used as a soil amendment to loosen clay soils and make them drain better when the cause of poor drainage is a high level of exchangeable sodium (alkali) rather than texture or compaction. Somewhat soluble in water, gypsum supplies soluble calcium to replace excess exchangeable sodium (alkali). Also used to reclaim sodic (salty) soils.

Harden off. The process in a plant of gradually becoming accustomed to colder weather in fall. This includes slowing down or stopping top growth so that the foliage will be hardy. (Young leaves are most likely to suffer frost damage.) Gardeners help plants harden off by reducing water and fertilizer in fall. Also refers to the gradual exposure of young seedlings to outdoor temperatures and sunlight after they've been grown in a greenhouse, indoors, or under lights.

Hardpan. A layer of hard, compacted soil of any type that's cemented together by minerals and almost impenetrable by roots or water. Often buried beneath a layer of good soil.

Hardscape. Any feature in a garden that's made of a construction material, including pools, decks, hot tubs, patios, steps, walks, walls, gazebos, pergolas, and planter boxes. Most gardens include some hardscape; some have more hardscape than landscape (areas of ground with plants growing in them).

Hardy. Describes a plant that can take various degrees of frost and freezing temperatures without dying. (Does not mean a strong or easy-to-grow plant.)

Head back. To cut back the growing end of a branch or young tree in order to stimulate branching farther back on the branch or trunk, thus redirecting growth.

Header. A hose that carries water from the water source to microtubing and emitters in a drip system.

Headers aren't all interchangeable; they and the various parts that are used to connect sections must be of the right size to fit.

Heel in. A way to keep bare-root plants from drying out when you can't plant them right away: laying the plants in the shade with their roots in a trench, covering the roots with soil, and keeping them damp.

Helix snail. *Helix aspersa,* our common brown garden snail.

Herb. Any plant used for medicine, fragrance, or flavoring. (Not all herbs are edible.) In botany, any nonwoody plant that dies down in winter.

Herbaceous border. A traditional flower border planted entirely with nonwoody plants.

Humus. The organic portion of soil, made up of largely decomposed animal and vegetable matter and usually light or dark brown in color. Nitrolized sawdust, leaf mold, peat moss, and manure are organic soil amendments that eventually become humus in soils, but they're not the same as humus.

Hybrid. The offspring of a cross, by intention or chance, between two plants that are more or less unlike. Some hybrids are sterile. Seeds from a hybrid plant don't produce plants like the parent.

Insecticidal soaps. A group of biodegradable fatty acids that are sold as environmentally safe sprays (such as Safer soap). They kill pests, especially soft-bodied pests such as aphids, on contact (by clogging their pores).

Integrated pest management (IPM). A system of balancing pest populations with populations of beneficial insects, so that few, if any, chemical sprays need to be used. When sprays are used, specific

sprays for the individual pest are chosen rather than broad-spectrum sprays that kill many beneficials.

June drop. Describes the dropping of many immature fruits, usually in early June but sometimes at other times. Nature's way of thinning fruit on trees that set more fruit than they can ripen.

Laterals. Side branches.

Layer. To propagate a plant by bending a living branch to the ground and burying a portion of it in soil while it's still attached to the parent plant, allowing the branch to root, and then cutting off and removing the rooted portion. (Prior to burying the branch portion, a slanting cut is made halfway through it; it's then brushed with rooting compound and held open by a sliver of wood or by a pebble. Once buried, it's usually pegged down on both sides or weighted down by a brick placed on top.)

Leggy. Describes a plant that tends to grow too tall with long, bare stalks below.

Legume. Any member of the Leguminosae, a family made up of plants having a pod shaped like a pea pod.

Loam. Technically, a soil type that is a combination of clay, sand, and silt. Loam soils vary greatly and are often described by such terms as "clay loam" or "sandy loam" depending on the percentages of their components. Also used popularly to describe any soil that's full of humus and is rich, crumbly, productive, and dark in color (as in "good garden loam").

Low chill. Describes a plant that needs few hours between 45°F and 32°F in order to bloom and bear fruit.

Manure. Animal excrement of

horses, cows, chickens, rabbits, or pigs; used for fertilizer and soil improvement. (Cat and dog droppings carry diseases and must never be used.)

Manure tea. A liquid fertilizer made by putting a shovelful of manure into a bucket of water and allowing it to stand overnight.

Microclimate. Small area within a climate zone where a plant will or won't grow because of factors of climate particular to that spot.

Microtubing. Quarter-inch plastic tubing used in drip systems to carry water to emitters. Most microtubing is of the same size and is thus interchangeable.

Mildew. Various fungal diseases (brown, powdery, and downy mildews) that grow on the surface of plant leaves and stems. They discolor and distort plant parts, sap plant energy, and can cause leaf drop.

Monocarpic. Describes a plant that blooms only once and then dies.

Mulch. A layer of loose organic matter applied to the surface of the soil to keep the ground cool, preserve moisture, stop the surface from cracking, cut down on weeds, and improve bacterial action. Also black plastic, agricultural fabrics, rocks, pebbles, and newspapers used in the same way.

Mushroom compost. Humus in which mushrooms have been grown; an inexpensive organic amendment largely made of manure and strati that can be bought bagged or in bulk, sometimes directly from growers. It may have a high salt content.

Native plant (or "native"). A plant that, in its original form, grows wild in a geographic region

such as California. Many native plants have been improved by selection and hybridization.

Native soil. Soil dug from a planting hole that's like the surrounding ground.

Naturalize. For a plant to multiply and come back year after year under normal garden conditions. Also for a plant to escape gardens and go wild, mixing in with and sometimes choking out native plants; examples are mustard, nasturtium, oxalis, pampas grass, statice, and valerian. Additionally, describes placing plants in natural-looking, less artificial settings in gardens—mounting an epiphyte on a tree branch, for example.

Nematode. A microscopic, occasionally parasitic worm that lives in soil. Root knot nematodes enter the roots of plants, causing swollen galls, called "root knots." The plant may become yellow and stunted, and its fruit may be small. Beneficial nematodes kill various soil pests and plant pests that touch the ground. They enter the pests' bodies, kill them with a bacteria, and then devour them. Some beneficial nematodes kill harmful ones by wrapping themselves around their victims and squeezing them to death.

Nitrogen. The chemical element, known by the symbol N, that is a colorless gas forming almost four-fifths of the atmosphere and that is part of all living things. It's absorbed by plant tissues in the form of a soluble salt (nitrate or ammonium), makes them grow, and contributes especially to top and green growth. The first number in the trio on a fertilizer package tells the percentage of nitrogen in the product.

Nitrolized wood shavings. An

organic soil amendment made of sawdust or ground wood, a by-product of sawmills, to which the amount of nitrogen (usually from sulfate of ammonia) necessary for its decomposition in soils has been added by the manufacturer prior to sale. Also sawdust or ground wood to which sufficient nitrogen for decomposition has been added by the gardener prior to tilling it into soil. (Some wood-based soil amendments are nitrolized; others are not. Whether they are is not always stated on the labels of bagged products, but most nursery managers can tell you.) Most wood shavings used today in soil amendments are fir based, but other types of wood are also used. Nitrolized redwood consists of sawdust and ground-up wood of redwood trees, to which the correct proportion of nitrogen has been added prior to sale; it's difficult to find but nonetheless available, and it's more acid than other wood products.

Node. The place on a plant from which leaves and axillary buds sprout.

Organic. In chemistry, any chemical compound that contains carbon. In gardening, anything that derives from plants or animals. *Organic gardeners* fertilize exclusively with organics and control pests with natural rather than chemical pesticides.

Pea stake. A plant stake, cut from shrubbery, with a straight piece to stick into the ground and many twigs to support plants as they grow.

Peat moss. A naturally occurring, usually acidic material found in peat bogs in cool, wet climates where dead moss has gradually built up and partially decomposed over hundreds or thousands of years.

Perennial. Technically, any nonwoody plant that lives for more than two years and produces flowers and seeds for more than one year from the same roots. Some perennials are evergreen; others die down in winter. Some plants often classed as perennials will eventually make woody stems when grown in Southern California. Some plants with fleshy roots, such as agapanthus and daylilies, are technically perennials but often classed with bulbs. Many perennials, including violas, pansies, and petunias, are customarily grown only as annuals.

Petal blight. A fungal or bacterial disease that afflicts flowers. It can ruin camellia and azalea blossoms by browning, discoloring, and rotting them.

pH. A symbol that stands for degree of acidity or alkalinity—for example, of soil—and which is measured on a scale numbered from 0 to 14 (7.0 is neutral). As the numbers decrease in value from 7.0 the soil is increasingly acid; as they rise above 7.0 the soil is increasingly alkaline.

Phosphorus. A nonmetallic chemical element that's known by the symbol P and is one of the three main ingredients in fertilizers. It contributes to root and flower growth and the overall health of plants. The second number in the trio on a fertilizer package tells the percentage of phosphorus in the product.

Photoperiodic. Responding to the length of daylight hours by the onset of a physical change, such as flowering. For example, chrysanthemums, which naturally bloom in fall, can be made to bloom at any time of year by artificially controlling the number of hours of daylight they undergo.

Photosynthesis. The method by which the chlorophyll in plants is acted on by sunlight, or appropriate artificial light, to change carbon dioxide and water (H_2O) into carbohydrates that feed the plant.

Pinch back. To prune off growing tips in order to make a plant bushier.

Pistil. The female organ of a flower, made up of the stigma, style, and ovary.

Pollen. A yellow dust usually produced inside the pollen sacs that make up the anther on top of the stamen of a flower; pollen grains (in seed plants, they are called "microspores") contain the male sex cells of seed plants.

Pollination. The transfer of pollen from the anthers (the male part of flowers) to the stigma (the female part). When bees, other insects, or the wind carry pollen from flower to flower on the same plant, the plants are self-pollinating. When plants need another plant, called a "pollinator," to supply pollen in order for them to bear fruit, they are cross-pollinating.

Pony pack. A small, oblong, undivided nursery container customarily holding six small transplants.

Potash. Potassium carbonate obtained from wood ashes, or potassium from any salt; expressed as K_2O and used in fertilizers. A common name for potassium.

Potassium. A chemical element that occurs abundantly in nature and is one of the three basic ingredients of fertilizers, known by the chemical symbol K. It contributes to flowering and overall plant health. The third number in the trio on a package of fertilizer tells the percentage of potassium in the product.

Pot on. Successively repotting a plant into a container that's just one size larger whenever its roots fill the pot.

Preemergent herbicide. A weed killer that kills germinating seeds.

Primary wilt. A stage when a plant barely begins to wilt from water stress. Signaled by a dull, lackluster look and the tips of the leaves turning down slightly. A lawn with primary wilt won't spring back when stepped on.

Pseudobulb. An aboveground, bulblike thickened stem on certain orchids, such as cymbidiums, that stores food for the plant.

Pup. A common name for the offshoots of some plants, including bromeliads and staghorn ferns, which produce sideshoots that can be separated from the parent plant to make new plants.

Rhizobia. A group of beneficial soil bacteria, each of which has a symbiotic relationship with a particular species of legume. Rhizobia help legumes take nitrogen directly from the air for nourishment.

Rhizome. A thickened stem that grows horizontally underground or on the surface of the ground, such as in bearded irises or calla lilies.

Rootbound. Describes a plant whose roots so fill a container that they've taken on its shape. The roots become thickly concentrated around the outside of the root ball, often wound around and around.

Rust. A fungal disease that attacks many plants, including snapdragons, hollyhocks, roses, and lawn grass. Yellow spots show through on the upper side of leaves where rusty pustules of brown powder occur on the underside.

Sand. A loose, gritty earth made up of tiny particles of rock. Grip a damp handful and it won't hold together. In its pure form sand contains little or no nutriment, but "sandy soils" usually contain a mixture of sand and humus and may also contain various small percentages of clay or silt.

Santa Ana. A dry wind, sometimes of gale force, that blows from the interior to the sea. High pressure over the Great Basin causes the westerly flow of air, which is heated and dried by compression as it flows over and down mountains and through canyons.

Scarify. To carefully nick or sand through the outer covering of seeds with hard seed coats, allowing them to germinate more easily.

Sepal. One section of the calyx of a flower. (The calyx is the outer covering that encloses and protects the flower while it is developing inside the bud.) After the flower opens, the calyx usually splits into individual sepals, though with some flowers like primroses it stays in one piece. Sepals are usually green and may be small, hairy, and insignificant, but with some flowers, including fuchsias, the sepals may be colorful and look somewhat like petals, though they are not. (See *corolla*.)

Shade cloth. A landscape fabric usually made of plastic that's mainly used for covering trellises, shade houses, and other structures; it creates an appropriate environment for shade plants, which are grown under it. Shade cloth is usually black or green in color, and it's available in weaves that provide shade in varying degree, including 25 percent, 50 percent, and 75 percent shade.

Shear. To clip plants on the outside like a hedge with hedge shears or an electric hedge clipper. Shearing results in dense outer foliage that shades out inner foliage, leaving bare branches in the center of the plant, a condition that doesn't harm hedges but may harm other plants.

Side-dress. To apply dry fertilizer, as a booster, on the ground on one or both sides of a vegetable row, and then water it into the soil. When black plastic mulch is in use, side-dressing is applied by pouring liquid fertilizer through holes made in the plastic, or foliar-feeding is substituted.

Silk. Sticky fibers that spill out of the tops of the ears of corn and are the female flower of the corn plant. Each fiber leads to one kernel of corn and must receive one grain of pollen in order to make that kernel grow. (See *tassel*.)

Sleeve drain. A pipe, often covered by gravel, that drains water from the bottom of a planting hole beneath the roots of a plant on a slope and releases it farther down the slope. It is constructed either by drilling a hole with water or machinery through hard soil, from a lower point on the hill, or by digging a trench that is later refilled.

Slow-release fertilizer. A fertilizer that's coated with a plastic or otherwise constituted in such a way that small, measured amounts of plant food are released over a period of time.

Soil amendment. Anything added to soil to improve its texture, structure, or pH. Some soil amendments are organic and break down to make humus. Others, including soil sulfur, lime, and gypsum, are inorganic.

Soil sulfur. A type of sulfur (a pale yellow, nonmetallic chemical element whose chemical symbol is S) that can be purchased in small or large bags at any nursery. It's used to acidify soil for acid-loving plants and to correct soils that have a high pH. The usual method of application is to sprinkle the recommended quantity on the ground and water it in.

Soil test. A chemical way to determine at least the pH of soils and soil mixes. More sophisticated soil tests determine some of the basic nutrients in soil.

Specialty plants. Plants that require special know-how or attention and that frequently have plant societies devoted to their culture.

Species. One kind of plant, or a group of plants, with a high number of similar characteristics that usually can interbreed only with each other. Designated by the uncapitalized second word in a botanical name. Also describes a plant in the form (or close to the form) in which it was originally found in the wild, as in "*Rosa banksiae* is a species rose."

Spike. A long, flowering stalk with flowers usually attached directly to it.

Sport. An entire plant that differs from the typical form of the plant, or a shoot of a plant that differs from the rest of the plant when it first occurs. Sports come about either from spontaneous mutation or from segregation. Many climbing roses, for example, have occurred as sports that began as one atypical shoot on a rosebush. All cole crops, such as Brussels sprouts, cauliflower, and cabbages, came from a series of sports that occurred over many centuries. They're all descendants of one ancestor, a wild plant that man segregated and grew as a crop.

Spreader-sticker. See *surfactant.*

Stamen. The male part of a flower consisting of the filament (stalk) and anther or anthers.

Stigma. The upper part of the pistil (the female part of the plant), which is sticky when receptive and which receives the male pollen during pollination.

Stolon. A stem (in some cases called a "runner") that grows aboveground or underground and that sprouts roots at the nodes, thus forming new plants. Bermuda, kikuyu, and zoysia are stoloniferous grasses; also, the runners of strawberries are stolons, as are the long shoots of currants and gooseberries, which, unable to support their weight, arch to the ground and sprout roots.

Subsoil. A layer of any kind of soil lying beneath a layer of topsoil.

Succulent. Any plant that stores water in leaves or stems that are thickened for the purpose. Aloes, cacti, crassulas, and most euphorbias are examples of succulents.

Sucker. On a rose, a cane that arises below the bud union and thus comes from the rootstock rather than the variety grafted onto it. On other plants, any usually unwanted, fast-growing, upright growth from roots, trunk, crown, or main branches. On tomatoes, the sprouts from axillary buds. (See also *water sprout.*)

Sump. An inefficient drainage system consisting of a small, deep hole dug in the center of the bottom of a planting hole and then filled with sand or ground bark, supposedly to drain off excess water. Not recommended; it soon fills with wa-

ter and does more harm than good. (See *chimney drain* and *sleeve drain.*)

Surfactant. A chemical product used to break down the surface tension of water. Some, often called "wetting agents," are used to help water penetrate soil. Others, often called "spreader-stickers," are mixed into sprays to make them more effective. Sprays containing surfactants cover leaves in a smooth film rather than in droplets.

Tassel. The male flower of the corn plant that emerges from the tops of stalks and bears pollen. (Some hybrid corn varieties sport a few distorted bisexual tassels or ears; they do no harm.)

Tensiometer. An instrument that measures soil moisture. It's made up of a handle, a probe to push down into the ground, and a dial that registers the moisture content of the soil below the surface.

Terminal bud. The bud at the tip of a branch or stem.

Thatch. In lawns, a layer of partially decomposed leaves, stems, and roots that forms between the earth and the grass blades.

Thermophotoperiodic. Describes a plant, such as an onion or a petunia, whose flowering and growth habit depend on the length of days combined with the temperature.

Topiary. The art of training plants into formalized and stylized shapes, such as circles, triangles, animals, or birds. Also the shaped plants themselves.

Topsoil. Any type of soil, whether based on sand, decomposed granite, loam, or clay, that's rich with humus and found in the top layer of soil, where plant roots live. In arid regions it can take centuries for nature to create a few

inches of natural topsoil. Commercial topsoil is often manmade by mixing decomposed granite, sand, or river-bottom silt with organic amendments.

Transpiration. The giving off of moisture from plant leaves into the air.

Tuber. A thickened stem, usually shorter, thicker, and rounder than a rhizome, that serves as a food-storage chamber and from which grows a plant. It grows totally or partially underground. A potato is a tuber.

Tuberous root. A thickened root that grows underground and has growth buds on top, in the old stem portion from which springs the plant. Dahlias and sweet potatoes grow from tuberous roots.

Variety. In taxonomy (the science of naming plants), the rank subordinate to subspecies (a name with varying meanings, usually a geographical difference) and above forma (a fifth name given to a plant by botanists to list a minor difference). However, in actual practice the variety is generally a third italicized name that's tacked onto the usual binomial (genus and species) to indicate a particular and distinct form of a species that's found in nature. For example, in the name *Pinus mugo mugo* the second *mugo* means a particular wild type of mugo pine that's different from others. All varieties first occur in nature (usually by spontaneous generation or mutation). Horticultural varieties (those that first occur under cultivation or that occurred first in nature but then persist only under cultivation by artificial means, such as propagation by cuttings) are more correctly called "cultivars." The names of cultivars are written in plain type and enclosed in single quotes, and they follow the italicized names, however many there may be. For example, in the name *Juniperus chinensis procumbens* 'Nana,' the first name is the genus, the second name is the species, the third name *(procumbens)* is the natural variety, and the fourth name ('Nana') is the man-made cultivar. Nevertheless, in common parlance most gardeners and many garden writers, including this one, often use the word "variety" loosely when referring to any plant to which a name has been given by its commercial producer or hybridizer—for example, in speaking of named zinnias or roses as varieties when actually they are more properly called "cultivars." *Mandevilla splendens* 'Alice du Pont', for example, is a particular cultivar of mandevilla.

Volunteer. A cultivated plant that comes up in a garden on its own accord and often in the wrong place, from a seed deposited by the wind, a bird, or by some other wild or domestic creature.

Warm-season flower. An annual, biennial, or perennial flowering plant that's native to a warm climate and thus grows fastest and flowers best during the warmest part of the year.

Warm-season lawn. A lawn variety that's best adapted to a warm tropical or subtropical climate and thus grows best and fastest during our warm late-spring, summer, and early-fall months. Examples are St. Augustine, Bermuda, and zoysia.

Warm-season vegetable. A vegetable that originated in a warm climate and thus grows best in warm temperatures.

Water sprout. A long, whippy sucker that sprouts, usually in summer, from the tops of branches or from the trunks of trees and shoots up rapidly.

Wetting agent. See *surfactant.*

BIBLIOGRAPHY

Ayensu, Edward S., et al. *Underexploited Tropical Plants with Promising Economic Value.* Washington, D.C.: National Academy of Sciences, 1976.

Bailey, Liberty Hyde, Ethel Zoe Bailey, and Staff of Liberty Hyde Bailey Hortorium. *Hortus Third: A Concise Dictionary of Plants Cultivated in the United States and Canada.* New York: Macmillan, 1976.

Ball, Vic, ed. *Ball Red Book.* 14th ed. Reston, Va.: Reston, 1985.

Barash, Cathy Wilkinson. *Edible Flowers: From Garden to Palate.* Golden, Colo.: Fulcrum, 1995.

Bartel, Janice R., and Sage Culpepper Belt. *A Guide to Botanical Resources of Southern California.* Los Angeles: Natural History Museum of Los Angeles County, 1977.

Barton, Barbara J. *Gardening by Mail: A Source Book.* 5th ed. New York: Houghton Mifflin, 1997.

Beley, Jim, ed., and Ortho Staff. *All About Azaleas, Camellias & Rhododendrons.* San Ramon, Calif.: Ortho Books, 1985.

Blackmore, Stephen, and Elizabeth Tootill, eds. *The Facts on File Dictionary of Botany.* Aylesbury, U.K.: Market House Books (published in U.S. by Facts on File), 1984.

Blomberry, Alec, and Tony Rodd. *Palms: An Informative, Practical Guide to Palms of the World: Their Cultivation, Care and Landscape Use.* London: Angus and Robertson, 1984.

Brenzel, Kathleen Norris, ed. *Sunset Western Landscaping.* Menlo Park, Calif.: Sunset Books, 1997.

Bryan, John. *Manual of Bulbs.* Portland, Oreg.: Timber Press, 1996.

Capon, Brian. *Botany for Gardeners: An Introduction and Guide.* Portland, Oreg.: Timber Press, 1990.

Carr, Anna. *Rodale's Color Handbook of Garden Insects.* Emmaus, Pa.: Rodale Press, 1983.

Carson, Rachel L. *Silent Spring.* Boston: Houghton Mifflin, 1962.

Chamberlin, Susan. *Hedges, Screens and Espaliers.* Tucson: HP Books, 1983.

Chatto, Beth. *The Dry Garden.* Sagaponack, N.Y.: Sagapress, 1996.

Clausen, Ruth Rogers, and Nicolas H. Ekstrom. *Perennials for American Gardens.* New York: Random House, 1989.

Clebsch, Betsy. *A Book of Salvias.* Portland, Oreg.: Timber Press, 1997.

Connelly, Kevin. *The Gardener's Guide to California Wildflowers.* Sun Valley, Calif.: Theodore Payne Foundation, 1991.

Courtright, Gordon. *Trees and Shrubs for Temperate Climates.* 3d ed. Portland, Oreg.: Timber Press, 1988.

———. *Tropicals.* Portland, Oreg.: Timber Press, 1988.

Cox, Jeff. *Perennial All Stars: The 150 Best Perennials for Great-Looking, Trouble-Free Gardens.* Emmaus, Pa.: Rodale Press, 1998.

Creasy, Rosalind. *Cooking from the Garden.* San Francisco: Sierra Club Books, 1988.

———. *The Complete Book of Edible Landscaping.* San Francisco: Sierra Club Books, 1982.

Cullmann, Willy, Erich Gotz, and Gerhard Groner. *The Encyclopedia of Cacti.* Sherborne, England: Alphabooks, 1986.

DiSabato-Aust, Tracy. *The Well-Tended Perennial Garden: Planting & Pruning Techniques.* Portland, Oreg.: Timber Press, 1998.

Doutt, Richard L. *Cape Bulbs.* Portland, Oreg.: Timber Press, 1994.

Everett, Thomas H. *The New York Botanical Garden Illustrated*

Encyclopedia of Horticulture. 10 vols. New York: Garland, 1981.

Farrell, Kenneth R., and Staff. *Agricultural Publications Catalogue, University of California Division of Agriculture and Natural Resources.* Special Publication 3020. Oakland: ANR Publications (University of California, 6701 San Pablo Ave., 94608), 1989.

Feathers, David, and Milton Brown, eds. *The Camellia: Its History, Culture, Genetics, and a Look Into Its Future Development.* Columbia, S.C.: R. L. Bryan, 1978.

Fell, Derek. *Annuals: How to Select, Grow and Enjoy.* Tucson: HP Books, 1981.

————. *Vegetables: How to Select, Grow and Enjoy.* Tucson: HP Books, 1982.

Graf, Alfred Byrd. *Exotica Pictorial Cyclopedia of Exotic Plants from Tropical and Near-tropic Regions.* E. Rutherford, N.J.: Roehrs, 1976.

Greenlee, John. *The Encyclopedia of Ornamental Grasses: How to Grow and Use Over 250 Beautiful and Versatile Plants.* Emmaus, Pa.: Rodale Press, 1992.

Harper, Pamela, and Frederick McGourty. *Perennials: How to Select, Grow and Enjoy.* Tucson: HP Books, 1985.

Harrington, Geri. *Grow Your Own Chinese Vegetables.* Pownal, Vt.: Garden Way, 1984.

Holmes, Roger, ed. *Taylor's Guide to Ornamental Grasses.* New York: Houghton Mifflin, 1997.

Hoyt, Roland Stewart. *Checklists for the Ornamental Plants of Subtropical Regions: A Handbook for Ready Reference.* Los Angeles: Livingston Press, 1938.

Hunter, Beatrice Trum. *Gardening Without Poisons.* Boston: Houghton Mifflin, 1964.

Jekyll, Gertrude. (Intro., Richard Bisgrove.) *The Illustrated Gertrude Jekyll.* Boston: Little, Brown, 1988.

Jekyll, Gertrude, and Edward Mawley. *Roses.* Rev., Stuart Graham Thomas. Salem, N.H.: Ayer, 1983.

Johnson, Eric, and Scott Millard. *How to Grow Wildflowers.* Tucson, Ariz.: Ironwood Press, 1997.

Johnson, Huey D., and Ronald B. Robie. *Plants for California Landscapes: A Catalogue of Drought Tolerant Plants.* Bulletin 209. Sacramento, Calif.: Department of Water Resources, 1979.

Jones, David L. *Palms Throughout the World.* Washington, D.C.: Smithsonian Institution Press, 1995.

Koehler, C. S. *Insect Pest Management Guidelines for California Landscape Ornamentals.* Publication 3317. Berkeley: University of California Division of Agriculture and Natural Resources, 1987.

Labadie, Emile L. *Native Plants for Use in the California Landscape.* Oakland, Calif.: Sierra City Press, 1978.

Lane, Clive. *Cottage Garden Annuals: Grown from Seed for Summer-Long Color.* Newton Abbot, U.K.: David & Charles, 1997.

Lathrop, Norma Jean. *Herbs: How to Select, Grow and Enjoy.* Tucson: HP Books, 1981.

Latymer, Hugo. *The Mediterranean Gardener.* New York: Barrons, in association with The Royal Botanic Gardens, Kew, 1990.

Lenz, Lee, W. *Native Plants for California Gardens.* Claremont, Calif.: Rancho Santa Ana Botanic Garden, 1977.

Lenz, Lee W., and John Dourley. *California Native Trees and Shrubs for Garden and Environmental Use in Southern California and Adjacent Areas.* Claremont, Calif.: Rancho Santa Ana Botanic Garden, 1981.

Levick, Melba, and Helaine Kaplan Prentice. *The Gardens of Southern California.* San Francisco: Chronicle Books, 1990.

Lindsay, Lowell, and Diana Lindsay. *The Anza-Borrego Desert Region.* Berkeley: Wilderness Press, 1985.

Loewer, Peter. *Step-by-Step Ornamental Grasses.* Des Moines: Better Homes & Gardens Books, 1995.

MacCaskey, Michael. *The Complete Guide to Basic Gardening.* Tucson: HP Books, 1986.

————. *Lawns and Ground Covers: How to Select, Grow and Enjoy.* Tucson: HP Books, 1982.

Martin, R. Sanford. *How to Prune Fruit Trees.* 10th ed. Van Nuys: Press of Document Engineering, 1978.

———. *How to Prune Western Shrubs.* Culver City, Calif.: Murray & Gee, 1947.

Mathias, Mildred, ed. *Flowering Plants in the Landscape.* Berkeley: University of California Press, 1982.

Milne, Lorus, and Margery Milne. *The Audubon Society Field Guide to North American Insects and Spiders.* New York: Alfred A. Knopf, 1980.

Munz, Philip A. *California Desert Wildflowers.* Berkeley: University of California Press, 1962.

———. *A Flora of Southern California.* Berkeley: University of California Press, 1974.

———. *Shore Wildflowers of California, Oregon, and Washington.* Berkeley: University of California Press, 1964.

Nottle, Trevor. *Gardens of the Sun.* Portland, Oreg.: Timber Press, 1996.

Padilla, Victoria. *Southern California Gardens.* Santa Barbara, Calif.: Allen A. Knoll, 1994.

Patent, Dorothy Hinshaw, and Diane E. Bilderback. *Garden Secrets: A Guide to Understanding How Your Garden Grows and How You Can Help It Grow Even Better.* Emmaus, Pa.: Rodale Press, 1982.

Paul, Anthony, and Yvonne Rees. *The Water Garden.* New York: Viking Press, 1986.

Perry, Robert C. *Landscape Plants for Western Regions: An Illustrated Guide to Plants for Water Conservation.* Claremont, Calif.: Land Design, 1992.

———. *Trees and Shrubs for Dry California Landscapes: Plants for Water Conservation.* San Dimas, Calif.: Land Design, 1981.

Peterson, Tru, ed. *The New A to Z on Fuchsias.* San Francisco: National Fuchsia Society, 1981.

Picart, François. *Escargots from Your Garden to Your Table: How to Control, Raise and Process the Common Garden Snail.* Santa Rosa, Calif.: F. Picart Snails (1550 Ridley Ave., 95401), 1978.

Quiros, Alice, and Barbara Young. *The World of Cactus and Succulents and Other Water Thrifty Plants.* San Francisco: Ortho Books, 1977.

Ray, Richard, and Michael Mac-Caskey. *Roses: How to Select, Grow and Enjoy* Tucson: HP Books, 1983.

Ray, Richard, and Lance Walheim. *Citrus: How to Select, Grow and Enjoy.* Tucson: HP Books, 1980.

Redfield, Margaret. *The Southern California Month-by-Month Flower Gardening Book.* Los Angeles: J. P. Tarcher, 1976.

Reilly, Ann. *Park's Success with Seeds.* Greenwood, S.C.: Geo. Park Seed, 1978.

Relf, Diane, Judy Schwab, Elissa Steeves, and Virginia Nathan, eds. *The Virginia Master Gardener Handbook.* Petersburg: Virginia Cooperative Extension Service, 1987.

Robinson, William. *The English Flower Garden.* Rev. ed., Graham Stuart Thomas. New York: Amaryllis Press, 1984.

Rodale, J. I., ed. *How to Grow Vegetables and Fruits by the Organic Method.* Emmaus, Pa.: Rodale Press, 1976.

Scheider, Alfred E. *Park's Success With Bulbs.* Greenwood, S.C.: Geo. Park Seed, 1981.

Schmidt, Marjorie. *Growing California Native Plants.* Berkeley: University of California Press, 1980.

Scott, George Harmon. *Bulbs: How to Select, Grow and Enjoy.* Tucson: HP Books, 1982.

Sedesko, Jerry. *The Butterfly Garden.* New York: Villard Books, 1991.

Sinnes, A. Cort, and Ortho Staff. *All About Fertilizers, Soils and Water.* San Francisco: Ortho Books, 1980.

Smaus, Robert. *52 Weeks in the California Garden.* Los Angeles: Los Angeles Times Syndicate, 1996.

———. Los Angeles Times *California Gardening: A Practical Guide to Growing Flowers, Trees, Vegetables and Fruits.* New York: Harry N. Abrams, 1983.

———. *The* Los Angeles Times *Planning and Planting the Garden.* New York: Harry N. Abrams, 1983.

Smith, Ken. *Western Home Landscaping.* Tucson: HP Books, 1978.

Smith, Michael D., ed. *The Ortho Problem Solver.* 4th ed. San Ramon, Calif.: Ortho, 1994.

Spellenberg, Richard. *The Audubon Society Field Guide to North American Wildflowers, Western Region.* New York: Alfred A. Knopf, 1979.

Starcher, Allison Mia. *Good Bugs for Your Garden.* Chapel Hill, N.C.: Algonquin Books of Chapel Hill, 1995.

Streatfield, David C. *California Gardens: Creating a New Eden.* New York: Abbeville Press, 1994.

Sunset Books and *Sunset* Magazine. *Garden Pools, Fountains & Waterfalls.* Menlo Park, Calif.: Lane, 1974.

———. *Lawns: How to Plant and Care for a Healthy Carpet of Green.* Menlo Park, Calif.: Sunset Books, 1997.

———. *Sunset Introduction to Basic Gardening.* Menlo Park, Calif.: Lane, 1981.

———. *Sunset Pruning Handbook.* Menlo Park, Calif.: Lane, 1975.

———. *Sunset Western Garden Book.* Menlo Park, Calif.: Sunset, 1995.

———. *Sunset Waterwise Gardening: Beautiful Gardens with Less Water.* Menlo Park, Calif.: Sunset Books, 1989.

———. *Sunset Western Garden Problem Solver.* Menlo Park, Calif.: Sunset Books, 1998.

Tanner, Ogden. *Living Fences: A Gardener's Guide to Hedges, Vines, and Espaliers.* New York: Houghton Mifflin, 1995.

Taylor, Norman. *Taylor's Guide to Annuals.* Rev. ed. Edited by Gordon P. DeWolf, Jr. Boston: Houghton Mifflin, 1986.

Tekulsky, Mathew. *The Butterfly Garden.* Boston: Harvard Common Press, 1985.

Uber, William C. *Water Gardening Basics.* Upland, Calif.: Dragonflyer Press (2460 N. Euclid Ave., 91786), 1988.

UC publications. *See* Farrell, *Agricultural Publications Catalogue.* (Many publications also available from local county Cooperative Extension offices.)

Walheim, Lance, and Robert L. Stebbins. *Western Fruit, Berries and Nuts: How to Select, Grow and Enjoy.* Tucson: HP Books, 1981.

Waters, George, and Norah Harlow, eds. *The Pacific Horticulture Book of Western Gardening.* Boston: David R. Godine, in association with the Pacific Horticultural Foundation, 1990.

Wright, John I. *Plant Propagation for the Amateur Gardener.* Poole, England: Blanford Books (distributed in U.S. by Stirling), 1983.

Wyman, Donald. *Wyman's Gardening Encyclopedia.* 2d ed. New York: Macmillan, 1986.

Yepsen, Roger B., Jr. *The Encyclopedia of Natural Insect and Disease Control.* Emmaus, Pa.: Rodale Press, 1984.

Yronwode, Catherine. *The California Gardener's Book of Lists.* Dallas: Taylor, 1998.

INDEX

100, 145; shade requirements of, 53, 186, 187; using sasanqua for winter color, 291; varieties of, 52–53, 70

Campanulas (bellflowers). *See also* Canterbury bells; Cup-and-saucer plants; planting time for, 93; using in tubs and hanging baskets, 130

Canary Island date palms, 220

Candia tulip *(tulipa saxatilis)*, 227

Candytuft, evergreen *(iberis sempervirens)*: color from, 236, 256; planting, 78, 93, 131, 278, 296

Candytuft, globe *(iberis umbellata)*, 256

Cane begonias. *See* Begonias

Cane berries, 42, 273, 299

Cannas, 75–76, 212

Cantaloupes. *See also* Melons, 136, 158, 200–201

Canterbury bells *(campanula medium)*, 131, 154, 190. *See also* Campanulas, Cup-and-saucer plants

Cape honeysuckle *(tecomaria capensis)*, 249

Cape mallow *(anisodontea)*, 94

Cape plumbago *(plumbago auriculata)*, 230, 275

Cape weed *(arctotheca calendula)*, 275

Carnations, 93

Carolina jessamine *(gelsemium sempervirens)*, 212, 249, 294

Carolina laurel cherry *(prunus caroliniana)*, 128

Carpenter bee, 202

Carpet bugle, 275

Carrots: direct seeding, 176; harvesting, 201; presprouting, 264; planting, 108, 136, 158, 200, 243, 262, 283, 303; preventing green shoulders on, 265; successive crops of, 110

Cassias (Gold medallion tree), 166, 215

Catalina cherry *(prunus lyonii)*, 271

Caterpillars, controlling, 39, 122, 125–126, 212

Catmint *(nepta faassenii)*, 131

Cauliflower: blanching, 303; harvesting, 60–61; planting, 86, 110, 222,

243, 262, 303; transplanting, 283

Celery: blanching, 86; how to grow, 302; planting, 86, 222, 243, 262, 303; transplanting, 283

Celosia, 93, 130, 154, 189

Cestrum fasciculatum 'Newellii', 297

Chamomile, 172

Chard, 108, 200. *See also* Swiss chard

Chasmanthe, 227

Chayote, 108, 158

Cherimoya trees, 102, 166

Cherry trees, 216

Chewings fescue *(festuca rubra commutata)*, 107

Chicory, 85

Chilling requirements, bare-root trees, 42

Chimney drains, 17, 34. *See also* Drainage

Chincherinchee *(ornithogalum thyrsoides)*, 227

Chinese elm *(ulmus parvifolia)*, 248

Chinese flame tree *(koelreuteria)*, 230, 249

Chinese fringe tree *(chionanthus retusus)*, 165

Chinese houses *(collinsia heterophylla)*, 260, 278

Chipper materials, soil amendments, 24

Chives, edible flowers of, 112

Chlorosis, 51, 193, 233

Chlorothalonil, 69

Christmas cactus *(schlumbergera bridgessii)*, 234. *See also* Zygocactus

Chrysanthemums: cutting back, 280; growing from cuttings, 97, 257; pruning and staking, 155; stopping fertilization of, 255

Cilantro, 136, 263

Cineraria *(senecio hybridus)*: care of, 152, 257; color from, 256, 277; fertilizing, 56, 78, 279; frost tenderness of, 295; partial shade and, 188; planting, 216, 236

Citrus trees: beneficial insects for, 68; brown rot control on lemons, 231; dwarf varieties of, 159; fertilization of, 50–51, 67, 97; frost protection for, 281; giant whiteflies and, 101; harvest-

ing, 230; irrigation of, 51–52, 182; pests of, 52, 67; planting, 97, 166; snail control and, 91; washing, 67–68

Clarkia: blooming period of, 152; planting, 56, 256, 278, 296

Clay soils, gypsum and, 19; irrigation and, 30; guidelines for, 32–34, 111; soil conditioners and, 210; improving, 20; soil textures and, 18

Clematis, 156–157

Cleome, 93, 154

Cleveland sage *(salvia clevelandii)*, 189, 271

Climate, 14–15, 269

Climbing roses. *See also* Roses; controlling ramblers, 183–184; pruning, 49, 183; rose categories and, 45; varieties of, 72, 184

Clivia: dividing, 250, 252; leaving in ground, 257; shade requirements of, 186, 187; varieties of, 71; when to purchase, 70

CloudCover, 150

Clumping bamboo, 103–104. *See also* Bamboo

Cobbitty daisy. *See* Marguerites

Cockscomb. *See* Celosia

Cole crops. *See also by individual type*, 60–61

Coleus: care of, 189; planting, 93, 130, 172; shade requirements of, 93, 186, 187

Columbine *(aquilegia)*, 93, 131, 154, 277

COMBAT, ant bait, 68, 129

Common sneezeweed *(helenium autumnale)*, 55, 297

Common thrift. *See* Thrift

Complete fertilizers, 23

Compost, 24, 76–78

Conifers, 190–191, 248

Container plants, 21, 23, 26, 210–211

Conventional drains, 17. *See also* drainage

Convolvulus, 131

Cool-season flowers, 255, 294

Cool-season grasses. *See also* Lawns; care of, 58–59, 260, 283, 303; dethatching, 260, 283; fertilizing, 157, 197, 260, 283, 303; irrigating, 197; mowing, 175, 197, 260; plant-